THE GROUNDWORK OF PRACTICAL NAVAL GUNNERY

A Study of the Principles and Practice of Exterior Ballistics, as Applied to Naval Gunnery
And of the
Computation and Use of Ballistic and Range Tables

BY PHILIP R. ALGER
Professor of Mathematics, U. S. Navy

Revised and Extended to Include the Formulæ and Methods of
Colonel James M. Ingalls, U. S. Army
By the Officers on Duty in the Department of Ordnance and Gunnery
United States Naval Academy
1914–15

SECOND EDITION

ANNAPOLIS, MD.
THE UNITED STATES NAVAL INSTITUTE
1917

PREFACE.

DEPARTMENT OF ORDNANCE AND GUNNERY.

U. S. NAVAL ACADEMY, ANNAPOLIS, MD., January 1, 1915.

1. Experience with the course of instruction of midshipmen in the science of exterior ballistics seemed to indicate that some modification of that course was necessary, especially in view of the fact that the Bureau of Ordnance in its work uses the formulæ and methods devised by Colonel James M. Ingalls, U. S. Army, in the place of those given by Professor Philip R. Alger, U. S. Navy, in the text book prepared by him and used at the Naval Academy up to this date, for the computation of the data contained in the following columns of the range tables prepared by the Bureau of Ordnance and officially issued to the service:

Column 2. Angle of departure.
Column 3. Angle of fall.
Column 4. Time of flight.
Column 5. Striking velocity.
Column 6. Drift.
Column 8. Maximum ordinate.
Column 10. Change of range for variation of ± 50 foot-seconds initial velocity.
Column 11. Change of range for variation of $\pm \Delta w$ in weight of projectile.
Column 12. Change of range for variation of density of air of ± 10 per cent.

2. Exterior ballistics is taught at the Naval Academy in order that the midshipmen, when they graduate and become officers, may be as familiar with the range tables, with the data contained in them, and with the methods by which this data is obtained and used,—in other words, with the use of the information which is furnished to aid them in using the guns successfully,—as the time available for this instruction will permit. This being the case, everything has been omitted that does not bear directly upon the point assumed to be at issue, and no formulæ have been retained that are not of use in connection with the practice of naval gunnery and the use of the range tables and of the gun afloat, or in the computation of the data contained in the range tables; except that certain preliminary formulæ and discussions have necessarily been retained as vitally requisite for a thorough understanding of the later and more practical parts of the work. An effort has been made to reduce the mathematical investigations to the lowest possible minimum consistent with a clear understanding of the practical portions of the work, in accordance with the views officially expressed by the Navy Department, by the Superintendent of the Naval Academy, and by the Academic Board; but the subject is one that is almost purely mathematical, and which requires considerable preliminary mathematical work (as is the case with the science of navigation) before the practical features can be properly understood. The preliminary discussions of the trajectory have therefore been retained, but have been restricted as much as possible; and, throughout, the work of revision has been carried out with the sole object in view of giving to the midshipmen, in the shortest possible time, a thorough practical knowledge of the underlying principles of naval gunnery and of the computation and use of the range tables.

3. In brief, the advantages sought by this revision of the text book previously in use are:

(a) An arrangement that would appear more logical and consecutive to a midshipman taking up the study of the subject for the first time.

(b) A more clear distinction between the methods and formulæ that are purely educational and those that are actually used in practice.

(c) The rendering more easily understood of quite a number of points in the older text book that seemed in the past to give great trouble to the midshipmen in their study of the subject.

(d) The modification of the problems given in the text book to make them apply to modern United States Naval Ordnance. The problems in the older text book dealt largely with foreign ordnance, and exclusively with guns, projectiles, velocities, etc., that are now obsolete, or nearly so; and, while many of the older problems have been retained as valuable examples of principles, a large number of problems dealing with present-day conditions and ordnance have been added.

(e) An effort has been made to give a complete discussion of the practical use of the range tables, a subject but lightly touched upon in the older text book. In order to accomplish this a large number of officers, in the Atlantic fleet and elsewhere, were requested to contribute such knowledge as they might have on this subject, and the matter received from them has been incorporated in the chapter on this subject. The discussion of this point should therefore include all the most up-to-date practice in the use of the range tables.

4. In preparing this revision for the purpose indicated in the preceding paragraphs, the logical treatment of the subject seemed to indicate its division under two general heads, as follows:

(A) The treatment of the trajectory as a plane curve; which, in turn, logically subdivides itself under two sub-heads, as follows:

(a) General definitions, etc.; the trajectory in vacuum; the resistance of the air and the retardation due thereto; the ballistic coefficient in its fullest form; the equation to the trajectory in air under certain specified and limited conditions; and the approximate determination of the elements of the trajectory by the use of the above special equation. In other words, the features that are of educational rather than of practical value, but which are necessary to an understanding of the practical methods that are to follow.

(b) The more exact and practical theories and formulæ; that is, the ones that are generally used in practical work. This subdivision is not a rigid one, as it will be seen that some of the approximate formulæ and methods are sufficiently accurate to permit of their use in practice, and they are so used; but the general statement of the subdivision may be accepted as logical, with this one reservation.

(B) A consideration of the variation of the actual trajectory from a plane curve, which treats of the influence upon the motion of the projectile of drift and wind, and of the effect upon the fall of the projectile relative to the target of motion of the gun and target. That is, having treated under the first division those computations that are not materially affected by the variations of the trajectory from a plane curve; in the second division we treat of the effect of such deviations upon accuracy of fire. In other words, there are here to be discussed the steps taken to overcome the inaccuracies in fire caused by the variation of the trajectory from a plane curve, in order to hit a moving target with a shot fired from a gun mounted on a moving platform, when there is a wind blowing.

5. Following these natural and logical divisions of the subject comes a full discussion of the range tables, column by column, and of the methods of computing the data contained in them, and of using this data after it has been computed and tabulated.

6. Following this comes a consideration of the processes necessary to ensure that the guns of a ship shall be so sighted that the shot in a properly aimed salvo will fall well bunched.

7. Following this again, comes naturally a consideration of the inherent errors of guns, and of the accuracy and probability of fire.

8. In accordance with the preceding statement of the natural and logical order in which the subject should be treated, this revised text book is therefore divided into six parts, as follows:

PART I.

Chapters 1 to 5 Inclusive.

GENERAL AND APPROXIMATE DEDUCTIONS.

Preliminary definitions and discussion. The trajectory in vacuum. The resistance of the atmosphere to the passage of a projectile through it, and the retardation in the motion of the projectile resulting from this resistance. The ballistic coefficient. The equation to the trajectory in air when Mayevski's exponent is taken as having a value of 2; and a comparison between this equation and that to the corresponding trajectory in vacuum. The derivation from this special equation to the trajectory in air of certain expressions for the approximate determination of the values of the elements of the trajectory.

PART II.

Chapters 6 to 12 Inclusive.

PRACTICAL METHODS.

The computation and use of the ballistic tables, and of the time and space integrals. The differential equations giving the relations between the several elements of the trajectory in air. Siacci's method. The time, space, altitude and inclination functions, and their computation and use. The ballistic formulæ. Ballistic problems.

PART III.

Chapters 13 to 15 Inclusive.

THE VARIATION OF THE TRAJECTORY FROM A PLANE CURVE.

The variation of the trajectory from a plane curve; the forces that cause this variation; and the consideration that it is necessary to give to it in the computations of exterior ballistics and in the use of the gun. Drift and the theory of sights. The effect upon the travel of the projectile of wind and of motion of the gun; and the effect of motion of the target upon the fall of the projectile relative to the target.

PART IV.

Chapters 16 to 17 Inclusive.

RANGE TABLES; THEIR COMPUTATION AND USE.

The computation of the data contained in the range tables and the practical methods of using this data.

PART V.

CHAPTERS 18 TO 19 INCLUSIVE.

THE CALIBRATION OF SINGLE GUNS AND OF A SHIP'S BATTERY.

The determination of the error of the setting of a sight for a given range; the adjustment of the sight to make the shot fall at a given range; and the sight adjustments necessary to make all the guns of a battery or ship shoot together.

PART VI.

CHAPTERS 20 TO 21 INCLUSIVE.

THE ACCURACY AND PROBABILITY OF GUNFIRE AND THE MEAN ERRORS OF GUNS.

The errors and inaccuracies of guns. The probability of hitting under given conditions, and whether or not it would be wise to attempt to hit under these conditions. The number of shots probably necessary to give a desired number of hits under certain given conditions, and the bearing of this point upon the wisdom of attempting an attack under the given conditions, having in mind its effect upon the total amount of ammunition available. The probabilities governing the method of spotting salvos by maintaining a proper number of "shorts."

9. No claim is made to originality in any part of this revision; it is merely a compilation of what is thought to be the best and most modern practice from the works of two noted investigators of the subject, namely, Professor Philip R. Alger, U. S. Navy, and Colonel James M. Ingalls, U. S. Army. This revised work is based on Professor Alger's text book on Exterior Ballistics (edition of 1906), and the additions to it concerning the Ingalls methods are from the Handbook of Problems in Exterior Ballistics, Artillery Circular N, Series of 1893, Adjutant General's Office (edition of 1900), prepared by Colonel Ingalls. Further information has been taken from Bureau of Ordnance Pamphlet No. 500, on the Methods of Computing Range Tables. The two chapters on the calibration of guns were taken from a pamphlet on that subject written by Commander L. M. Nulton, U. S. Navy, for use in the instruction of midshipmen, and Chapter 15 was furnished by officers on duty at the Naval Proving Ground at Indian Head.

10. To summarize, it may be said that the belief is held that the only reason for teaching the science of exterior ballistics to midshipmen and the only reason for expecting officers to possess a knowledge of its principles is in order that they may intelligently and successfully use the guns committed to their care. So much as is necessary for this purpose is therefore to be taught the undergraduate and no more; and, as the information necessary for the scientific use of a gun is contained in the official range table for that gun, it may be said that this revision of the previous text book on the subject has been founded upon the question:

"What is a range table, how is the information contained in it obtained, and how is it used?"

With a very few necessary and important exceptions, such as the computations necessary in determining the marking of sights, the text of the book follows closely the question laid down above.

11. For the use of the midshipmen in connection with this revised text book, a reprint has been made of Table II for the desired initial velocities, from the Ballistic Tables computed by Major J. M. Ingalls, U. S. Army, Artillery Circular M, 1900; a reprint of the table from Bureau of Ordnance Pamphlet No. 500, for use in connection with Column 12 of the Range Tables; and a partial reprint of the Range

Tables for Naval Guns issued by the Bureau of Ordnance; these being in addition to the tables previously available for midshipmen in the older text book. It is believed that these reprints will render available a range of practical problems far exceeding anything that has heretofore been possible for the instruction of midshipmen, and that by their use they will be graduated and commissioned with a far wider knowledge of the meaning and use of these tables, and of the underlying principles of naval gunnery than has ever been the case before.

12. The work of revision was done by the Head of Department, assisted by certain officers of the Department, and by criticisms and suggestions from numerous other officers, on duty elsewhere as well as at the Naval Academy. Thanks are due to all those who helped in the work, and especially to Lieutenant (j. g.) C. T. Osburn, U. S. N., Lieutenant (j. g.) W. S. Farber, U. S. N., and Lieutenant (j. g.) N. L. Nichols, U. S. N. Lieutenant Osburn carefully scrutinized the text, checked all sample problems worked in the text, and independently worked and checked the results of all the examples given at the ends of the chapters. Lieutenants Farber and Nichols checked all the solutions given in the appendix, and Lieutenant Nichols prepared the drawings for all the figures.

L. H. CHANDLER,
Captain, U. S. Navy, Head of Department.

U. S. Naval Academy, Annapolis, Md., August 1, 1917.

Advantage has been taken of the opportunity, presented in the publication of a second edition, to eliminate all errors discovered in the previous edition during three years of use for instructional purposes at the Naval Academy; to make minor changes in form (principally in Appendix A) designed to facilitate the use of this work; to insert additional explanatory paragraphs to the discussion on correction for wind and speed, Chapters 14 and 17; and to insert additional problems, 13 and 14, Chapter 17, with forms for their solution (Forms 27A and 27B, Appendix A). This material was assembled and prepared for publication by Lieut. Commander C. C. Soule, U. S. N. So well has this work met the requirements of the Naval Academy course that no change is at present contemplated or desired.

J. W. GREENSLADE,
Commander, U. S. Navy,
Head of Department of Ordnance and Gunnery.

CONTENTS.

PRELIMINARY.

PART III.

THE VARIATION OF THE TRAJECTORY FROM A PLANE CURVE.

PART IV.

RANGE TABLES; THEIR COMPUTATION AND USE.

PART V.

THE CALIBRATION OF SINGLE GUNS AND OF A SHIP'S BATTERY.

PART VI.

THE ACCURACY AND PROBABILITY OF GUNFIRE AND THE MEAN ERRORS OF GUNS

APPENDIX A.

APPENDIX B.

APPENDIX C.

TABLE OF SYMBOLS EMPLOYED.

1. The symbols employed in this book are given in the following table. So far as possible they are those employed by the computers of the Bureau of Ordnance in their work of preparing range tables, etc.; but a considerable number of additional symbols have been found necessary in a text book treatment of the subject.

2. In quite a number of cases it has been found necessary or advisable to use the same symbol to represent two or more different quantities; but such quantities are, as a rule, widely different from each other, and a reasonable amount of care will easily prevent any confusion from arising from this cause.

3. The symbols employed are:

PERTAINING TO THE TRAJECTORY AS A PLANE CURVE.

SYMBOL. QUANTITY REPRESENTED BY IT.

R'....Range in yards on an inclined plane.
X'....Range in feet on an inclined plane.
R....Horizontal range in yards.
X....Horizontal range in feet.
ϕ....Angle of departure.
ω....Angle of fall.
ψ....Angle of elevation.
ψ'....Angle of projection.
p....Angle of position.
j....Angle of jump.
v....Remaining velocity in foot-seconds at any point of the trajectory.
V....Initial velocity in foot-seconds.
v_o....Remaining velocity at the vertex in foot-seconds.
v_ω....Remaining velocity at point of fall (or striking velocity) in foot-seconds.
v_h....Horizontal velocity at any point of the trajectory in foot-seconds.
v_v....Vertical velocity at any point of the trajectory in foot-seconds.
u....Pseudo velocity at any point of the trajectory in foot-seconds.
U....Pseudo velocity at the muzzle of the gun in foot-seconds; $U = V$.
u_o....Pseudo velocity at the vertex in foot-seconds.
u_ω....Pseudo velocity at the point of fall in foot-seconds.
(x, y)....Coordinates of any point of the trajectory in feet.
(x_o, y_o)....Coordinates of the vertex in feet.
Y....Ordinate of the vertex in feet; $Y = y_o$.
t....Elapsed time of flight from the muzzle to any point of the trajectory in seconds.
T....Time of flight from muzzle to point of fall in seconds.
t_o....Time of flight from muzzle to vertex in seconds.
θ....Angle of inclination of the tangent to the trajectory at any point to the horizontal.

PERTAINING TO THE PROJECTILE.

w....Weight of the projectile in pounds.
Δw....Variation from standard in weight of projectile in pounds.
d....Diameter of the projectile in inches.
c....Coefficient of form of the projectile.
C....Ballistic coefficient. When written with numerical subscripts, as 1, 2, 3, etc., the several symbols represent successive approximate values of C as appearing in the computations. The same system of subscripts is used for a similar purpose with a number of other symbols.
β....The integration factor of the ballistic coefficient; normally $\beta = 1$.
K....Constant part of the ballistic coefficient for any given projectile, given by the formula $K = \frac{w}{cd^2}$.

PERTAINING TO ATMOSPHERIC CONDITIONS.

δ_1....Standard density of the atmosphere, in work taken as unity.

δ....Density of the atmosphere at the time of firing, and subsequently representing the ratio $\frac{\delta}{\delta_1} = \frac{\delta}{1}$.

f....Altitude factor of the ballistic coefficient.

PERTAINING TO WIND AND SPEEDS.

W....Real wind; force in feet per second.

β....Angle between wind and line of fire.

W_x....Component of W in line of fire in feet per second.

W_{12x}....Wind component in feet per second of 12 knots in line of fire.

W_z....Component of W perpendicular to line of fire in feet per second.

W_{12z}....Wind component in feet per second of 12 knots perpendicular to the line of fire.

X....Range in feet without considering wind.

X'....Range in feet considering wind.

V....Initial velocity in foot-seconds without considering wind.

V'....Initial velocity in foot-seconds considering wind.

ϕ....Angle of departure without considering wind.

ϕ'....Angle of departure considering wind.

T....Time of flight in seconds without considering wind.

T'....Time of flight in seconds considering wind.

ΔX_W....Variation in range in feet due to W_x.

ΔX_{12W}....Variation in range in feet due to a wind component of 12 knots in the line of fire.

ΔR_W....Variation in range in yards due to W_x.

ΔR_{12W}....Variation in range in yards due to a wind component of 12 knots in the line of fire.

γ....Angle between the trajectories relative to the air and relative to the ground.

D_W....Deflection in yards due to W_z.

D_{12W}....Deflection in yards due to a wind component of 12 knots perpendicular to the line of fire.

G....Motion of gun in feet per second.

G_x....Component of the motion of the gun in the line of fire in feet per second.

G_{12x}....Motion of gun in line of fire in feet per second for a component of motion of gun in that line of 12 knots.

G_z....Component of the motion of the gun perpendicular to the line of fire in feet per second.

G_{12z}....Motion of gun perpendicular to line of fire in feet per second for a component of motion of gun of 12 knots in the same direction.

ΔX_G....Variation in range in feet resulting from G_x.

ΔX_{12G}....Variation in range in feet due to a motion of the gun of 12 knots in the line of fire.

ΔR_G....Variation in range in yards resulting from G_x.

ΔR_{12G}....Variation in range in yards due to a motion of the gun of 12 knots in the line of fire.

D_G....Deflection in yards due to G_z.

D_{12G}....Deflection in yards due to the motion of the gun of 12 knots perpendicular to the line of fire.

T....Motion of target in feet per second.

T_x....Component of the motion of the target in the line of fire in feet per second.

T_{12x}....Motion of target in line of fire in feet per second for a component of motion of target in that line of 12 knots.

T_z....Component of the motion of the target perpendicular to the line of fire in feet per second.

T_{12z}....Motion of target perpendicular to line of fire in feet per second for a component of motion of target of 12 knots in the same direction.

ΔX_T....Variation in range in feet resulting from T_x.

ΔX_{12T}....Variation in range in feet due to a motion of the target of 12 knots in the line of fire.

ΔR_T....Variation in range in yards resulting from T_x.

ΔR_{12T}....Variation in range in yards due to a motion of the target of 12 knots in the line of fire.

D_T....Deflection in yards due to T_z.

D_{12T}....Deflection in yards due to a motion of the target of 12 knots perpendicular to the line of fire.

a....Angle of real wind with the course of the ship.

a'....Angle of apparent wind with the course of the ship.

W'....Velocity of the real wind in knots per hour.

W''....Velocity of the apparent wind in knots per hour.

PERTAINING TO THE THEORY OF PROBABILITY.

X....Axis of; axis of coordinates lying along range, for points over or short of the target.

Y....Axis of; axis of coordinates in vertical plane through target for points above or below the center of the target.

Z....Axis of; axis of coordinates in vertical plane through target for points to right or left of the center of target.

(z_1, y_1), etc....Coordinates of points of impact in vertical plane through target.

Σz....Summation of z_1, z_2, etc.

Σy....Summation of y_1, y_2, etc.

n....Number of shot.

γ_z....Mean deviation along axis of Z, that is, above or below.

γ_y....Mean deviation along axis of Y, that is, to right or left.

γ_x....Mean deviation along axis of X, that is, in range.

P....Probability that the deviation of a single shot will be numerically less than the given quantity a.

$\frac{a}{\gamma}$....Argument for probability table.

PERTAINING TO VARIATIONS IN THE BALLISTIC ELEMENTS.

ΔX....Variation in the range in feet.

ΔR....Variation in the range in yards.

$\Delta(\sin 2\phi)$....Variation in the sine of twice the angle of departure.

Δ_{VA}....Quantity appearing in Table II of the Ballistic Tables in the Δ_V column pertaining to "A." With figures before the subscript V it shows the amount of variation in V for which used. (Be careful not to confuse this symbol with ΔV or δV.)

δV....Variation in the initial velocity. (Be careful not to confuse this symbol with Δ_{VA} or ΔV.)

ΔV....Difference between V for two successive tables in Table II. (Be careful not to confuse this symbol with Δ_{VA} or δV.)

ΔV_w....Variation in the initial velocity in foot-seconds due to variation in the weight of the projectile in pounds. Figures before the w show the amount of variation in that quantity in pounds.

ΔX_V....Variation in range in feet due to a variation in V in foot-seconds. Figures before the V show the amount of variation in that quantity in foot-seconds.

ΔR_V....Variation in range in yards due to a variation in V in foot-seconds. Figures before the V show the amount of variation in that quantity in foot-seconds.

ΔC....Variation in the ballistic coefficient in percentage.

ΔX_C....Variation in range in feet due to a variation in C in percentage. Figures before the C show the amount of variation in that quantity in percentage.

ΔR_C....Variation in range in yards due to a variation in C in percentage. Figures before the C show the amount of variation in that quantity in percentage.

$\Delta\delta$.... Variation in δ in percentage.

ΔX_δ.... Variation in range in feet due to a variation in δ in percentage. Figures before the δ show the amount of variation in that quantity in percentage.

ΔR_δ.... Variation in range in yards due to a variation in δ in percentage. Figures before the δ show the amount of variation in that quantity in percentage.

Δw.... Variation in w in pounds.

ΔX_w.... Variation in range in feet due to a variation in w in pounds. Figures before the w show the amount of variation in that quantity in pounds.

$\Delta X'_w$.... That part of ΔX_w in feet which is due to the reduction in initial velocity resulting from Δw.

$\Delta X''_w$.... That part of ΔX_w in feet which is due to Δw directly.

ΔR_w.... Variation in range in yards due to a variation in w in pounds. Figures before the w show the amount of variation in that quantity in pounds.

$\Delta R'_w$.... That part of ΔR_w in yards which is due to the reduction in initial velocity resulting from Δw.

$\Delta R''_w$.... That part of ΔR_w in yards which is due to Δw directly.

H.... Change in height of point of impact on a vertical screen through the target, in feet, due to a change of ΔR in R in yards. Figures as subscripts to the H show the change in R necessary to give that particular value of H.

MATHEMATICAL AND MISCELLANEOUS.

g.... Acceleration due to gravity in foot-seconds per second; $g = 32.2$.

dx.... Differential increment in x.

dy.... Differential increment in y.

ds.... Differential increment along the curve, that is, in s.

dv.... Differential increment in v.

dt.... Differential increment in t.

du.... Differential increment in u.

a.... Mayevski's exponent.

A.... Mayevski's coefficient.

R.... Total air resistance in pounds.

R_f.... Total air resistance in pounds under firing conditions.

R_s.... Total air resistance in pounds under standard conditions.

ρ.... Radius of curvature of the trajectory at any point in feet.

k.... The value of $\frac{A}{C}$, in which A is Mayevski's constant and C is the ballistic coefficient.

ϵ.... The base of the Naperian system of logarithms; $\epsilon = 2.7183$.

n.... The ratio between the range in vacuum and the range in air for the same angle of departure.

T_v.... Value of the time integral in seconds for remaining velocity v.

T_V.... Value of the time integral in seconds for initial velocity V.

S_v.... Value of the space integral in feet for remaining velocity v.

S_V.... Value of the space integral in feet for initial velocity V.

T_u.... Value of the time function in seconds for pseudo velocity u.

T_V.... Value of time function in seconds for initial velocity V.

S_u.... Value of space function in feet for pseudo velocity u.

S_V.... Value of space function in feet for initial velocity V.

A_u.... Value of altitude function for pseudo velocity u.

A_V.... Value of altitude function for initial velocity V.

I_u.... Value of inclination function for pseudo velocity u.

I_V.... Value of inclination function for initial velocity V.

S_{u_ω}.... Value of space function in feet for pseudo velocity u_ω.

S_{u_0}.... Value of space function in feet for pseudo velocity u_0.

T_{u_ω}.... Value of time function in seconds for pseudo velocity u_ω.

T_{u_0}....Value of time function in seconds for pseudo velocity u_0.
A_{u_ω}....Value of altitude function for pseudo velocity u_ω.
A_{u_0}....Value of altitude function for pseudo velocity u_0.
I_{u_ω}....Value of inclination function for pseudo velocity u_ω.
I_{u_0}....Value of inclination function for pseudo velocity u_0.
ΔS....Difference between two values of the space function.
ΔT....Difference between two values of the time function.
ΔA....Difference between two values of the altitude function.
ΔI....Difference between two values of the inclination function.
z....General expression for value of argument in Column 1 of Table II of the Ballistic Tables, for any point of the trajectory; $z = \frac{x}{C}$.
Z....Special expression for value of argument in Column 1 of Table II of the Ballistic Tables, for the whole trajectory; $Z = \frac{X}{C}$.
a, b, a', t'.... General values of Ingalls' secondary functions.
A, B, A', T'...., A'' and $B' = \frac{B}{A}$ } Special value of Ingalls' secondary functions for whole trajectory.
ϕ_x....Angle of departure for a horizontal distance x.
$\mu = \frac{k^2}{R^2}$ ....A ratio used in computing the drift; in which k is the radius of gyration of the projectile about its longitudinal axis, and R is the radius of the projectile.
$\frac{\lambda}{h}$ ....A special ratio used in computing the drift.
n....The twist of the rifling, used in computing the drift.
D'....Ingalls' secondary function for drift.
D....Drift in yards.
l....Sight radius in inches.
D....Deflection in yards (used with R in yards in deflection computations).
d....Distance in inches which the sliding leaf is set over to compensate for the deflection D in yards.
i....Permanent sight-bar angle.
h....Sight bar height in inches.
E....Penetration of armor in inches.
K....Constant used in computing penetration of armor.
K'....Constant used in computing penetration of armor.
h....Height of target in feet.
S....Danger space in general.
α...., β...., γ.... } Angles for plotting fall of shot in calibration practice.
(a, a')...., (b, b')...., (c, c')...., (d, d').... } Coordinates of point of fall of shot for plotting in calibration practice.

LETTERS OF THE GREEK ALPHABET USED AS SYMBOLS.

Letter.	Pronunciation.	Letter.	Pronunciation.	Letter.	Pronunciation.
α	Alpha.	θ	Theta.	Σ or σ	Sigma.
β	Beta.	λ	Lambda.	ϕ	Phi.
γ	Gamma.	μ	Mu.	ψ	Psi.
Δ or δ	Delta.	π	Pi.	ω	Omega.
ϵ	Epsilon.	ρ	Rho.		

PART I.

GENERAL AND APPROXIMATE DEDUCTIONS.

INTRODUCTION TO PART I.

Part I of this text book includes the preliminary definitions and discussions, from which we pass to the derivation of the equation to the trajectory in a non-resisting medium, and thence to the principle of the rigidity of the trajectory in vacuum.

As the next step comes the discussion of the resistance of the atmosphere to the passage of a projectile through it, and of the retardation in the motion of the projectile resulting from this resistance; and following this, a consideration of the ballistic coefficient in all its forms; and following this again, a statement of Mayevski's general and special formulæ for retardation, that is, of the general formula, and of the numerical results of experiments to determine the resistance and retardation.

We are then prepared to take up the derivation of the equation to the trajectory in air, having determined the forces that act upon a projectile in flight. We will find that it is only possible to determine such an expression for certain given velocities, but having thus determined it, we will be able to get a comparison between the trajectories in vacuum and in air under similar conditions (for the special conditions under which we were able to derive the equation to the trajectory in air). We can also derive certain formulæ for determining approximate values of the elements of the trajectory in air, by the use of the equation above described.

This completes the preliminary, educational and approximate consideration of the trajectory as a plane curve, and enables us to pass on, in Part II, to the more practical methods actually employed by artillerists in making such computations as are necessary for the successful use of guns. It must be noted, however, that some of the approximate methods given in Part I give results that are sufficiently accurate to render them available for general use, and that these results are actually so used in practice.

CHAPTER 1.

DEFINITIONS AND INTRODUCTORY EXPLANATIONS.

Symbols Introduced.

R'....Range in yards on an inclined plane.
X'....Range in feet on an inclined plane.
R....Horizontal range in yards.
X....Horizontal range in feet.
ϕ....Angle of departure.
ω....Angle of fall.
p....Angle of position.
j....Angle of jump.
ψ....Angle of elevation.
ψ'....Angle of projection.
V....Initial velocity in foot-seconds.
v....Remaining velocity at any point in the trajectory in foot-seconds.
v_0....Remaining velocity at the vertex in foot-seconds.
v_ω....Remaining velocity at the point of fall, or striking velocity, in foot-seconds.
v_h....Horizontal velocity at any point of the trajectory in foot-seconds.
v_v....Vertical velocity at any point of the trajectory in foot-seconds.
u....Pseudo velocity at any point of the trajectory in foot-seconds.
U....Pseudo velocity at the muzzle of the gun in foot-seconds; $U=V$.
u_0....Pseudo velocity at the vertex in foot-seconds.
u_ω....Pseudo velocity at the point of fall in foot-seconds.

1. **Ballistics** is the science of the motion of projectiles, and is divided into two branches; namely, interior ballistics and exterior ballistics. Definitions.

2. **Interior ballistics** is that branch of the science which treats of the motion of the projectile while in the gun and of the phenomena which cause and attend this motion.

3. **Exterior ballistics** is that branch of the science which treats of the motion of the projectile after it leaves the gun. The investigations to be conducted under exterior ballistics therefore begin at the instant when the projectile leaves the muzzle of the gun.

4. There are certain definitions connected with the travel of the projectile after it leaves the gun, and certain symbols which are used to represent the quantities covered by these definitions. These definitions and symbols will now be given.

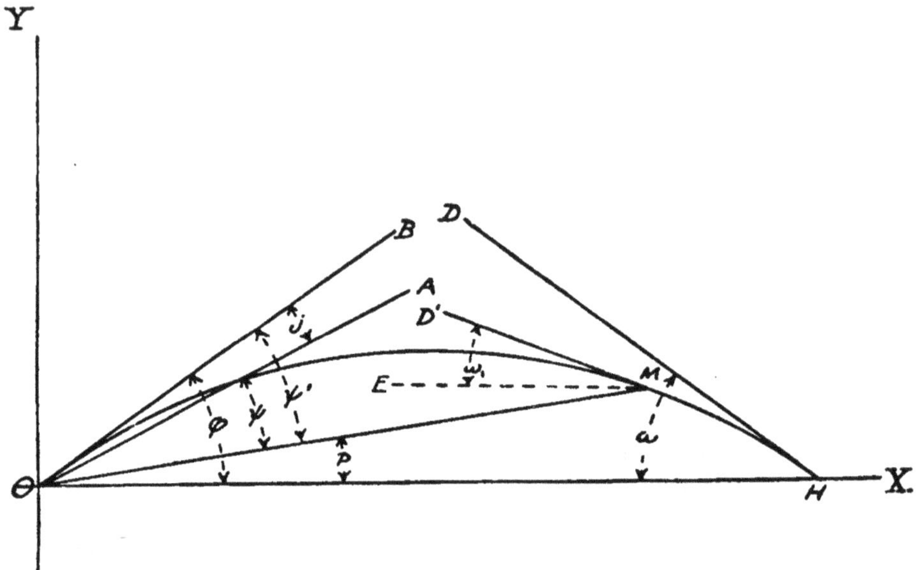

FIGURE 1.

ELEMENTS OF TRAJECTORY.

$BOH = \phi =$ Angle of Departure.	$OM = X' =$ Range.
$H =$ Point of Fall, Horizontal Range.	$BOM = \psi' =$ Angle of Projection.
$DHO = \omega =$ Angle of Fall.	$BOA = j =$ Angle of jump.
$OH = X =$ Horizontal Range.	$AOM = \psi =$ Angle of Elevation.
$OM =$ Line of Position.	$\phi = \psi + j + p = \psi' + p.$
$MOH = p =$ Angle of Position.	When $p = 0.$ $\phi = \psi' = \psi + j.$
$D'ME = \omega' =$ Angle of Fall.	When $p = j = 0,$ $\phi = \psi = \psi'.$

5. The **trajectory** is the curve traced by the projectile in its flight from the muzzle of the gun to the first point of impact, which point of impact is called the **point of fall**; in other words, it is the path of the projectile between those two points considered as a curve.

6. The **elements of the trajectory**, broadly considered, are certain quantities which are now to be defined, such as the initial velocity, range, time of flight, etc., which enter into the mathematical consideration of the trajectory.

7. The **range** is the distance in a straight line from the gun to the point of fall. It will be denoted by R' when given in yards and by X' when given in feet.

8. When the point of fall is in the same horizontal plane as the gun, the range is called the **horizontal range**. It will be denoted by R when given in yards and by X when given in feet. Unless otherwise stated, in discussions and problems, the term **range** will always mean **horizontal range**.

9. The **line of departure** is the line in which the projectile is moving when it leaves the gun. It is tangent to the trajectory at its origin, and, with modern guns, it practically coincides with the axis of the bore of the gun.

10. The **angle of departure** is the angle between the tangent to the trajectory at the origin, that is the line of departure, and the horizontal plane. It will be denoted by ϕ.

11. The **angle of fall** is the angle between the tangent to the trajectory at the point of fall and the horizontal plane. It will be denoted by ω.

12. The **line of position** is the straight line from the gun to the target. As it coincides with the line of vision through the sight when the gun is properly aimed, it is sometimes called the **line of sight.**

13. The **angle of position** is the angle between the line of position and the horizontal plane. It will be denoted by p; and is positive when the target is higher than the gun, and negative when the target is lower than the gun.

14. The **angle of elevation** is the angle between the axis of the bore of the gun and the line of position at the instant before firing. It will be denoted by ψ.

15. The **angle of projection** is the angle between the axis of the bore of the gun and the line of position at the instant the projectile leaves the muzzle. It will be denoted by ψ'.

16. The **angle of jump** or **jump** is the difference between the angle of projection (ψ') and the angle of elevation (ψ); in other words, it is the vertical angle which the axis of the gun describes under the shock of firing during the interval from the ignition of the powder charge to the exit of the projectile from the gun. It will be denoted by j; positive when the muzzle of the gun jumps upward, and negative when it jumps downward. Jump is generally positive, but not invariably so.

17. The **muzzle velocity** or **initial velocity** is the velocity with which the projectile is supposed to leave the muzzle of the gun. It is measured in feet per second, foot-seconds (denoted by f. s.), and is often indicated by the abbreviation I. V. It will be denoted by V. As it is impracticable in practice, for reasons that will be readily apparent, to actually measure the velocity of the projectile at the instant it leaves the muzzle, it is the custom to determine it by actual measurements at a known distance from the gun, that distance being as small as possible and still keep the necessary measuring apparatus from being destroyed by the blast from the gun. Having determined the velocity at this known short distance from the gun, it is the custom to then compute, by formulæ to be derived later, what the velocity would have been at the muzzle had the conditions at the muzzle and from the muzzle to the point of measurement been the same as at that latter point. Actually, however, the projectile, immediately after leaving the muzzle, is surrounded by gases moving even more rapidly than the projectile itself, and experiments have shown that the velocity increases instead of decreases during a travel, which, for large guns, may be as much as fifty yards after leaving the gun. Thus the initial or muzzle velocity used in exterior ballistics is really a fictitious quantity not actually existent when the projectile leaves the muzzle, but which may be more accurately defined as the velocity with which it would be necessary to project the projectile from the muzzle *into still air* in order to have it describe the actual trajectory. **Initial velocity.**

18. The **remaining velocity** at any point in the trajectory is the actual velocity in foot-seconds at that point in a line which is tangent to the trajectory at that point. It will be denoted by v. At the vertex it is denoted by v_0.

19. The **striking velocity** is the remaining velocity at the point of fall. It will be denoted by v_ω.

20. The **horizontal velocity** at any point in the trajectory is the horizontal component of the remaining velocity at that point. It will be denoted by v_h.

21. The **vertical velocity** at any point of the trajectory is the vertical component of the remaining velocity at that point. It will be denoted by v_v.

22. The **pseudo velocity** is an assumed velocity, at any point of the trajectory, parallel to the line of departure, such that its horizontal component is the horizontal velocity at that point. It is a most important quantity in ballistic computations, and

will be denoted by u. At the muzzle it becomes U, and is equal to V; at the vertex it becomes u_0; and at the point of fall it becomes u_ω.

23. The two following assumptions, which are sufficiently correct for all present practical purposes, are made throughout:

1. The force of gravity throughout the trajectory acts in parallel lines perpendicular to the horizontal plane at the gun; the value of g being 32.2 f. s. s.

2. The dimensions of the gun are negligible in comparison with the trajectory. For convenience we may therefore suppose the trajectory to begin at the axis about which the gun is being elevated or depressed, and we will take the horizontal plane through that axis to be the horizontal plane through the gun.

24. Figure 1 represents a trajectory, O indicating the position of the gun or origin, and OH the horizontal plane. Then $BOH=\phi$ is the angle of departure; H the point of fall on the horizontal plane; $DHO=\omega$ is the angle of fall; and $OH=X$ (or R) is the horizontal range. If the target be at M, then OM is the line of position; $MOH=p$ is the angle of position; $D'ME=\omega'$ is the angle of fall; and $OM=X'$ (or R') is the range. $BOM=\psi'$ is the angle of projection, which coincides with the angle of departure, ϕ, when the angle of position, p, is zero. OA represents the position of the axis of the bore at the instant before firing, and OB its position at the instant the projectile leaves the muzzle, the angle between them, $BOA=j$, being the angle of jump. The angle $AOM=\psi$ is the angle of elevation. It will be seen that $\phi=\psi+j+p=\psi'+p$; and that when $p=0$ this becomes $\phi=\psi'=\psi+j$.

25. In studying these definitions it should be noted that in them, as given for the various angles, the angle of departure (ϕ) and the angle of fall (ω) are the only ones that are measured from the horizontal plane, except that of course the position angle (p) is by its very definition the angle between the line of position and that plane. The angle of elevation (ψ) and the angle of projection (ψ') are measured from the line of position. Of course when we are working with horizontal ranges, which is generally the case, and when there is no jump, which is also generally the case (when $p=0$ and $j=0$), then the angle of elevation, angle of projection, and angle of departure all become the same, that is, $\phi=\psi=\psi'$.

26. Being now familiar with certain definitions relating to the trajectory, we may undertake its consideration in a general way. If it were possible to fire the gun and have the whole travel of the projectile take place in a non-resisting medium, as in vacuum for instance, it is apparent that, after it has acquired its initial velocity, the only force acting upon the projectile during its flight is the force of gravity. The derivation of the equation to the trajectory in vacuum and the investigation of its elements therefore becomes a very simple matter, as will be seen in the next chapter.

27. It is also apparent that, as the flight of the projectile necessarily takes place in a resisting medium, that is the atmosphere, there must really be in actual practice, in addition to the force of gravity, a force acting upon it during flight due to the atmospheric resistance. Such being the case, it is evident that the investigation of the trajectory in vacuum, while most necessary from an educational standpoint, must necessarily be of comparatively little real value in the solution of practical problems in gunnery.

28. It is proposed, in this text book, to first discuss the trajectory in vacuum, in order to derive from it such general knowledge as is of value in later work. Then an equation to the trajectory in air will be derived for certain special conditions, in order that it may be compared with the equation to the trajectory in vacuum for the same angle of departure and initial velocity. It will be shown, however, that neither of the above equations is very serviceable for the solution of practical problems in service gunnery with modern velocities, and other mathematical formulæ will be deduced which, while not general equations to the complete trajectory in air as a whole, will nevertheless express the relations that always exist between certain elements of that trajectory. These formulæ will be generally true for all velocities, and will be in such form that practical results can be obtained by their use.

29. These expressions having been deduced, it will be shown how they are used in the computation of the data contained in the range tables; and thence, conversely, how the data contained in those tables can be used in service aboard ship.

30. The assumption that the trajectory in vacuum is a plane curve, as already stated, is based upon the fact that, under these conditions the only force acting upon the projectile in flight is the force of gravity, and as this force acts solely in the vertical plane through the projectile, it is evident that there is no force present to divert the projectile from the original plane of fire. When the flight takes place in air, however, in addition to the force of gravity, we have the atmospheric resistance acting to retard the flight of the projectile, and it is assumed that this resistance acts at every point in the trajectory along the tangent to the curve at such point. This retarding force therefore always acts in the original vertical plane of fire, if our assumption be correct, and therefore the trajectory in air also remains a plane curve.

31. It will be shown later, however, that this assumption, that the resistance of the air always acts in the original vertical plane of fire, is in error, and that the trajectory in air is not exactly a plane curve; but it will also be shown that the errors in the computed values of ranges, angles, times, etc., based on formulæ derived on the assumption that the trajectory is a plane curve, are so small that such results may be considered as practically correct for all desired purposes of this nature. It will also be shown, however, that when it comes to the question of computations involving the actual hitting of a given target, there are forces that enter to divert the projectile from the original vertical plane of fire enough to cause it to fail to hit the point aimed at unless allowance be made for them, even though they are not of sufficient moment to introduce serious errors into computed values of ranges, angles, times, etc.

EXAMPLES.

Note to Examples in this Book.—In very many cases one example gives in tabular form the data for a considerable number of separate problems. In giving out examples, therefore, give one problem in the example to each midshipman.

1. For the following angles of elevation and jump, what are the corresponding angles of projection and departure, the position angle being zero? Draw a curve showing each angle.

Problem.	DATA.		ANSWERS.
	Angle of elevation.	Angle of jump.	Angle of projection = angle of departure.
1	3° 00′	+ 5′	3° 05′
2	2 00	+ 3	2 03
3	2 15	+ 5	2 20
4	3 05	— 5	3 00
5	3 35	+ 5	3 40
6	9 50	—10	9 40

2. For the following angles of elevation, jump and position, what are the corresponding angles of projection and departure? Draw curves showing all angles.

Problem.	DATA.			ANSWERS.	
	Angle of elevation.	Angle of jump.	Angle of position.	Angle of departure.	Angle of projection.
1...........	2° 00′	+5′	+15° 00′	+17° 05′	+2° 05′
2...........	3 00	−3	+12 15	+15 12	+2 57
3...........	3 00	−7	−10 30	− 7 37	+2 53
4...........	2 00	+4	−12 07	−10 03	+2 04
5...........	3 00	+6	+11 15	+14 21	+3 06
6...........	5 00	−5	+10 16	+15 11	+4 55
7...........	4 00	+6	− 9 37	− 5 31	+4 06
8...........	6 00	−8	− 6 22	− 0 30	+5 52

3. A target is at a horizontal distance of 3000 yards from the gun, and is 750 feet higher than the gun above the water. Compute the angle of position by the use of logarithms. *Answer.* $p=4° \ 45' \ 49''$.

4. A target is at a horizontal distance of 10,000 yards from the gun, and is on the water 1500 feet below the level of the gun, the latter being in a battery on a hill. Compute the angle of position by the use of logarithms.

Answer. $p=(-)2° \ 51' \ 45''$.

5. A target is at a horizontal distance of 1924 yards from the gun, and is 1123 feet higher above the water than the gun. Find, by the use of the traverse tables, the angle of position and the distance in a straight line from the gun to the target in yards. *Answers.* $p=11° \ 00' \ 00''$. $R'=1960$ yards.

6. A target is at a horizontal distance of 1860 yards from the gun, and it is on the water 1238 feet below the level of the gun, the latter being in a battery on a hill. Find, by the use of the traverse tables, the angle of position and the distance in a straight line from the gun to the target in yards.

Answers. $p=(-)12° \ 30' \ 31''$. $R'=1905.23$ yards.

CHAPTER 2.

THE EQUATION TO THE TRAJECTORY IN A NON-RESISTING MEDIUM AND THE THEORY OF THE RIGIDITY OF THE TRAJECTORY IN VACUUM.

New Symbols Introduced.

(x, y).... Coordinates of any point of the trajectory in feet.

(x_0, y_0).... Coordinates of the highest point, or vertex, of the trajectory in feet.

θ.... Angle of inclination of the tangent to the trajectory at any point to the horizontal.

t.... Elapsed time of flight from the muzzle to any point on the trajectory in seconds.

t_0.... Elapsed time to the vertex of the trajectory in seconds.

T.... Time of flight from the muzzle to the point of fall in seconds.

g.... Acceleration due to gravity in foot-seconds per second; $g = 32.2$.

dx.... Differential increment in x.

dy.... Differential increment in y.

ds.... Differential increment along the curve, that is, in s.

32. The resistance of the air to the motion of a projectile animated with the high velocity given by a modern gun is so great that calculations which neglect it are of little practical value at the present day, except to aid in a comprehension of the underlying principles of exterior ballistics and to permit comparisons to be made between the travel of a projectile in a non-resisting and in a resisting medium. For these purposes, however, the study of the motion of a projectile in vacuum is of the utmost value, and therefore this chapter will be devoted to this subject, which, through its simplicity, furnishes a valuable groundwork for the correct understanding of the more complex problems which arise when account is taken of the atmospheric resistance.

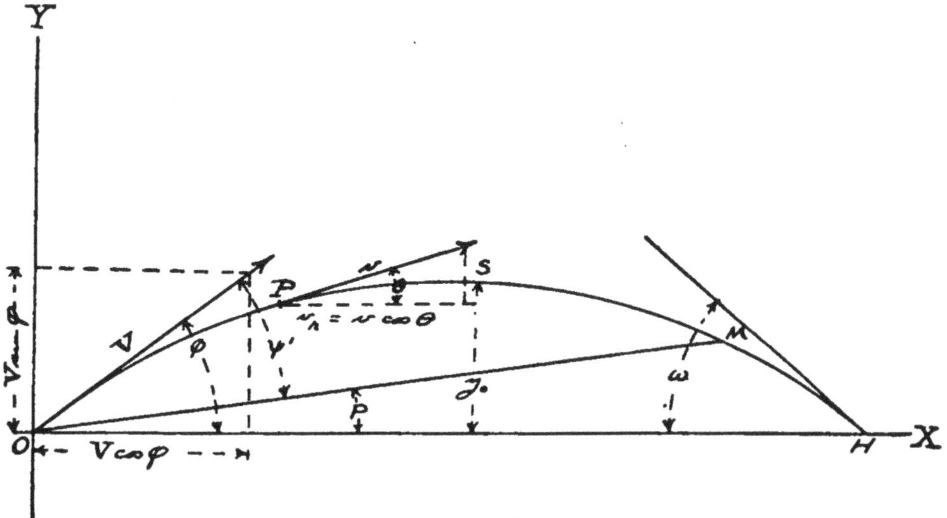

FIGURE 2.

33. Figure 2 represents the trajectory in vacuum, the origin, O, being taken at the gun, the axis of Y vertical, and the axis of X horizontal. The line marked V is the line of departure, and by its length represents the initial velocity, V; the vertical and horizontal components of which are $V \sin \phi$ and $V \cos \phi$, respectively. The remaining velocity, v, at any point of the trajectory, P, whose coordinates are (x, y), and its horizontal component, v_h, are also represented. Letting θ represent the angle at which the tangent to the trajectory at the point P is inclined to the horizontal, we have $v_h = v \cos \theta$.

34. Since the only force acting on the projectile after it leaves the gun is the vertical force of gravity, the projectile will remain throughout its travel in the vertical plane through the line of departure, and the trajectory will be a plane curve.

Primary equations.

35. Let t be the elapsed time from the origin to any point P, whose coordinates are (x, y); and then from the figure we evidently have:

$$x = tV \cos \phi \qquad y = tV \sin \phi - \tfrac{1}{2}gt^2 \tag{1}$$

Equation to trajectory in vacuum.

as $\frac{1}{2}gt^2$ represents the vertical acceleration (in this case negative) due to the action of the force of gravity during the time t. Eliminating t between the two equations given above we have

$$y = x \tan \phi - \frac{gx^2}{2V^2 \cos^2 \phi} \tag{2}$$

and (2) is the equation to the trajectory in vacuum, which trajectory, from the form of its equation, is evidently a parabola with a vertical axis.

36. From the above equation various expressions may be derived from which we can readily determine the values of the different elements of the curve.

Angle of inclination.

37. Differentiating (2) and putting $\tan \theta$ for $\frac{dy}{dx}$, we get

$$\tan \theta = \tan \phi - \frac{gx}{V^2 \cos^2 \phi} \tag{3}$$

which gives the inclination of the curve to the horizontal at any point.

Horizontal range.

38. Putting $y = 0$ in (2), we find two values of x, the first zero, and the second $\frac{V^2 \sin 2\phi}{g}$; consequently the horizontal range, OH, is given by

$$X = \frac{V^2 \sin 2\phi}{g} \tag{4}$$

This shows that, for a given initial velocity, the range increases with the angle of departure up to $\phi = 45°$, when it reaches its maximum value of $\frac{V^2}{g}$; and that the same range is given by either of two angles of departure, one as much greater than 45° as the other is less than 45°.

Variations in angle of inclination.

39. From (3) we see that, as x increases, θ decreases from its initial value of ϕ, until it becomes zero when $\tan \phi = \frac{gx}{V^2 \cos^2 \phi}$; that is, when

$$x = \frac{V^2 \cos^2 \phi \tan \phi}{g} = \frac{V^2 \cos^2 \phi \sin \phi}{g \cos \phi} = \frac{V^2 \sin \phi \cos \phi}{g}$$

$$= \frac{V^2 \sin 2\phi}{2g}{}^{*}, \text{ or, as } X = \frac{V^2 \sin 2\phi}{g}, \text{ when } x = \frac{X}{2}$$

We also see that after this value of x is reached, the value of θ becomes negative, as $\frac{gx}{V^2 \cos^2 \phi}$ then becomes greater than $\tan \phi$; and that for $x = X$, $\theta = -\phi$. That is to say, the highest point or vertex, S, of the curve is midway of the range, and the angle of fall, ω, is equal to the angle of departure, ϕ.

* $\sin 2\phi = 2 \sin \phi \cos \phi$.

40. The maximum ordinate is obtained by putting $x=\frac{X}{2}=\frac{V^2 \sin 2\phi}{2g}$ in (2), whence we have for the coordinates (x_0, y_0) of the vertex **Coordinates of vertex.**

$$x_0=\frac{V^2 \sin 2\phi}{2g}=\frac{X}{2} \qquad y_0=\frac{V^2 \sin^2 \phi}{2g}=\frac{X \tan \phi}{4} \tag{5}$$

This value of y_0 is directly given from the fact that the vertical component of the initial velocity is $V \sin \phi$, since the height to which a body will rise in vacuum is equal to the square of the vertical velocity divided by $2g$.

41. The vertical and horizontal components of the velocity at any time being respectively $\frac{dy}{dt}=V \sin \phi - gt$ and $\frac{dx}{dt}=V \cos \phi$, we have for the remaining velocity at any point (x, y) **Remaining velocity.**

$$v^2=\left(\frac{ds}{dt}\right)^2=\left(\frac{dy}{dt}\right)^2+\left(\frac{dx}{dt}\right)^2=V^2 \sin^2 \phi - 2gtV \sin \phi + g^2t^2 + V^2 \cos^2 \phi \,^*$$

$$=V^2-2gtV \sin \phi + g^2t^2 = V^2 - 2g\left(Vt \sin \phi - \frac{gt^2}{2}\right)$$

whence we have

$$v=\sqrt{V^2-2gy} \tag{6}$$

as from the second equation of (1) we have

$$y=Vt \sin \phi - \tfrac{1}{2}gt^2$$

Thus we see that where $y=0$, both at the origin and at the point of fall on the horizontal plane, $v=V$, or the striking velocity is the same as the initial velocity. Also, putting $y=y_0=\frac{V^2 \sin^2 \phi}{2g}$, we have for the velocity at the vertex $v_0=V \cos \phi$, which of course it must be, since the vertical component of the velocity has been destroyed by gravitation, while the original horizontal component of the initial velocity remains unchanged throughout the trajectory.

42. Since the horizontal velocity is constant and equal to $V \cos \phi$, it is evident that the time to any point whose abscissa is x is given by $t=\frac{x}{V \cos \phi}$, and so the duration of the trajectory, or time of flight, T, is given by **Time of flight.**

$$T=\frac{X}{V \cos \phi}=\sqrt{\frac{2X \tan \phi}{g}} \tag{7}$$

The second of these values is obtained directly from the consideration that if gravity did not act the projectile would rise to the height $(X \tan \phi)$ while moving X horizontally, and so the distance which it falls from the tangent to the curve at the origin under the action of gravity during the time of flight T is given by

$$X \tan \phi = \tfrac{1}{2}gT^2$$

43. To determine the range, X', on an inclined plane, let (x_1, y_1) be the coordinates of the target M, in Figure 2, p being the angle of position, and $\psi'=\phi-p$ the angle of projection. Then from (2) we get **Range on an incline.**

$$\tan p=\frac{y_1}{x_1}=\tan \phi - \frac{gx_1}{2V^2 \cos^2 \phi} \qquad x_1=\frac{2V^2}{g}\cos^2 \phi(\tan \phi - \tan p)$$

But $$\tan \phi - \tan p = \frac{\sin \phi \cos p - \cos \phi \sin p}{\cos \phi \cos p}=\frac{\sin(\phi-p)}{\cos \phi \cos p}$$

Therefore $$x_1=\frac{2V^2}{g}\times\frac{\sin(\phi-p)\cos \phi}{\cos p}=\frac{2V^2}{g}\times\frac{\sin \psi' \cos(\psi'+p)}{\cos p}$$

Whence, since $X'=x_1 \sec p$, we have

$$X'=\frac{2V^2}{g}\times\frac{\sin \psi' \cos(\psi'+p)}{\cos^2 p} \tag{8}$$

* $\sin^2 \phi + \cos^2 \phi = 1$.

Angle of departure on an incline.

44. To determine the angle of departure necessary to give a given range on an inclined plane, we have

$$y_1 = x_1 \tan\phi - \frac{g x_1^2}{2V^2 \cos^2\phi}$$

But $x_1 = X' \cos p$ and $y_1 = X' \sin p$; therefore

$$X' \sin p = X' \cos p \tan\phi - \frac{g X'^2 \cos^2 p}{2V^2 \cos^2\phi}$$

or $$2X'V^2 \cos p \sin\phi \cos\phi - 2X'V^2 \sin p \cos^2\phi - gX'^2 \cos^2 p = 0$$

But $\sin\phi \cos\phi = \frac{1}{2} \sin 2\phi$ and $\cos^2\phi = \frac{1}{2}(1 + \cos 2\phi)$, therefore

$$X'V^2(\sin 2\phi \cos p - \cos 2\phi \sin p) = gX'^2 \cos^2 p + X'V^2 \sin p$$

whence $$\sin(2\phi - p) = \frac{gX'}{V^2} \cos^2 p + \sin p \qquad (9)$$

45. If p were zero, as the angle of departure was ψ', we would have for the horizontal range from (8), $X = \frac{2V^2}{g} \sin\psi' \cos\psi'$, and so the ratio of the range on an inclined plane to the horizontal range, for the same angle of projection, would be

$$\frac{X'}{X} = \frac{\cos(\psi' + p)}{\cos\psi' \cos^2 p} = \sec p(1 - \tan\psi' \tan p) \qquad (10)$$

The value of the second member of (10) is very nearly unity so long as ψ' and p are small angles, being, for example, 0.9992 for $\psi' = 3°$, $p = 5°$; and it therefore follows that, **with small angles of projection and position, we may consider the range as independent of the angle of position.**

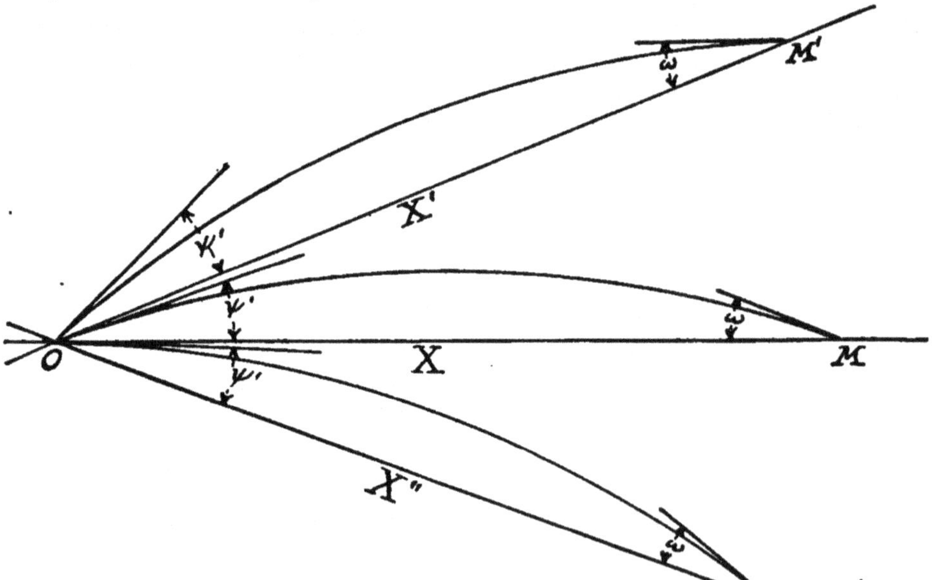

FIGURE 3.

Theory of the rigidity of the trajectory.

46. The assumption in the last line of the preceding paragraph is called the assumption of the rigidity of the trajectory, and evidently consists in supposing that the gun, trajectory, and line of position (a chord of the trajectory) may be turned through a vertical angle, as illustrated in Figure 3, without any change of form. The trajectory is assumed to be rigid in practice when the same sight graduations are used in firing a gun at objects at different heights, or when the gun itself is at different heights relative to the target.

47. As an example of the mathematical work relative to the trajectory in vacuum, and to show the proper logarithmic forms for such work, suppose we have given, in vacuum, an angle of elevation (ψ) of 7° 50′, an angle of jump (j) of +10′, an initial velocity of 2600 f. s., and an angle of position (p) of zero; and desire to compute the horizontal range, time of flight, striking velocity, angle of fall, coordinates of vertex, and time to and remaining velocity at the vertex. (Use Table VI where convenient.)

$$\phi=\psi'=\psi+j;\quad X=\frac{V^2\sin 2\phi}{g};\quad T=\frac{X}{V\cos\phi};\quad v_\omega=V;\quad \omega=\phi$$

$$x_0=\frac{X}{2};\quad y_0=\frac{X\tan\phi}{4};\quad t_0=\frac{T}{2};\quad v_0=V\cos\phi$$

$V=2600$	2 log 6.82994	colog 6.58503—10		log 3.41497
$\phi=8°\ 00'$		sec 0.60425	tan 9.14780—10	cos 9.99575—10
$2\phi=16°\ 00'$	sin 9.44034—10			
$g=32.2$	colog 8.49214—10			
4			colog 9.39794—10	
$X=57865.5'$	log 4.76242	log 4.76242	log 4.76242	
$T=22.475$		log 1.35170		
$y_0=2033.1$			log 3.30816	
$v_0=2574.65$				log 3.41072

Results.

$R=19288.5$ yards.	$x_0=9644.25$ yards.
$T=22.475$ seconds.	$y_0=2033.1$ feet.
$\omega=8°\ 00'$.	$t_0=11.2375$ seconds.
$v_\omega=2600$ f. s.	$v_0=2574.65$ f. s.

48. And, again, suppose the angle of position (p) to be 30°, the angle of projection (ψ') to be 2° 25′ 45″, and the initial velocity 2900 f. s.; and it is desired to find the range on the incline and the time of flight, both in vacuum.

$$X'=\frac{2V^2}{g}\times\frac{\sin\psi'\cos(\psi'+p)}{\cos^2 p};\ \cos p=\frac{x}{X'};\ \text{therefore, } x=X'\cos p, \text{ and}$$

$$t=\frac{x}{V\cos\phi},\ \text{whence } T=\frac{X'\cos p}{V\cos\phi},\ \text{where } \phi=\psi'+p$$

$V=2900$		2 log 6.92480	colog 6.53760−10
$p=30°\ 00'\ 00''$	sec 0.06247	2 sec 0.12494	cos 9.93753−10
$\psi'=2°\ 25'\ 45''$		sin 8.62721−10	
$\phi=32°\ 25'\ 45''$		cos 9.92637−10	sec 0.07363
$g=32.2$	log 1.50786	colog 8.49214−10	
2		log 0.30103	
$X'=24916.5$		log 4.39649	log 4.39649
$T=8.8155$			log 0.94525

Results. $R'=8305.5$ yards. $T=8.8155$ seconds.

EXAMPLES.

1. If the initial velocity and angle of departure are as given in the first two columns of the following table, compute the horizontal and vertical components of the velocity at the point of origin, in vacuum. Give results obtained by both the use of logarithms and by the use of the traverse tables without logarithms.

Problem.	DATA.		ANSWERS.			
	Initial velocity. f. s.	Angle of departure.	By logs.		By traverse tables.	
			v_h. f. s.	v_v. f. s.	v_h. f. s.	v_v. f. s.
1	1000	2° 00′ 00″	999	35	999	35
2	1100	3 15 42	1098	63	1098	63
3	1250	4 25 16	1246	96	1246	96
4	1400	5 10 25	1394	126	1394	126
5	1500	10 12 14	1476	266	1476	265
6	1750	7 30 00	1735	228	1735	229
7	2000	5 00 00	1992	174	1992	174
8	2400	9 21 15	2368	390	2368	390
9	2600	12 37 54	2537	569	2537	569
10	2900	17 24 24	2767	868	2767	868

NOTE.—It will be seen from the above that the traverse tables give the results correctly to the nearest foot-second, which is all that is required in ordinary work.

2. The data being as given in the first three columns of the following table, find the results, in vacuum, required by the other columns.

Problem.	DATA.			ANSWERS.				
	Initial velocity. f. s.	Angle of elevation.	Angle of jump.	Angle of departure.	Horizontal range. Yds.	Time of flight. Secs.	Angle of fall.	Striking velocity. f. s.
1	1000	5° 27′	+ 7′	5° 34′	1999	6.03	5° 34′	1000
2	1100	4 32	+ 3	4 35	1995	5.46	4 35	1100
3	1250	3 33	− 3	3 30	1971	4.74	3 30	1250
4	1400	2 15	− 5	2 10	1533	3.29	2 10	1400
5	1500	7 22	+ 6	7 28	6002	12.11	7 28	1500
6	1750	8 12	0	8 12	8951	15.50	8 12	1750
7	2000	12 37	− 7	12 30	17500	26.89	12 30	2000
8	2400	7 50	−10	7 40	15767	19.89	7 40	2400
9	2600	3 07	+ 3	3 10	7719	8.92	3 10	2600
10	2900	16 35	+ 5	16 40	47840	51.66	16 40	2900

3. Given the initial velocities and angles of departure in the table below, compute the coordinates of the vertex, and the time to and remaining velocity at the vertex, in vacuum.

Problem.	DATA. Initial velocity. f. s.	Angle of departure.	ANSWERS. x_0. Yds.	y_0. Feet.	t_0. Secs.	v_0. f. s.
1	1000	5° 34′	999	146	3.01	995
2	1100	4 35	998	120	2.73	1096
3	1250	3 30	986	90	2.37	1248
4	1400	2 10	767	44	1.64	1399
5	1500	7 28	3001	590	6.05	1487
6	1750	8 12	4475	967	7.75	1732
7	2000	12 30	8750	2910	13.44	1953
8	2400	7 40	7884	1592	9.94	2379
9	2600	3 10	3860	320	4.46	2596
10	2900	16 40	23920	10742	25.83	2778

4. A body is projected in vacuum with $V=1000$ f. s., and an angle of departure of 30°. Where is it after 3 seconds? Where after 10 seconds?

Answers. 3 seconds. $x=1500\sqrt{3}$ feet. $y=1355$ feet.
10 seconds. $x=5000\sqrt{3}$ feet. $y=3390$ feet.

5. A body is projected in vacuum from the top of a tower 200 feet high, with a velocity of 50 f. s., and an angle of departure of 60°. Find the range on the horizontal plane through the foot of the tower, and the time of flight.

Answers. Range=128 feet. Time=5.12 seconds.

6. What is the angle of departure in vacuum in order that the horizontal range may be: (a) Equal to the maximum ordinate of the trajectory; and (b), equal to three times the maximum ordinate?

Answers. (a) 75° 57′ 51″. (b) 53° 07′ 48″.

7. Compute the initial velocity and angle of departure in vacuum in order that the projectile may be 100 feet high at a horizontal distance from the gun of a quarter of a mile, and may have a horizontal range of one mile.

Answers. For 1 mile=5280 feet. 5° 46′ 05″. 922 f. s.
For 1 mile=6080 feet. 5° 00′ 07″. 1062 f. s.

8. The angle of position is 45°, the angle of projection is 1° 16′ 31″, and the initial velocity is 1500 f. s. Compute the range on the incline and the time of flight, in vacuum. *Answers.* $R'=1433$ yards. $T=2.93$ seconds.

9. What must be the angle of projection in vacuum for an initial velocity of 400 f. s. in order that the range may be 2500 yards on a plane that descends at an angle of 30°?

Answer. Angle of projection. 34° 35′ 56″ or 85° 24′ 04″.

10. A body is projected in vacuum with an angle of departure of 60°, and an initial velocity of 150 f. s. Compute the coordinates of its position and its remaining velocity after 5 seconds; also the direction of its motion.

Answers. $x=375$ feet. $y=247$ feet.
$\theta=(-)22° 31′ 25″$. $v=81$ f. s.

11. A 12″ mortar shell weighing 610 pounds, fired with an initial velocity of 591 f. s., and an angle of departure of 73°, gave an observed horizontal range in air of 1939 yards, and a time of flight of 36 seconds. What would the range and time of flight have been in vacuum? *Answers.* $R = 2022$ yards. $T = 35.10$ seconds.

12. The measured range in air of a 12″ shell of 850 pounds weight, fired with 2800 f. s. initial velocity, and an angle of departure of 7° 32′, was 11,900 yards, and the time of flight was 19.5 seconds. What would the range and time of flight have been in vacuum? *Answers.* $R = 21{,}097$ yards. $T = 22.8$ seconds.

CHAPTER 3.

THE RESISTANCE OF THE AIR, THE RETARDATION RESULTING THEREFROM, AND THE BALLISTIC COEFFICIENT.

New Symbols Introduced.

w.... Weight of projectile in pounds.
d.... Diameter of projectile in inches.
a.... Mayevski's exponent.
A.... Mayevski's constant.
R.... Total air resistance in pounds.
R_f.... Total air resistance under firing conditions in pounds.
R_s.... Total air resistance under standard conditions in pounds.
δ_1.... Standard density of air, taken as unity.
δ.... Density of air at time of firing, and subsequently representing the ratio $\frac{\delta}{\delta_1} = \frac{\delta}{1}$.
c.... Coefficient of form of the projectile.
C.... Ballistic coefficient.
f.... Altitude factor.
β.... Integration factor.
Y.... Maximum ordinate, or ordinate of the vertex, in feet; $Y = y_0$.
dv.... Differential increment in v.
dt.... Differential increment in t.
K.... Constant part of ballistic coefficient for a given projectile; $K = \frac{w}{cd^2}$.

49. The first investigations of the resistance offered by the air to and the resultant retardation in the travel of the projectile were in the nature of practical experiments conducted from time to time by a number of persons, and indeed, although later mathematical investigations have led to a fuller understanding of the subject, the formulæ still in use for the determination of atmospheric resistance and the retardation resulting from it are the results of these experiments; in other words, they are partly empirical, and not purely mathematical. The list of men who conducted these experiments includes many names prominent in the records of scientific research, such as Tartaglia, Galileo, Newton, Bernouilli (Ber-nō-yē), Robins, Count Rumford, Dr. Hutton, Wheatstone, Bashforth, Mayevski (Mäijévski) and Zaboudski (Zäböŭdski). The results of Bashforth's experiments, as expressed in formulæ by Mayevski, and modified and extended by Zaboudski, form the basis upon which calculations for resistance and retardation still rest. **Measurement of retardation.**

50. As it is manifestly simpler to determine experimentally the retardation produced in the flight of a projectile than it is to attempt to measure the atmospheric pressure opposing its motion, the experiments have naturally taken that direction. To measure the retardation, a gun is given a very slight elevation, and the velocity of the projectile is measured at two points sufficiently far apart to make the two velocities (v_1 and v_2) appreciably different, and yet near enough together to ensure, as closely as possible, that the resistance of the air does not change from one point of measurement to the other. The two pairs of screens used for measuring the velocities should be at about the same level, so that the effect of gravity may be neglected.

Having determined these two velocities, it is evident that the retardation of the projectile while traveling the distance, x, between the two points of measurement is v_1-v_2. Let w be the weight of the projectile, R the resistance of the air in pounds (total resistance). Then, since the work done by the resistance must equal the loss of energy of the projectile, we have

$$Rx=\frac{w}{2g}(v_1^2-v_2^2)$$

whence.

$$R=\frac{w}{2gx}(v_1^2-v_2^2) \qquad (11)$$

where R is taken to be the total resistance of the air in pounds which corresponds to the mean velocity $\frac{v_1+v_2}{2}$.

As an example of the use of the above formula, suppose we have a 12″ projectile weighing 870 pounds, fired through two pairs of screens 300 feet apart, and the measured velocity at the first pair was 2819 f. s. and at the second pair was 2757 f. s. These measured velocities are the mean velocities for the spaces traversed between the two screens of each pair, that is, we may assume that each velocity is the velocity at the point midway between the two screens of its own pair. The distance given as 300 feet is the distance between the midway points of each pair of screens.

Also, for determining the value of $(v_1^2-v_2^2)$, we know that $v_1^2-v_2^2=(v_1+v_2)(v_1-v_2)$, and the work becomes:

$v_1+v_2=5576$		log 3.74632
$v_1-v_2=62$		log 1.79239
$w=870$		log 2.93952
$x=300$	log 2.47712	colog 7.52288−10
$2g=64.4$	log 1.80889	colog 8.19111−10
$R=15567.5$ pounds		log 4.19222

in which R is the resistance for the mean of the two measured velocities, that is, for $\frac{v_1+v_2}{2}=2788$ f. s.

Experimental results. **51.** As the result of many such measurements with different projectiles and different velocities, it has been shown that the resistance of the air is proportional to:

1. The cross-sectional area of the projectile; or, what is the same thing, the square of its diameter, which is the caliber.
2. The density of the air; or, what is the same thing, the weight of a cubic foot of the air.
3. A power of the velocity, of which the exponent varies with the velocity, but may be considered as a constant within certain limits of velocity.
4. A coefficient which varies with the velocity, with the form of the projectile, and with the assumed value of the exponent; but which may be considered as a constant for any given projectile between the same limits of velocity for which the exponent is considered as a constant.

Mayevski's formula. **52.** In accordance with these four experimentally determined laws, we may write a general formula expressing the retardation of a projectile caused by the atmospheric resistance to its flight; which is Mayevski's formula. It would be:

$$\text{Retardation}=\frac{dv}{dt}=-A\frac{\delta c d^2}{w}v^a \qquad (12)$$

in which a is Mayevski's exponent, A is Mayevski's constant coefficient, c is the coefficient of form of the projectile, d the diameter of the projectile, w the weight of the projectile, and v the velocity. The acceleration, which is negative in this case, is of course represented by $\frac{dv}{dt}$.

53. The quantity δ in the above equation represents the ratio of the density of half-saturated air for the temperature of the air and barometric height at the time of firing to the density of half-saturated air for 15° C. (59° F.) and 750 mm. (29.5275″) barometric height. The values of δ for different readings of the barometer (in inches) and thermometer (in degrees Fahrenheit) may be found in Table III of the Ballistic Tables.

54. In the above expression, c is the coefficient of form of the projectile. It will be readily understood that if certain results are obtained with a projectile of a given shape, a change in the shape of the projectile will change the results. Therefore the factor c is introduced, and values for it for different projectiles are determined experimentally, as explained later.

55. Mayevski adopted as standard the form of projectile in most common use at the time he conducted his experiments, which was one about three calibers in length, with an ogival head the radius to the curve of which ogive was two calibers, and for that projectile called the value of c unity. He also used a temperature of 59° F. and a barometric height of 29.5275″ as standard, thus reducing the value of δ to unity also. His general expression then becomes

$$\frac{dv}{dt} = -A\frac{d^2}{w}v^n \tag{13}$$

By determining velocities experimentally as explained in paragraph 50, he proceeded, on this formula as a basis, to derive specific laws for finding the retardation at different velocities.

56. As the result of these experiments he derived the following expressions:

v between 3600 f. s. and 2600 f. s.

$$\frac{dv}{dt} = -A_1\frac{d^2}{w}v^{1.55} \qquad \log A_1 = 7.60905-10$$

v between 2600 f. s. and 1800 f. s.

$$\frac{dv}{dt} = -A_2\frac{d^2}{w}v^{1.7} \qquad \log A_2 = 7.09620-10$$

v between 1800 f. s. and 1370 f. s.

$$\frac{dv}{dt} = -A_3\frac{d^2}{w}v^2 \qquad \log A_3 = 6.11926-10$$

v between 1370 f. s. and 1230 f. s.

$$\frac{dv}{dt} = -A_4\frac{d^2}{w}v^3 \qquad \log A_4 = 2.98090-10 \tag{14}$$

v between 1230 f. s. and 970 f. s.

$$\frac{dv}{dt} = -A_5\frac{d^2}{w}v^5 \qquad \log A_5 = 6.80187-20$$

v between 970 f. s. and 790 f. s.

$$\frac{dv}{dt} = -A_6\frac{d^2}{w}v^3 \qquad \log A_6 = 2.77344-10$$

v between 790 f. s. and 0 f. s.

$$\frac{dv}{dt} = -A_7\frac{d^2}{w}v^2 \qquad \log A_7 = 5.66989-10$$

57. From the above expressions, by using the appropriate one, the retardation for any velocity in foot-seconds may be calculated for the standard projectile and standard condition of atmosphere as adopted by Mayevski; and thence for any other projectile or atmospheric condition by applying the proper multipliers. Of course the total resistance of the air in pounds (R) may be found by multiplying the mass of the projectile by the retardation, so we have

$$R = A\frac{d^2}{w}v^a \times \frac{w}{g} = A\frac{d^2}{g}v^a \qquad (15)$$

58. For instance, given a 6″ shell weighing 105 pounds, traveling with a velocity of 2500 f. s.; to find the resistance and retardation under standard atmospheric conditions, provided it be a standard shell.

$$\frac{dv}{dt} = -A\frac{d^2}{w}v^a \qquad R = A\frac{d^2}{g}v^a$$

For 2500 f. s., Mayevski's constants are $a = 1.7$ and $\log A = 7.09620 - 10$.

$v = 2500$	log 3.39794		loglog 0.53121
$a = 1.7$			log 0.23045
$v^a =$	log 5.77640		loglog 0.76166
$A =$	log 7.09620 − 10		
$d^2 = 36$	log 1.55630		
Ad^2v^a	log 4.42890	log 4.42890	
$w = 105$	log 2.02119		
$g = 32.2$		log 1.50786	
$\frac{dv}{dt} = -255.69$ f. s.	log 2.40771		
$R = 833.75$ pounds		log 2.92104	

In the case of the experimental firing, suppose the above shell gave measured velocities of 2525 f. s. and 2475 f. s. at two points 488.88 feet apart, to find the resistance:

$$R = \frac{w}{2gx}(v_1^2 - v_2^2) = \frac{w}{2gx}(v_1 + v_2)(v_1 - v_2)$$

$v_1 + v_2 = 5000$		log 3.69897
$v_1 - v_2 = 50$		log 1.69897
$w = 105$		log 2.02119
$2g = 64.4$	log 1.80889	colog 8.19111 − 10
$x = 488.88$	log 2.68920	colog 7.31080 − 10
$R = 833.75$ pounds		log 2.92104

59. These results being only for standard conditions, we must introduce another factor if we desire results for any other conditions. This factor is known as the ballistic coefficient, and is denoted by C. It is a most important quantity to which great attention must be paid and which we must strive to thoroughly understand, for it enters constantly into nearly every problem in exterior ballistics. It represents the combination of the different elements already explained as well as some other elements which will now be discussed.

60. Introducing the ballistic coefficient, equation (12) becomes:

$$\frac{dv}{dt} = -\frac{A}{C}v^a \qquad (16)$$

In other words, the values resulting from the use of the specific formulæ given in (14) must be divided by C for the individual case and conditions in order to get results for any other than standard conditions.

61. The value of C in its most complete form is given by the expression: **Ballistic coefficient.**

$$C=\frac{\delta_1 fw}{\beta\delta cd^2} \qquad (17)$$

in which

w = the weight of the projectile in pounds.
d = the diameter of the projectile in inches (caliber of the gun).
c = the coefficient of form of the projectile.
f = the altitude factor.
β = the integration factor.
δ = the density of the air at the time of firing.
δ_1 = the adopted standard density of the air.

62. Considering these factors in detail:

Weight and diameter. w and d are standard characteristics of the projectile, and need no special remark.

Coefficient of form. c is a quantity representing the form of the projectile. It may readily be conceived that for a projectile more sharply pointed than the standard its value would be less than unity and that the shell would suffer less retardation than the standard projectile (for the modern 12", long-pointed shell, for instance, $c=0.61$), whereas for a blunter shell, its value would exceed unity (for a flat-headed projectile the value of c is probably greater than 2). It has been found that the value of c depends to some extent upon the smoothness and the length of the projectile, but that it depends primarily upon the shape of the head. Apparently the form of the head near its junction with the cylindrical body is also a most important factor in determining the resistance of the air to the flight of the projectile. The U. S. Navy method of determining the value of c for any projectile by experimental firing will be explained later. (See page 167, Par. 260.)

Density factor. δ_1 represents the adopted standard density of the air, which has been taken as the density of half-saturated air for 15° C. (59° F.) and 750 mm. (29.5275") barometric height. δ represents the density of half-saturated air for the given temperature and barometric height at the time of firing. Assuming that $\delta_1=1$ for the standard condition, Table III of the Ballistic Tables has been computed for the values of $\frac{\delta}{\delta_1}$ for different readings of the thermometer in degrees Fahrenheit and barometer in inches; and as $\frac{\delta}{\delta_1}$ then becomes $\frac{\delta}{1}$, when this table is used, $\frac{\delta}{\delta_1}$ may be replaced by δ in the formulæ. Hereafter the symbol δ will be used to represent this ratio, and (17) then becomes $C=\frac{fw}{\beta\delta cd^2}$, in which δ is taken from Table III.

Altitude factor. f is a factor which enters in cases in which we can no longer assume that the density of the air is the same at all points of the trajectory, owing to the fact that the path of the projectile rises to a considerable height above the level of the gun, or passes to a considerable vertical distance below the level of the gun, as when firing from an elevated battery down to the water. In such cases, f, which is known as the altitude factor, must enter into the computation of the value of the ballistic coefficient. f is the ratio of the density of the air at the gun to the mean density of the air through which the projectile actually passes. The mean height of the projectile during flight is ordinarily taken as two-thirds the height of the vertex of the trajectory, which would be exact were the trajectory in air a true parabola. This is therefore ordinarily practically correct, and the mean density of the air is taken to be the same as the density at a height of $\frac{2}{3}Y$. The value of f for any height in feet will be found in Table V of the Ballistic Tables.

For firing when gun and target are in approximately the same horizontal plane, correction for altitude is ordinarily a needless refinement for trajectories for which the time of flight does not exceed about 12 seconds. (This time of flight corresponds to 9700 yards for Gun " N.") In computing range table data, the correction for altitude is generally started when such correction would produce a variation in the angle of departure of about one minute in arc.

In all problems in which the vertical distance of the point aimed at above or below the horizontal plane of the gun is such that the rigidity of the trajectory cannot be

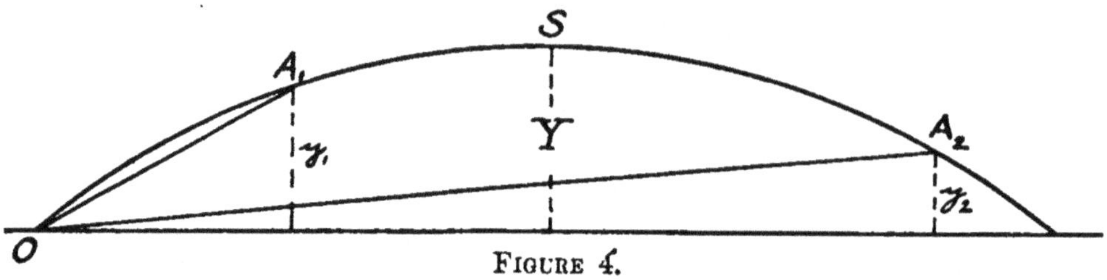

FIGURE 4.

taken for granted, the ballistic coefficient should be corrected for altitude; and an examination of Figure 4 will show that the mean height of the trajectory from gun to target is less or greater than two-thirds the height of the target above the horizontal plane of the gun according as the target is nearer to or further from the gun than the vertex of the complete trajectory. Thus, if the target be at A_1, the mean height of the arc OA_1 is less than $\frac{2}{3}y_1$, and approaches $\frac{y_1}{2}$ more and more as A_1 is nearer and nearer O; while if the target be at A_2 the mean height of the arc OA_2 is greater than $\frac{2}{3}y_2$, being about equal to y_2 when the abscissa of A_2 is $\frac{3}{4}X$. If, therefore, all possible refinements are to be introduced into the calculations, the relative positions of target and vertex must be determined before fixing the value of f. Generally speaking, however, it will be sufficiently accurate to give f the value corresponding to $Y=\frac{2}{3}y_1$.

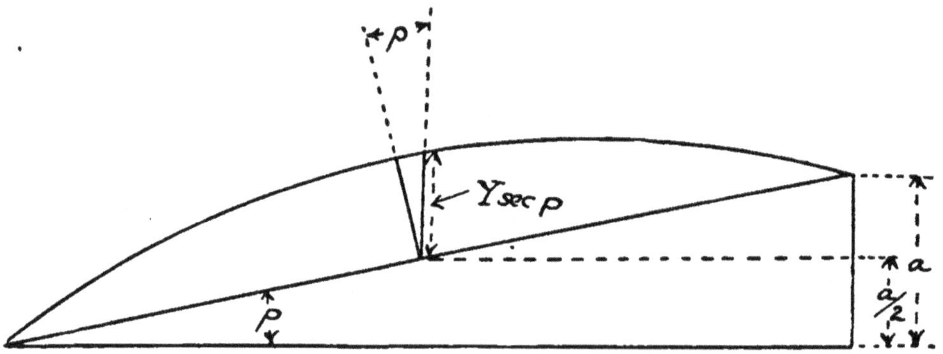

FIGURE 5.

The two preceding paragraphs explain how to determine the value of f for either: (1) A horizontal trajectory with a maximum ordinate sufficiently great to make it necessary to correct for altitude; or (2) in the case in which there is a material difference in height between the gun and the target. For the third possible case, a very likely one in naval operations, that of long-range firing at an elevated target, it is apparent that we have here both of the conditions calling for the use of the factor f as previously discussed. **In the light of what has been said, an approximate rule that would probably not lead to material error in most cases, is to take the value of f**

from the table for a height equal to two-thirds the maximum ordinate or two-thirds the height of the target, whichever of the two gives the greater height.

The rule given in the preceding subparagraph is of course only approximate, and a reference to Figure 5 will show at once that a closer approximation to the mean height of travel would really be $\frac{1}{2}a+\frac{2}{3}Y \sec p$, and that the value of f would then be taken from the table for the height determined by the above expression (not for two-thirds of it). It is believed, however, that the first rule given is sufficiently accurate for all ordinary cases; although special consideration should be given to this point in all cases involving peculiar conditions.

β is a quantity known as the integration factor, and will be explained later. (See page 83.) For the present it may be assumed to be equal to unity, and it will therefore disappear from the formula for the value of the ballistic coefficient for all our practical purposes. **Integration factor.**

63. C, as given in its fullest form in paragraph 61, is sometimes known as the reduced ballistic coefficient, the form used by Mayevski, $C=\frac{w}{cd^2}$, being called the ballistic coefficient. The expression for the value of this ballistic coefficient should always be remembered in its fullest form, however, and the different factors entering into it allowed to drop out by becoming unity as the conditions of actual firing approach the standard conditions.

64. Suppose we desire to find the value of the ballistic coefficient for the 12″ gun, $w=870$, $c=0.61$, for 30.14″ barometer and 24.5° F., when the highest point of the trajectory is 3333 feet. The formula is $C=\frac{fw}{\delta cd^2}$. We could work it out directly from this formula, but where investigations are to be carried out in regard to any one particular gun and projectile, it is convenient to work out the combined value of the constant factors for that projectile, that is, for w, c and d^2, and having once determined this, thereafter for the given gun and projectile we have only to apply δ and f to this constant to get the value of the ballistic coefficient under the given conditions. Expressed mathematically this is:

$$K=\frac{w}{cd^2} \qquad C=\frac{f}{\delta}K$$

and for the above problem the work becomes:

$w=870$		log 2.93952
$c=.61$	log 9.78533−10	colog 0.21467
$d^2=144$	log 2.15836	colog 7.84164−10
$K=9.9045$		log 0.99583

Now, from Table III, for 30.14″ and 24.5°, we find $\delta=1.0947$. And, from Table V, for a height of $\frac{2\times 3333}{3}=2222$ feet, we find $f=1.059$. Hence, for our special case, we have

$K=$		log 0.99583
$f=1.059$		log 0.02490
$\delta=1.0947$	log 0.03929	colog 9.96071−10
$C=9.5816$		log 0.98144

65. Referring to the second part of paragraph 58, we see that we found experimentally that a certain resistance existed at the time of firing to the passage of a certain projectile through the air. Let us now suppose that the coefficient of form of the projectile used was $c=0.61$, and that the barometer stood at 30.14″, and the thermometer at 24.5° F. at the time of firing. What would be, from this experimental firing, the resistance to a standard projectile under standard atmospheric conditions? The air on firing, being more dense than standard, the resistance would be less under standard conditions, that is, $R_s = \frac{1}{\delta} R_f$. The projectile used being more tapering than the standard, would pass more easily through the air, and the resistance to the standard projectile would be more than that measured, that is, $R_s = \frac{1}{c} R_f$; and combining, $R_s = \frac{1}{\delta c} R_f$

$R_f = 833.75$ .... log 2.92104
$\delta = 1.0947$ ....log 0.03929..................colog 9.96071−10
$c = .61$ ....log 9.78533−10..............colog 0.21467

$R_s = 1248.6$ pounds .... log 3.09642

66. Suppose that we have given that, for a 12″ gun: $w = 870$; $c = 0.61$; two measured velocities at points 920 feet apart were 2840 f. s. and 2810 f. s.; to determine the resistance, and then discuss the difference between the results obtained by actual firing and by the use of Mayevski's formula. For simplicity in computation, consider the atmospheric conditions as standard. By Mayevski's formula

$$R = A\frac{cd^2}{g}v^a;\quad \text{Mean velocity} = 2825 \text{ f. s.};\quad a = 1.55;\quad \log A = 7.60905 - 10$$

$v = 2825$ ......log 3.45102...............................loglog 0.53794
$a = 1.55$ .... log 0.19033

$v^a =$ .... log 5.34900.................loglog 0.72827
$c = .61$ .... log 9.78533−10
$A =$ .... log 7.60905−10
$d^2 = 144$ .... log 2.15836
$g = 32.2$ ....log 1.50786....colog 8.49214−10

$R = 2476.7$ pounds .... log 3.39388

By actual firing: $R = \frac{w}{2gx}(v_1^2 - v_2^2) = \frac{w}{2gx}(v_1 + v_2)(v_1 - v_2)$

$v_1 + v_2 = 5650$ .... log 3.75205
$v_1 - v_2 = 30$ .... log 1.47712
$w = 870$ .... log 2.93952
$2g = 64.4$ ....log 1.80889................colog 8.19111−10
$x = 920$ ....log 2.96379................colog 7.03621−10

$R = 2488.9$ pounds .... log 3.39601

If by our experimental firing we find as above that the resistance is 2488.9 pounds for the given projectile, when moving with a velocity of 2825 f. s., and assuming that at this velocity the resistance varies as the 1.55th power of the velocity, what would be the value of Mayevski's constant A in this case?

$$R = A\frac{cd^2}{g}v^a \quad \text{therefore} \quad A = \frac{g}{cd^2v^a}R$$

$R = 2488.9$ .... log 3.39601
v^a (from preceding problem)...log 5.34900................colog 4.65100−10
$g = 32.2$ .... log 1.50786
$c = 0.61$ ....log 9.78533−10............colog 0.21467
$d^2 = 144$ ....log 2.15836................colog 7.84164−10

$A = .0040849$ .... log 7.61118−10

But Mayevski gives for A for this velocity a value of $A = .0040649$, of which $\log A = 7.60905 - 10$.

This difference simply means that Mayevski's value is the mean of a large number of values obtained by experimental firings, such as the one worked out above; and that the value of A found above is the one resulting from a single firing only. The difference between them therefore simply represents the difference between a mean value resulting from many experiments and one of the many individual values that go to make up such a mean.

NOTE.—See Chapter 15 for a more full discussion of the coefficient of form, the subject being there treated according to the most modern practical methods now employed in the U. S. Navy. In this later consideration a different method of determining the values of the coefficient of form and ballistic coefficient is employed, and in fact a somewhat different conception of what the coefficient of form really is is adopted. A comprehension of the methods of this present chapter is however very necessary in understanding the explanations contained in Chapter 15.

EXAMPLES.

1. Compute the value of K $\left(C = \frac{fw}{\delta c d^2} = \frac{f}{\delta} K\right)$ in the ballistic coefficient in the cases given in the following table; giving the values of log K and colog K. Do not use Table VI of the Ballistic Tables in these computations; as this question calls for the computation of the data contained in that table.

Problem.	DATA.				ANSWERS.		
	Gun.				$K = \frac{w}{cd^2}$.		
	d. In.	*w.* Lbs.	*c.*	*V.* f. s.	*K.*	log *K.*	colog *K.*
A..........	3	13	1.00	1150	1.4444	0.15970	9.84030 — 10
B..........	3	13	1.00	2700	1.4444	0.15970	9.84030 — 10
C..........	4	33	0.67	2900	3.0783	0.48832	9.51168 — 10
D..........	5	50	1.00	3150	2.0000	0.30103	9.69897 — 10
E..........	5	50	0.61	3150	3.2787	0.51570	9.48430 — 10
F..........	6	105	0.61	2600	4.7814	0.67956	9.32044 — 10
G..........	6	105	1.00	2300	2.9166	0.46489	9.53511 — 10
H..........	6	105	0.61	2800	4.7814	0.67956	9.32044 — 10
I..........	7	165	1.00	2700	3.3673	0.52728	9.47272 — 10
J..........	7	165	0.61	2700	5.5201	0.74195	9.25805 — 10
K..........	8	260	0.61	2750	6.6598	0.82346	9.17654 — 10
L..........	10	510	1.00	2700	5.1000	0.70757	9.29243 — 10
M..........	10	510	0.61	2700	8.3605	0.92224	9.07776 — 10
N..........	12	870	0.61	2900	9.9045	0.99583	9.00417 — 10
O..........	13	1130	1.00	2000	6.6863	0.82519	9.17481 — 10
P..........	13	1130	0.74	2000	9.0355	0.95596	9.04404 — 10
Q..........	14	1400	0.70	2000	10.2040	1.00877	8.99123 — 10
R..........	14	1400	0.70	2000	10.2040	1.00877	8.99123 — 10

2. Using the values of K found in example 1 preceding, determine the values of δ, f, and log C for the conditions given in the following table. Correct for maximum ordinate or for height of target according to rule, but consider every trajectory whose time of flight is greater than five seconds as requiring correction for altitude.

Problem	DATA. Gun. d. In.	w. Lbs.	c.	V. f.s.	R'nge. Yds.	Time of flight. Secs.	Max. ord. Feet.	Value of log K.	Diff. in ht. of gun and target. Feet.	Atmosphere. Bar. In.	Ther. °F.	ANSWERS. δ.	f.	log C.
A...	3	13	1.00	1150	2600	8.25	277	0.15970	300	30.33	24.7	1.1011	1.0050	0.12004
B...	3	13	1.00	2700	4400	9.25	366	0.15970	150	30.13	17.5	1.1113	1.0063	0.11660
C...	4	33	0.67	2900	3900	5.10	105	0.48832	200	29.92	15.7	1.1080	1.0037	0.44538
D..	5	50	1.00	3150	4300	6.18	154	0.30103	225	29.83	12.4	1.1135	1.0040	0.25606
E...	5	50	0.61	3150	4300	5.19	108	0.51570	90	29.57	29.3	1.0644	1.0022	0.48956
F...	6	105	0.61	2600	14800	31.56	4215	0.67956	1200	29.45	33.8	1.0502	1.0753	0.68982
G...	6	105	1.00	2800	4000	5.56	124	0.46489	350	29.37	39.4	1.0352	1.0060	0.45247
H..	6	105	0.61	2800	3700	4.57	85	0.67956	200	29.07	43.2	1.0170	1.0037	0.67384
I...	7	165	1.00	2700	7000	11.76	563	0.52728	None	28.95	48.7	1.0009	1.0095	0.53100
J...	7	165	0.61	2700	7400	10.61	455	0.74195	175	28.83	50.3	0.9936	1.0081	0.74824
K..	8	260	0.61	2750	8300	11.49	532	0.82346	450	28.73	52.8	0.9852	1.0091	0.83387
L...	10	510	1.00	2700	10100	16.57	1116	0.70757	500	28.58	69.3	0.9475	1.0193	0.73029
M..	10	510	0.61	2700	11000	15.69	997	0.92224	1100	28.47	95.7	0.8936	1.0190	0.97927
N..	12	870	0.61	2900	23500	37.61	5758	0.99583	1500	28.36	97.4	0.8867	1.1061	1.09185
O...	13	1130	1.00	2000	10400	21.53	1889	0.82519	700	28.27	99.8	0.8790	1.0328	0.89522
P...	13	1130	0.74	2000	11300	22.28	2005	0.95596	508	28.21	74.8	0.9243	1.0351	1.00513
Q...	14	1400	0.70	2000	14100	28.36	3264	1.00877	800	28.20	71.3	0.9310	1.0583	1.06443
R...	14	1400	0.70	2600	14400	21.83	1925	1.00877	700	28.71	84.6	0.9225	1.0335	1.05811

3. Given the measured velocities of a projectile at two points, as determined by experimental firing, as given in the following table, determine the resistance of the air at the mean velocity between the two points of measurement. If the atmospheric conditions at the time of firing were as given, what would be the corresponding resistance under standard atmospheric conditions?

Problem.	DATA. Projectile. d. In.	w. Lbs.	Dist. between points of measurement. Yds.	Measured velocities at. First point. f. s.	Second point. f. s.	ANSWERS. R_f. Lbs.	DATA. Atmosphere. Bar. In.	Ther. °F.	ANSWERS. R_s. Lbs.
1..........	3	13	80	2650	2600	220.78	28.00	50	228.55
2..........	5	60	90	2250	2200	767.76	29.00	60	783.43
3..........	6	105	95	2550	2500	1444.5	30.00	70	1454.7
4..........	7	165	100	2680	2580	4492.2	30.50	80	4539.8
5..........	12	870	105	2870	2800	17022.0	31.00	90	17281.0
6..........	13	1130	110	1910	1880	6045.5	30.00	0	5257.0
7..........	14	1400	125	2540	2460	23188.0	29.00	25	22021.0
8..........	6	70	200	1951	1874	533.55	29.53	59	533.55

4. Under the conditions given in the following table, compute the total atmospheric resistance to the passage of the projectile, and the resultant retardation in foot-seconds.

Problem.	DATA.						ANSWERS.	
	Projectile.			Velocity. f. s.	Atmosphere.		Retardation. f. s.	Resistance. Lbs.
	d. In.	w. Lbs.	c.		Bar. In.	Ther. °F.		
1..............	3	13	1.00	2300	30.00	20	493.39	199.19
2..............	5	60	1.00	1500	31.00	55	130.53	243.23
3..............	6	105	0.61	1300	29.00	47	44.23	144.24
4..............	7	165	0.61	2700	28.50	82	141.16	723.33
5..............	12	870	0.61	2850	29.45	90	86.92	2348.40
6..............	13	1130	0.95	1100	30.15	95	13.74	482.27
7..............	14	1400	0.70	850	28.67	64	3.43	149.27
8..............	14	1400	0.70	2500	29.33	75	70.20	3052.20
9..............	3	13	0.93	650	30.40	80	12.54	5.06

5. What is the resistance of the air to a baseball of 3″ diameter, weighing 8 ounces, moving at 100 f. s.; supposing the resistance of a sphere to be 1.25 times that of a standard ogival; and what would be its retardation?

Answers. Resistance, 0.16337 pound.
Retardation, 10.521 foot-seconds.

6. Given the data in the following tables, compute the value of the constant A in Mayevski's formula, for each individual case.

Problem.	DATA.								ANSWERS.
	Projectile.			δ.	Velocity. f. s.	Resistance. Lbs.	Retardation. f. s.	Value of n.	Value of A.
	d. In.	w. Lbs.	c.						
1...........	6	70	1.00	1.0000	1912.5	533.6	......	1.70	0.001259
2...........	6	70	1.00	1.0200	1818.0	491.8	......	1.70	0.00124023
3...........	6	70	1.00	1.0200	1859.5	1248.6	......	1.70	0.0030296
4...........	12	870	0.61	0.9354	2850.0	......	86.92	1.55	0.0040649
5...........	14	1400	0.70	0.9610	850.0	......	3.4328	3.00	0.000000059353
6...........	14	1400	0.70	0.9606	2500.0	3052.4	......	1.70	0.001248

7. A 6″ projectile, weight 70 pounds, is fired through screens, and the velocities measured at two points 200 yards apart are 1951 f. s. and 1874 f. s. What was the mean resistance of the air? *Answer.* 533.57 pounds.

8. A 6″ ogival-headed projectile, weight 70 pounds, is fired through screens 150 yards apart, and its velocities at the first and at the second pairs of screens are 1846 f. s. and 1790 f. s., respectively. A 6″ flat-headed projectile of the same weight is fired through the same screens, and gives velocities of 1929 f. s. and 1790 f. s., respectively. What was the resistance of each projectile? If the first was a standard projectile, what was the coefficient of form of the second?

Answers. First, $R=$ 491.82 pounds.
Second, $R=$1248.65 pounds.
Coefficient of form of second=2.5388.

9. A 12″ projectile, weight 850 pounds, gave measured velocities of 1979 f. s. and 1956 f. s. at points 500 feet apart. What was the mean resistance of the air? If the density of the air at the time of firing was 1.02 times the standard density, what would be the resistance in a standard atmosphere?

Answers. $R_f=$2389.0 pounds. $R_s=$2342.2 pounds.

10. Determine the resistance of the air to and the consequent retardation of a standard 3″ projectile, weight 13 pounds, when moving: (1) at 2800 f. s.; (2) at 2000 f. s.

Answers. (1) Resistance=250.34 pounds. Retardation=620.09 f. s.
(2) Resistance=142.67 pounds. Retardation=353.38 f. s.

11. Determine the resistance of the air and the consequent retardation in the following cases. (Standard atmosphere; and $c=1.00$ in each case.)

Problem.	DATA. Projectile. d. In.	DATA. Projectile. w. Lbs.	DATA. Velocity. f. s.	ANSWERS. Resistance. Lbs.	ANSWERS. Retardation. f. s.
1	4	33	2800	445.1	434.3
2	4	33	2000	253.6	247.5
3	6	100	2800	1001.4	322.4
4	6	100	2000	570.7	183.8
5	8	250	2800	1780.2	229.3
6	8	250	2000	1014.5	130.7
7	10	500	2800	2781.5	179.1
8	10	500	2000	1585.2	102.1
9	12	850	2800	4005.4	151.7
10	12	850	2000	2282.7	86.5
11	12.5	802.5	1400	1251.6	50.2
12	12.5	1000.0	1400	1251.6	40.3

CHAPTER 4.

THE EQUATION TO THE TRAJECTORY IN AIR WHEN MAYEVSKI'S EXPONENT IS EQUAL TO 2.

New Symbols Introduced.

ρ....Radius of curvature, in feet, of the trajectory at any point.

k....The ratio $\frac{A}{C}$, where A is Mayevski's constant, and C is the ballistic coefficient.

ϵ....The base of the Naperian system of logarithms; $\epsilon=2.7183$.

n....The ratio of the range in vacuum to the range in air for the same angle of departure.

67. Mayevski's equations, as given in (14) and (16), show that, strictly speaking, A and a can only be regarded as constants in the general expression for the retardation caused by the resistance of the air

$$\frac{dv}{dt}=-\frac{A}{C}v^a \qquad (18)$$

within certain limited ranges of the value of the velocity, v. As will shortly be seen, in the attempt to derive the equation to the trajectory in air, it will be possible to succeed in cases where the value of a is an integer, that is, for cases within the range of the formulæ in (14) where the value of v lies between 1800 f. s. and 1370 f. s. ($a=2$), or within the lower limits where $a=3$, 5 or 2 again; and, unfortunately, these limits do not include the initial velocities for modern high-powered guns. This is true, as will be seen, because the derivation of the required equation involves the integration of certain expressions in which the value of a must appear as an exponent, and it is impossible to make such integrations except when a is a whole number. The equation which we will derive will therefore only be correct for the limited range of values of v for which $a=2$. Could all the integrations be performed, for the decimal as well as for the integral values of a, a series of equations to the trajectory for the different limits of the initial velocity, could be derived and tabulated in the same way in which Mayevski's expressions for retardation shown in (14) were tabulated, but as it is, for the reason given, such equations cannot be derived for the initial velocities that are used at the present day; namely, from 1800 f. s. up, so some other method of obtaining solutions must be found. This is done by the use of certain differential equations, as will be explained later.

68. Meanwhile it is of value to follow through the derivation of the equation to the trajectory in air when $a=2$, both for educational purposes and in order to make a comparison with the equation to the same curve in vacuum. We must remember, however, that this equation will only be correct for initial velocities for which $a=2$ in (14), and that for all other initial velocities results obtained by its use will be only approximate.

69. Assuming that the axis of the projectile coincides with the tangent to its path at every point, which is very nearly the case with modern rifled guns, the resultant action of the resistance of the air will likewise coincide with the axis, and the trajectory will be the same as if the mass of the projectile were concentrated at its center of gravity and moved under the action of two forces only, one the constant Forces acting.

vertical force of gravity, w, and the other the variable resistance of the air, $\frac{w}{g} \times \frac{A}{C} v^2$, acting in the tangent. Figure 6 represents the trajectory, which is, of course, a plane curve, under the foregoing suppositions, and Figure 6(a) represents the two forces acting upon the projectile at any point, the resistance of the air being denoted by $\frac{w}{g} f$, in which f is the retardation, $\frac{dv}{dt}$, which we are now taking as proportional to v^2

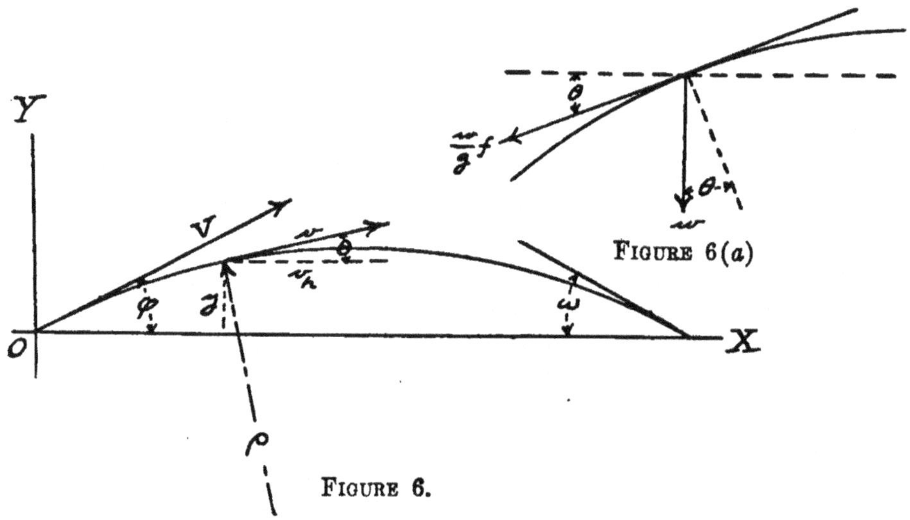

FIGURE 6(a)

FIGURE 6.

70. Taking vertical and horizontal axes at the point of departure, O, let V be the initial velocity, ϕ the angle of departure, v the velocity at any point whose coordinates are (x, y), and v_h the horizontal component of the velocity at that point. ρ is the radius of curvature of the curve at that point. Then, letting $k = \frac{A}{C}$ in equation (18), we can put $\frac{dv}{dt} = -kv^2$, and, since w has no horizontal component, the acceleration parallel to the axis of X is given by

$$\frac{d^2x}{dt^2} = -kv^2 \cos\theta \tag{19}$$

but $\frac{d^2x}{dt^2} = \frac{dv_h}{dt}$, $v \cos\theta = v_h$, and $v = \frac{ds}{dt}$; whence (19) may be written

$$\frac{dv_h}{dt} = -kv_h \frac{ds}{dt}. \tag{20}$$

$$\frac{dv_h}{v_h} = -kds \tag{21}$$

and integrating (21) between corresponding limits of v_h and s we get

$$\log_e v_h \Big]_{v_h}^{V\cos\phi} = -ks\Big]_s^0 \qquad \log_e \frac{V\cos\phi}{v_h} = ks \qquad v_h = V\cos\phi\, \epsilon^{-ks} \tag{22}$$

Next resolving along the normal, since the acceleration towards the center of curvature is given by the expression $\frac{v^2}{\rho}$, ρ being the radius of curvature at that point, we have

$$\frac{v^2}{\rho} = g\cos\theta \tag{23}$$

But $v = v_h \sec\theta$, and $\rho = -\frac{ds}{d\theta}$, whence (23) may be written

$$v_h^2 \sec^2\theta\, d\theta = -g\cos\theta\, ds = -g dx \text{ (as } dx = ds\cos\theta\text{)}; \sec^2\theta\, d\theta = -\frac{g dx}{v_h^2} \qquad (24)$$

Now substituting in (24) the value of v_h given in (22), we get

$$\sec^2\theta\, d\theta = -\frac{g}{V^2\cos^2\phi}\epsilon^{2ks}dx \qquad (25)$$

71. In the case of the flat trajectory, in which the angle of departure does not exceed 4° or 5°, the difference between the values of s and x is so small that it may be practically disregarded, and x may be substituted for s in (25), giving, after integration,*

$$\tan\theta\Big]_{\phi}^{\theta} = -\frac{g}{2kV^2\cos^2\phi}\epsilon^{2kx}\Big]_0^x \qquad \tan\theta = \tan\phi - \frac{g}{2kV^2\cos^2\phi}(\epsilon^{2kx}-1) \quad (26)$$

But ϵ^{2kx}, when expanded by Maclaurin's theorem, equals †

$$1+2kx+2k^2x^2+\tfrac{4}{3}k^3x^3+\ldots.$$

so that

$$\epsilon^{2kx}-1 = 2kx(1+kx+\tfrac{2}{3}k^2x^2+\ldots.)$$

whence, substituting in (26) and writing $\frac{dy}{dx}$ for $\tan\theta$, we have

$$\frac{dy}{dx} = \tan\phi - \frac{gx}{V^2\cos^2\phi}(1+kx+\tfrac{2}{3}k^2x^2+\ldots.)$$

or, integrating between corresponding limits of x and y,

$$y = x\tan\phi - \frac{gx^2}{2V^2\cos^2\phi}(1+\tfrac{2}{3}kx+\tfrac{1}{3}k^2x^2+\ldots.) \qquad (27)$$

But the greatest value of kx is always a small fraction in any trajectory flat enough to justify the substitution of x for s which has already been made; hence we may neglect the terms beyond k^2x^2 in the expansion, and write for the equation to the trajectory in air when $a=2$

Equation to trajectory in air when $a=2$.

$$y = x\tan\phi - \frac{gx^2}{2V^2\cos^2\phi}(1+\tfrac{2}{3}kx+\tfrac{1}{3}k^2x^2) \qquad (28)$$

---

* The integration in paragraph 71 is as follows: From (25)

$$\int_{\phi}^{\theta}\sec^2\theta\, d\theta = -\frac{g}{V^2\cos^2\phi}\int_0^x \epsilon^{2kx}dx$$

From calculus we know that $\int\sec^2\theta\, d\theta = \tan\theta + C_1$, C_1 being the constant of integration. From calculus we know that $\int\epsilon^y dy = \epsilon^y + C_2$, C_2 being the constant of integration. Now let $y = 2kx$ and the above becomes

$$\int\epsilon^{2kx}d(2kx) = 2k\int\epsilon^{2kx}dx = 2k\epsilon^{2kx} + C_2$$

whence

$$\int\epsilon^{2kx}dx = \frac{1}{2k}\int\epsilon^{2kx}d(2kx) = \frac{1}{2k}\epsilon^{2kx} + C_2$$

The integration between the limits given above therefore becomes

$$(\tan\theta + C_1) - (\tan\phi + C_1) = -\frac{g}{V^2\cos^2\phi}\left[\left(\frac{1}{2k}\epsilon^{2kx}+C_2\right)-\left(\frac{1}{2k}\epsilon^0+C_2\right)\right]$$

or

$$\tan\theta = \tan\phi - \frac{g}{V^2\cos^2\phi}\times\frac{1}{2k}\left(\epsilon^{2kx}-1\right)$$

† The expansion in paragraph 71 is: From either algebra or calculus we have that

$$\epsilon^y = 1+y+\frac{y^2}{\lfloor 2}+\frac{y^3}{\lfloor 3}+\frac{y^4}{\lfloor 4}+\ldots\text{etc.}$$

whence, if we let $y = 2kx$ we have

$$\epsilon^{2kx} = 1+2kx+\frac{4k^2x^2}{2}+\frac{8k^3x^3}{3\times 2}+\frac{16k^4x^4}{4\times 3\times 2}+\ldots\text{etc.}$$

or

$$\epsilon^{2kx} = 1+2kx(1+kx+\tfrac{2}{3}k^2x^2+\tfrac{1}{3}k^3x^3+\ldots\text{etc.})$$

72. Comparing this equation with (2), it will be seen that its first two terms represent the trajectory in vacuum, and that it only differs from the latter by having other terms, subtractive like the second, and containing higher powers of k and x.

73. The value of k in the equation to the trajectory in air (28) just deduced is, as already stated, $\frac{A}{C}$, where A is the experimentally determined coefficient, and $C=\frac{w}{\delta c d^2}$ is the ballistic coefficient. As a matter of general interest, it may be stated that, for the value of $A=0.0001316$, the value assigned to A by Mayevski when $a=2$, the value of k for our naval guns from the 6-pounder up to the 13″ gun, varies from about 0.00011006 to about 0.00002022, for the standard projectile and standard density of the air.

The ratio n

74. If we put $y=0$ in equation (28), we get for values of x, one equal to zero, denoting the origin, and another, the range X, given by

$$X(1+\tfrac{2}{3}kX+\tfrac{1}{3}k^2X^2)=\frac{V^2\sin 2\phi}{g} \tag{29}$$

But the second member of (29) is the range in vacuum for the same initial velocity, V, and the same angle of departure, ϕ, so we see that the expression

$$1+\tfrac{2}{3}kX+\tfrac{1}{3}k^2X^2=\frac{X(\text{in vacuum})}{X(\text{in air})}$$

This ratio will be found to play an important part in many ballistic problems, and will hereafter be designated by the letter n. Hence we have for the range in air the expression

$$X=\frac{V^2\sin 2\phi}{gn} \tag{30}$$

or, if it be desired to find the value of n for a given range,

$$n=\frac{V^2\sin 2\phi}{gX} \tag{31}$$

75. Since k is a very small fraction, the value of n, which is evidently unity for $X=0$, increases slowly with X, and for moderate values of X is only slightly greater than unity. These deductions follow from the form of the equation

$$1+\tfrac{2}{3}kX+\tfrac{1}{3}k^2X^2=n$$

Assumptions made.

76. It is well to summarize here that the following suppositions have been made in deriving the equation to the trajectory in air when $a=2$, and these suppositions must be held to be correct in all consideration of this equation; and the equation is inaccurate to whatever degree results from the lack of correctness of any one or more of these assumptions:

1. That $a=2$, and that the corresponding value of A is correct.
2. That the axis of the projectile coincides with the tangent to the trajectory at every point, and that the resistance of the air will therefore act along the same tangent.
3. That the curve is so flat that we may consider $dx=ds$ without material error.
4. That kx is so small in value that any term involving powers higher than k^2x^2 may be neglected.

77. The following examples show the form for work under the formulæ derived in this chapter. It must be remembered, be it again said, that these formulæ are derived on the assumptions given in the preceding paragraph, and results obtained by their use are therefore only approximately correct for the usual present-day initial velocities.

For a 6″ gun, given that the initial velocity is 2600 f. s., and that an angle of departure of 4° 14′ 30″ gives a range of 7000 yards, to compute the value of the ratio between the ranges in vacuum and in air for that angle of departure; that is, the value of n.

$$n=\frac{V^2 \sin 2\phi}{gX}$$

$V=2600$	log 3.41497	2 log	6.82994
$2\phi=8°\ 29'\ 00''$		sin	9.16886−10
$g=32.2$	log 1.50786	colog	8.49214−10
$X=21000$	log 4.32222	colog	5.67778−10
$n=1.4748$		log	0.16872

78. Given that the angle of departure for the 12″ gun of 2900 f. s. initial velocity ($w=870$ pounds; $c=0.61$) for a range of 10,000 yards is 4° 13′ 12″, compute the approximate value of the ordinate at a distance of 2000 yards from the gun, and compare it with the ordinate in vacuum at the same point for the same angle of departure.

In vacuum $\qquad y=x\tan\phi-\dfrac{gx^2}{2V^2\cos^2\phi}$

In air $\qquad y=x\tan\phi-\dfrac{ngx^2}{2V^2\cos^2\phi}$ where $n=\dfrac{V^2\sin 2\phi}{gX}$

Work in Vacuum.

$x=6000$	log 3.77815		2 log 7.55630
$\phi=4°\ 13'\ 12''$	tan 8.86797−10	sec 0.00118	2 sec 0.00236
$g=32.2$			log 1.50786
2		log 0.30103	colog 9.69897−10
$V=2900$	log 3.46240	2 log 6.92480	2 colog 3.07520−10
442.710	log 2.64612		
69.294			log 1.84069
$y=373.416$			

Work in Air.

From work in vacuum; $x\tan\phi=442.71$ and $\dfrac{gx^2}{2V^2\cos^2\phi}=69.294$.

$V=2900$	log 3.46240	2 log	6.92480
$2\phi=8°\ 26'\ 24''$		sin	9.16665−10
$g=32.2$		colog	8.49214−10
$X=30000$	log 4.47712	colog	5.52288−10
$n=1.2778$		log	0.10647
$\dfrac{gx^2}{2V^2\cos^2\phi}=69.294$		log	1.84069
$\dfrac{ngx^2}{2V^2\cos^2\phi}=88.544$		log	1.94716
$x\tan\phi=442.710$			
$y=354.166$			

Ordinate at 2000 yards .... In vacuum ......373.416 feet.
In air ....354.166 feet.

EXAMPLES.

1. Determine the value of the radius of curvature of the trajectory at the point of departure for a muzzle velocity of 2000 f. s., and an angle of departure (1) of 3°, and (2) of 8°.

Answers. For 3°, 124,390 feet. For 8°, 125,443 feet.

2. In the two cases given in Example 1 preceding, the striking velocities are 1600 f. s. and 1240 f. s., respectively, and the angles of fall are 3° 29′ and 11° 08′, respectively. Compute the radii of curvature at the point of fall.

Answers. For 3°, 79,648.5 feet. For 8°, 48,667.0 feet.

3. Using the equation to the trajectory in air when $a=2$, compute the value of n and the approximate angle of departure in each of the following cases:

Problem.	DATA.				ANSWERS.	
	Gun. In.	Value of k.	Initial Velocity. f. s.	Range. Yds.	n.	Angle of departure.
1............	6	0.00004738	2400	1000	1.101	0° 32′
2............	6	0.00004738	2400	2000	1.216	1 03
3............	6	0.00004738	2400	3000	1.345	1 56
4............	8	0.00003369	2400	1000	1.071	0 31
5............	8	0.00003369	2400	2000	1.148	1 06
6............	8	0.00003369	2400	3000	1.233	1 47
7............	10	0.00002632	2400	1000	1.055	0 30
8............	10	0.00002632	2400	2000	1.114	1 04
9............	10	0.00002632	2400	3000	1.177	1 42
10............	12	0.00002229	2400	1000	1.046	0 30
11............	12	0.00002229	2400	2000	1.095	1 03
12............	12	0.00002229	2400	3000	1.147	1 39

4. A 6″ gun with 2900 f. s. initial velocity gave a measured range of 5394 yards for an angle of departure of 3° 03′ 51″. Compute the value of n from the firing.

Answer. $n=1.72290$.

5. A 6″ gun with 2900 f. s. initial velocity gave a measured range of 2625 yards for an angle of departure of 1° 07′ 49″. Compute the value of n from the firing.

Answer. $n=1.308$.

6. Given the data in the first six columns of the following table, compute the ordinates of the trajectory for each of the given abscissæ, in both vacuum and air, using the equation to the trajectory when $a=2$. In working in air, first determine the value of n for the given range corresponding to the given angle of departure, then determine the value of k from this by using the formula $n=1+\frac{2}{3}kX$ (neglecting the square and higher powers of kX), and the required ordinates by the use of the value of k thus found:

Problem.	DATA.						ANSWERS.	
	Gun. In.	Initial velocity. f. s.	Weight of projectile. Lbs.	Angle of departure.	Range. Yds.	Abscissa. Yds.	Ordinates in feet.	
							Vacuum.	Air.
1.	12	2800	850	2° 11′	5000	1000	95.9	95.0
2.	12	2800	850	2 11	5000	2000	154.7	147.7
3.	12	2800	850	2 11	5000	3000	176.5	153.0
4.	12	2800	850	2 11	5000	4000	161.4	105.5
5.	12	2800	850	2 11	5000	5000	109.2	000.0
6.	6	2000	100	1 17	3000	1000	50.0	48.2
7.	6	2900	100	1 17	3000	2000	65.5	51.7
8.	6	2900	100	1 17	3000	3000	46.5	00.0
9.	3	2800	13	1 01	2000	500	22.0	21.5
10.	3	2800	13	1 01	2000	1000	34.8	30.7
11.	3	2800	13	1 01	2000	1500	38.3	24.5
12.	3	2800	13	1 01	2000	2000	32.5	00.0

CHAPTER 5.

APPROXIMATE DETERMINATION OF THE VALUES OF THE ELEMENTS OF THE TRAJECTORY IN AIR WHEN MAYEVSKI'S EXPONENT IS EQUAL TO 2. THE DANGER SPACE AND THE COMPUTATION OF THE DATA CONTAINED IN COLUMN 7 OF THE RANGE TABLES.

New Symbols Introduced.

h.... Height of target in feet.

S.... Danger space in feet or yards according to work.

79. Before presenting for discussion the more exact computations of the elements of the trajectory by the use of the ballistic tables, we will in this chapter deduce formulæ by means of which the values of those elements can be determined with a sufficient degree of approximation for certain purposes; and it will be seen later that a few of these formulæ are sufficiently exact in their results to enable us to use them practically. Remember that the inaccuracies in these formulæ result from the assumptions upon which the derivation of the equation to the trajectory in air was based, as enumerated in paragraph 76 of the preceding chapter. For our present purposes we will take as the equation to the trajectory in air the one given in (28), but simplified by the omission of higher powers of kx than the first. The equation then becomes

$$y=x\tan\phi-\frac{gx^2}{2V^2\cos^2\phi}\left(1+\tfrac{2}{3}kx\right) \qquad (32)$$

In this equation k can no longer be considered as strictly constant, but its value, when found for any one value of ϕ, may be used over a considerable range of values of ϕ, since it increases slowly with increases of range, provided the trajectory be reasonably flat. We shall still denote by n the ratio of the range in vacuum to the range in air, which is now given by

$$n=1+\tfrac{2}{3}kX$$

Approximate horizontal range. **80.** To determine the approximate horizontal range, put $y=0$ in (32), and solve for x. An x factor will divide out, so one value of x is zero, for the origin, as was to be expected, and the remaining equation is

$$\frac{gX}{2V^2\cos^2\phi}\left(1+\tfrac{2}{3}kX\right)=\tan\phi \qquad (33)$$

It is at once apparent that this is an awkward equation for logarithmic work, and furthermore not very accurate for work with five place logarithmic tables owing to the decimal value of k.

Angle of fall. **81.** Differentiating (32) we get

$$\frac{dy}{dx}=\tan\theta=\tan\phi-\frac{gx}{V^2\cos^2\phi}(1+kx) \qquad (34)$$

But the angle of fall, ω, is the negative of the value of θ at the point of fall, where $x=X$, hence

$$\tan\omega=-\tan\phi+\frac{gX}{V^2\cos^2\phi}(1+kX)$$

and since $\dfrac{2V^2\sin\phi\cos\phi}{g}=nX$, this may be written

$$\tan\omega=-\tan\phi+\frac{2\tan\phi}{n}(1+kX)=\tan\phi\left(\frac{2+2kX-n}{n}\right)$$

Also from $1+\frac{2}{3}kX=n$ we get $2kX=3(n-1)$, whence

$$\tan\omega=\tan\phi\left(2-\frac{1}{n}\right) \qquad (35)$$

From (35) we see that the angle of fall is always greater than the angle of departure, but can never reach double the latter.*

82. Returning to equation (22) and writing $\frac{dx}{dt}$ for v_h, and x for s, we have **Time of flight.**

$$\frac{dx}{dt}=V\cos\phi\epsilon^{-kx}$$

Separating the variables and integrating between corresponding limits †

$$\int_0^X \epsilon^{kx}dx=V\cos\phi\int_0^T dt \qquad \frac{\epsilon^{kX}-1}{k}=TV\cos\phi$$

Expanding ϵ^{kX} and neglecting higher powers than the second ‡

$$X\left(1+\frac{kX}{2}\right)=TV\cos\phi$$

but from $1+\frac{2}{3}kX=n$ we get that $1+\frac{kX}{2}=\frac{3n+1}{4}$, therefore

$$T=\frac{3n+1}{4}\times\frac{X}{V\cos\phi} \qquad (36)$$

* This follows from the form of the expression, for from paragraph 75 we know that $n=1+\frac{2}{3}kX+\frac{1}{3}k^2X^2$, from which we see that n is unity when $X=0$ and increases very slowly with X, k being a very small decimal. Therefore $\frac{1}{n}$ is always less than unity and $2-\frac{1}{n}$ is always greater than unity; and the angle of fall must therefore always be greater than the angle of departure. Also as n must always be greater than unity for any real range, then $\frac{1}{n}$ must always be a positive real number, and therefore the value of $2-\frac{1}{n}$ must always be less than 2; therefore the angle of fall can never become twice as great as the angle of departure.

† The integration in paragraph 82 is as follows: From integral calculus

$$\int\epsilon^y dy=\epsilon^y+C$$

C being the constant of integration. Now let $y=kX$ and we have

$$\int\epsilon^{kX}dX=\frac{1}{k}\int\epsilon^{kX}d(kX)=\frac{1}{k}(\epsilon^{kX})+C$$

Therefore $$\int_0^X\epsilon^{kX}dX=V\cos\phi\int_0^T dt$$

becomes $$\left(\frac{\epsilon^{kX}}{k}+C\right)-\left(\frac{\epsilon^0}{k}+C\right)=(V\cos\phi\times T+C_1)-(V\cos\phi\times 0+C_1)$$

C_1 being the constant of integration in the second term. The above becomes

$$\frac{\epsilon^{kX}-1}{k}=VT\cos\phi$$

‡ The expansion of ϵ^{kX} following the integration is as follows: From either calculus or algebra we know that

$$\epsilon^y=1+y+\frac{y^2}{\underline{|2}}+\frac{y^3}{\underline{|3}}+\ldots\text{etc.}$$

and substituting kX for y, and neglecting the higher powers than the square, we have

$$\epsilon^{kX}=1+kX+\frac{k^2X^2}{2}$$

whence $$\epsilon^{kX}-1=kX+\frac{k^2X^2}{2}$$

and $$\frac{\epsilon^{kX}-1}{k}=X+\frac{kX^2}{2}=X\left(1+\frac{kX}{2}\right)$$

whence $$X\left(1+\frac{kX}{2}\right)=VT\cos\phi$$

As the range in vacuum for the same values of V and ϕ would be nX, then $\frac{nX}{V\cos\phi}$ is the time of flight in vacuum, and so we see that the time of flight in air is always less than it would be in vacuum, approaching three-fourths the latter's value as a minimum.* For flat trajectories, $\cos\phi$ may, of course, be taken as unity.

Remaining velocity.

83. Equation (22), with the substitution of x for s, gives the value of the horizontal component of the velocity at any point in the trajectory, and since the striking velocity is the horizontal velocity at the point of fall multiplied by $\sec\omega$, we have

$$v_\omega = v_{h_\omega}\sec\omega = \frac{V\cos\phi}{\epsilon^{kX}\cos\omega}$$

whence, putting for ϵ^{kX} the first two terms of its expansion, and calling $\frac{\cos\phi}{\cos\omega}$ equal to unity,

$$v_\omega = \frac{V}{1+kX} = \frac{2}{3n-1}\,V \tag{37}$$

The striking velocity, therefore, is always less than the initial velocity, being reduced to $\frac{V}{4}$ when $n=3$, a value which it seldom reaches.†

Coordinates of vertex.

84. Since the trajectory is horizontal at its highest point, we obtain the abscissa (x_0) of the vertex by putting $\theta=0$ in (34), thus getting $\frac{V^2\sin 2\phi}{2g} = x_0(1+kx_0)$, and since $\frac{V^2\sin 2\phi}{g} = nX$, this may be written $x_0(1+kx_0) = \frac{nX}{2}$, a quadratic equation, the solution of which gives $x_0 = \frac{-1+\sqrt{1+2knX}}{2k}$ which, since $kX=\frac{3}{2}(n-1)$, may be written

$$x_0 = \frac{\sqrt{1+3n(n-1)}-1}{3(n-1)}\,X \tag{38}$$

if we divide both numerator and denominator of the second term of (38) by n we get

$$x_0 = \frac{\sqrt{\frac{1}{n^2}+3-\frac{3}{n}}-\frac{1}{n}}{3-\frac{3}{n}}\,X$$

from which we see that when n is infinity, the value of x_0 becomes $\frac{X}{\sqrt{3}} = 0.58X$,

---

* We know that $n = 1 + \frac{2}{3}kX + \frac{1}{3}k^2X^2$, therefore n increases slowly with the range and is always greater than unity. Therefore $3n$ is always greater than 3 and $3n+1$ is always greater than 4 but less than $4n$. Therefore $\frac{3n+1}{4n}$ is always less than unity, and as $\frac{nX}{V\cos\phi}$ is the time of flight in vacuum, the time of flight in air, which is $T = \frac{3n+1}{4n} \times \frac{nX}{V\cos\phi}$ must be always less than $\frac{nX}{V\cos\phi}$; that is, the time of flight in air is always less than it would be in vacuum. We also see that $\frac{3n+1}{4n} = \frac{3n}{4n} + \frac{1}{4n} = \frac{3}{4} + \frac{1}{4n}$, and therefore that if n becomes infinitely great then $\frac{3n+1}{4n}$ becomes $\frac{3}{4}$, which is evidently the maximum possible value of $\frac{3n+1}{4n}$; and we therefore see than the time of flight in air cannot be less than three-fourths of the time of flight in vacuum.

† As in the note to paragraph 82, n is necessarily greater than unity, therefore $3n-1$ is necessarily greater than 2, and $\frac{2}{3n-1}$ is therefore necessarily less than unity; therefore the final velocity is always less than the initial velocity.

from which we see that the abscissa of the vertex is always greater than half the range but never reaches $0.58X$.*

The ordinate of the vertex may be obtained by substituting the value of x_0 obtained from (38) in the equation to the trajectory (32), but an equally accurate and much simpler determination is given by

$$y_0 = \frac{gT^2}{8} \tag{39}$$

This assumes the height of the vertex to be that from which a body would fall freely (in vacuum) in half the time of flight. Actually the vertical velocity of the projectile is reduced by air resistance, but since the time the projectile takes to describe the descending branch of the trajectory is somewhat greater than half the time of flight, the air resistance is approximately allowed for by equation (39).

85. As an example of the use of the foregoing formulæ, we will compute the various elements of the 500-yard trajectory of the old pattern United States magazine rifle, for which the initial velocity is 2000 f. s., and the angle of departure for the given range is 0° 31′ 35″. After finding the value of n, we may, as the angles are small, use ϕ and ω in place of their tangents, and the formulæ then are

$$n = \frac{V^2 \sin 2\phi}{gX}; \quad \omega = \left(2 - \frac{1}{n}\right)\phi; \quad T = \frac{3n+1}{4} \times \frac{X}{V \cos\phi}; \quad v_\omega = \frac{2}{3n-1} V;$$

$$x_0 = \frac{\sqrt{1+3n(n-1)}-1}{3(n-1)} X; \quad y_0 = \frac{gT^2}{8}$$

$V=2000$	log 3.30103		2 log 6.60206
$2\phi=1°\ 03'\ 10''$			sin 8.26418−10
$g=32.2$	log 1.50786		colog 8.49214−10
$X=1500$	log 3.17609		colog 6.82391−10
$n=1.5216$			log 0.18229
$\frac{1}{n}=0.6572$			colog 9.81771−10
$2-\frac{1}{n}=1.3428$	log 0.12801		
$3n=4.5648$			
$3n+1=5.5648$		log 0.74545	
$3n-1=3.5648$	log 0.55204		colog 9.44796−10
$\phi=31.6'$	log 1.49969	sec 0.00002	
4	log 0.60206	colog 9.39794−10	
$X=1500$		log 3.17609	
$V=2000$	log 3.30103	colog 6.69897−10	log 3.30103
2			log 0.30103
$\omega=42.43'$	log 1.62770		
$T=1.0434$		log 0.01847	
$v_\omega=1122$			log 3.05002

* Let us suppose that $\frac{\sqrt{1+3n(n-1)}-1}{3(n-1)} = \frac{1}{2}$. Solving this quadratic for n, we find that under these conditions $n=1$; and therefore if n be greater than unity the value of the left-hand member above must be greater than ½; therefore the value of x_0 must always be greater than $\frac{X}{2}$ for a trajectory in air; and, as $x_0 = 0.58X$ when n is infinity, we also see that the value of x_0 can never reach $0.58X$.

$n=1.5216$

$3n=4.5648$ ..log 0.65942

$n-1=0.5216$ ..log 9.71734−10

$3(n-1)=1.5648$ .... log 0.19446......colog 9.80554−10

$3n(n-1)=2.3810$ ..log 0.37676

$1+3n(n-1)=3.3810$ ..log 0.52905

$\sqrt{1+3n(n-1)}=1.8388$.½ log 0.26453

$\sqrt{1+3n(n-1)}-1=0.8388$ .... log 9.92366−10

$X=1500$ .... log 3.17609

$x_0=804.05$ .... log 2.90529

$T=1.0434$ ..log 0.01847......2 log 0.03694

$g=32.2$ .... log 1.50786

8 ......log 0.90309......colog 9.09691−10

$y_0=4.3824$ .... log 0.64171

$\omega=0°\ 42'\ 24''$.	$x_0=268.02$ yards.
$T=1.0434$ seconds.	$y_0=4.3824$ feet.
$v_\omega=1122$ f. s.	

86. As another example, take the case of the 6″ gun with $V=2400$ f. s., and an angle of departure of 2°, for which the range is 3100 yards.

$$n=\frac{V^2 \sin 2\phi}{gX}\ ;\ \tan\omega=\tan\phi\left(2-\frac{1}{n}\right);\ T=\frac{3n+1}{4}\times\frac{X}{V\cos\phi}\ ;\ v_\omega=\frac{2}{3n-1}V$$

$V=2400$ ....log 3.38021........................2 log 6.76042

$2\phi=4°$ .... sin 8.84358−10

$g=32.2$ ....log 1.50786........................colog 8.49214−10

$X=9300$ ....log 3.96848........................colog 6.03152−10

$n=1.3417$ .... log 0.12766

$\frac{1}{n}=0.7453$ ....colog 9.87234−10

$2-\frac{1}{n}=1.2547$ ....log 0.09854

$3n=4.0251$

$3n+1=5.0251$ .... log 0.70115

$3n-1=3.0251$ ..log 0.48074....................................colog 9.51926−10

$\phi=2°$ ....tan 8.54308−10.. sec 0.00026

4 ....log 0.60206..................colog 9.39794−10

$X=9300$ .... log 3.96848

$V=2400$ ....log 3.38021..................colog 6.62979−10.. log 3.38021

2 .... log 0.30103

$\omega=2°\ 30'\ 38''$ ....tan 8.64162−10

$T=4.871$ .... log 0.68762

$v_\omega=1586.7$ .... log 3.20050

$\omega=2°\ 30'\ 38''$.

$T=4.871$ seconds.

$v_\omega=1586.7$ f. s.

87. If the value of n be known, k may be found from $n=1+\frac{2}{3}kX$, and then by substituting the proper value of x in the equation to the trajectory (32), the corresponding value of y, the ordinate of the trajectory at a distance x from the gun may be computed; and this was the way in which the last problems in the examples under the last chapter were worked. If, however, we know the angles of departure corresponding to various ranges (which data is contained in the range table for the gun) the approximate value of y for any value of x, for the trajectory for a given range, may be more readily found as follows. Referring to Figure 7, let (x', y') be the coordinates of the point M on the trajectory for which $\phi=\psi'+p$. Then, by the principle of the rigidity of the trajectory, if the angle of departure were ψ', the horizontal range would equal OM, or what is practically the same thing, x'. Consequently, if we take from the range table the angle of departure for a range x', and subtract it from the angle of departure for the given trajectory, the result will be the angle p. Then $y'=x' \tan p$.

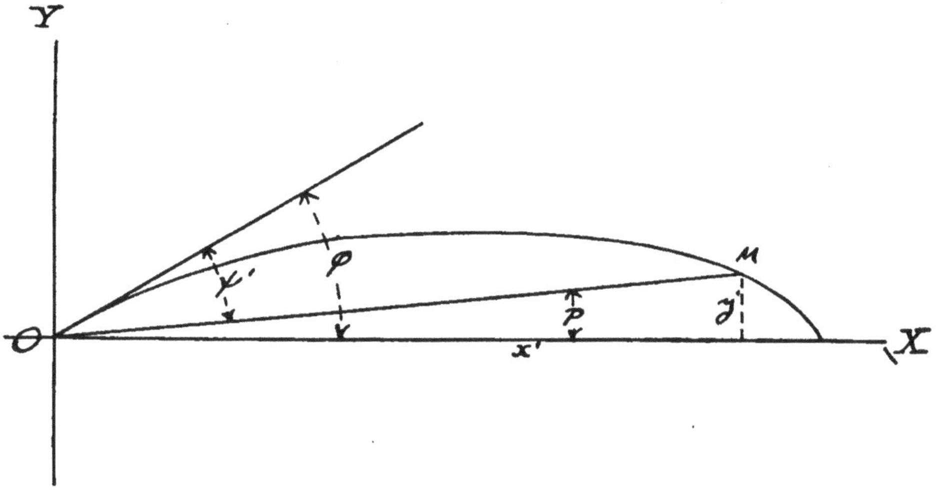

FIGURE 7.

88. By the term "danger space" is meant an interval of space, between the point of fall and the gun, such that the target will be hit if situated at any point in that space. In other words, **it is the distance from the point of fall through which a target of the given height can be moved directly towards the gun and still have the projectile pass through the target.** Therefore, within the range for which the maximum ordinate of the trajectory does not exceed the height of the target, the danger space is equal to the range, and such range is known as the "danger range." Referring to Figure 8, $AH=S$ is the danger space for a target of height $AB=h$, in the case of the trajectory OBH. It will be seen from Figure 8 that, when the value of h is very small in comparison with the range, the danger space is given with sufficient accuracy by the formula **Danger space.**

$$S=h \cot \omega \qquad (40)$$

This assumes that the tangent at the point of fall is identical with the curve from H to B, whereas it really passes above B, so that the result given by (40) is somewhat too small.

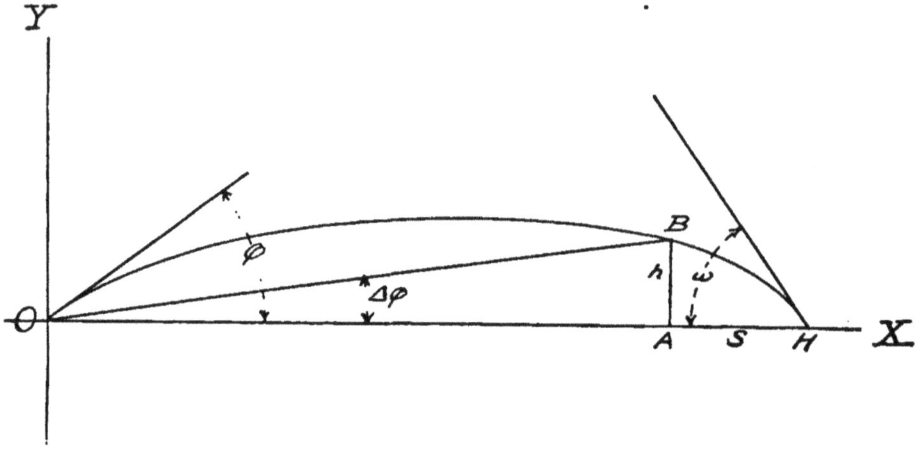

FIGURE 8.

89. A more accurate formula for the danger space is deduced as follows: Calling the very small angle $AOB=\Delta\phi$, we have, very nearly, $\tan\Delta\phi=\frac{h}{X}$ and $\tan\omega=\frac{h}{S}$, whence, equating the two values of h derived from the preceding expressions,

$$h=X\tan\Delta\phi=S\tan\omega,$$

or, as $\Delta\phi$ is very small, $X\Delta\phi=S\tan\omega$, or, since $\Delta\phi=\frac{h}{X-S}$, $\frac{hX}{X-S}=S\tan\omega$,

whence $$S=h\cot\omega\left(\frac{X}{X-S}\right)=h\cot\omega\left(1+\frac{S}{X}+\frac{S^2}{X^2}+\ldots\right)$$

whence, neglecting the higher powers of the fraction $\frac{S}{X}$, and putting for S in the expression its approximate value of $h\cot\omega$

$$S=h\cot\omega\left(1+\frac{h\cot\omega}{X}\right) \tag{41}$$

90. As a further example of the use of the equations derived in this chapter in determining the approximate values of the quantities concerned, we have the following: Given that, for the 6″ gun ($w=105$, $c=0.61$), the initial velocity is 2600 f. s., and that the angle of departure for a range of 5500 yards is 3° 02′ 24″; to find the approximate values of the angle of fall, time of flight and striking velocity.

$$n=\frac{V^2\sin 2\phi}{gX}\ ;\ \tan\omega=\tan\phi\left(2-\frac{1}{n}\right);\ T=\frac{3n+1}{4}\times\frac{X}{V\cos\phi}\ ;\ v_\omega=\frac{2}{3n-1}V$$

$V=2600$ .... log 3.41497	........................2 log	6.82994
$2\phi=6°\ 04'\ 48''$	.... sin	9.02491−10
$g=32.2$ .... log 1.50786	........................colog	8.49214−10
$X=16500$ .... log 4.21748	........................colog	5.78252−10
$n=1.3474$	.... log	0.12951
$\frac{1}{n}=0.74215$	........................colog	9.87049−10

$2-\frac{1}{n}=1.25785$ .... log 0.09963

$3n=4.0422$

$3n+1=5.0422$ .... log 0.70262

$3n-1=3.0422$ ..log 0.48319.................................... colog 9.51681−10

$\phi=3°\ 02'\ 24''$ .... tan 8.72516−10.. sec 0.00061

4 ....log 0.60206.................... colog 9.39794−10

$X=16500$ .... log 4.21748

$V=2600$ ....log 3.41497.................. colog 6.58503−10.. log 3.41497

2 .... log 0.30103

$\omega=3°\ 49'\ 19''$ .... tan 8.82479−10

$T=8.011$ .... log 0.90368

$v_\omega=1709.3$ .... log 3.23281

$\omega=3°\ 49'\ 19''$.

$T=8.011$ seconds.

$v_\omega=1709.3$ f. s.

To find the approximate co-ordinates of the vertex for the trajectory given above.

$$x_0=\frac{\sqrt{1+3n(n-1)}-1}{3(n-1)}X;\quad y_0=\frac{gT^2}{8}$$

$n=1.3474$

$3n=4.0422$ ..log 0.60662

$n-1=0.3474$ ..log 9.54083−10

$3(n-1)=1.0422$ .... log 0.01795...... colog 9.98205−10

$3n(n-1)=1.4043$ ..log 0.14745

$1+3n(n-1)=2.4043$ ..log 0.38099

$\sqrt{1+3n(n-1)}=1.5506$. $\frac{1}{2}$ log 0.19050

$\sqrt{1+3n(n-1)}-1=0.5506$ .... log 9.74084−10

$X=16500$ .... log 4.21748

$x_0=8716$ .... log 3.94037

$T=8.011$ ...log 0.90368......2 log 1.80736

$g=32.2$ .... log 1.50786

8 ....log 0.90309...... colog 9.09691−10

$y_0=258.30$ .... log 2.41213

$x_0=2905.3$ yards.

$y_0=258.30$ feet.

For the conditions given in the preceding problem, to find the danger space for a target 20 feet high. There are two formulæ possible, of which the longer is the more exact, and is the one used in computing the values of the danger space for a 20-foot target given in Column 7 of the range tables. It should be used whenever exactness is required. We will compute by both and compare the results.

$$S=h\cot\omega \qquad S=h\cot\omega\left(1+\frac{h\cot\omega}{X}\right)$$

$h=20$ ....log 1.30103
$\omega=3°\ 49'\ 19''$ .....cot 1.17519

$S=h\cot\omega=299.38$ ....log 2.47622......log 2.47622..........log 2.47622
$X=16500$..........................log 4.21748

$\frac{h\cot\omega}{X}=0.0181$ ....log 8.25875−10

$\frac{h\cot\omega}{X}+1=1.0181$ ....log 0.00779

$S=304.8$ ....log 2.48402

By approximate formula...... 99.795 yards.
By more exact formula.......101.600 yards.

The variation in the above more exact result from the value given in the range table is due to the fact that the value of the angle of fall used above is only approximate.

Standard problem. Throughout this book, in working sample problems showing the computation of the data for the range tables, the work will be done in each case for what will be known as the "standard problem" of the book. This will be for a range of 10,000 yards, for the 12″ gun for which $V=2900$ f. s., $w=870$ pounds, and $c=0.61$. This is the gun for which the range table is Bureau of Ordnance Pamphlet No. 298; which table is given in full in the edition of the Range and Ballistic Tables, printed for the use of midshipmen in connection with this text book. For this gun and range, we know, by methods that will be explained later, that the angle of fall, ω, is 5° 21′ 10″; therefore, to determine the danger space for a target 20 feet high, at the given range, the work for getting the data in Column 7 of the Range Table is as follows:

$$S=h\cot\omega\left(1+\frac{h\cot\omega}{X}\right)$$

As we desire our result in yards, however, we may reduce all units of measurement in the formula to yards, and the expression then becomes

$$S_{20}=\frac{h}{3}\cot\omega\left(1+\frac{\frac{h}{3}\cot\omega}{R}\right)$$

$\frac{h}{3}=6.6667$ .... log 0.82391..........log 0.82391

$\omega=5°\ 21'\ 10''$ .... cot 1.02827..........cot 1.02827

$R=10000$ ......log 4.00000......colog 6.00000−10

$\frac{\frac{h}{3}\cot\omega}{R}=0.0071$ .... log 7.85218−10

$1+\frac{\frac{h}{3}\cot\omega}{R}=1.0071$ ....log 0.00307

$S_{20}=71.655$ yards ....log 1.85525

91. We can now make a comparison between the trajectory in vacuum and that in air for the same initial velocity and angle of departure.

Figure 9 represents on the same scale the trajectories in air and in vacuum of a 12″ projectile weighing 870 pounds, $c=0.61$, fired with an initial velocity of 2900 f. s., at an angle of departure of 4° 13.2′; the range in vacuum for this angle of departure being 38315.3 feet (12771.7 yards), and in air of standard density, being 30,000 feet or 10,000 yards. In the figure the ordinates of both curves are exaggerated ten times as compared with the abscissæ, in order that the curve may be seen.

If gravity did not act, the projectile would move in the tangent to the curve OQ_1Q_2, and in traveling the horizontal distance $x=OA$, would rise to the height

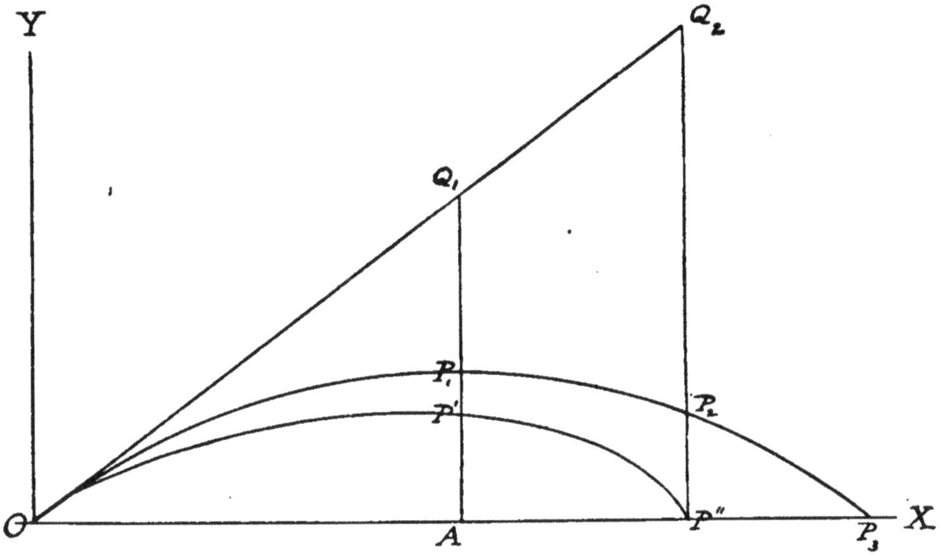

FIGURE 9.

Comparison between Trajectory in Vacuum and that in Air for same ϕ and same *I. V.*

$AQ_1 = x \tan\phi$. In this case, assuming $x=20{,}000$ feet from the gun, we would have:

$x=20000$ ....log 4.30103
$\phi=4°\ 13.2'$ ....tan 8.86797−10

$y=1475.7$ feet ....log 3.16900

The attraction of gravity, however, pulls the projectile down $Q_1P_1 = \dfrac{gX^2}{2V^2\cos^2\phi}$ while it moves OA horizontally, and so for the ordinate of the trajectory in vacuum we have

$$AP_1 = y_1 = x\tan\phi - \frac{gx^2}{2V^2\cos^2\phi}$$

We have already computed the value of $x\tan\phi$ as above and found it to be 1475.7 feet. Therefore, computing the second term of the right-hand member of the above equation, we have

$g=32.2$ .... log 1.50786
$x=20000$ ....log 4.30103......2 log 8.60206
2 ....log 0.30103......colog 9.69897−10
$v=2900$ ....2 colog 3.07520−10
$\phi=4°\ 13.2'$ ....2 sec 0.00236

$\dfrac{gx^2}{2V^2\cos^2\phi} =$ 769.93 feet.................. log 2.88645
$x\tan\phi = 1475.7$ feet

$AP_1 = y_1 = x\tan\phi - \dfrac{gx^2}{2V^2\cos^2\phi} =$ 705.8 feet

When the resistance of the air also acts, retarding the motion of the projectile, it takes longer for it to move OA horizontally, and so gravity has longer to act, and it has fallen the further distance

$$P_1P' = \frac{gx^2}{2V^2 \cos^2 \phi} \left(\tfrac{2}{3}kx + \tfrac{1}{3}k^2x^2\right)$$

and the ordinate of the trajectory in air is

$$AP' = y_2 = x \tan \phi - \frac{gx^2}{2V^2 \cos^2 \phi} \left(1 + \tfrac{2}{3}kx + \tfrac{1}{3}k^2x^2\right)$$

or

$$y_2 = x \tan \phi - \frac{gnx^2}{2V^2 \cos^2 \phi}$$

in which

$$n = \frac{V^2 \sin 2\phi}{gX}$$

$V = 2900$ .... 2 log 6.92480
$2\phi = 8°\ 26.4'$ .... sin 9.16646 − 10
$g = 32.2$ .... colog 8.49214 − 10
$X = 30000$ .... log 4.47712 .... colog 5.52288 − 10

$n = 1.277$ .... log 0.10628
$\frac{gx^2}{2V^2 \cos^2 \phi} =$ .... log 2.88645

$\frac{gnx^2}{2V^2 \cos^2 \phi} = 983.4$ .... log 2.99273
$x \tan \phi = 1475.7$

$y_2 = 492.3$

In the particular case represented, the projectile reached the ground after having traveled, in air, the horizontal distance $X = OP'' = 30{,}000$ feet; but if it had moved in vacuum it would, at that range, have been at P_2, at a height of 481.2 feet above P''.

$$P_2P'' = x \tan \phi - \frac{gx^2}{2V^2 \cos^2 \phi} \quad \text{(in vacuum)}$$

so at $x = 30{,}000$ feet, we solve for P_2P''

$x = 30000$ .... log 4.47712 .... 2 log 8.95424
$\phi = 4°\ 13.2'$ .... tan 8.86797 .... 2 sec 0.00236
$g = 32.2$ .... log 1.50786
2 .... colog 9.69897 − 10
$V = 2900$ .... 2 colog 3.07520 − 10

$x \tan \phi = 2213.5$ .... log 3.34509

$\frac{gx^2}{2V^2 \cos^2 \phi} = 1732.3$ .... log 3.23863
$P_2P'' = 481.2$ feet

$$n = \frac{\text{Range in vacuum}}{\text{Range in air}}, \text{ whence range in vacuum} = nX$$

$n = 1.277$ .... log 0.10628
$X = 30000$ .... log 4.47712

Range in vacuum = 38315.83 .... log 4.58340

The exaggeration of the ordinates in order to present a serviceable figure, as well as the arithmetical results, shows how flat is the trajectory, according to the most modern standards. It may also be noted from the figure, as we have already pointed out, that the vertex of the curve in air is reached after a shorter horizontal travel than is the case for the trajectory in vacuum.

EXAMPLES.

1. From the data given in the first four columns of the following table, compute the value of n, and thence the approximate values of the angle of fall, time of flight and striking velocity in each case.

Problem.	DATA.				ANSWERS.			
	Gun. In.	Initial velocity. f. s.	Angle of departure.	Range. Yds.	n.	Angle of fall.	Time of flight. Secs.	Striking velocity. f. s.
1........	6	2900	1° 07′ 49″	2625	1.308	1° 24′	3.34	1984
2........	6	2900	3 03 51	5394	1.723	4 21	8.62	1391
3........	4	2900	1 07 26	2600	1.313	1 24	3.32	1973
4........	4	2900	3 03 47	5166	1.798	4 25	8.56	1320
5........	4	2900	5 02 58	6599	2.313	7 53	13.60	977
6........	*	2000	1 33 00	1000	2.239	2 24	2.90	700
7........	12	2400	3 33 00	5900	1.249	4 15	8.77	1747
8........	12	2250	1 11 00	2000	1.082	1 16	2.83	2004
9........	13	2300	1 08 00	2000	1.083	1 13	2.77	2046

* Small arm.

2. A 6″ gun, with 2900 f. s. initial velocity, with an angle of departure of 1° 07′ 49″, gives a range of 2625 yards, an angle of fall of 1° 24′ 00″ and a time of flight of 3.34 seconds. Find the coordinates of the vertex and the danger space for a target 20 feet high.

Answers. $x_0=1382$ yards. $y_0=45$ feet. $S=301$ yards.

3. A 6″ gun with 2900 f. s. initial velocity, with an angle of departure of 3° 03′ 51″, gives a range of 5394 yards, a time of flight of 8.61 seconds and an angle of fall of 4° 22′ 00″. Find the coordinates of the vertex, also the danger space for a target 20 feet high.

Answers. $x_0=2926$ yards. $y_0=298$ feet. $S=89$ yards.

4. The range table of the 3″ gun of 2800 f. s. initial velocity gives an angle of departure of 1° 01′ 00″ for a range of 2000 yards, and shows that the range changes 100 yards for each 4′ change in the angle of departure. Find the ordinates of the trajectory for that range at points 1700, 1800 and 1900 yards from the gun.

Answers. 5.93, 4.19, 2.21 yards, respectively.

5. The angle of fall for the 2000-yard trajectory of the 3″ gun is 1° 26′ 00″. Compute the danger space for a target 20 feet high.

Answer. $S=302$ yards.

PART II.

PRACTICAL METHODS.

INTRODUCTION TO PART II.

Taking up the more practical part of the study of exterior ballistics, we here find that certain expressions may be derived that are not equations to the trajectory in air itself as a whole, but which do express with sufficient accuracy for all practical purposes certain relations that exist between the values of the several elements of the trajectory. Furthermore, these expressions are generally true, for all initial velocities, wherein they differ from the equation to the trajectory in air which we have heretofore been using, which, as we know, was only true for initial velocities for which Mayevski's exponent, *a*, was equal to 2. As was the case in our effort to derive an equation to the trajectory in air, we also find that, owing to the differential character of the expressions which we are now about to investigate, direct solutions are not always possible; but, as was not the case with the equation to the special trajectory, we will see that, thanks to the ingenuity of Major Siacci, it is possible to obtain solutions in all cases by the use of certain artificial mathematical methods. These methods are sufficiently accurate for our purposes in all cases and are comparatively simple of application after they are understood, and are therefore entirely satisfactory for all practical purposes.

We will also see that, although the mathematical expressions involved contain a number of more or less complicated integral expressions, the working out of which for every problem which we wish to solve would be laborious in the extreme, this labor has already been performed for us by different investigators of the subject, notably Colonel Ingalls, and the results tabulated in Tables I and II of the Ballistic Tables; and that, by the use of these tables, the labor of computation by means of the formulæ in question may be simplified to a very great degree and reduced to a minimum.

The investigation of these methods and the solution of problems by them constitute Part II of this book, and complete the consideration of the trajectory as a plane curve.

CHAPTER 6.

THE TIME AND SPACE INTEGRALS; THE COMPUTATION OF THEIR VALUES FOR DIFFERENT VELOCITIES, AND THEIR USE IN APPROXIMATE SOLUTIONS.

New Symbols Introduced.

T_v.... Value of the time integral in seconds for remaining velocity v.
T_V.... Value of the time integral in seconds for initial velocity V.
S_v.... Value of the space integral in feet for remaining velocity v.
S_V.... Value of the space integral in feet for initial velocity V.

Time integral.

92. Returning now to Mayevski's equation for the retardation due to atmospheric resistance, namely, $\frac{dv}{dt} = -\frac{A}{C}v^a$, we see that it may be written, after separation of the variables

$$dt = -\frac{C}{A} \times \frac{dv}{v^a} \tag{42}$$

in which A and a are Mayevski's constants and C is the reduced ballistic coefficient

$$\left(C = \frac{fw}{\delta c d^2}\right)$$

Suppose now a projectile to travel so nearly horizontally that its velocity is not affected by gravitation, but is only affected by air resistance; then the integration of (42) between corresponding limits, t_1 and t_2 of t, and v_1 and v_2 of v, will give the elapsed time (t_2-t_1) corresponding to the loss of velocity (v_1-v_2). We will assume the velocity at the origin of time (v_1) to be 3600 f. s., as that is the upper limit of initial velocities for which the values of Mayevski's constants have been experimentally determined (3600 f. s. is also well above all present-day service initial velocities, and this point of origin will therefore answer all practical purposes until initial velocities are greatly increased over any present practice), and will therefore have $t_1=0$ seconds, and $v_1=3600$ f. s.; and we will designate by T_v the elapsed time from the origin until the velocity is reduced to v. Then we have

$$\int_0^{T_v} dt = -\frac{C}{A}\int_{3600}^{v} \frac{dv}{v^a} \tag{43}$$

by integrating which we get

$$T_v = \frac{C}{A} \times \frac{1}{a-1}\left(\frac{1}{v^{a-1}} - \frac{1}{(3600)^{a-1}}\right) \tag{44}$$

Substituting in (44) the values of A and a given in the first of Mayevski's special equations (14), we get

$$T_v = C\left(\frac{[2.65059]}{v^{0.55}} - 4.9502\right)^* \tag{45}$$

and the value of this, computed for any value of v between 3600 f. s. and 2600 f. s., is the time in seconds which it takes for the air resistance to reduce the velocity of the projectile whose ballistic coefficient is C from 3600 f. s. to v f. s., when v lies between 3600 f. s. and 2600 f. s.

---

* The number enclosed in brackets is the logarithm of the constant and not the constant itself.

Below 2600 f. s. the values of A and a change to those given in the second of Mayevski's special equations (14), and with the new values the limits of integration change also, and we have

$$\int_{T_{2600}}^{T_v} dt = -\frac{C}{A}\int_{2600}^{v} \frac{dv}{v^a}$$

whence

$$T_v = T_{2600} + \frac{C}{A} \times \frac{1}{a-1}\left(\frac{1}{v^{a-1}} - \frac{1}{(2600)^{a-1}}\right)$$

which, after substituting the values of A and a, and that of T_{2600} as computed from (45), reduces to

$$T_v = C\left(\frac{[3.05870]}{v^{0.7}} - 3.6880\right)^*$$

and the value of this, computed for any value of v between 2600 f. s. and 1800 f. s. is the time in seconds it takes for the air resistance to reduce the velocity of a projectile whose ballistic coefficient is C from 3600 f. s. to v f. s., when v lies between 2600 f. s. and 1800 f. s.

Proceeding in a similar manner with the other values of A and a, each integration being performed between the limits which correspond to the particular values of A and a used, we obtain the following expressions for T_v:

v between 3600 f. s. and 2600 f. s.

$$T_v = C\left(\frac{[2.65059]}{v^{0.55}} - 4.9502\right)$$

v between 2600 f. s. and 1800 f. s.

$$T_v = C\left(\frac{[3.05870]}{v^{0.7}} - 3.6880\right)$$

v between 1800 f. s. and 1370 f. s.

$$T_v = C\left(\frac{[3.88074]}{v} - 1.8837\right)$$

v between 1370 f. s. and 1230 f. s.

$$T_v = C\left(\frac{[6.71807]}{v^2} + 0.8790\right) \qquad (46)^*$$

v between 1230 f. s. and 970 f. s.

$$T_v = C\left(\frac{[12.59607]}{v^4} + 2.6089\right)$$

v between 970 f. s. and 790 f. s.

$$T_v = C\left(\frac{[6.92553]}{v^2} - 1.8801\right)$$

v between 790 f. s. and 0 f. s.

$$T_v = C\left(\frac{[4.33011]}{v} - 15.460\right)$$

NOTE.—The above formulæ give numerical values to five places only. In actually computing the tables, the numerical values were carried out correctly to seven or more places.

Space integral.

93. Multiplying both sides of equation (42) by v, we get $v dt = -\frac{C}{A} \times \frac{dv}{v^{a-1}}$, and putting ds for $v dt$ in this, we have

$$ds = -\frac{C}{A} \times \frac{dv}{v^{a-1}} \qquad (47)$$

* The numbers enclosed in brackets are the logarithms of the constants and not the constants themselves.

and the integration of this equation between corresponding limits, s_1 and s_2 of s, and v_1 and v_2 of v, will give the space traversed (s_2-s_1), while the velocity is reduced by the atmospheric resistance from v_1 to v_2, supposing again that the path of the projectile is so nearly horizontal that the effect of gravitation on the velocity in the trajectory may be neglected. We will assume that the origin of space, as well as the origin of time, coincides with the value of 3600 f. s. for v, or $s_1=0$ and $v_1=3600$; and we will designate by S_v the space passed over from the origin to the point where the velocity is reduced to v. Thus we have

$$\int_0^{S_v} ds = -\frac{C}{A}\int_{3600}^{v}\frac{dv}{v^{a-1}}$$

which integrates to

$$S_v=\frac{C}{A}\times\frac{1}{a-2}\left(\frac{1}{v^{a-2}}-\frac{1}{(3600)^{a-2}}\right) \tag{48}$$

Substituting in (48) the values of A and a given in the first of Mayevski's special formulæ (14), we get

$$S_v=C(21780.9-[2.73774]v^{0.45})^{*} \tag{49}$$

and the value of this, computed for any value of v between 3600 f. s. and 2600 f. s., is the space in feet passed over by a projectile whose ballistic coefficient is C, while the atmospheric resistance reduces its velocity from 3600 f. s. to v f. s.

Proceeding similarly for the different values of A and a between the different limits of velocity, exactly as was done in the case of the time integrals, we obtain the following expressions for S_v:

v between 3600 f. s. and 2600 f. s.

$$S_v=C(21780.9-[2.73774]v^{0.45})$$

v between 2600 f. s. and 1800 f. s.

$$S_v=C(31227.1-[3.42668]v^{0.8})$$

v between 1800 f. s. and 1370 f. s.

$$S_v=C(62875.3-[4.24296]\log v)$$

v between 1370 f. s. and 1230 f. s.

$$S_v=C\left(\frac{[7.01910]}{v}+365.69\right) \tag{50*}$$

v between 1230 f. s. and 970 f. s.

$$S_v=C\left(\frac{[12.72101]}{v^{3}}+6034.5\right)$$

v between 970 f. s. and 790 f. s.

$$S_v=C\left(\frac{[7.22656]}{v}-5571.4\right)$$

v between 790 f. s. and 0 f. s.

$$S_v=C(158436.8-[4.69232]\log v)$$

NOTE.—The above formulæ give numerical values to five places only. In computing the tables, the numerical values were carried out correctly to seven or more places.

* The numbers enclosed in brackets are the logarithms of the constants and not the constants themselves.

94. T_v and S_v are known as the "time function" and "space function," respectively, and their values have been computed for values of v from 3600 f. s. to 500 f. s., on the supposition that C is unity, and their values for the different velocities will be found in Table I of the Ballistic Tables under the headings T_u and S_u, with the velocities in the column headed u as an argument. The reason for representing the velocities in this table by the symbol u will be explained in a subsequent chapter. To apply them to any projectile for any given atmospheric conditions it is only necessary to multiply the tabular values by the particular value of C for the given projectile and atmospheric conditions.

Meaning of S and T

95. It must be clearly borne in mind just what the values of T_u and S_u tabulated in these two columns mean; that is, that they are *the time elapsed and the space covered, respectively, while the velocity of the projectile whose ballistic coefficient is unity is being reduced from 3600 f. s. to v f. s. by the atmospheric resistance.* Therefore, if we wish to find how long it takes the atmospheric resistance to reduce the velocity of a projectile whose ballistic coefficient is unity from v_1 f. s. to v_2 f. s., we would find T_{v_1} and T_{v_2} from Table I, using the values of v_1 and v_2 as arguments in the column headed u, and then we would have $T=T_{v_2}-T_{v_1}$, and similarly for the space covered we would have $S=S_{v_2}-S_{v_1}$. If the value of the ballistic coefficient be not unity, then these two equations would become

$$T=C(T_{v_2}-T_{v_1}) \tag{51}$$
$$S=C(S_{v_2}-S_{v_1}) \tag{52}$$

96. The above can perhaps be best illustrated by a reference to Figure 10, which represents the complete trajectory from the point where $V=3600$ f. s. as an origin to its end, where $v_\omega=0$. Now remembering the assumption that the trajectory is

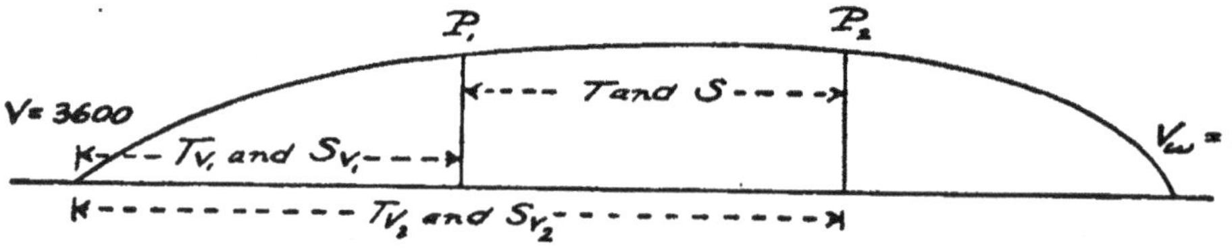

FIGURE 10.

supposed to be so flat that it is practically a straight line, and supposing P_1 and P_2 are points on it at which the remaining velocities are those under consideration, namely, v_1 and v_2, respectively. Then manifestly from the figure, the value of T is the difference between the values of T_{v_1} and T_{v_2}, and the value of S is the difference between the values of S_{v_1} and S_{v_2}, which graphic representation, with the addition of the ballistic coefficient, gives the expressions contained in (51) and (52).

NOTE.—The curve shown in Figure 10 must not be taken as literally and mathematically correct. It is simply used to illustrate the point. While the distances are marked as both T and S they do not literally represent both times and spaces.

97. Suppose we wish to find how long it will take the atmospheric resistance, under standard conditions, to reduce the velocity of a 6", 105-pound projectile from its initial velocity of 2600 f. s. to 2000 f. s., and through what space the projectile would travel while its velocity is being so reduced, the value of the ballistic coefficient being taken as unity. From Table I we see that the reduction from 3600 f. s. to 2600 f. s. would take 0.970 second, during which time the projectile would travel 2967.1 feet. That is, $T_{2600}=0.970$ second and $S_{2600}=2967.1$ feet. Similarly for the reduction from 3600 f. s. to 2000 f. s. $T_{2000}=1.909$ seconds and $S_{2000}=5106.1$ feet. Therefore

$$T=T_{2000}-T_{2600}=1.909-0.970=0.939 \text{ second, and}$$
$$S=S_{2000}-S_{2600}=5106.1-2967.1=2139 \text{ feet.}$$

If the ballistic coefficient were not unity, then we would have $T=0.939\times C$ and $S=2139\times C$. The variation from unity of the ballistic coefficient may, of course, be caused by a variation in any of its factors, such as coefficient of form, density of atmosphere, etc.

98. By means of equations (51) and (52), if we have given the ballistic coefficient, one of the velocities, and any one of the other quantities, we can find the remaining quantities.

99. Suppose that a 6″ projectile weighs 105 pounds; that its coefficient of form is 0.61; and that it has an initial velocity of 2562 f. s.; and that we desire to know its velocity after it has traveled 3 seconds, and also how far it will travel in that time; when the barometer stands at 30.00″ and the thermometer at 40° F.

$$C=\frac{w}{\delta c d^2};\ T=C(T_{v_2}-T_{v_1}),\ \text{or}\ T_{v_2}=\frac{T}{C}+T_{v_1};\ S=C(S_{v_2}-S_{v_1})$$

$w=105$ .... log 2.02119
$\delta=1.056$ ....log 0.02366......colog 9.97634−10
$c=0.61$ ....log 9.78533−10..colog 0.21467
$d^2=36$ ....log 1.55630......colog 8.44370−10

$C=$ .... log 0.65590......colog 9.34410−10
$T=3$ .... log 0.47712

$\frac{T}{C}=0.66255$ .... log 9.82122−10
$T_{v_1}=1.01840$ From Table I.

$T_{v_2}=1.68095$ whence
$v_2=2122.2$ f. s. From Table I.
Also $S_{v_2}=4637.2$ From Table I.
$S_{v_1}=3091.6$ From Table I.

$S_{v_2}-S_{v_1}=1545.6$ .... log 3.18910
$C=$ .... log 0.65590

$S=6998.4$ feet .... log 3.84500

Therefore the

Remaining velocity ....2122.2 foot-seconds.
Space traversed ....2332.8 yards.

100. Again, suppose we have a 12″ projectile weighing 870 pounds, coefficient of form 0.61, which has a remaining velocity of 2521 f. s. after traveling 4000 yards through air in which the barometer stands at 30.00″ and the thermometer at 68° F.; and that we wish to determine its initial velocity and time of flight to that point.

$$C=\frac{w}{\delta c d^2}\ ;\ S=C(S_{v_2}-S_{v_1}),\ \text{whence}\ S_{v_1}=S_{v_2}-\frac{S}{C}\ ;\ T=C(T_{v_2}-T_{v_1})$$

$w=870$ .... log 2.93952
$\delta=0.997$ ....log 9.99870−10..colog 0.00130
$c=0.61$ ....log 9.78533−10..colog 0.21467
$d^2=144$ ....log 2.15836......colog 7.84164−10

$C=$ .... log 0.99713......colog 9.00287−10
$S=12000$ .... log 4.07918

$\frac{S}{C}=1208.0$ .... log 3.08205

$S_{v_2}=3227.5$ From Table I.

$S_{v_1}=2019.5$ hence
$v_1=2900$ f. s. From Table I.
Also $T_{v_2}=1.072$ From Table I.
$T_{v_1}=0.625$ From Table I.

$T_{v_2}-T_{v_1}=0.447$ .... log 9.65031−10
$C=$ .... log 0.99713

$T=4.4406$ .... log 0.64744

Therefore the initial velocity was 2900 f. s., and the elapsed time was 4.4406 seconds.

101. Again, suppose the projectile given in the preceding paragraph started with an initial velocity of 2900 f. s., and traveled for 3 seconds, under atmospheric conditions as given; how far did it go in that time?

$C=$ as before. $T=C(T_{v_2}-T_{v_1})$, hence $T_{v_2}=\frac{T}{C}+T_{v_1}$; $S=C(S_{v_2}-S_{v_1})$

$C=$ as in preceding paragraph........................colog 9.00287−10
$T=3$ .... log 0.47712

$\frac{T}{C}=0.302$ .... log 9.47999−10

$T_{v_1}=0.625$ From Table I.

$T_{v_2}=0.927$ hence
$v_2=2635$ f. s. From Table I.
Also $S_{v_2}=2853.6$ From Table I.
$S_{v_1}=2019.4$ From Table I.

$S_{v_2}-S_{v_1}=$ 834.2 ....log 2.92127
$C=$ ....log 0.99713

$S=8287$ ....log 3.91840

Therefore the space traversed was 2762.3 yards.

102. The foregoing methods are of course only strictly applicable to such parts of the trajectory as may without material error be considered as straight lines, since in deducing (51) and (52) we have entirely neglected the effect of gravitation. They will give sufficiently accurate results when applied to any arc of a trajectory if the length of the arc be not materially greater than the length of its chord, and if the latter's inclination to the horizontal be not greater than 10° to 15°; but they are principally applied to the entire trajectories of guns fired with angles of departure not exceeding 3° or 4°, giving the striking velocity and time of flight for ranges as great as 5000 yards, in the case of medium and large guns of high initial velocity, with as much accuracy as is obtainable by any other method of computation. It will be seen later that these formulæ may be correctly employed in dealing with the pseudo velocity, and that the formulæ then become generally serviceable.

103. By means of the formulæ derived in this chapter we may see how to determine by experimental firing the value of the coefficient of form of any given projectile. To do this the projectile may be fired through two pairs of screens at a known distance apart, and the velocity measured at each pair of screens. Considering the first pair of screens, which gave a measured velocity of v_1, we know that this measured velocity is the mean velocity for the distance between the two screens of the first pair, that is, it is the actual velocity at a point half way between the two screens of the first pair; and similarly for the second pair of screens. Therefore the points of measurement giving the distance traversed while the velocity is being reduced from v_1 to v_2 are the two points half way between the two screens of each pair, respectively. It will also be understood that this distance between the two pairs of screens must be great enough to furnish a material reduction in the velocity, but not great enough to violate the assumption on which we have been working; namely, that the force of gravity does not affect the flight of the projectile while traversing the distance under consideration. Also, to avoid introducing errors resulting from the action of gravity, the two pairs of screens should be in the same horizontal plane. We then have the formulæ:

$$S=C(S_{v_2}-S_{v_1}),\text{ or, as } C=\frac{w}{\delta c d^2},\text{ for such firing}$$

$$S=\frac{w}{\delta c d^2}(S_{v_2}-S_{v_1}),\text{ from which}$$

$$c=\frac{w}{\delta d^2}\times\frac{S_{v_2}-S_{v_1}}{S} \qquad (53)$$

from which we can solve for the value of c from the observed velocities, by the use of Table I of the Ballistic Tables.

104. As an example of the above, a Krupp 11.024″ gun fired a projectile weighing 760.4 pounds through two pairs of screens 328.1 feet and 6561.7 feet, respectively, from the gun, giving measured velocities of 1694.6 f. s. and 1483.3 f. s., respectively, at the pairs of screens. The value of δ at the time of firing being 1.013, find the value of c for the projectile used. Using formula (53), we have

$S_{v_2}=7389.5$	From Table I.			
$S_{v_1}=6377.3$	From Table I.			
$S_{v_2}-S_{v_1}=1012.2$				log 3.00527
$w=760.4$				log 2.88104
$\delta=1.013$	log 0.00561			colog 9.99439−10
$d=11.024$	log 1.04234	2 log 2.08468		2 colog 7.91532−10
$S=6233.6$	log 3.79474			colog 6.20526−10
$c=1.003$				log 0.00128

Actually this result should have come out $c=1.00$, as the projectile fired was similar to those actually used in the experiments to determine the values of A and α for standard projectiles, but the unavoidable errors in the measurements of velocities, slight variations in the projectiles themselves, the effect of wind and of the variable density of the air at the different points in the path of the projectile, all produce variations in the experimentally determined values of c, so that only the mean of a great number of determinations can be safely considered as reliable.

105. Again, for a 6″ gun, two velocities were measured, $v_1=2550$ f. s. and $v_2=1667$ f. s., at 250 feet and 5000 yards from the muzzle, respectively. If the barometer stood at 30.50″ and the thermometer at 0° F. at the moment of firing, compute the value of the coefficient of form of the projectile used, which weighed 105 pounds.

$$c=\frac{w}{\delta d^2}\times\frac{S_{v_2}-S_{v_1}}{S}$$

$S_{v_2}=6502.1$			
$S_{v_1}=3131.2$			
$S_{v_2}-S_{v_1}=3370.9$			log 3.52775
$w=105$			log 2.02119
$\delta=1.169$	log 0.06781	colog	9.93219 − 10
$d^2=36$	log 1.55630	colog	8.44370 − 10
$S=14750$	log 4.16879	colog	5.83121 − 10
$c=0.57021$			log 9.75604 − 10

It is to be noted that the distance between the two points of measurement in this case is rather large for our assumption in regard to gravity, and the result is therefore probably not very accurate.

106. The value of c may also be determined by a comparison of actual with computed ranges, but the causes of variation in the actual ranges are so numerous that nothing less than consistent results given by many series of shots should cause the acceptance as correct of any value of c thus determined. As a matter of fact this is the method of determining the value of c now in use in our navy, as explained in a later chapter.

107. We have now arrived at a point where we may see how to determine experimentally the initial or muzzle velocity of a projectile, as defined in paragraph 17 of Chapter 1. To do this, we actually measure its velocity at a known distance from the gun, and then, by the formulæ and methods given in this chapter, we may compute the velocity that complies with the given definition of initial velocity; namely, a fictitious velocity, not actually existent when the projectile leaves the gun, but with which the projectile would have to be projected from the muzzle into still air in order to describe its actual trajectory.

Determination of initial velocity.

108. For instance, a 12″ projectile weighing 850 pounds was fired through two screens 100 and 200 feet from the muzzle of the gun, respectively, and the time of flight between the two screens was 0.047 second. All conditions being standard, including the coefficient of form of the projectile, compute the initial velocity.

$$C=\frac{w}{d^2}\qquad S=C(S_{v_2}-S_{v_1})$$

The shell traveled 100 feet (the distance between the screens) in 0.047 second, therefore the measured velocity was $\frac{100}{.047}=2127.7$ f. s., and this, being the mean velocity between the two screens, is the actual velocity at a point midway between them, that is, at a point 150 feet from the muzzle of the gun. Therefore, we have, $S=150$ feet and $v_2=2127.7$ f. s., and desire to compute v_1.

$w=850$		log 2.92942		
$d^2=144$	log 2.15836	colog 7.84164 − 10		
$C=$		log 0.77106	colog	9.22894 − 10
$S=150$				log 2.17609
$\frac{S}{C}=$ 25.4				log 1.40503

$S_{v_2}=4616.5$	From Table I.
$S_{v_1}=4591.1$	whence
$v_1=2134.5$ f.s.	From Table I.

That is, the initial velocity in this case is 2134.5 foot-seconds.

EXAMPLES.

NOTE.—The answers to these problems, being obtained by the use of formulæ and methods discussed in this chapter, all depend for their accuracy upon the correctness of the assumption that in every case the effect of gravity upon the flight of the projectile is negligible for the portion of the trajectory involved. They are, therefore, only accurate within the limits imposed by this assumption.

1. Given the data in the first five columns of the following table and two velocities; or one velocity and either S and T, compute the data in the other two of the last four columns.

Problem.	Projectile.			Atmosphere.		v_1. f. s.	v_2. f. s.	S. Feet.	T. Secs.
	d. In.	w. Lbs.	c.	Bar. In.	Ther. °F.				
A.	3	13	1.00	28.00	0	1150	935	3978.0	3.8810
B.	3	13	1.00	29.00	5	2700	2300	1763.3	0.7078
C.	4	33	0.67	30.00	10	2900	2552	3024.2	1.1110
D.	5	50	1.00	31.00	20	3150	2003	6720.9	2.6819
E.	5	50	0.61	30.00	30	3150	2561	5549.4	1.9556
F.	6	105	0.61	29.00	40	2600	2013	9779.2	4.2756
G.	6	105	1.00	28.00	50	2800	2247	5581.0	2.2253
H.	6	105	0.61	28.25	60	2800	2474	5289.8	2.0087
I.	7	165	1.00	29.50	70	2700	2313	4471.5	1.7897
J.	7	165	0.61	30.75	80	2700	2133	10799.0	4.4980
K.	8	260	0.61	31.00	90	2750	2541	4562.4	1.7241
L.	10	510	1.00	30.00	95	2700	2114	10942.0	4.5808
M.	10	510	0.61	29.00	100	2700	2316	11920.0	4.7642
N.	12	870	0.61	28.00	85	2900	2154	27530.0	11.0280
O.	13	1130	1.00	29.00	75	2000	1833	4746.7	2.4774
P.	13	1130	0.74	29.53	59	2000	1756	9042.8	4.8340
Q.	14	1400	0.70	30.00	52	2000	1900	3947.9	2.0289
R.	14	1400	0.70	29.00	45	2600	2343	8767.7	3.5527

2. Given the data contained in the first seven columns of the following table, compute the value of the coefficient of form of the projectile in each case.

Problem.	DATA.							ANSWERS.
	Projectile.		Value of δ.	Distance of pairs of screens from gun.*		Measured velocities at.		Value of c.
	d. In.	w. Lbs.		First pair. Feet.	Second pair. Yds.	First pair. f. s.	Second pair. f. s.	
A.	3	13	1.057	75	500	1100	1017	1.00570
B.	3	13	0.989	150	1000	2650	2090	1.00120
C.	4	33	1.111	150	1500	2875	2390	0.67250
D.	5	50	1.062	200	1500	3130	2399	1.01260
E.	5	50	0.899	200	1200	3130	2830	0.59322
F.	6	105	0.950	200	1200	2550	2348	0.62045
G.	6	105	1.107	250	900	2750	2461	1.01390
H.	6	105	1.009	250	800	2760	2620	0.60165
I.	7	165	0.937	250	900	2650	2448	0.97983

* The distance given in these columns is in each case the distance from the muzzle of the gun to a point midway between the two screens composing the pair.

3. Given the data for actual firing contained in the first six columns of the following table, compute the initial velocity of the gun in each case.

Problem.	DATA.							ANSWERS.
	Projectile.			Distance of screens from gun.		Value of δ.	Elapsed time between screens. Secs.	Initial velocity. f. s.
	d. In.	w. Lbs.	c.	First screen. Feet.	Second screen. Feet.			
J.........	7	165	0.61	150	350	0.925	0.074	2716
K.........	8	260	0.61	200	400	1.021	0.074	2717
L.........	10	510	1.00	250	450	0.899	0.074	2722
M.........	10	510	0.61	250	450	1.125	0.075	2681
N.........	12	870	0.61	250	450	0.937	0.071	2828
O.........	13	1130	1.00	250	550	1.015	0.153	1976
P.........	13	1130	0.74	250	550	0.954	0.149	2024
Q.........	14	1400	0.70	250	600	1.115	0.176	2001
R.........	14	1400	0.70	250	600	0.913	0.136	2585

4. The initial velocity of a 3″ 13-pound projectile, $c=1.00$, is 2800 f. s. Atmospheric conditions being standard, what are the elapsed times until its velocity is reduced to 2600 f. s., 2400 f. s. and 2200 f. s.?

Answers. 0.341, 0.729 and 1.176 seconds.

5. The initial velocity of a 3″ 13-pound projectile, $c=1.00$, is 2800 f. s. Atmospheric conditions being standard, what are the spaces traversed while the velocity is being reduced to 2600 f. s., 2400 f. s. and 2200 f. s.?

Answers. 922, 1890 and 2917 feet.

6. A 12″ projectile weighing 850 pounds, $c=1.00$, has an initial velocity of 2400 f. s. What is the remaining velocity at 1000, at 2000 and at 3000 yards range; first in an atmosphere of standard density; and, second, when the thermometer is at 82° F., and the barometer at 29.20″?

Answers. 2256, 2118, 1986 f. s.
2264, 2133, 2008 f. s.

7. A 12″ projectile weighing 850 pounds, $c=1.00$, has an initial velocity of 2400 f. s. What is the time of flight for 1000, for 2000 and for 3000 yards range; when the temperature is 82° F., and the barometer is at 29.20″?

Answers. 1.283, 2.647, 4.092 seconds.

8. How long does it take a 6″ projectile weighing 100 pounds, having an initial velocity of 2000 f. s., to travel 1000, 2000 and 3000 yards, and what is the remaining velocity at each range; the temperature being 44° F., and the barometer at 30.15″?

Answers. 1.614, 3.492, 5.668 seconds.
1725, 1485, 1282 f. s.

9. A Krupp 5.91″ gun, projectile weighing 112.2 pounds, having an initial velocity of 1667.6 f. s., in experimental firing under standard atmospheric conditions, gave as a mean of ten shots, measured velocities of 1656 f. s. at 164 feet from the gun, and 1358 f. s. at 4921 feet from the gun. Compute the velocities at those ranges and from a comparison between the observed and computed ranges, determine the coefficient of form of the projectile used.

Answers. Computed velocities ....1656....1363 f. s.
Observed velocities ....1656....1358 f. s.
Value of c............1.00

10. A Krupp 5.91" gun, projectile weighing 112.2 pounds, having an initial velocity of 1763.6 f. s., in experimental firing under standard atmospheric conditions, gave measured velocities of 1740.7 f. s. at 328 feet from the gun, and 1369 f. s. at 6562 feet from the gun. Compute the velocities at those ranges, and from a comparison between the observed and the computed ranges, determine the coefficient of form of the projectile used.

Answers. Computed velocities..1740.....1348 f. s.
Observed velocities...1740.7...1369 f. s.
Value of c..........1.00

11. A Krupp 12" gun, projectile weighing 1001 pounds, having an initial velocity of 1721.7 f. s., in experimental firing under standard atmospheric conditions, gave measured velocities of 1711 f. s. at 328 feet from the gun; 1692 f. s. at 984 feet from the gun, and 1518 f. s. at 6562 feet from the gun. Compute the velocities at those ranges, and from a comparison between the observed and computed ranges, determine the coefficient of form of the projectile used.

Answers. Computed velocities..1711....1690....1521 f. s.
Observed velocities...1711....1692....1518 f. s.
Value of c..........1.00

12. A 4.72" gun, firing a projectile weighing 45 pounds, $c=1.00$, in experimental firing, when the thermometer was at 65° F. and the barometer at 30.43", gave a measured velocity of 2204 f. s. at a point 175 feet from the muzzle. What was the initial velocity? *Answer.* 2228 f. s.

13. A Krupp 11.024" gun, projectile weighing 760.4 pounds, in experimental firing, under atmospheric conditions when $\delta=1.013$, gave measured velocities of 1746 f. s. and 1529 f. s. at points 328 and 6562 feet from the gun, respectively. Compute the value of the coefficient of form of the projectile used.

Answer. $c=0.9992$.

14. A flat-headed, 6" projectile, weighing 70 pounds, when fired through two pairs of screens 150 feet apart, gave measured velocities at those two points of 1881 f. s. and 1835 f. s. Atmospheric conditions being standard at the time of firing, compute the value of the coefficient of form of the projectile.

Answer. $c=2.46$.

15. A Krupp 9.45" gun, projectile weighing 474 pounds, in experimental firing, under atmospheric conditions when $\delta=1.06$, gave measured velocities of 1719 f. s. and 1460 f. s. at points 328 feet and 6562 feet, respectively, from the gun. Compute the value of the coefficient of form of the projectile used. *Answer.* $c=0.9969$.

CHAPTER 7.

THE DIFFERENTIAL EQUATIONS GIVING THE RELATIONS BETWEEN THE SEVERAL ELEMENTS OF THE GENERAL TRAJECTORY IN AIR. SIACCI'S METHOD. THE FUNDAMENTAL BALLISTIC FORMULÆ. THE COMPUTATION OF THE DATA GIVEN IN THE BALLISTIC TABLES, AND THE USE OF THE BALLISTIC TABLES.

New Symbols Introduced.

u.... Pseudo velocity at any point of the trajectory in foot-seconds.
du.... Differential increment in u.
S_u.... Value of space function in feet for pseudo velocity u.
S_V.... Value of space function in feet for initial velocity V.
T_u.... Value of time function in seconds for pseudo velocity u.
T_V.... Value of time function in seconds for initial velocity V.
A_u.... Value of altitude function for pseudo velocity u.
A_V.... Value of altitude function for initial velocity V.
I_u.... Value of inclination function for pseudo velocity u.
I_V.... Value of inclination function for initial velocity V.

109. From the hypothesis already made in paragraph 69 that the resultant atmospheric resistance acts in the line of the projectile's axis, which itself coincides with the tangent to the trajectory at every point, it follows that the trajectory is a plane curve. For, if a vertical plane be passed through the gun and through any point of the trajectory, that plane will contain the only two forces acting upon the projectile while it is at that point, namely, gravity and the resistance of the air; and so their resultant will lie in that plane also, and there will be no force tending to draw the projectile from that plane, and so the next consecutive point of the curve must lie in the same plane also; and so on to the end.

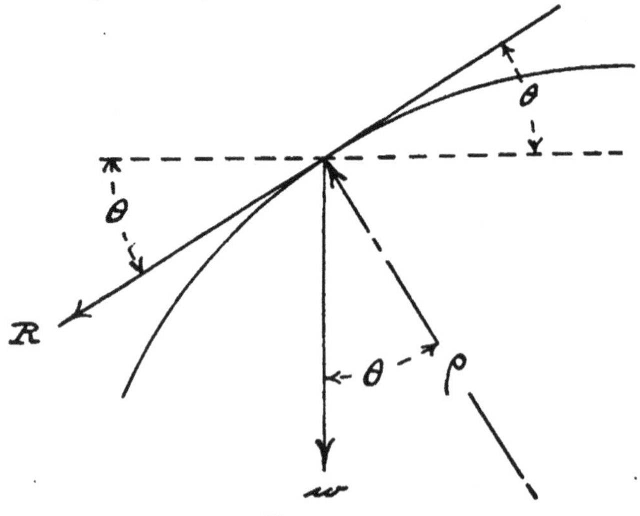

FIGURE 11.

Derivation of the differential equations.

110. Figure 11 represents a portion of the trajectory with the two forces acting upon the projectile, namely, its weight, w, acting vertically downward, and the resistance of the air, $R=\frac{w}{g}\times\frac{A}{C}v^n$, acting along the tangent to the curve in a direction opposite to that in which the projectile is moving. Kinetic equilibrium results from the balancing of these two forces by the inertia forces $\frac{w}{g} \times \frac{dv}{dt}$ acting in the tangent, and $\frac{w}{g} \times \frac{v^2}{\rho}$ acting in the normal, ρ being the radius of curvature of the curve at the point under consideration.* Resolving forces along the normal to the trajectory, the inertia force $\frac{w}{g} \times \frac{v^2}{\rho}$, commonly called the centrifugal force, must balance the resolved part of w along the same line, whence we have $\frac{w}{g} \times \frac{v^2}{\rho} = w \cos \theta$,

or $$\frac{v^2}{\rho} = g \cos \theta \qquad (54)$$

In other words, the acceleration towards the center of curvature is the resolved part of g in that direction. But the radius of curvature $\rho = -\frac{ds^*}{d\theta}$, whence

$$v^2 d\theta = -g \cos \theta \, ds = -g dx, \text{ or } g dx = -v^2 d\theta \qquad (55)$$

111. Dividing each side of (55) by dt and putting v_h for $\frac{dx}{dt}$, we have

$$g v_h = -v^2 \frac{d\theta}{dt}, \text{ whence } g dt = -\frac{v^2 d\theta}{v_h} = -\frac{v^2 d\theta}{v \cos \theta},$$

whence $$g dt = -v \sec \theta \, d\theta \qquad (56)$$

112. By putting $\cot \theta \, dy$ for dx in (55) we get

$$g \cot \theta \, dy = -v^2 d\theta \text{ or } g dy = -v^2 \tan \theta \, d\theta \qquad (57)$$

113. By putting $\cos \theta \, ds = dx$ in (55) we get

$$g \cos \theta \, ds = -v^2 d\theta \text{ or } g ds = -v^2 \sec \theta \, d\theta \qquad (58)$$

114. Now resolving horizontally, since the horizontal component of the atmospheric resistance, $\frac{w}{g} \times \frac{A}{C} v^a \cos \theta$, is the only force which acts to produce horizontal acceleration, $\frac{d^2x}{dt^2} = \frac{dv_h}{dt}$, which in this case is negative acceleration, we have

$$\frac{dv_h}{dt} = \frac{d(v \cos \theta)}{dt} = -\frac{A}{C} v^a \cos \theta$$

but from (56) we know that $g dt = -v \sec \theta \, d\theta$, therefore the above expression becomes

$$g d(v \cos \theta) = \frac{A}{C} v^{(a+1)} d\theta \qquad (59)$$

115. Grouping the expressions derived above together, we have — The differential equations.

$$g d(v \cos \theta) = \frac{A}{C} v^{(a+1)} d\theta \qquad (60)$$
$$g dx = -v^2 d\theta \qquad (61)$$
$$g dt = -v \sec \theta \, d\theta \qquad (62)$$
$$g dy = -v^2 \tan \theta \, d\theta \qquad (63)$$
$$g ds = -v^2 \sec \theta \, d\theta \qquad (64)$$

and these equations, (60) to (64) inclusive, are the differential equations giving the relations between the several elements of the trajectory; and, could (60) be integrated, thus giving a finite relation between v and θ, one of those variables could

* See any standard work on the subject for the derivation of this expression.

be eliminated from equations (61) to (64) inclusive, and then values of x, y, t and s could all be obtained.

116. Since we cannot integrate (60), it is necessary to resort to methods of approximation, and a method devised by Major F. Siacci (Sē-ā́-chē), of the Italian Army, has been generally adopted by artillerists because of its comparative simplicity and readiness of application. It is to be noted that in all the preceding chapters discussing the trajectory in air and deriving mathematical expressions in regard to it, we have dealt with approximate methods only, and we now see that we are again, and for our final and most approved methods, driven to fall back upon another approximate system. However, this one, Siacci's method, has been found to be accurate within all necessary limits for ordinary ballistic problems, and for our purposes we may consider it as exact, in contradistinction to the more approximate methods that we have hitherto considered. It should not be forgotten, however, that the method is not literally exact, and that it might be possible, under unusual and peculiar conditions, that results might vary appreciably from those actually existent in practice. It is not ordinarily necessary to consider this point, but should some unusual and peculiar problem present itself, it would be necessary to consider whether the conditions were such as to introduce material inaccuracies into results obtained by the ordinary methods.

117. Taking rectangular axes in the plane of fire; origin at the gun; X, as always, horizontal, and positive in the direction of projection; Y, as always, vertical, and positive upward; let V, in Figure 12, be the initial velocity, and ϕ the angle of departure, and let v be the remaining velocity at any point, P, of the trajectory. Revolving v horizontally, we have $v \cos \theta$, and, parallel to the line of departure

$$u = v \cos \theta \sec \phi \tag{65}$$

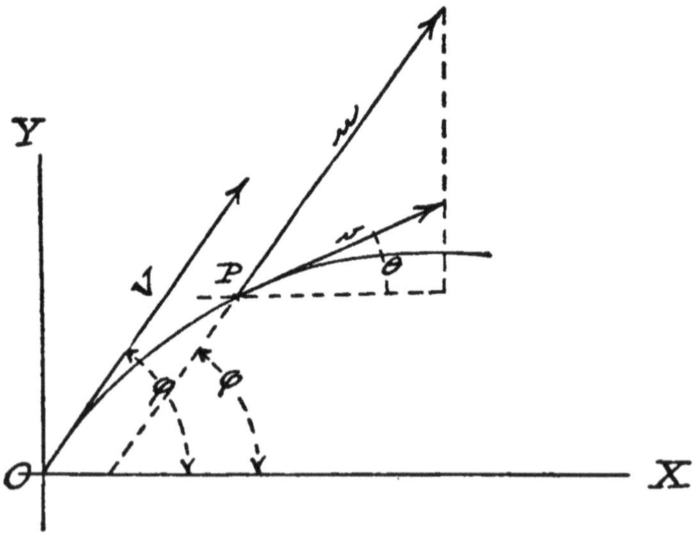

FIGURE 12.

Pseudo velocity.

118. The quantity u, which is represented in Figure 12, is known as the "pseudo velocity" (see definition in paragraph 22), and its use in the solution of practical ballistic problems is due to Major Siacci, and is the essence of his method. It will readily be seen that $u = V$ at the origin, where $\theta = \phi$, and also at another point in the descending branch of the trajectory where $\theta = -\phi$. At the vertex, where $\theta = 0$, the pseudo velocity differs most from the true velocity, its value there being $u = v \sec \phi$, but if ϕ be small the difference is very small, and for flat trajectories (ϕ not greater than about 5°), u may be considered as equal to v throughout the entire trajectory without material error.

119. Substituting $u \cos\phi$ for $v \cos\theta$ and $\frac{u \cos\phi}{\cos\theta}$ for v in (60), we get Siacci's method.

$$gdu = \frac{A}{C} \times \frac{\cos^a\phi}{\cos^{(a+1)}\theta} u^{(a+1)} d\theta$$

whence

$$\frac{gC}{A} \times \frac{du}{u^{(a+1)}} = \frac{\cos^a\phi}{\cos^{(a-1)}\theta} \sec^2\theta \, d\theta \qquad (66)$$

Now the value of a definite integral remains unchanged when for any variable under the integral sign is substituted a constant which is the mean value of that variable between the limits of integration. Thus for the variable quantity * $\frac{\cos^{(a-2)}\phi}{\cos^{(a-1)}\theta}$ we may substitute a constant, β, thereby enabling (66) to be integrated without introducing any error, provided we assign to β its proper value. It may be said here that, for all practical purposes, in the use of the methods of exterior ballistics in connection with the ordinary problems of naval gunnery, β may always be considered as equal to unity without exceeding the limits of accuracy within which we are otherwise able to work. In certain special classes of firing this value of $\beta=1$ cannot be used without introducing material error, the principal such classes being mortar and high-angle firing; but as these are not methods within the province of ordinary naval gunnery, the value of $\beta=1$ will be adopted in the formulæ throughout the rest of this book, and the factor β will be allowed to disappear from the formulæ, as, when it is equal to unity, it does not affect the results obtained by their use. (For a further discussion of the value of β, see Alger's Text Book on Exterior Ballistics, Edition of 1906, page 58, *et seq.*, and other standard works on the subject.) We know that

$$\cos^a\phi = \cos^{(a-2+2)}\phi = \cos^{(a-2)}\phi \cos^2\phi$$

and by substituting

$$\beta = \frac{\cos^{(a-2)}\phi}{\cos^{(a-1)}\theta} \text{ in } \frac{\cos^a\phi}{\cos^{(a-1)}\theta} \text{ we have } \frac{\cos^a\phi}{\cos^{(a-1)}\theta} = \beta\cos^2\phi$$

whence, by substitution in (66) and expressing the direct integration, we get

$$\frac{gC}{A}\int_u^V \frac{du}{u^{(a+1)}} = \beta\cos^2\phi \int_\theta^\phi \sec^2\theta \, d\theta \qquad (67)$$

Now if we call $-\frac{2g}{A}\int\frac{du}{u^{(a+1)}} = I_u$, then (67) becomes, after integration,

$$\tan\phi - \tan\theta = \frac{C}{2\cos^2\phi}(I_u - I_V) \text{ or } \tan\theta = \tan\phi - \frac{C}{2\cos^2\phi}(I_u - I_V) \qquad (68)$$

120. Now let us put $\frac{u\cos\phi}{\cos\theta}$ for v in (61), and we will have

$$gdx = -u^2\cos^2\phi \sec^2\theta \, d\theta$$

or, substituting for $\sec^2\theta \, d\theta$ its value from (66)

$$gdx = -\frac{gC}{A} \times \frac{du}{u^{(a-1)}}$$

whence

$$\int_0^x dx = -C\int_V^u \frac{1}{A} \times \frac{du}{u^{(a-1)}} \qquad (69)$$

* The constant factor $\cos^{(a-2)}\phi$ is taken out with the variable factor $\frac{1}{\cos^{(a-1)}\theta}$ for the reason that their product, the mean value of which we call β, differs very little from unity.

whence $$x=C(S_u-S_V) \tag{70}$$

in which S_u stands for $-\frac{1}{A}\int\frac{du}{u^{(a-1)}}$

121. Proceeding in exactly the same way with (62), we get

$$gdt=-u\cos\phi\sec^2\theta\,d\theta=-\frac{C}{\cos\phi}\times\frac{g}{A}\times\frac{du}{u^a}$$

or
$$\int_0^t dt=-\frac{C}{\cos\phi}\int_V^u\frac{1}{A}\times\frac{du}{u^a}$$

or
$$t=\frac{C}{\cos\phi}(T_u-T_V) \tag{71}$$

in which T_u stands for $-\frac{1}{A}\int\frac{du}{u^a}$

122. Now, multiplying (68) by the differential of (70), and putting dy for $\tan\theta\,dx$, we have

$$dy-\tan\phi\,dx=\frac{C^2}{2\cos^2\phi}(I_u-I_V)\times\frac{1}{A}\times\frac{du}{u^{(a-1)}}$$

and by putting $-\frac{1}{A}\int I_u\times\frac{du}{u^{(a-1)}}=A_u$, this becomes, after integrating,

$$y-x\tan\phi=-\frac{C}{2\cos^2\phi}[A_u-A_V-I_V(S_u-S_V)]$$

and, finally, dividing by (70), we get

$$\frac{y}{x}=\tan\phi-\frac{C}{2\cos^2\phi}\left(\frac{A_u-A_V}{S_u-S_V}-I_V\right) \tag{72}$$

Note that in this substitution that A_u means the A function of u, otherwise known as the altitude function, this A having of course nothing in common with the constant A on the other side of the equation.

The ballistic formulæ. **123.** The formulæ given in equations (65), (68), (70), (71) and (72) are known as the ballistic equations, and are the ones on which are based all the principal problems in exterior ballistics. They are here repeated, grouped, for convenience, as follows:

$$x=C(S_u-S_V) \tag{73}$$

$$\frac{y}{x}=\tan\phi-\frac{C}{2\cos^2\phi}\left(\frac{A_u-A_V}{S_u-S_V}-I_V\right) \tag{74}$$

$$\tan\theta=\tan\phi-\frac{C}{2\cos^2\phi}(I_u-I_V) \tag{75}$$

$$t=\frac{C}{\cos\phi}(T_u-T_V) \tag{76}$$

$$v=u\cos\phi\sec\theta \tag{77}$$

124. These ballistic formulæ express the values of

(a) The two coordinates of any point of the trajectory;

(b) The tangent of the angle of inclination of the curve to the horizontal at any point of the trajectory:

(c) The time of flight to any point of the trajectory; and

(d) The remaining velocity at any point in the trajectory directly as functions of

1. A new variable, u, known as the pseudo velocity, and already defined;
2. The ballistic coefficient;
3. The angle of departure; and
4. The initial velocity.

The formulæ could therefore be used in solving problems by working out the values for each case represented by the symbols S, A, I and T, with their appropriate subscript letters in each case; but, in order to facilitate the process, the values of these integrals corresponding to all necessary velocities have been worked out and made available in the columns of Table I of the Ballistic Tables. For all velocities between 3600 f. s. and 500 f. s., using the velocities as arguments in the left-hand column of the table, headed u, we may find the corresponding values of the desired integrals, under the appropriate columns, headed, respectively, S_u, A_u, I_u and T_u.

The time function.

125. As shown by (71), the value of the definite integral $-\frac{1}{A}\int_V^u \frac{du}{u^a}$ (when multiplied by $\frac{C}{\cos\phi}$) measures the time of flight from a point where the pseudo velocity is V to one where it is u. We have represented this definite integral by $T_u - T_V$, and we require a table from which its value may be taken for any given values of V and u. But, as explained in Chapter 6, the values of $T_v(T_u)$ in Table I were calculated by the use of the formula

$$T_v = \frac{1}{A}\int_{3600}^{v} \frac{dv}{v^a}$$

and the integral given above is the same as this, except that u, a velocity, is substituted for v, a velocity; so that the results for the same velocity, whether real or pseudo, would be the same, and what we formerly called T_v is the same thing that we now designate $T_u - T_{3600}$. Consequently, we have always that $T_{u_2} - T_{u_1} = T_{v_2} - T_{v_1}$, and the tabulated time functions may be used indiscriminately for either real or pseudo velocities, provided the proper quantity be taken as an argument.

The space function.

126. In the same way, in (70), the value of the integral $-\frac{1}{A}\int_V^u \frac{du}{u^{(a-1)}}$, which we have represented by $S_u - S_V$, measures (when multiplied by C) the horizontal space traversed while the pseudo velocity changes from V to u, and, as the values of S_u in Table I, as explained in Chapter 6, were calculated by the use of the formula

$$S_v = -\frac{1}{A}\int_{3600}^{v} \frac{dv}{v^{(a-1)}}$$

and the integral given above is the same as this, except that u, a velocity, has been substituted for v, a velocity, so that the results for the same velocity, whether pseudo or real, would be the same, and what we formerly called S_v is the same thing that we now designate $S_u - S_{3600}$. Consequently, we now have $S_{u_2} - S_{u_1} = S_{v_2} - S_{v_1}$, and the tabulated values of the space function, S_u, may be used indiscriminately for either real or pseudo velocities, provided the proper quantity be taken as an argument.

The inclination function.

127. As shown by (68), the value of the definite integral $-\frac{2g}{A}\int_V^u \frac{du}{u^{(a+1)}}$ (when multiplied by $\frac{C}{2\cos^2\phi}$) measures the change in the tangent of the inclination of the trajectory from the point where pseudo velocity is V to the point where it is u. We have represented this definite integral by $I_u - I_V$, and we require a table from which its value, for any given values of V and u may be taken. To supply this, the values of $-\frac{2g}{A}\int_{\infty}^{u} \frac{du}{u^{(a+1)}}$ have been computed for values of u from 3600 f. s. to 500 f. s., and placed in Table I under the heading I_u, with u as an argument in the left-hand column. Then, as in the case of the time and space functions, we always have $I_{u_2} - I_{u_1} = I_{v_2} - I_{v_1}$, and these values may be used for either true or pseudo velocities indiscriminately, provided the proper argument be used. It would have been equally well to have tabulated the values of $-\frac{2g}{A}\int_{3600}^{u}\frac{du}{u^{(a+1)}}$, making $I_{3600}=0$ instead of $I_{3600}=.03138$, as is the case with the integration performed as indicated for a lower limit of infinity. This would have made the series of values of the inclination function, like those of the space, time and altitude functions, begin at the imagined origin where $u=3600$ f. s., but as we deal entirely with differences, the point of origin is immaterial.

128. The equations from which I_u are computed are obtained by substituting successive values of A and a in

$$I_u=-\frac{2g}{A}\int\frac{du}{u^{(a+1)}}$$

and integrating, the first integration being between infinity and u (u from 3600 f. s. to 2600 f. s.); the second between 2600 and u (u from 2600 to 1800); the third between 1800 and u (u between 1800 and 1370); and so on; the results being as follows:

u between 3600 f. s. and 2600 f. s.

$$I_u=\frac{[4.00897]}{u^{1.55}}$$

u between 2600 f. s. and 1800 f. s.

$$I_u=\frac{[4.48170]}{u^{1.7}}+0.00452$$

u between 1800 f. s. and 1370 f. s.

$$I_u=\frac{[5.38806]}{u^{2}}+0.01776$$

u between 1370 f. s. and 1230 f. s.

$$I_u=\frac{[8.35032]}{u^{3}}+0.06083$$

u between 1230 f. s. and 970 f. s.

$$I_u=\frac{[14.30751]}{u^{5}}+0.10912$$

u between 970 f. s. and 790 f. s.

$$I_u=\frac{[8.55778]}{u^{3}}-0.05028$$

u between 790 f. s. and 0 f. s.

$$I_u=\frac{[5.83743]}{u^{2}}-0.41960$$

The numbers enclosed in brackets are the logarithms of the constants and not the constants themselves. (78)

NOTE.—The above formulæ give numerical values correct to five places only. In computing the tables the numerical values were carried out correctly to seven or more places.

The altitude function.

129. As explained in paragraph 122, A_u-A_V stands for the value of the definite integral $-\frac{1}{A}\int_V^u I_u\frac{du}{u^{(a-1)}}$, or, substituting for I_u its value of $-\frac{2g}{A}\int\frac{du}{u^{(a+1)}}$, we have

$$A_u-A_V=-\frac{2g}{A^2a}\int_V^u\frac{du}{u^{(2a-1)}}$$

and in order that the value of this integral may be found for any given values of V and u, the values of $-\frac{2g}{A^2a}\int_{3600}^{u}\frac{du}{u^{(2a-1)}}$ have been computed for values of u from 3600 f. s. to 500 f. s., and will be found in Table I under the heading A_u, with values of u as arguments in the left-hand column. Then, as in the case of the space, time and inclination functions, we have always $A_{u_2}-A_{u_1}=A_{v_2}-A_{v_1}$, and the tabulated values of the altitude function may be used for either real or pseudo velocities indiscriminately, provided the proper argument be used.

130. The equations from which the values of A_u are computed are obtained by substituting the successive values of A and a in the expression

$$A_u=-\frac{2g}{A^2a}\int\frac{du}{u^{(2a-1)}}$$

and integrating, exactly as was done in Chapter 6 in finding the values of T_v, except that the values of I_u to be substituted in the integral expression for the value of A_u-A_V must include the constants of integration whose values are given in (78). The results are:

u between 3600 f. s. and 2600 f. s.

$$A_u=\frac{[6.35853]}{u^{1.1}}-279.64$$

u between 2600 f. s. and 1800 f. s.

$$A_u=\frac{[7.23937]}{u^{1.4}}-[1.08179]u^{0.2}-39.264$$

u between 1800 f. s. and 1370 f. s.

$$A_u=\frac{[8.96777]}{u^2}-[2.49233]\log u+1052.0$$

u between 1370 f. s. and 1230 f. s.

$$A_u=\frac{[14.76736]}{u^4}+\frac{[5.80321]}{u}-57.984$$

u between 1230 f. s. and 970 f. s.

$$A_u=\frac{[26.60254]}{u^6}+\frac{[11.75890]}{u^3}+329.62$$

u between 970 f. s. and 790 f. s.

$$A_u=\frac{[15.18228]}{u^4}-\frac{[5.92791]}{u}+624.05$$

u between 790 f. s. and 0 f. s.

$$A_u=\frac{[9.86650]}{u^2}+[4.31515]\log u-68192.0$$

(79) The numbers enclosed in brackets are the logarithms of the constants and not the constants themselves.

NOTE.—The above formulæ give numerical values correct to five places only. In computing the tables the numerical values were carried out correctly to seven or more places.

131. In the preceding work in this chapter we have followed the methods given by Professor Alger in his most excellent book on Exterior Ballistics, which are the generally accepted methods, and have derived certain ballistic formulæ as given in equations (73) to (77) inclusive. We have also shown how the values of the space (S_u), time (T_u), inclination (I_u) and altitude (A_u) functions for varying values of the real or pseudo velocities have been computed and made readily available in Table I of the Ballistic Tables. Professor Alger accepts the results already obtained as being sufficient for all practical purposes, and uses these equations in the form in which we already have them (rearranged to suit each special problem) in the solution of ballistic problems. Colonel Ingalls, however, proceeded still further with the reduction of these formulæ, and by most noteworthy mathematical work succeeded in getting resulting expressions that vastly reduce the labor of the computer below that involved in the use of the formulæ as they stand above. These reductions are somewhat involved, but, when once carried through, so simplify the solutions of problems and reduce the labor connected therewith, that Ingalls' methods have become generally accepted for work of this nature. Their acceptance and use involved the computation of another extensive table, Table II of the Ballistic Tables, but with this table and Ingalls' formulæ, the work of the computer is reduced to a minimum. Ingalls' methods and formulæ may be more appropriately considered in the solution of certain special problems, and the study of them is therefore deferred to the next chapter.

Use of Table I. 132. As an example of the use of Table I, let us suppose that it is desired to take from it the values of the four functions corresponding to a velocity, either real or pseudo, of 2727 f. s.

For determining the value of S_u, we have: For $u=2720$, $S_u=2581.1$, and the difference between that value and the value for the next tabulated value of u, namely, $u=2740$, is, by subtraction or as given in the difference column headed Δ_S, 63.4; that is, a change of 20 f. s. (at this part of the table; note the reduction in the tabulated intervals as the velocity decreases) in the velocity changes the value of the space function 63.4. (Note that the difference given in the Δ columns is in each case that between the value of the function on the same line and the one on the line next below it.) Therefore, for $u=2727$ f. s., we have

$$S_u=2581.1-\frac{63.4\times 7}{20}=2581.1-22.2=2558.9$$

or

$$S_u=2517.7+\frac{63.4\times 13}{20}=2517.7+41.2=2558.9$$

and similarly

$$A_u=97.94+\frac{3.05\times 13}{20}=97.94+1.98=99.92$$

$$I_u=.04791+\frac{.00055\times 13}{20}=.04791+.00036=.04827$$

$$T_u=.802+\frac{.023\times 13}{20}=.802+.015=.817$$

133. And, similarly, suppose that we want to find the value of the real or pseudo velocity (which one it is depends upon the formula in use) corresponding to a value of $I_u=.05767$.

The nearest tabular value to this is $I_u=.05775$, corresponding to $u=2430$ f. s., from which, by interpolation,

$$u(\text{or } v)=2430+\frac{8\times 10}{37}=2430+2.2=2432.2 \text{ f. s.}$$

134. If we had desired to find the value of A_u corresponding to the value of $I_u=.05767$ given above, we could find u as just described, and then find the value of A_u thus

$$A_u=151.46-\frac{1.97\times 2.2}{10}=151.46-0.43=151.03$$

or we could proceed without finding the value of u, thus

$$A_u = 151.46 - \frac{8 \times 10}{37} \times \frac{1.97}{10} = 151.46 - 0.43 = 151.03$$

This latter method will frequently be found necessary in the use of Table II, and it should be practiced until it can be done quickly and accurately.

135. As an example of the problems that may be solved by the methods indicated in this chapter, let us suppose we have a 3″ gun, standard projectile weighing 13 pounds, with an initial velocity of 2800 f. s., and that the angle of departure for a horizontal range of 3000 yards is 1° 53′; and that we desire to determine the pseudo velocity and the horizontal distance traversed at the moment when the projectile has been in flight 4 seconds; atmospheric conditions being standard.

$$C = \frac{w}{d^2}\ ;\ t = \frac{C}{\cos\phi}(T_u - T_V) \text{ whence } T_u = \frac{t\cos\phi}{C} + T_V;\ x = C(S_u - S_V)$$

$w = 13$ .... log 1.11394

$d^2 = 9$ ....log 0.95424......colog 9.04576−10

$C =$ .... log 0.15970......colog 9.84030−10

$t = 4$ .... log 0.60206

$\phi = 1°\ 53'$ .... cos 9.99977−10

$\frac{t\cos\phi}{C} = 2.768$ .... log 0.44213

$T_V = 0.734$ From Table I.

$T_u = 3.502$ whence $u = 1411$ f. s. From Table I.

$S_u = 7769.2$ From Table I.

$S_V = 2329.1$ From Table I.

$S_u - S_V = 5440.1$ .... log 3.73561

$C =$ .... log 0.15970

$x = 7858$ .... log 3.89531

Pseudo velocity ....1411 f. s.

Distance traveled ....2619 yards.

EXAMPLES.

1. In the 4000-yard trajectory of a 3″ gun ($V = 2800$ f. s.), $\phi = 3°\ 10'$, $\omega = 6°\ 00'$, v_0 (velocity at vertex) $= 1600$ f. s. and $v_\omega = 1050$ f. s. What are the pseudo velocities at the three points where the velocities are given?

Answers. 2800, 1602, 1046 f. s.

2. In the 4000-yard trajectory of a 6″ gun ($V = 2400$ f. s.), $\phi = 2°\ 52'$, $\omega = 4°\ 09'$, $v_0 = 1780$ f. s. and $v_\omega = 1377$ f. s. What are the pseudo velocities at the point of departure, vertex and point of fall?

Answers. 2400, 1782, 1375 f. s.

3. In the 8000-yard trajectory of a 12″ gun ($V = 2250$ f. s.), $\phi = 6°\ 23'$, $\omega = 8°\ 58'$, $v_0 = 1690$ f. s. and $v_\omega = 1347$ f. s. What are the pseudo velocities at the point of departure, vertex and point of fall?

Answers. 2250, 1701, 1339 f. s.

4. In the 10,000-yard trajectory of an 8″ gun ($V = 2300$ f. s.), $\phi = 11°\ 00'$, $\omega = 18°\ 14'$, $v_0 = 1340$ f. s. and $v_\omega = 1036$ f. s. What are the pseudo velocities at the point of departure, vertex and point of fall?

Answers. 2300, 1365, 1000 f. s.

5. The 4000-yard trajectory of a 3″ gun ($V=2800$ f. s., $w=13$ pounds) has $\phi=3°\ 10'$. What is the pseudo velocity at a point horizontally distant from the gun 2000 yards, and what is the time of flight to that point?

Answers. 1671 f. s.; 2.791 seconds.

6. The 4000-yard trajectory of a 6″ gun ($V=2400$ f. s., $w=100$ pounds) has $\phi=2°\ 52'$. What is the pseudo velocity at a point horizontally distant from the gun 2000 yards, and what is the time of flight to that point?

Answers. 1829 f. s.; 2.856 seconds.

7. In the 4000-yard trajectory of a 5″ gun ($V=2550$ f. s., $w=50$ pounds), $\phi=3°\ 01'$. What is the pseudo velocity at a point horizontally distant from the gun 2200 yards, and what is the inclination of the curve at that point?

Answers. 1683 f. s.; 0° 07′ 12″.

8. In the 6000-yard trajectory of a 6″ gun ($V=2300$ f. s., $w=100$ pounds), $\phi=5°\ 53'$. What is the pseudo velocity after 1000 and after 2000 yards horizontal travel, and what are the ordinates of the trajectory at those distances?

Answers. 2010 and 1747 f. s.; 279 and 485 feet.

9. In the 3000-yard trajectory of a 3″ gun ($V=2800$ f. s., $w=13$ pounds), $\phi=1°\ 53'$. What are the pseudo velocities and what the horizontal distances traveled after 1, 2 and 3 seconds flight?

Answers. 2276, 1898 and 1619 f. s.; 840, 1529 and 2117 yards.

10. Determine the reduced ballistic coefficient for a 10″, 500-pound projectile of standard form, if the temperature and barometric height at the gun be 84° F. and 29.12″, and the time of flight be 16 seconds. If the initial velocity be 2000 f. s., given the above time of flight, find the range and the pseudo velocity at the point of fall.

Answers. $C=5.432$; $R=7927$ yards; $u_\omega=1151$ f. s.

11. Determine the reduced ballistic coefficient for an 8″, 250-pound projectile of standard form, the temperature being 46° F., and the barometer 30.11″, the time of flight being 22 seconds. If the initial velocity be 2300 f. s. and the angle of departure be 11° 00′, find u_ω from the given value of the time of flight, and then find the range. *Answers.* $C=3.8581$; $u_\omega=974.3$ f. s.; $R=9947$ yards.

CHAPTER 8.

THE DERIVATION AND USE OF SPECIAL FORMULÆ FOR FINDING THE ANGLE OF DEPARTURE, ANGLE OF FALL, TIME OF FLIGHT AND STRIKING VELOCITY FOR A GIVEN HORIZONTAL RANGE AND INITIAL VELOCITY; THAT IS, THE DATA CONTAINED IN COLUMNS 2, 3, 4 AND 5 OF THE RANGE TABLES. INGALLS' METHODS.

New Symbols Introduced.

u_ω.... Pseudo velocity at the point of fall.

v_ω.... Remaining velocity at point of fall, or striking velocity.

S_{u_ω}.... Value of the space function for pseudo velocity u_ω.

T_{u_ω}.... Value of the time function for pseudo velocity u_ω.

A_{u_ω}.... Value of the altitude function for pseudo velocity u_ω.

I_{u_ω}.... Value of the inclination function for pseudo velocity u_ω.

S_{u_0}.... Value of the space function for pseudo velocity u_0.

T_{u_0}.... Value of the time function for pseudo velocity u_0.

A_{u_0}.... Value of the altitude function for pseudo velocity u_0.

I_{u_0}.... Value of the inclination function for pseudo velocity u_0.

ΔS.... Difference between two values of the space function.

ΔT.... Difference between two values of the time function.

ΔA.... Difference between two values of the altitude function.

ΔI.... Difference between two values of the inclination function.

$z = \frac{x}{C}$ .... General expression for value of argument for Column 1 of Table II.

$Z = \frac{X}{C}$ .... Special expression for value of argument for Column 1 of Table II.

a...
b...
a'...
t'... } General values of Ingalls' secondary functions.

A...
B...
A'...
T'...
$B' = \frac{B}{A}$...
A''... } Special values of Ingalls' secondary functions for whole trajectory.

C_1, C_2, C_3, etc.... Successive values of C. The same system of notation by subscripts also applies for successive approximate values of other quantities where such use of them is necessary.

136. As already deduced, the six fundamental ballistic formulæ are:

$$C=\frac{fw}{\delta cd^2} \tag{80}$$

$$x=C(S_u-S_V) \tag{81}$$

$$\frac{y}{x}=\tan\phi-\frac{C}{2\cos^2\phi}\left(\frac{A_u-A_V}{S_u-S_V}-I_V\right) \tag{82}$$

$$\tan\theta=\tan\phi-\frac{C}{2\cos^2\phi}(I_u-I_V) \tag{83}$$

$$t=C\sec\phi(T_u-T_V) \tag{84}$$

$$v=u\cos\phi\sec\theta \tag{85}$$

137. It will be seen from the above that special formulæ may be derived to fit all particular cases, which special formulæ will contain only the quantities contained in the above fundamental equations; that is, quantities that are either known or contained in the Ballistic Tables, or the values of which are to be found.

Transformation of ballistic formulæ.

138. Let us apply these formulæ to the special case under consideration, that is, to the derivation of special formulæ for computing the values shown in Columns 2, 3, 4 and 5 of the range tables. For the complete horizontal trajectory we may substitute in the fundamental equations as given above, as follows: $x=X$, $y=0$, $t=T$, $v=v_\omega$ and $\theta=-\omega$. If we make these substitutions we get:

From (80) $$C=\frac{fw}{\delta cd^2} \tag{86}$$

From (81) $$S_{u_\omega}=S_V+\frac{X}{C} \tag{87}$$

From (82) $$\tan\phi=\frac{C}{2\cos^2\phi}\left(\frac{A_{u_\omega}-A_V}{S_{u_\omega}-S_V}-I_V\right)$$

$$\frac{2\sin\phi\cos^2\phi}{\cos\phi}=\sin 2\phi=C\left(\frac{A_{u_\omega}-A_V}{S_{u_\omega}-S_V}-I_V\right) \tag{88}$$

From (83) $$\tan(-\omega)=\tan\phi-\frac{C}{2\cos^2\phi}(I_{u_\omega}-I_V)$$

and substituting in this the value of $\tan\phi$ given above we get

$$\tan\omega=\frac{C}{2\cos^2\phi}\left(I_{u_\omega}-\frac{A_{u_\omega}-A_V}{S_{u_\omega}-S_V}\right) \tag{89}$$

From (84) $$T=C\sec\phi(T_{u_\omega}-T_V) \tag{90}$$

From (85) $$v_\omega=u_\omega\cos\phi\sec\omega \tag{91}$$

139. Considering the above expressions, we may note that, with the exception of the quantities that we desire to find, all the quantities contained in them are either known or else may be found in the Ballistic Tables (exclusive of Table II). Professor Alger uses them in this form, in his text book, for computing the values of the unknown quantities in those expressions. As an example of his methods we will now solve a problem by the use of the above formulæ as they stand, and without using Table II of the Ballistic Tables.

Alger's method.

140. For the 12″ gun, $V=2900$ f. s., $w=870$ pounds, $c=0.61$, atmosphere at standard density, to compute the values of the angle of departure, angle of fall, time of flight, and striking velocity, for a horizontal range of 10,000 yards (without using Table II) by Alger's method.

$$C=\frac{fw}{cd^2}\ ;\ S_{u_\omega}=S_V+\frac{X}{C}\ ;\ \sin 2\phi=C\left(\frac{A_{u_\omega}-A_V}{S_{u_\omega}-S_V}-I_V\right)$$

$$\tan\omega=\frac{C}{2\cos^2\phi}\left(I_{u_\omega}-\frac{A_{u_\omega}-A_V}{S_{u_\omega}-S_V}\right);\ T=C\sec\phi(T_{u_\omega}-T_V)\ ;\ v_\omega=u_\omega\cos\phi\sec\omega$$

We cannot get a correct result without determining the value of f; but let us disregard that for the moment nevertheless, and proceed for the present as though $f=1$. The value of C for standard conditions could be taken from Table VI, and this will usually be done to save labor, but for this first problem we will compute it.

$w=870$ .... log 2.93952
$c=0.61$ ....log 9.78533−10..colog 0.21467
$d^2=144$ ....log 2.15836......colog 7.84164−10

$C=$ .... log 0.99583......colog 9.00417−10
$X=30000$ .... log 4.47712

$\frac{X}{C}=\Delta S=3029.0$ .... log 3.48129

From Table I.

$S_V=2019.4$

$S_{u_\omega}=5048.4$ $A_{u_\omega}=253.05$ $T_{u_\omega}=1.880$
$u_\omega=2014.8$ $A_V=75.09$ $T_V=0.625$ $I_V=0.4388$

$\Delta A=177.96$ $\Delta T=1.255$

$\Delta A=177.96$ ....log 2.25032
$\Delta S=3029$ ....log 3.48129

$\frac{\Delta A}{\Delta S}=.05875$ ....log 8.76903−10
$I_V=.04388$

$\frac{\Delta A}{\Delta S}-I_V=.01487$ ....log 8.17231−10

$\Delta T=1.255$ .... log 0.09864
$C=$ ....log 0.99583...... log 0.99583

$2\phi=8°\ 28'\ 09''$......................sin 9.16814−10
$\phi=4°\ 14'\ 05''$................................. sec 0.00119

$T=12.464$ .... log 1.09566

Let us now determine the approximate maximum ordinate for the above trajectory. To do this we have

$$Y=\frac{gT^2}{8}$$

$T=12.464$ ....log 1.09566................2 log 2.19132
$g=32.2$ .... log 1.50786
8 ....log 0.90309................colog 9.09691−10

$Y=625.3$ .... log 2.79541
$\frac{2}{3}Y=416.87$ feet, whence, from Table V, $f=1.0105$.

We will now repeat the preceding process, using the found value of f to correct the original value of C, in which f was considered as unity, and introducing consecutive subscripts to the several symbols to represent successive approximate found values.

```
C_1 = ........................log 0.99583
f_1 = 1.0105 .................log 0.00454

C_2 = ........................log 1.00037............colog 8.99963-10
X = 30000 ............................................ log 4.47712

ΔS = 2997.4 .......................................... log 3.47675
S_V = 2019.4                     From Table I.

S_uω = 5016.8        A_uω = 250.60     T_uω = 1.864     I_uω = .07722
u_ω = 2022.9         A_V = 75.09       T_V = 0.625      I_V = .04388

                     ΔA = 175.51       ΔT = 1.239

ΔA = 175.51 .................log 2.24430
ΔS = 2997.4 .................log 3.47675                 I_uω = .07722

ΔA/ΔS = .05855 ..............log 8.76755-10              ΔA/ΔS = .05855

I_V = .04388                                       I_uω - ΔA/ΔS = .01867

ΔA/ΔS - I_V = .01467 .....log 8.16643-10

I_uω - ΔA/ΔS = .01867 ..................... log 8.27114-10
ΔT = 1.239 ...................................log 0.09307
C_2 = ...........log 1.00037...... log 1.00037......log 1.00037
2 ...........................colog 9.69897-10
u_ω = 2022.9 ...........................................log 3.30598

2φ = 8° 26′ 35″ ..sin 9.16680-10
φ = 4° 13′ 18″ ..................2 sec 0.00236......sec 0.00118..cos 9.99882-10

ω = 5° 22′ 00″ .................. tan 8.97284-10..............sec 0.00191

T = 12.434 ...................................log 1.09462
v_ω = 2026.3.............................................log 3.30671
```

Results. $\phi = 4^\circ\ 13'\ 18''$
$\omega = 5^\circ\ 22'\ 00''$
$T = 12.434$ seconds.
$v_\omega = 2026.3$ foot-seconds.

It will be noted that the two values of T found above, first by using f as unity, and second by using the first found value of f, differ so very slightly that a value of f found from the second value of T would not be sufficiently different from the first to materially affect the value of the ballistic coefficient. Therefore we concluded that the limit of accuracy of the method had been reached, and proceeded to use the values already derived to find the values of the other unknown elements. For a longer range it would probably be necessary to repeat the work again, and get a second, and perhaps even a third value of f.

141. The above is the method employed by Professor Alger, and it will be noted that considerable mathematical work is required. Colonel Ingalls further reduced the formulæ in such a way that, while the original work of reduction of formulæ is much greater and is somewhat involved, nevertheless the work to be done by the computer in practical cases is very much reduced, thereby reducing the amount of labor involved and time expended in computing a range table, as well as reducing the probability of error in doing the work. He computed an additional table, Table II of the Ballistic Tables, to assist in this. We will now follow through his method.

142. From equation (83) we have

$$\tan\phi=\tan\theta+\frac{C}{2\cos^2\phi}(I_u-I_V)$$

and if we substitute this value in (82) we get

$$\frac{y}{x}=\tan\theta+\frac{C}{2\cos^2\phi}\left(I_u-\frac{A_u-A_V}{S_u-S_V}\right) \tag{92}$$

143. Let us now introduce into the fundamental equations (80) to (85) inclusive, and into (92) four so-called "secondary functions," as follows:

Ingalls' secondary functions in general.

$$a=\frac{A_u-A_V}{S_u-S_V}-I_V \tag{93}$$

$$b=I_u-\frac{A_u-A_V}{S_u-S_V} \tag{94}$$

$$a'=a+b=I_u-I_V \tag{95}$$

$$t'=T_u-T_V \tag{96}$$

The fundamental equations then become

From (80) $$C=\frac{fw}{\delta cd^2} \tag{97}$$

From (81) $$x=C(S_u-S_V) \tag{98}$$

From (82) and (92)

$$\frac{y}{x}=\tan\phi-\frac{aC}{2\cos^2\phi}=\tan\theta+\frac{bC}{2\cos^2\phi} \tag{99}$$

From (83) $$\tan\theta=\tan\phi-\frac{a'C}{2\cos^2\phi} \tag{100}$$

From (84) $$t=Ct'\sec\phi \tag{101}$$

From (85) $$v=u\cos\phi\sec\theta \tag{102}$$

144. Now Ingalls' Ballistic Tables, Table II, give values for a, b, a' and t' for different values of V and of $z=\frac{x}{C}$, so that, in any given problem, knowing V and x, we can compute the value of z from the proper formula, and then take the corresponding values of the secondary functions from Table II.

145. For a complete horizontal trajectory, however, certain other simplifications become possible, if we have Table II available for use. The relations between ϕ, ω, T and v_ω, and the other elements of the trajectory involve the complete curve from the gun to the point of fall in the same horizontal plane with the gun. Under these conditions we have that

Secondary functions for entire trajectory.

$$y=0;\quad \frac{y}{x}=0;\quad \text{and } \theta=-\omega$$

When this is the case our equations become:

$$C=\frac{fw}{\delta cd^2} \tag{103}$$

$$X=C(S_{u_\omega}-S_V) \tag{104}$$

$$\tan\phi=\frac{C}{2\cos^2\phi}\left(\frac{A_{u_\omega}-A_V}{S_{u_\omega}-S_V}-I_V\right)$$

or, as $2\tan\phi\cos^2\phi=2\sin\phi\cos\phi=\sin 2\phi$

$$\sin 2\phi=C\left(\frac{A_{u_\omega}-A_V}{S_{u_\omega}-S_V}-I_V\right) \tag{105}$$

$$\tan\omega=-\tan\phi+\frac{C}{2\cos^2\phi}(I_{u_\omega}-I_V)$$

Substituting in this the value of $\tan\phi$ from the first expression used in deducing equation (105) we get

$$\tan\omega=\frac{C}{2\cos^2\phi}\left(I_{u_\omega}-\frac{A_{u_\omega}-A_V}{S_{u_\omega}-S_V}\right) \tag{106}$$

$$T=C\sec\phi(T_{u_\omega}-T_V) \tag{107}$$

$$v_\omega=u_\omega\cos\phi\sec\omega \tag{108}$$

146. Now let us take another set of secondary functions, or rather a set of special values of the regular secondary functions, as follows:

$$A=\frac{A_{u_\omega}-A_V}{S_{u_\omega}-S_V}-I_V \tag{109}$$

$$B=I_{u_\omega}-\frac{A_{u_\omega}-A_V}{S_{u_\omega}-S_V} \tag{110}$$

$$A'=A+B=I_{u_\omega}-I_V \tag{111}$$

$$T'=T_{u_\omega}-T_V \tag{112}$$

Ingalls' ballistic formulæ. **147.** Now by combining these special values of the secondary functions given in equations (109) to (112) inclusive with the formulæ in (103) to (108) inclusive, we get

$$C=\frac{fw}{\delta cd^2} \tag{113}$$

$$X=C(S_{u_\omega}-S_V) \tag{114}$$

$$\sin 2\phi=AC \tag{115}$$

From (115) we have that $C=\frac{\sin 2\phi}{A}$, and we also have that

$$\tan\omega=\frac{BC}{2\cos^2\phi}\text{ or }C=\frac{2\cos^2\phi\tan\omega}{B}$$

therefore $\quad\frac{\sin 2\phi}{A}=\frac{2\cos^2\phi\tan\omega}{B}$

whence we have $\quad\tan\omega=B'\tan\phi \qquad (116)$

in which $B'=\frac{B}{A}$, and tabulated values of $\log B'$ will be found in Table II.

$$T=CT'\sec\phi \tag{117}$$

$$v_\omega=u_\omega\cos\phi\sec\omega \tag{118}$$

148. It will readily be seen, as already stated, that, as A, B, A' and T' are only special values of a, b, a' and t', the values of both sets of secondary functions, the general and the special, may be taken from Table II, provided we enter the table with the proper argument in each case, that is, with the corresponding values of V and of $z=\frac{x}{C}$ or $Z=\frac{X}{C}$, z being of course for any point in the trajectory whose abscissa is x, and Z being for the entire horizontal trajectory, where the abscissa is the range X. And, as stated above, values of $\log B$ may also be taken from Table II as required, with the same arguments.

149. We therefore see that, by certain somewhat involved mathematical processes, Colonel Ingalls put the ballistic formulæ into such form that their use involves the least possible amount of logarithmic work. By the use of equations (113) to (118) inclusive, we can find the value of ϕ, ω, T and v_ω, by Ingalls' methods, provided we have Table II from which to take the values of the secondary functions, and provided we make no correction for altitude. Before we proceed to computations, however, we must find out how to determine the value of f, and, as a preliminary to this, we must consider the values of the elements at another important point of the trajectory, that is, at its highest point, summit, or vertex. This question is more fully discussed in a later chapter, but a certain preliminary consideration of it is necessary here in order to enable us to correct for f in using the formulæ just derived. The coordinates, etc., at the vertex are denoted by the symbols already used, with the subscript zero.

150. At the vertex (x_0, y_0), we have that $\theta=0$; hence at this point the fundamental equations become: **Ingalls' formulæ for vertex.**

$$C=\frac{fw}{\delta c d^2} \qquad (119)$$

By putting $\theta=0$ in the expression for $\tan\theta$ we get

$$\tan\phi=\frac{C}{2\cos^2\phi}(I_{u_0}-I_V), \text{ or } \sin 2\phi=C(I_{u_0}-I_V)$$

or

$$I_{u_0}=I_V+\frac{\sin 2\phi}{C} \qquad (120)$$

$$x_0=C(S_{u_0}-S_V) \qquad (121)$$

$$\frac{y_0}{x_0}=\tan\phi-\frac{C}{2\cos^2\phi}\left(\frac{A_{u_0}-A_V}{S_{u_0}-S_V}-I_V\right) \qquad (122)$$

$$t_0=C\sec\phi(T_{u_0}-T_V) \qquad (123)$$

$$v_0=u_0\cos\phi \qquad (124)$$

151. Alger solves for the elements at the vertex by the use of the above expressions and of Table I. Ingalls, however, simplifies the work of the computer by some further preliminary reductions, as he did in the preceding case. The important point at issue in the present problem is to find a simple expression for finding the value of the ordinate of the vertex, in order to find the value of f. Ingalls, by a somewhat involved mathematical process which we will not follow through in this chapter, finally reduced the formulæ to give the following expression for the value of the maximum ordinate:

$$Y=A''C\tan\phi \qquad (125)$$

152. The values of A'' for different conditions he computed and tabulated in Table II, with values of V and of $\frac{\sin 2\phi}{C}$ as arguments; the latter, for reasons that will be explained later, being taken as the value of a'_0 at the vertex. That is, compute the value of $\frac{\sin 2\phi}{C}$ from the given data; and then use it, under the proper page in the table for the known value of V, as an argument in the A' column, to find the value of A'' from its own column. Then solve (125) to determine the maximum ordinate. A full explanation of the reasons for using this value of $\frac{\sin 2\phi}{C}$ as an argument in the A' column of the table will be given in the next chapter. **Finding value of A'' from A'.**

In further explanation of this point let us recall the fact that we have derived certain formulæ relating to the trajectory, and that each of these formulæ has in it one or more somewhat involved integral expressions. In reducing these formulæ to serviceable shape we replaced these integral expressions by certain symbols, each such symbol representing one particular one of these integral expressions. Now by the labor of previous investigators, notably Ingalls, the values of each one of these integral expressions have been computed for all possible useful conditions and the results tabulated in the several columns of the Ballistic Tables, under the several symbols which we used to represent these integral expressions.

Let us consider the trajectory $ONPQ$ in Figure 13. The ballistic formulæ represent certain relations existing between the elements of the trajectory at any point. For the point P, for instance, the equations would contain certain integral expressions which we have called the "secondary functions," and have represented by a, a', b, b' (of which the logarithm is always used), and t', and also the pseudo velocity u. Now for this particular point, P, the integral expressions in each of the formulæ must be integrated between the proper limits for that particular point and their numerical values for this special case determined; a space integral being given the limits x and 0 for instance. Instead of having to actually perform this integration in each case, however, Colonel Ingalls has already done the work for us; and we simply compute the value of the argument $z=\frac{x}{C}$, and, knowing V, we can take from Table II each of the numerical results of integration between the proper limits that we desire. So for each point of the curve there is a special numerical value of each of the integrals represented by the symbols a, a', etc.

In a subsequent chapter we will use values so found for different points of the curve, but for the present we are dealing with the entire trajectory, and want to find the values of the functions for the point of fall, Q. Therefore, x becomes X, the range, and our integral expressions are represented by A, A', B, B' and T', and u becomes u_ω. Knowing V, we therefore compute the value of $Z=\frac{X}{C}$, and thence from Table II we

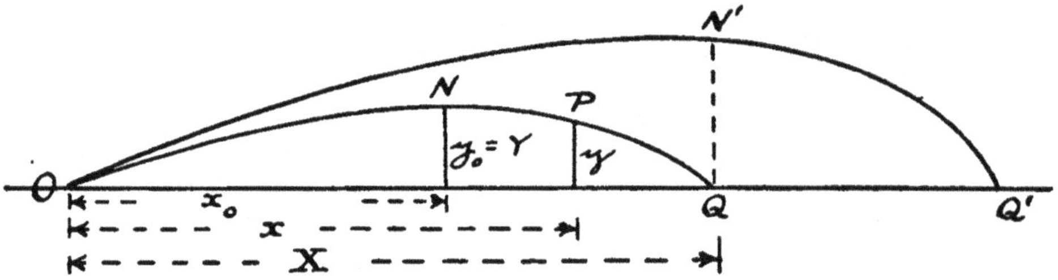

FIGURE 13.

may find the correct values of each of the integral expressions represented by the symbols A, A', etc., and also of the pseudo velocity at the point of fall, u_ω. Keep it firmly in mind that these particular symbols and values, A, A', etc., are only special symbols and values of the general symbols a, a', etc., at one particular point of the trajectory, that is, at the point of fall, or, expressed in another way, that they *pertain to the entire trajectory* and not to any part thereof or to any other point of the curve than the point of fall.

Similarly, for the vertex, where $x=x_0$, we have another set of special values, but here another symbol (which also represents an integral expression) A'' has been introduced. So we would have as our special symbols for the vertex a_0, a_0', A'', b_0, b_0' and t_0', and the pseudo velocity u_0. Remember that A'' pertains exclusively to the vertex, and to no other point of the curve. If we only knew the value of x_0, we could find the numerical values of each of the symbols for the vertex (each an integral expression integrated for the proper limits for the vertex) by computing the value of $z_0=\frac{x_0}{C}$, and thence with that value and the value of V as arguments taking them from Table II just as for any other case. *But we do not know the value of x_0.* Fortunately, however, it happens to be a fact (susceptible of mathematical proof, as will be shown in a later chapter) that the value of A for the point of fall is always numerically equal to the value of a_0' for the vertex. Now we have already a method of finding the value of A for the point of fall when we know the range and the initial velocity, and having found that value of A, we know that, because of the coincidence stated above, we have also the value of a_0' for the vertex, for the values of these two functions are numerically the same.

Now we are trying to find the value of A'', an integral expression relating solely to the vertex, and from what has been said above we know that we have found the value of another function of the vertex; namely, a_0'. Therefore, with our found value of a_0' *in the A' column of the table,* we interpolate across to the A'' column to find the proper value of A'' for substitution in the formula $Y=y_0=A''C \tan \phi$.

The question has been frequently asked why, given $Z=\frac{X}{C}$, we cannot take out the corresponding value of A'' direct. The answer to this question is that *Z is for the point of fall for the entire trajectory only;* therefore, if we do this we will get the value of A'' corresponding, *not to our vertex N,* but to the vertex of another trajectory entirely, that is, of the trajectory $ON'Q'$, which vertex lies vertically over the point Q, the point of fall of the trajectory with which we are working.

The value of z_0 for our correct trajectory may be found from our found value of a_0' by interpolating back from it in the A' column to the Z column by the use of equation number (128); and having found this we may then find the value of x_0 from the expression $x_0=z_0C\left(\text{as } z_0=\frac{x_0}{C}\right)$, which is a process employed in a later chapter. From this found value of z_0 we may also take from the tables the values of the other secondary functions for the vertex, a_0, b_0, $\log b_0'$ and t_0', and of the pseudo velocity at the vertex, u_0. *But to get the correct value of A'' it must be taken out by cross interpolation as already described,* and not by finding first z_0 and then working with a found value of z_0 as an argument.

There are points in this explanation which are perhaps not mathematically perfect, but it is hoped that these explanations will nevertheless lead the student to a better practical understanding of the reason why, when we have found a numerical value for A for the whole trajectory, we go over with it to the A' column when we wish to interpolate to get the value of the integral expression A'' and that of $z_0=\frac{x_0}{C}$, both of which values pertain solely to the vertex.

153. Before proceeding further, let us now investigate the manner of using Table II. Suppose we have $Z=2760$ and $V=1150$, and we wish to find the value of the secondary function A. Looking in the table for $V=1150$, and working from $Z=2700$, we have, by the ordinary methods of interpolation, **Use of tables.**

$$A=.07643+\frac{.00322\times 60}{100}=.07643+.00193=.07836$$

Now suppose we had had $Z=2700$ and $V=1175$, we would have had

$$A=.07643+\frac{(-.00496)\times 25}{50}=.07643-.00248=.07395$$

Now suppose, to combine the two, we had had $Z=2760$ and $V=1175$, then we would have had

$$A=.07643+\frac{.00322\times 60}{100}+\frac{(-.00496)\times 25}{50}=.07643+.00193-.00248=.07588$$

Expressing this algebraically, we would have had **Interpolation formula.**

$$A=A_t+\frac{Z-Z_t}{100}\Delta_{ZA}+\frac{V-V_t}{\Delta V}\Delta_{VA}$$

where A_t is the next lower tabular value of A below the desired value, Z_t and V_t

are the next lower tabular values of Z and V below the given values; ΔV is the difference between successive tabular values of V (that is, 50 f. s. for the table $V=1150$ to 1200 f. s., and 100 f. s. for all other tables given in the tables to be used with this book). ΔZ is always 100 for all tables, and it is therefore allowed to remain in numerical form in the above algebraic expression. Δ_{ZA} and Δ_{VA} are the differences given in the proper line of the Δ columns pertaining to A. Care must be taken to use the proper signs for all the quantities given in the above expression. It will also be seen at once that any other one of the secondary functions may be substituted for A in the above expression provided we exercise due care in regard to the signs. It must also be noted that the formula applies for the *next lower* tabular values only. If we work from the *nearest* tabular values, there would be a change of signs in the expression if the *nearest* tabular value happens to be the *next higher* tabular value in any case.

Interpolation formulæ. Repeating the expression just derived, and also solving it for Z and V, we get

$$A=A_t+\frac{Z-Z_t}{100}\Delta_{ZA}+\frac{V-V_t}{\Delta V}\Delta_{VA} \qquad (126)^*$$

$$V=V_t+\frac{\Delta V}{\Delta_{VA}}\left[(A-A_t)-\frac{Z-Z_t}{100}\Delta_{ZA}\right] \qquad (127)^*$$

$$Z=Z_t+\frac{100}{\Delta_{ZA}}\left[(A-A_t)-\frac{V-V_t}{\Delta V}\Delta_{VA}\right] \qquad (128)^*$$

From the first of these we find the value of A, given Z and V (or of any other of the secondary functions in place of A). From (127) we can find V, and from (128) we can find Z, given Z or V respectively, and A or any other secondary function in its place. The expressions of course simplify greatly when working with a tabular value of either Z or V, in which case $Z-Z_t$ or $V-V_t$ becomes zero.

Cross interpolation formula from A' to A'' 154. In practice it is often necessary to find the value of A'' corresponding to a found value of A, knowing V, in finding the value of the maximum ordinate, as will be shown later, under circumstances when we do not care to know the value of Z or of any other of the secondary functions. To do this, that is, to find the double interpolation formula for crossing direct from A' to A'' without finding Z, knowing V, substitute in (126) expressed for A'', the value of Z found from (128) expressed for A'. The resultant expression is

$$A''=A_t''-\frac{V-V_t}{\Delta V}\times\frac{\Delta_{VA'}\Delta_{ZA''}}{\Delta_{ZA'}}+\frac{V-V_t}{\Delta V}\Delta_{VA''}+(A'-A_t')\frac{\Delta_{ZA''}}{\Delta_{ZA'}} \qquad (129)^*$$

If we are working with a tabular value of V, which is fortunately generally the case, then $V-V_t=0$, and the above formula simplifies greatly, becoming

$$A''=A_t''+(A'-A_t')\frac{\Delta_{ZA''}}{\Delta_{ZA'}} \qquad (130)^*$$

As examples, suppose we have $V=1175$ and $Z=2760$, and desire to find the corresponding values of the secondary functions. Then $V-V_t=25$ and $Z-Z_t=60$, and we have

$$A=.07643+\frac{.00322\times60}{100}+\frac{(-.00496)\times25}{50}=.07643+.00193-.00248=.07588$$

$$A'=.1631+\frac{.0072\times60}{100}+\frac{(-.0096)\times25}{50}=.1631+.00432-.0048=.16262$$

---

* It must be noted that the interpolation formulæ here derived for use with Table II of the Ballistic Tables, neglect second and higher differences. They therefore give results that are accurate only within certain limits, which limits are sufficiently narrow to permit the formulæ to be used for the purposes for which employed in this text book. A caution must be given, however, against using them for other purposes without ascertaining whether or not they will give sufficiently accurate results for the purpose in view. A case where they cannot be successfully used is given in Chapter 14. (See foot-note to paragraph 239, Chapter 14.)

$$B = .0866 + \frac{.004\times 60}{100} + \frac{(-.0046)\times 25}{50} = .0866 + .0024 - .0023 = .0867$$

$$\log B' = .05465 + \frac{.00149\times 60}{100} + \frac{.00522\times 25}{50} = .05465 + .00089 + .00261 = .05815$$

$$u = 948.5 + \frac{(-5.3)\times 60}{100} + \frac{22.6\times 25}{50} = 948.5 - 3.18 + 11.3 = 956.62$$

$$T' = 2.613 + \frac{.106\times 60}{100} + \frac{(-.08)\times 25}{50} = 2.613 + .0636 - .04 = 2.6366$$

$$D' = 117 + \frac{10\times 60}{100} + \frac{(-6)\times 25}{50} = 117 + 6 - 3 = 120$$

155. Suppose we had been given $u = 956.62$ and $Z = 2760$, and wanted to find the value of V, knowing it to be between 1150 and 1200 f. s. From (127)

$$V = 1150 + \frac{50}{22.6}\left(8.12 - \frac{(-5.3)\times 60}{100}\right) = 1150 + 25 = 1175$$

And we could proceed similarly with the other secondary functions.

Now suppose that we know that $V = 2775$ and that $A = .20235$, and desire to find the corresponding value of A''. Then from (129) we have

$$A'' = 4935 - \frac{75}{100}\times\frac{(-.0143)\times 74}{.0056} + \frac{75\times 11}{100} + \frac{.00225\times 74}{.0056}$$

$$A'' = 4935 + 141.7 + 8.3 + 29.7 = 5114.7\ *$$

156. Returning now to our formulæ, and having found an expression for the value of the maximum ordinate, on the basis that the mean density of the air through which the projectile travels is the same as that at a point two-thirds the maximum ordinate above the gun (which is absolutely true for a uniformly varying atmosphere and for a trajectory that is a true parabola); and starting with Chauvenet's discussion of atmospheric refraction, Colonel Ingalls, by another rather involved mathe-

* It must be noticed here, as well as elsewhere throughout this text book, that interpolations are carried out to more decimal places than is strictly justifiable for the limits of accuracy obtainable with the ballistic and logarithmic tables used. The rule adopted for instruction of midshipmen has been to have them carry out all interpolations to five working decimal places, as five place logarithmic tables are standard at the Naval Academy; thus 2534.7, 2.5347, .0025347, etc. This has been found advisable, not because it is expected to attain more accurate results thereby, but in order that a comparison of the relative accuracy of the tabular and logarithmic work of all midshipmen may be secured. Due consideration was given to all possible methods of attaining this object, and the only available rule that could be given them that would not depend upon individual judgment in any case and yet that would fit all cases was the one that is set forth above. Under it, with a given set of data, all midshipmen should secure the same results (within decimal differences in the last place), and therefore their results can be compared and relative marks fairly awarded. In service, however, this practice would simply be an apparent effort to attain an impossible degree of accuracy, which might in some cases, indeed, introduce small errors into the work that would otherwise be avoided by a less rigorous rule for interpolations. Only an experienced mathematical judgment can tell to what degree each process of interpolation should be carried in each separate case, and this is not possessed by midshipmen. Some simple, absolute rule was therefore necessary for them, and this being a simple, invariable rule, it is believed that the end justifies the means in this particular. This note should be a caution against attempts in service to attain impossible accuracy of results by excessive carrying out of interpolations.

matical process which it is unnecessary to follow through, derives an equation for determining the value of f as follows:

$$\log\log f = \log Y + 5.01765 - 10 \qquad (131)$$

Ingalls' solution by successive approximations.

157. With the aid of the formulæ of Colonel Ingalls already given, we may now proceed to the solution of the original problem already solved by Alger's method, as given in paragraph 140, by the methods used in preparing the range tables by the expert computers of the Bureau of Ordnance. The data is the same as before.

$$C_1 = \frac{w}{cd^2}\text{; argument for Table II, } Z = \frac{X}{C}\text{; } \sin 2\phi = AC$$

$w = 870$		log 2.93952	
$c = 0.61$	log 9.78533 − 10	colog 0.21467	
$d^2 = 144$	log 2.15836	colog 7.84164 − 10	
$C_1 =$		log 0.99583	colog 9.00417 − 10
$X = 30000$			log 4.47712
$Z_1 = 3029$			log 3.48129

For $V = 2900$ (table for $V = 2900$ to 3000), for $Z = 3029$, we have $A_1 = .014882$

$A = .014882$	log 8.17266 − 10
$C_1 =$	log 0.99583
$2\phi_1 = 8°\ 28'\ 34''$	sin 9.16849 − 10

$\phi_1 = 4°\ 14'\ 17''$....First approximation, disregarding f.

Having obtained the preceding approximation to the value of ϕ, we may now proceed to determine a second approximation to the value of the same quantity, and this time we can correct for a value of f, using equations (125) and (131).

$$Y = A''C \tan\phi \qquad \log\log f = \log Y + 5.01765 - 10$$

For finding A'' from Table II we use $a_{0_1}' = \frac{\sin 2\phi}{C} = .014882$, as already determined, as an argument, in its proper column. For this the table gives for

$$A' = .0148 \quad \Delta_{ZA'} = .0012 \quad A'' = 849 \quad \Delta_{ZA''} = 57$$

therefore

$$A_1'' = 849 + \frac{.000082 \times 57}{.0012} = 852.9$$

$A_1'' = 852.9$			log 2.93090
$C_1 =$			log 0.99583
$\phi_1 = 4°\ 14'\ 17''$			tan 8.86983 − 10
$Y_1 =$			log 2.79656
Constant			log 5.01765 − 10
$f_1 =$	log 0.00652		loglog 7.81465 − 10
$C_1 =$	log 0.99583		
$C_2 =$	log 1.00235		colog 8.99765 − 10
$X = 30000$			log 4.47712
$Z_2 = 2983.8$			log 3.47477

From Table II, $A_2 = .014599$

$A_2 = .014599$ .... log 8.16432 − 10
$C_2 =$ .... log 1.00235

$2\phi_2 = 8°\ 26'\ 26''$ .... sin 9.16667 − 10
$\phi_2 = 4°\ 13'\ 13''$.... Second approximation.

Having obtained the above second approximation to the value of ϕ, we see that it differs from the first approximation by over one minute of arc, and we therefore cannot assume that the second value is sufficiently accurate. We therefore repeat the above process to get a third approximation.

From above work $Z_2 = 2983.8$ and $A_2 = a_{0_2}' = .014559$, which gives, from Table II,

$$A_2'' = 793 + \frac{.000859 \times 56}{.0011} = 836.73$$

$A_2'' = 836.7$ .... log 2.92257
$C_2 =$ .... log 1.00235
$\phi_2 = 4°\ 13'\ 13''$ .... tan 8.86800 − 10

$Y_2 =$ .... log 2.79292
Constant .... log 5.01765 − 10

$f_2 =$ .... log 0.00646 .... loglog 7.81057 − 10
$C_1 =$ .... log 0.99583

$C_3 =$ .... log 1.00229 .... colog 8.99771 − 10
$X = 30000$ .... log 4.47712

$Z_3 = 2984.1$ .... log 3.47483

Hence from Table II, as before,

$$A_3 = .014602$$

$A_3 = .014602$ .... log 8.16438 − 10
$C_3 =$ .... log 1.00231

$2\phi_3 = 8°\ 26'\ 28''$ .... sin 9.16669 − 10
$\phi_3 = 4°\ 13'\ 14''$.... Third approximation.

This value is only one second in value different from the second approximation, and is therefore practically correct; but we see that there is still a small difference between the last two successive values of C, and as we desire to determine accurately and definitely a correct value of C for use in further work, we will proceed with another approximation.

$$A_3 = .014602$$

$$A_3'' = 793 + \frac{.000901 \times 56}{.0011} = 838.9$$

$A_3'' = 838.9$ .... log 2.92371
$C_3 =$ .... log 1.00231
$\phi_3 = 4°\ 13'\ 14''$ .... tan 8.86803 − 10

$Y_3 =$ .... log 2.79405
Constant .... log 5.01765 − 10

$f_3 =$ .... log 0.00648 .... loglog 7.81170 − 10
$C_1 =$ .... log 0.99583

$C_4 =$ .... log 1.00231

Now we see that $C_4 = C_3$, and that we have therefore reached the limit of accuracy possible by the method of successive approximations and have verified the value of C, and no further work in this connection is therefore necessary. We therefore have for further work in connection with this trajectory:

$$\phi = 4° \ 13' \ 14'' \qquad Z = 2984.1 \qquad \log C = 1.00231$$

To determine the angle of fall, time of flight and striking velocity, we have, from (116), (117) and (118)

$$\tan \omega = B' \tan \phi \qquad T = CT' \sec \phi \qquad v_\omega = u_\omega \cos \phi \sec \omega$$

From Table II

$$\log B' = .10371 \qquad T' = 1.2332 \qquad u_\omega = 2026.1$$

$B' =$	log 0.10371		
$C =$		log 1.00231	
$\phi = 4° \ 13' \ 14''$	tan 8.86803−10	sec 0.00118	cos 9.99882−10
$T' = 1.2332$		log 0.09103	
$u_\omega = 2026.1$			log 3.30666
$\omega = 5° \ 21' \ 11''$	tan 8.97174−10		sec 0.00190
$T = 12.43$		log 1.09452	
$v_\omega = 2029$			log 3.30738

Hence we have as the solutions to this problem

$$\phi = 4° \ 13' \ 14''.$$
$$\omega = 5° \ 21' \ 11''.$$
$$T = 12.43 \text{ seconds.}$$
$$v_\omega = 2029 \text{ f. s.}$$

These are the correct and final results, and it will be observed that they are the values which appear in Columns 2, 3, 4 and 5 of the range table for this gun, for a range of 10,000 yards. We have therefore learned how to compute the values for these columns in the range tables. In a later chapter will be given the forms used by the computers in actually computing the data for the range tables.

NOTE.—The mathematical processes carried through in the preceding chapters may be briefly and generally described as follows:

1. Considering the forces acting on the projectile in flight, that is, the force of gravity and the atmospheric resistance, and dealing with differential increments at any point of the trajectory, certain equations are derived (from the laws of physics governing motion) which show the relations existing between these differential increments in the different elements of the trajectory at the given point. These are not equations to the curve itself as a whole, but simply express the relations between the differential increments referred to above. Could they be integrated in general form, they could be generally used for solutions, but such integration is impossible owing to fractional exponents, and some other method must be adopted. The accepted method is known as Siacci's method, from its deviser, its essential point being the introduction into the computations of a new quantity known as the "pseudo velocity," which was defined in paragraph 22, page 23. By the introduction of this quantity, it becomes possible to reduce the differential equations to certain others that are known as the "ballistic formulæ," which are used in the practical solutions of ballistic problems. Each of these formulæ contains certain integral expressions, which are represented in the formulæ by the symbols A, I, S and T (the altitude, inclination, space and time functions), and the values of these functions for any given velocity, whether real or pseudo, may be found in Table I of the Ballistic Tables. That is, the tabulated values of

these functions are simply the values of the given integral expressions when integrated between the proper limits for the given velocity.

2. As stated above, these several functions are merely values of certain rather involved integral expressions, the values of which for any given velocity may be found in Table I. Different subscripts to the symbols are used to represent the values at different points of the trajectory; thus S_ω is the value of the space function for the point of fall, S_0 for the vertex, etc.

3. Professor Alger took the ballistic formulæ as they stood after the reductions described above, and put them in the form desired for any particular problem. Any necessary changes for this purpose were simply algebraic and trigonometrical transformations in order to get the value of the desired unknown quantity expressed in terms of the ones that are known. He then solved in each case, taking the necessary values of the integral expressions I, A, S and T from Table I.

4. The successive approximation feature (and this description fits every such case, whether Alger or Ingalls) becomes necessary because, when we start a ballistic problem we usually do not know the maximum height of flight of the projectile. We therefore work the problem by first disregarding this height, that is, by considering that the density of the air throughout the flight is constant and equal to that at the gun. We know this to be wrong, however, and that our first result can therefore be only approximate. Therefore by using our first result we determine the maximum ordinate (Alger by one formula and the use of a table; and Ingalls by the use of different formulæ but by computation without the use of any table) and from that the altitude factor of the ballistic coefficient. This approximate value of f we apply to our first value of the ballistic coefficient, and then repeat our computations, thereby getting a second result, which is still approximate, but more nearly correct than the first one. By continually repeating this process we will finally get to a point where repeated computations make no change in the value of the ballistic coefficient, and at that point the limit of accuracy of our methods, whatever they may be, has been reached, and our result is as nearly correct as it is possible to get by the adopted methods. Taking the final value of the ballistic coefficient thus obtained as correct, we can then proceed to the final solution of the problem.

5. Ingalls further simplified the ballistic formulæ so that their use would be less difficult. In these formulæ there are certain integral expressions involving the values of I, A, S and T for the point of fall and for the vertex, that is, I_ω, I_0, etc., and certain constantly repeating combinations of these integrals. Ingalls substituted for these constantly repeating combinations of integrals certain other quantities which he called "secondary functions," and represented by the symbols A, A', A'', B, B', T', etc., and thereby derived new and simpler formulæ involving those secondary functions and the pseudo velocity, u. He also computed the values of the secondary functions with the expressions integrated between all useful limits (that is, of the integral forms which they represent) and tabulated them in Table II of the Ballistic Tables. To solve by his methods, we therefore take his forms of the ballistic formulæ, properly transposed to put all known quantities in the right-hand member and the desired unknown quantity as the left-hand member of each expression, and then solve; taking the values of the secondary functions that we need from Table II. To use this table we must know for use as arguments the value of the initial velocity and also the quotient of the horizontal distance traveled divided by the ballistic coefficient, that is, of $z = \frac{x}{C}$ or $Z = \frac{X}{C}$

The above paragraphs of this note indicate the manner in which a student should try to retain in his mind the general features of the mathematical processes described in this text book. Each student, in addition to learning the text of each chapter in detail should endeavor to formulate in his own mind a general understanding of the processes described in the chapter in accordance with the general method illustrated above for the fundamental processes of exterior ballistics.

EXAMPLES.

1. Given the values of V and Z contained in the first two columns of the following table, take from Table II of the Ballistic Tables the corresponding values of $A, A', B, \log B', u, T'$ and D'.

Problem.	DATA.		ANSWERS.						
	$Z=\frac{X}{C}$.	V.	A.	A'.	B.	$\log B'$.	u.	T'.	D'.
1	3370	1150	.09855	.21279	.11431	.06440	914.07	3.3323	192.10
2	1763	1150	.04755	.09963	.05214	.03935	1002.5	1.6510	46.780
3	6982	1150	.23947	.54902	.30961	.11151	763.85	7.6714	1055.3
4	1326	2000	.01200	.02550	.01354	.04989	1683.3	0.72534	9.2600
5	4173	2000	.04992	.12123	.07132	.15484	1175.2	2.7711	136.57
6	7652	2000	.12736	.33625	.20885	.21477	919.40	6.1727	786.12
7	1943	2600	.01087	.02365	.01274	.06869	2050.8	0.84207	11.860
8	3756	2600	.02489	.05904	.03414	.13693	1619.7	1.8427	59.240
9	9743	2600	.12187	.35927	.23739	.28950	921.85	7.0604	1139.1
10	10742	2600	.14759	.43913	.29149	.29561	873.90	8.1739	1599.4
11	1818	2700	.00931	.02005	.01074	.06345	2169.1	0.75228	9.1800
12	4747	2700	.03210	.07981	.04774	.17323	1484.6	2.3925	101.82
13	5561	2700	.04095	.10630	.06536	.20376	1332.6	2.9718	162.49
14	7937	2700	.07613	.21928	.14322	.27450	1050.0	5.0092	514.14
15	9541	2700	.10868	.32365	.21501	.29617	948.95	6.6211	988.58
16	1856	2900	.00823	.01777	.00959	.06326	2331.8	0.71408	8.5600
17	2942	2900	.01434	.03253	.01818	.10215	2037.1	1.2126	24.840
18	3839	2900	.02034	.04814	.02787	.13558	1813.6	1.6795	50.170
19	4815	2900	.02809	.06988	.04176	.17277	1595.8	2.2535	90.750
20	8634	2900	.07677	.22861	.15189	.29651	1044.3	5.3016	592.50
21	3231	3100	.01404	.03213	.01808	.10982	2119.6	1.2026	27.620
22	5742	3100	.03182	.08283	.05106	.20430	1530.2	2.6633	129.36
23	8841	3100	.06943	.21036	.14094	.30760	1076.3	5.1291	553.84
24	10305	3100	.09566	.30074	.20504	.33126	974.70	6.5632	998.90

NOTE FOR INSTRUCTOR.—In exercising class in these interpolations, give to each midshipman one problem from each of the tables given in this and in the following five examples.

2. Given the values of V and Z contained in the two first columns of the following table, take from Table II of the Ballistic Tables the corresponding values of $A, A', B, \log B', u, T'$ and D'.

Problem.	DATA.		ANSWERS.						
	$Z=\frac{X}{C}$.	V.	A.	A'.	B.	$\log B'$.	u.	T'.	D'.
1	2200	1162	.05974	.12640	.06666	.04798	981.92	2.0769	73.800
2	5500	1173	.17257	.38758	.21499	.09544	826.98	5.7299	581.96
3	8100	1187	.28019	.65643	.37621	.12808	735.41	9.0104	1492.5
4	1800	2030	.01654	.03592	.01936	.06810	1606.6	0.99900	17.400
5	4200	2057	.04764	.11600	.06828	.15644	1200.5	2.7176	131.02
6	7700	2082	.12004	.32104	.20103	.22389	932.58	6.0389	755.90
7	3100	2618	.01902	.04359	.02456	.11167	1779.7	1.4399	35.460
8	7300	2643	.06832	.19222	.12389	.25853	1087.5	4.5167	403.81
9	9400	2663	.10854	.32104	.21254	.29194	950.71	6.5537	961.42
10	5100	2730	.03494	.08853	.05364	.18625	1433.0	2.6048	122.00
11	6100	2750	.04581	.12240	.07660	.22305	1271.0	3.3235	205.50
12	8700	2779	.08543	.25263	.16723	.29158	1012.8	5.5986	668.13
13	5500	2913	.03410	.08787	.05378	.19836	1465.8	2.6889	131.57
14	8200	2954	.06667	.19629	.12959	.28890	1093.6	4.7975	471.02
15	9700	2982	.09156	.28154	.19002	.31698	989.76	6.1909	860.34
16	4600	3140	.02210	.05408	.03198	.16032	1804.6	1.9410	66.000
17	7000	3150	.04291	.11930	.07645	.25060	1322.5	3.4925	232.00
18	9900	3160	.08423	.26398	.17978	.32934	1009.4	6.0338	819.60

3. Given the values of V and Z contained in the first two columns of the following table, take from Table II of the Ballistic Tables the corresponding values of $A, A', B, \log B', u, T'$ and D'.

Problem.	DATA.		ANSWERS.						
	$Z=\frac{X}{C}$.	V.	A.	A'.	B.	log B′.	u.	T'.	D'.
1.	2730	1157	.07670	.16392	.08716	.05583	950.07	2.6336	119.16
2.	5980	1169	.19258	.43558	.24299	.10109	806.72	6.3303	713.94
3.	8730	1182	.31173	.73709	.42530	.13503	712.68	9.9097	1814.7
4.	1036	2028	.01807	.03947	.02138	.07330	1576.1	1.0858	20.160
5.	4757	2048	.05773	.14368	.08599	.17296	1131.5	3.2098	187.20
6.	7915	2063	.12780	.34164	.21386	.22372	918.22	6.3151	833.56
7.	3342	2628	.02082	.04836	.02753	.12076	1731.1	1.5724	42.840
8.	7539	2644	.07243	.20534	.13292	.26385	1067.8	4.7373	450.35
9.	9526	2684	.10970	.32588	.21624	.29471	946.98	6.6413	994.18
10.	5433	2733	.03848	.09921	.06078	.19856	1373.2	2.8391	147.01
11.	6214	2748	.04734	.12721	.07993	.22720	1253.1	3.4172	218.04
12.	8848	2763	.08944	.26494	.17552	.29272	1000.7	5.7785	719.75
13.	5584	2925	.03464	.08970	.05506	.20142	1457.0	2.7347	136.13
14.	8282	2944	.06853	.20229	.13369	.29045	1084.3	4.8913	492.76
15.	9748	2962	.09391	.28840	.19452	.31627	983.28	6.2813	890.22
16.	4632	3148	.02221	.05445	.03224	.16136	1802.8	1.0536	67.200
17.	7148	3155	.04439	.12447	.08010	.25606	1300.2	3.5998	248.31
18.	9923	3163	.08449	.26497	.18052	.32979	1008.6	6.0511	825.65

4. Given the values of V contained in the first column and of the secondary functions contained in the second column of the following table, take from Table II of the Ballistic Tables the corresponding values of Z.

Problem.	DATA.		ANSWERS.
	V.	Secondary function.	Z.
1.	1157	$A = 0.06256$	2278.0
2.	1172	$A' = 0.12163$	2150.4
3.	2030	$B = 0.03845$	2911.0
4.	2053	$T' = 1.0956$	1971.0
5.	2075	$A = 0.04133$	3833.7
6.	2615	$A' = 0.03115$	2428.3
7.	2691	$B = 0.14932$	8061.7
8.	2743	$T' = 1.0756$	2522.7
9.	2772	$A = 0.01793$	3241.8
10.	2784	$A' = 0.23795$	8468.7
11.	2947	$B = 0.01932$	3123.1
12.	2962	$T' = 5.2227$	8669.3
13.	3121	$A = 0.00985$	2457.2
14.	3178	$A' = 0.19555$	8761.7
15.	3191	$T' = 5.1563$	9040.5

5. Given the value of Z contained in the first column, the value of the secondary function contained in the second column, and the limits near which the value of V lies contained in the third column of the following table, take from Table II of the Ballistic Tables the corresponding value of V.

Problem.	DATA.			ANSWERS.
	$Z=\frac{X}{C}$.	Secondary function.	Limits of V.*	V.
1	1732	$A=$ 0.04632	1150–1200	1154.9
2	4140	$A'=$ 0.27837	1150–1200	1137.0
3	1232	$B=$ 0.01273	2000–2100	1962.4
4	4381	$u=$ 1154.7	2000–2100	2007.4
5	8175	$T'=$ 6.7324	2000–2100	2007.5
6	2222	$A=$ 0.01278	2600–2700	2595.9
7	4444	$A'=$ 0.07735	2600–2700	2602.0
8	2551	$B=$ 0.01693	2700–2800	2715.0
9	5743	$u=$ 1298.4	2700–2800	2693.0
10	9107	$T'=$ 6.2333	2700–2800	2668.9
11	3232	$A=$ 0.01607	2900–3000	2909.6
12	6474	$A'=$ 0.12087	2900–3000	2916.8
13	1334	$B=$ 0.00555	3100–3200	3080.0
14	4321	$u=$ 1835.2	3100–3200	3089.0
15	8448	$T'=$ 4.7867	3100–3200	3090.1

* These limits determine the table to be used; in some cases it will be found that the interpolation gives a value of V lying outside of the limits indicated.

6. Given the values of V and of A contained in the first two columns of the following table, take from Table II of the Ballistic Tables the corresponding values of A'', without determining the corresponding value of Z.

Problem.	DATA.		ANSWERS.
	V.	A.	A''.
1	1150	0.19787	1699.6
2	1179	0.32995	2692.0
3	1192	0.40843	3234.5
4	2000	0.04932	1236.5
5	2053	0.15563	3009.1
6	2086	0.37543	5293.2
7	2600	0.05837	2154.4
8	2677	0.12647	3752.0
9	2689	0.27563	5805.7
10	2700	0.02543	1194.3
11	2750	0.10023	3376.6
12	2772	0.00995	547.19
13	2900	0.03613	1786.5
14	2932	0.13333	4357.5
15	2988	0.30057	6760.3
16	3118	0.20475	5880.7
17	3150	0.27777	6877.5
18	3173	0.02975	1774.1

7. Compute by Ingalls' method for standard atmospheric conditions, using successive approximations, the values of the angle of departure, angle of fall, time of flight and striking velocity in the following cases.

Problem.	DATA.					ANSWERS.			
	Projectile.			Velocity. f. s.	Range. Yds.	ϕ.	ω.	T. Secs.	v_ω. f. s.
	d. In.	w. Lbs.	c.						
A........	3	13	1.00	1150	2130	5° 39.1′	6° 46′	6.56	867
B........	3	13	1.00	2700	3720	2 59.3	5 33	6.94	1074
C........	4	33	0.67	2900	3825	1 43.4	2 20	4.98	1843
D........	5	50	1.00	3150	4370	2 11.4	3 44	6.33	1408
E........	5	50	0.61	3150	4465	1 44.8	2 25	5.44	1941
F........	6	105	0.61	2600	12690	11 03.4	19 38	24.70	1104
G........	6	105	1.00	2800	3875	1 55.7	2 41	5.34	1712
H........	6	105	0.61	2800	3622	1 32.3	1 51	4.46	2134
I........	7	165	1.00	2700	7230	5 00.7	8 31	12.32	1221
J........	7	165	0.61	2700	7357	3 57.4	5 30	10.54	1650
K........	8	260	0.61	2750	8390	4 15.3	5 49	11.62	1735
L........	10	510	1.00	2700	10310	6 40.8	11 09	17.05	1293
M........	10	510	0.61	2700	11333	6 07.6	8 30	16.30	1653
N........	12	870	0.61	2900	21650	12 30.9	19 55	33.59	1441
O........	13	1130	1.00	2000	10370	11 15.2	16 09	21.45	1168
P........	13	1130	0.74	2000	11111	10 58.0	14 44	21.57	1281
Q........	14	1400	0.70	2000	14220	14 48.8	20 15	28.68	1251
R........	14	1400	0.70	2600	14370	8 32.4	11 55	21.76	1577

8. Given the data contained in the first eight columns of the following table, compute in each case the values of ϕ, ω, T and v_ω, by Ingalls' method, using Table II, and using in each case the value of f from Table V corresponding to the maximum ordinate given in the table below.

Problem.	DATA.								ANSWERS.			
	Projectile.			Atmosphere.		V. f. s.	R. Yds.	Max. ord. Feet.	ϕ.	ω.	T. Secs.	v_ω. f. s.
	d. In.	w. Lbs.	c.	Bar. In.	Ther. °F.							
A........	3	13	1.00	Standard	..	1150	2550	265	7° 03.4′	8° 40′	8.07	832
B........	3	13	1.00	Standard	..	2700	3450	158	2 36.4	4 42	6.20	1122
C........	4	33	0.67	Standard	..	2900	4000	112	1 49.8	2 31	5.27	1802
D........	5	50	1.00	29.00	20	3150	3870	108	1 52.1	3 06	5.46	1475
E........	5	50	0.61	29.50	22	3150	3850	80	1 28.0	1 58	4.61	2011
F........	6	105	0.61	30.00	25	2600	14530	3798	15 42.4	28 31	32.04	1036
G........	6	105	1.00	30.15	27	2800	4570	169	2 33.0	3 55	6.82	1476
H........	6	105	0.61	30.25	30	2800	4030	101	1 47.2	2 14	5.11	2010
I........	7	165	1.00	30.33	33	2700	6030	363	3 55.2	6 22	9.85	1301
J........	7	165	0.61	30.50	35	2700	6540	328	3 28.3	4 46	9.29	1676
K........	8	260	0.61	30.67	40	2750	8080	485	4 10.0	5 45	11.32	1698
L........	10	510	1.00	31.00	45	2700	9090	807	5 52.9	9 23	14.80	1320
M........	10	510	0.61	30.75	50	2700	10070	784	5 20.3	7 17	14.28	1691
N........	12	870	0.61	30.33	60	2900	22030	4801	13 23.2	21 56	35.37	1377
O........	13	1130	1.00	30.25	70	2000	10560	1037	11 39.1	16 51	22.08	1154
P........	13	1130	0.74	29.50	80	2000	11050	1830	10 45.6	14 19	21.24	1299
Q........	14	1400	0.70	29.00	90	2000	14020	3204	14 09.7	19 00	27.67	1284
R........	14	1400	0.70	28.75	100	2600	14590	1960	8 23.2	11 23	21.63	1645

9. Compute by Alger's method, without using Table II, the values of ϕ, ω, T and v_ω, from the data contained in the following table, correcting for altitude in each case by successive approximations.

Problem.	DATA.									ANSWERS.			
	Projectile.			Atmosphere.			V. f. s.	R'nge. Yds.	Wind* compon't. f. s.	ϕ.	ω.	T. Secs.	v_ω. f. s.
	d. In.	w. Lbs.	c.	Bar. In.	Ther. °F.	Value of δ.							
1......	3	13	1	Standard	..	......	2800	2000	None	1° 00.9′	1° 25′	2.70	1671
2......	5	50	1	Standard	..	......	2550	3000	None	1 54.4	2 49	4.76	1439
3......	6	100	1	Standard	..	......	2300	4000	None	3 07.5	4 31	6.97	1321
4......	8	250	1	Standard	..	......	2300	4000	None	2 45.1	3 36	6.38	1552
5......	12	850	1	Standard	..	......	2250	5000	None	3 26.0	4 15	7.88	1626
6......	11.024	760.4	1	.....	..	1.0306	1733	2260	+ 19	2 21.5	2 36	4.27	1480
7......	11.024	760.4	1	.....	..	1.0058	1733	6788	— 14	8 25.7	11 01	14.64	1173
8......	6	100	1	30.05	70	......	2900	9700	None	8 53.3	17 58	19.80	987
9......	12	850	1	30.19	59	......	2827	11566	None	6 55.0	11 14	18.16	1364
10.....	11.024	760.4	1	.....	..	1.0174	1733	11207	— 12	17 32.7	24 33	28.06	1046
11.....	15.75	2028	1	Standard	..	......	1805	1094	None	0 57.8	1 00	1.86	1712
12.....	15.75	2028	1	Standard	..	......	1805	3281	None	3 06.2	3 27	5.91	1542
13.....	15.75	2028	1	Standard	..	......	1805	5468	None	5 36.4	6 42	10.43	1391
14.....	3	13	1	Standard	..	......	2800	2000	None	1 00.7	1 26	2.79	1672
15.....	3	15	1	Standard	..	......	2628	1883	None	1 00.0	1 21	2.66	1720
16.....	5	60	1	Standard	..	......	2900	3000	None	1 21.2	1 50	3.91	1837
17.....	5	55	1	Standard	..	......	2097	3095	None	1 21.7	1 55	4.02	1796

* The sign + means a wind with the flight of the projectile, and a — sign a wind against it. Therefore, in problem 6, say, in order to get the desired range we would have to proceed as though the initial velocity were really 1733 — 19 = 1714 f. s. and there were no wind, and compute results accordingly.

NOTE.—The above problems in Example 9 are taken from Alger's text book, and cover guns of older date, both U. S. Navy and foreign. Note the difference between this data and modern weights and velocities; and observe care to use correct data as given in the table.

CHAPTER 9.

THE DERIVATION AND USE OF SPECIAL FORMULÆ FOR FINDING THE COORDINATES OF THE VERTEX AND THE TIME OF FLIGHT TO AND THE REMAINING VELOCITY AT THE VERTEX, FOR A GIVEN ANGLE OF DEPARTURE AND INITIAL VELOCITY, WHICH INCLUDES THE DATA GIVEN IN COLUMN 8 OF THE RANGE TABLES.

158. Equations (74) and (75) are

Ballistic formulæ.

$$\frac{y}{x}=\tan\phi-\frac{C}{2\cos^2\phi}\left(\frac{A_u-A_V}{S_u-S_V}-I_V\right) \tag{132}$$

$$\tan\theta=\tan\phi-\frac{C}{2\cos^2\phi}\,(I_u-I_V) \tag{133}$$

and by eliminating I_V from the above we get

$$\frac{y}{x}=\tan\theta+\frac{C}{2\cos^2\phi}\left(I_u-\frac{A_u-A_V}{S_u-S_V}\right) \tag{134}$$

159. Equation (76) is

$$t=C\sec\phi(T_u-T_V) \tag{135}$$

160. Equations (132), (133), (134) and (135) may be written

$$\frac{y}{x}=\tan\phi-\frac{aC}{2\cos^2\phi}=\tan\theta+\frac{bC}{2\cos^2\phi} \tag{136}$$

$$\tan\theta=\tan\phi-\frac{a'C}{2\cos^2\phi} \tag{137}$$

$$t=Ct'\sec\phi \tag{138}$$

by the introduction of the general forms, a, a', b and t' of Ingalls' secondary functions, as explained in the last chapter.

161. Equations (136) and (137) may be written

Transformation of equations.

$$\frac{y}{x}=\tan\phi\left(1-\frac{aC}{\sin 2\phi}\right) \tag{139}$$

$$\tan\theta=\tan\phi\left(1-\frac{a'C}{\sin 2\phi}\right) \tag{140}$$

Substituting in these the value of $\sin 2\phi=AC$ from (115), we get

$$\frac{y}{x}=\frac{\tan\phi}{A}\,(A-a)=\frac{C}{2\cos^2\phi}\,(A-a) \tag{141}$$

$$\tan\theta=\frac{\tan\phi}{A}\,(A-a')=\frac{C}{2\cos^2\phi}\,(A-a') \tag{142}$$

162. Now by taking the first two members of each of the above equations, that is,

Equations for ordinate and inclination.

$$y=\frac{\tan\phi}{A}\,(A-a)x \tag{143}$$

$$\tan\theta=\frac{\tan\phi}{A}\,(A-a') \tag{144}$$

we can readily find the values of y and θ corresponding to any given value of x for any given trajectory; that is, by computing the ordinates and angles of inclination corresponding to any necessary number of abscissæ, we are in a position to actually plot the trajectory to scale, provided we have determined or know the values of ϕ,

V, X and C for that trajectory; for a knowledge of the values of V and of $Z=\frac{X}{C}$ is necessary to enable us to use Table II.

163. The quantity a varies with x, and must be taken from the "A" column of Table II with V and $z=\frac{x}{C}$ as arguments. Similarly, a' must be taken from the "A'" column with the same arguments.

164. For the vertex, we know that $\theta=0$, and (144) therefore becomes, for that particular point,

$$\frac{\tan\phi}{A}(A-a_0')=0$$

and, as $\frac{\tan\phi}{A}$ cannot be equal to zero, then we must have

$$A-a_0'=0 \quad \text{or} \quad A=a_0' \tag{145}$$

165. Also, if we suppose $\theta=-\phi$ at some point in the descending branch of the trajectory, which point manifestly exists, as in that branch the value of θ varies from zero at the vertex to $-\omega$ at the point of fall, and we have seen that ω is always numerically greater than ϕ, equation (142) will become for that point

$$\tan(-\phi)=\frac{\tan\phi}{A}(A-a'_{-\phi})$$

or

$$A-a'_{-\phi}=-A$$

or

$$a'_{-\phi}=2A \tag{146}$$

whence, from (145) and (146)

$$a_0'=A=\tfrac{1}{2}a'_{-\phi}$$

166. Substituting a_0' for A in (141) and designating symbols relating to the vertex by the subscript zero, we get

$$\frac{y_0}{x_0}=\frac{a_0'-a_0}{a_0'}\tan\phi=\frac{b_0}{a_0'}\tan\phi$$

whence

$$y_0=\frac{b_0x_0}{a_0'}\tan\phi=C\frac{b_0x_0}{a_0'C}\tan\phi$$

The secondary function A''

167. Now if we let $A''=\frac{b_0x_0}{a_0'C}=\frac{b_0z_0}{a_0'}$, in which A'' may be taken from Table II, using V and $a_0'=A=\frac{\sin 2\phi}{C}$, we will have the expression for the summit ordinate, or ordinate of the vertex

$$y_0=Y=A''C\tan\phi \tag{147}$$

It will be observed that a_0' is a special value of A', this latter symbol referring to the entire trajectory. This value of the ordinate at the vertex, y_0, is ordinarily denoted by Y in work.

168. We have already shown that, for the whole trajectory, $A=\frac{\sin 2\phi}{C}$, and also that, *for the vertex of the curve,* $a_0'=A$, and from this we see that, *for that particular point* $a_0'=\frac{\sin 2\phi}{C}$; and we also know that a_0' is merely the special value of A' for that particular point in the trajectory, namely, the vertex. Hence if we know the values of ϕ, V and C, we can compute this particular value of A', namely, a_0', from the expression $a_0'=\frac{\sin 2\phi}{C}$; and then, as this is a special value of A', we may look for it in the A' column of Table II, and by interpolation in the usual manner we may take from that table the corresponding value of A''; and, in fact, the corresponding values of any other of the secondary functions for the vertex. This explains the reasons for the method of determining the value of A'' described and used in the last chapter.*

169. We also find, in the Z column corresponding to the above interpolation, the value of $z_e = \frac{x_e}{C}$; and we therefore have

$$x_e = Cz_e \tag{148}$$

170. Assembling the equations already derived, we see that our formulæ for finding the elements at the vertex are — Equations for vertex.

$$y_e = Y = A''C \tan\phi \tag{149}$$

$$x_e = Cz_e \tag{150}$$

$$t_e = Ct_e' \sec\phi \tag{151}$$

$$v_e = u_e \cos\phi \tag{152}$$

171. Let us now proceed with our standard problem, the 12" gun, for which $V=2900$ f. s., $w=870$ pounds and $c=0.61$, for which, at 10,000 yards range, we have already determined in the last chapter that $\log C = 1.00231$, $Z=2984.1$ and $\phi = 4°\ 13'\ 14''$.

$$Y = A''C\tan\phi \qquad x_e = Cz_e \qquad t_e = Ct'\sec\phi \qquad v_e = u_e\cos\phi$$

From Table II

$A = .01408 + \frac{.00062 \times 84.1}{100} = .014601$ { for the entire trajectory, which equals a_e' for the vertex. This could also be determined by solving $A = \frac{\sin 2\phi}{C}$ for the above values instead of taking it from the table.

$A'' = 793 + \frac{9 \times 56}{11} = 838.87$ { by using the value of A given above as an argument in the A' column, and working, as should always be done, from the *next lower tabular value.*

$z_e = 1500 + \frac{100 \times .0009}{.0011} = 1581.8$

$t_e' = .565 + \frac{.041 \times 81.9}{100} = .59858$

$u_e = 2435 - \frac{30 \times 81.9}{100} = 2410.4$

$C=$	log 1.00231	log 1.00231	log 1.00231	
$A''=838.87$	log 2.92370			
$\phi=4°\ 13'\ 14''$	tan 8.86803−10		sec 0.00116	cos 9.99882−10
$z_e=1581.9$		log 3.19918		
$t_e'=.59858$			log 9.77712−10	
$u_e=2410.4$				log 3.38209
$Y=622.36$	log 2.79404			
$x_e=15903.3$		log 4.20149		
$t_e=6.034$			log 0.78061	
$v_e=2403.9$				log 3.38091

$x_e = 5301.1$ yards. $\qquad t_e = 6.034$ seconds.

$Y = 622.36$ feet. $\qquad v_e = 2403.9$ foot-seconds.

---

* See paragraph 152.

172. Had we not known the correct value of C, as corrected for altitude, but had only known ϕ and V, the work would then have been by successive approximations, as follows:

$V = 2900$ f. s. $\quad \phi = 4°\ 13'\ 14''$ $\quad w = 870$ pounds $\quad c = 0.61$

$Y = A''C \tan\phi$ $\quad \log\log f = \log Y + 5.01765 - 10$ $\quad x_0 = Cz_0$

$t_0 = Ct_0' \sec\phi$ $\quad v_0 = u_0 \cos\phi$

$w=870$			log	2.93952
$c=0.61$	log	9.78533−10	colog	0.21467
$d^2=144$	log	2.15836	colog	7.84164−10
$C_1=$			log	0.99583 ...... colog 9.00417−10
$2\phi=8°\ 26'\ 28''$			sin	9.16670−10
$a_{0_1}'=.01482$			log	8.17087−10

From Table II, with .01482 in the A' column as an argument,

$$A_1'' = 849 + \frac{.2 \times 100}{12} \times \frac{57}{100} = 849 + 1 = 850$$

$A_1''=850$			log	2.92942
$C_1=$			log	0.99503
$\phi=4°\ 13'\ 14''$			tan	8.86803−10
$Y_1=$			log	2.79328
Constant			log	5.01765−10
$f_1=$	log	0.00647	loglog	7.81093−10
$C_1=$	log	0.99583		
$C_2=$	log	1.00230	colog	8.99770−10
$2\phi=8°\ 26'\ 28''$			sin	9.16670−10
$a_{0_2}'=.0146$			log	8.16440−10

From Table II as above

$$A_2'' = 793 + \frac{9 \times 56}{11} = 793 + 46 = 839$$

$A_2''=839$			log	2.92376
$C_2=$			log	1.00230
$\phi=4°\ 13'\ 14''$			tan	8.86803−10
$Y_2=622.43$			log	2.79409
Constant			log	5.01765−10
$f_2=$	log	0.00648	loglog	7.81174−10
$C_1=$	log	0.99583		
$C_3=$	log	1.00231	colog	8.99769−10
$2\phi=8°\ 26'\ 28''$			sin	9.16670−10
$a_{0_3}'=.0146$			log	8.16439−10

As these last two successive values of a_0' are equal, we have evidently reached the limit of accuracy in our approximations, and we have for the remainder of the problem

$$a_0' = .0146 \quad \text{and} \quad \log C = 1.00231$$

Also, from log Y_2 as found above, we have that $Y=622.43$ feet, and from Table II

$$z_0=1581.8 \qquad t_0'=.59854 \qquad u_0=2410.5$$

$C=$ ....log 1.00231....log 1.00231
$\phi=4°\ 13'\ 14''$ ....sec 0.00118........cos 9.99882−10
$z_0=1581.8$ ....log 3.19915
$t_0'=.59854$ ....log 9.77709−10
$u_0=2410.5$ ....log 3.38093

$x_0=15902.3$ ....log 4.20146

$t_0=6.0336$ ....log 0.78058

$v_0=2404.0$ ....log 3.38093

$x_0=5300.7$ yards.
$Y=622.43$ feet.
$t_0=6.0366$ seconds.
$v_0=2404.0$ foot-seconds.

173. If we desire to plot any particular trajectory to scale, we can determine the ordinate corresponding to any given abscissa, and also the angle of inclination of the curve at the given point as follows:

We have from (143) and (144)

$$y=\frac{\tan\phi}{A}(A-a)x \tag{153}$$

and

$$\tan\theta=\frac{\tan\phi}{A}(A-a') \tag{154}$$

Suppose we wish to plot the 10,000-yard trajectory for our standard problem, for which we now know that $\phi=4°\ 13'\ 14''$ and log $C=1.00231$.

$2\phi=8°\ 26'\ 28''$ .... sin 9.16670−10
$C=$ ....colog 8.99769−10

$A=.014601$ .... log 8.16439−10
$a_0'=A=.014601$

$$A''=793+\frac{.00901\times 56}{.0011}=838.87 \qquad z_0=1500+\frac{100\times .000901}{.0011}=1581.9$$

$A''=838.87$ ....log 2.92370
$C=$ ....log 1.00231..........log 1.00231
$\phi=4°\ 13'\ 14''$ ....tan 8.86803−10
$z_0=1581.9$ ....log 3.19918

$y_0=Y=622.35$ ....log 2.79404

$x_0=15903$ ....log 4.20149

The coordinates of the vertex are therefore 5301 yards in range and 622.35 feet in altitude.

174. In the equations given we now find the value of $\frac{\tan\phi}{A}$ for the given trajectory, having the value of A as above.

$\phi=4°\ 13'\ 14''$ .... log 8.86803−10
$A=.014601$ ....log 8.16439−10...........colog 1.83561

$\frac{\tan\phi}{A}=5.054$ .... log 0.70364

and our equations become

$$y=5.054(.014601-a)x \qquad \tan\theta=5.054(.014601-a')$$

175. The following table gives the results of work with these equations for abscissæ varying by 1000 yards for this trajectory, some of the cases being worked out below:

Abscissæ. Yards.	Ordinates. Feet.	θ.	Remarks.
0	0	4° 13′ 14″	Origin.
1000	203.58	3 31 57	
2000	370.06	2 48 55	
3000	497.25	2 02 20	
4000	581.62	1 10 37	
5000	620.81	0 17 11	
5301	622.35	0 00 00	Vertex.
6000	610.34	(—)0 41 35	
7000	547.66	(—)1 43 08	
8000	427.21	(—)2 50 43	
9000	246.44	(—)4 04 16	
10000	0	(—)5 21 34	Point of fall; $\theta = -\omega$.

Work for 3000 yards:

$C =$ ....colog 3.99769−10

$x = 9000$ .... log 3.95424

$z = 895.21$ .... log 2.95193

$a = .00326 + \dfrac{.00043 \times 95.21}{100} = .003669$ $a' = .0067 + \dfrac{.0009 \times 95.21}{100} = .007557$

$A = .014601$ $A = .014601$

$a = .003669$ $a' = .007557$

$A - a = .010932$ ....log 8.03870−10

$A - a' = .007044$ ....log 7.84782−10

$\dfrac{\tan\phi}{A} = 5.054$ ....log 0.70364..........log 0.70364

$x = 9000$ ....log 3.95424

$y = 497.25$ ....log 2.69658

$\theta = 2°\ 02'\ 20''$ ....tan 8.55146−10

Work for 8000 yards:

$C =$ ....colog 8.99769−10

$x = 24000$ .... log 4.38021

$z = 2387.3$ .... log 3.37790

$a = .01059 + \dfrac{.00056 \times 87.3}{100} = .011079$ $a' = .0233 + \dfrac{.0013 \times 87.3}{100} = .024435$

$A = .014601$ $A =$ .014601

$a = .011079$ $a' =$ .024435

$A - a = .003522$ ....log 7.54679−10

$A - a' = (-).009834$ ....(−)log 7.99273−10

$\dfrac{\tan\phi}{A} = 5.054$ ....log 0.70364...... log 0.70364

$x = 24000$ ....log 4.38021

$y = 427.21$ ....log 2.63064

$\theta = (-)2°\ 50'\ 43''$ ....(−)tan 8.69637−10

The work for the point of fall, that is, for an abscissa of $x=10,000$ yards, becomes:

$C=$ .... colog 8.99769−10
$x=30000$ .... log 4.47712

$z=2984.1$ .... log 3.47481

$a=.01408+\frac{.00062\times 84.1}{100}=.014601$ $a'=.0319+\frac{.0015\times 84.1}{100}=.033162$

$A=.014601$	$A=.014601$
$a=.014601$	$a'=.033162$

$A-a=0$

$A-a'=(-).018561$ .... (−)log 8.26860−10

$\frac{\tan\phi}{A}=5.054$ .... log 0.70364

$\theta=(-)5°\ 21'\ 34''$ .... (−)tan 8.97224−10

$y=0$

176. A reversal of the original formulæ would enable us to find the abscissa corresponding to any given ordinate; but there are some practical difficulties in the way of a simple use of the formulæ for this purpose, and as it is not a usual case it is not considered necessary to go into the matter here. **Reverse formulæ.**

EXAMPLES.

1. Given the data contained in the following table, compute the values of x_0, $y_0(Y)$, t_0 and v_0 by Ingalls' method, using Table II, and correcting for altitude in each case by computing successive approximations to the value of C.

Problem.	DATA.							ANSWERS.			
	Projectile.			Atmosphere.		ϕ.	Velocity. f. s.	x_0. Yds.	$y_0=Y$. Feet.	t_0. Secs.	v_0. f. s.
	d. In.	w. Lbs.	c.	Bar. In.	Ther. °F.						
A	3	13	1.00	28.00	100	6° 52′ 54″	1150	1340	257	3.88	958
B	3	13	1.00	28.40	95	2 40 24	2700	2106	171	3.00	1659
C	4	33	0.67	29.15	93	1 50 00	2900	2196	113	2.55	2300
D	5	50	1.00	29.90	87	1 53 12	3150	2272	127	2.62	2154
E	5	50	0.61	30.00	84	1 45 48	3150	2453	123	2.65	2460
F	6	105	0.61	30.10	79	14 01 06	2600	8529	3827	13.88	1373
G	6	105	1.00	30.70	75	2 18 48	2800	2407	160	3.00	2075
H	6	105	0.61	30.90	73	1 44 06	2800	2091	100	2.43	2393
I	7	165	1.00	31.00	67	5 20 18	2700	4227	686	6.01	1667
J	7	165	0.61	30.75	58	3 41 36	2700	3747	393	4.75	2088
K	8	260	0.61	30.50	49	4 03 06	2750	4292	493	5.31	2154
L	10	510	1.00	30.17	35	6 30 06	2700	5483	1067	7.58	1766
M	10	510	0.61	30.00	29	5 52 42	2700	5849	984	7.49	2054
N	12	870	0.61	29.75	23	13 49 48	2900	12661	5365	16.90	1803
O	13	1130	1.00	29.33	18	10 40 18	2000	5353	1676	9.65	1418
P	13	1130	0.74	29.00	15	10 08 42	2000	5542	1610	9.58	1535
Q	14	1400	0.70	28.50	10	13 54 00	2000	7245	2938	12.89	1471
R	14	1400	0.70	28.25	5	8 14 06	2600	7468	1770	10.01	1950

2. Given the data contained in the following table, compute the values of x_0, y_0 (Y), t_0 and v_0 by Ingalls' method, using Table II, and correcting for f for the mean altitude during flight given in Column 8 of the table. (Note that this is not the maximum ordinate.)

Problem.	DATA.								ANSWERS.			
	Projectile.			Atmosphere.		ϕ.	Velocity. f. s.	Mean height of flight. Feet.	x_0. Yds.	$y_0=Y$. Feet.	t_0. Secs.	v_0. f. s.
	d. In.	w. Lbs.	c.	Bar. In.	Ther. °F.							
A....	3	13	1.00	28.15	0	5° 14′ 18″	1150	100	1032	150	2.97	966
B....	3	13	1.00	28.75	5	2 48 54	2700	120	2011	176	3.00	1524
C....	4	33	0.67	29.00	10	1 18 42	2900	40	1619	59	1.85	2371
D....	5	50	1.00	29.30	20	1 44 12	3150	72	2070	106	2.44	2131
E....	5	50	0.61	29.70	25	1 39 24	3150	72	2278	107	2.47	2436
F....	6	105	0.61	29.90	30	9 18 54	2600	1257	6378	1841	9.77	1514
G....	6	105	1.00	30.00	40	1 48 36	2800	68	1971	101	2.41	2167
H....	6	105	0.61	30.15	50	1 37 54	2800	60	1976	89	2.29	2416
I....	7	165	1.00	30.33	60	4 38 00	2700	360	3856	536	5.34	1744
J....	7	165	0.61	30.50	70	3 37 18	2700	254	3709	381	4.67	2110
K....	8	260	0.61	30.67	75	4 07 12	2750	344	4391	512	5.42	2165
L....	10	510	1.00	30.90	80	6 36 24	2700	744	5649	1113	7.76	1789
M....	10	510	0.61	31.00	85	5 57 06	2700	680	6009	1019	7.64	2081
N....	12	870	0.61	30.75	90	9 04 36	2900	1706	9655	2564	11.92	2065
O....	13	1130	1.00	30.00	95	10 21 36	2000	1076	5408	1626	9.56	1471
P....	13	1130	0.74	29.50	100	10 48 54	2000	1220	5908	1851	10.30	1560
Q....	14	1400	0.70	29.00	80	14 02 42	2000	2018	7472	3043	13.16	1502
R....	14	1400	0.70	28.00	60	8 23 54	2600	1238	7783	1869	10.33	1989

3. Knowing that $y=\frac{\tan\phi}{A}(A-a)x$ and that $\tan\theta=\frac{\tan\phi}{A}(A-a')$, derive expressions for the values of y and $\tan\theta$ in terms of a, a', x and of the numerical coefficients, for any point in each of the trajectories given below, atmospheric conditions being standard.

Problem.	DATA.							ANSWERS.	
	Projectile.			V. f. s.	R. Yds	Value of log C.	ϕ.	$y=$	$\tan\theta=$
	d. In.	w. Lbs.	c.						
A...	3	13	1.00	1150	2130	0.16152	5° 39′ 06″	$0.73236(.135125-a)x$	$0.73236(.135125-a')$
B...	3	13	1.00	2700	3720	0.16179	2 59 18	$0.72758(.071750-a)x$	$0.72758(.071750-a')$
C...	4	33	0.67	2900	3825	0.48936	1 43 24	$1.54425(.019483-a)x$	$1.54425(.019483-a')$
D...	5	50	1.00	3150	4370	0.30272	2 11 24	$1.00530(.038037-a)x$	$1.00530(.038037-a')$
E...	5	50	0.61	3150	4465	0.51695	1 44 48	$1.64560(.018531-a)x$	$1.64560(.018531-a')$
F...	6	105	0.61	2600	12690	0.70596	11 03 24	$2.63750(.074085-a)x$	$2.63750(.074085-a')$
G...	6	105	1.00	2800	3875	0.46608	1 55 48	$1.46400(.023017-a)x$	$1.46400(.023017-a')$
H...	6	105	0.61	2800	3622	0.68039	1 32 18	$2.39700(.011203-a)x$	$2.39700(.011203-a')$
I...	7	165	1.00	2700	7230	0.53374	5 00 42	$1.72170(.050924-a)x$	$1.72170(.050924-a')$
J...	7	165	0.61	2700	7357	0.74663	3 57 24	$2.80300(.024675-a)x$	$2.80300(.024675-a')$
K...	8	260	0.61	2750	8390	0.82912	4 15 18	$3.39220(.021932-a)x$	$3.39220(.021932-a')$
L...	10	510	1.00	2700	10310	0.71990	6 49 48	$2.66130(.045010-a)x$	$2.66130(.045010-a')$
M...	10	510	0.61	2700	11333	0.93343	6 07 36	$4.33860(.024739-a)x$	$4.33860(.024739-a')$
N...	12	870	0.61	2900	21650	1.04355	12 30 54	$5.79990(.038272-a)x$	$5.79990(.038272-a')$
O...	13	1130	1.00	2000	10370	0.84469	11 15 12	$3.63520(.054735-a)x$	$3.63520(.054735-a')$
P...	13	1130	0.74	2000	11111	0.97554	10 58 00	$4.90370(.039516-a)x$	$4.90370(.039516-a')$
Q...	14	1400	0.70	2000	14220	1.04355	14 48 48	$5.91410(.044718-a)x$	$5.91410(.044718-a')$
R...	14	1400	0.70	2600	14370	1.02872	8 32 24	$5.46220(.027492-a)x$	$5.46220(.027492-a')$

NOTE.—Values of R and $\log C$ are taken from the results of work in Example 7, Chapter 8.

4. For the trajectories given in the preceding example (Example 3) compute the abscissa and ordinate of the vertex; and the ordinate and inclination of the curve at each of the points whose abscissæ are given below, and also at the point of fall.

ANSWERS.

Problem.	Vertex.		Point of fall.		For different abscissæ.					
	x_0. Yds.	$y_0=Y$. Feet.	y_0. Feet.	$\theta=-\omega$.	x_1. Yds.	y_1. Feet.	θ_1.	x_2. Yds.	y_2. Feet.	θ_2.
A...	1112	175	0.	(—) 6° 45.0′	750	154.5	2° 02.9′	1800	96.7	(—) 4° 24.8′
B...	2160	200	0.08	(—) 5 32.4	1000	133.0	2 00.5	3000	149.2	(—) 2 29.4
C...	2056	100	0.	(—) 2 19.9	1000	71.7	0 59.2	3000	73.7	(—) 1 07.2
D...	2476	163	0.05	(—) 3 44.4	1000	98.3	1 31.9	3000	152.7	(—) 0 46.5
E...	2414	120	0.64	(—) 2 24.7	1000	75.8	1 07.8	3000	111.2	(—) 0 34.8
F...	7329	2534	(—)1.61	(—)19 38.2	4000	1910.7	6 34.8	9000	2332.6	(—) 4 50.6
G...	2097	115	0.49	(—) 2 40.6	1000	81.1	1 08.1	3000	87.9	(—) 1 11.0
H..	1888	80	0.03	(—) 1 50.8	1000	61.1	0 47.3	3000	48.1	(—) 1 07.7
I...	4102	620	0.37	(—) 8 30.6	2000	433.7	3 11.3	4000	618.9	(+) 0 11.2
J...	3990	450	0.19	(—) 5 29.1	2000	328.0	2 14.3	4000	448.6	0 00.0
K..	4511	544	0.43	(—) 5 46.7	2000	388.1	2 37.3	4000	535.9	(+) 0 35.7
L...	5799	1184	0.17	(—)11 08.4	3000	869.7	4 00.3	9000	629.4	(—) 7 08.8
M..	6146	1075	(—)0.30	(—) 8 29.0	3000	769.4	3 33.0	9000	770.2	(—) 4 12.5
N..	12154	4581	0.38	(—)19 55.7	9000	4209.5	4 20.3	19000	2360.4	(—)13 14.0
O...	5675	1873	(—)1.47	(—)16 10.0	3000	1411.2	6 15.0	9000	980.3	(—)10 47.5
P...	5976	1879	0.33	(—)14 44.2	3000	1376.5	6 11.5	9000	1272.3	(—) 8 02.4
Q...	7714	3339	(—)0.25	(—)20 15.0	3000	2006.0	10 06.3	9000	3220.6	(—) 3 28.2
R...	7810	1915	0.47	(—)11 54.7	3000	1141.0	5 47.7	9000	1857.2	(—) 1 48.8

NOTE.—Of course, the found values of the ordinate and of the angle of inclination at the point of fall should be numerically equal to zero and to the angle of fall, respectively. The actual results obtained by the above work show the degree of accuracy of the method.

CHAPTER 10.

THE DERIVATION AND USE OF SPECIAL FORMULÆ FOR FINDING THE HORIZONTAL RANGE, TIME OF FLIGHT, ANGLE OF FALL, AND STRIKING VELOCITY FOR A GIVEN ANGLE OF DEPARTURE AND INITIAL VELOCITY.

Ballistic formulæ transformed. 177. For this problem we use expressions that have already been derived, namely, equations (113), (115), (116), (117) and (118); in some cases somewhat transposed, as follows (neglecting the altitude factor):

$$C=\frac{w}{\delta cd^2} \qquad (155)$$

$$A=\frac{\sin 2\phi}{C} \qquad (156)$$

$$X=CZ \qquad (157)$$

$$\tan \omega=B' \tan \phi \qquad (158)$$

$$T=CT' \sec \phi \qquad (159)$$

$$v_\omega=u_\omega \cos \phi \sec \omega \qquad (160)$$

178. As no account is taken of the altitude factor in the above expression, we cannot use our standard problem at present, so we will take a different case for our first solution, and one at such a short range that the altitude factor may be neglected without material error. Let us therefore compute the values of X, ω, T and v_ω for an angle of departure of 1° 02′ 24″, for the 5″ gun for which $V=3150$ f. s., $w=50$ pounds and $c=0.61$, for a barometer reading of 30.00″ and a thermometer reading of 50° F.

From Table VI.

$K=$	log 0.51570		
$\delta=1.035$	log 0.01494		
$C=$	log 0.50076	colog	9.49924−10
$2\phi=2°\ 04'\ 48''$		sin	8.55984−10
$A=.01146$		log	8.05908−10

From which, from Table II, we get

$$Z=2700+\frac{100}{.00052}\left(\frac{50\times.00072}{100}+.01146-.01119\right)=2700+121.1=2821.1$$

$$\log B'=.0945+\frac{.0035\times 21.1}{100}-\frac{.0015\times 50}{100}=.09449$$

$$u_\omega=2235-\frac{27\times 21.1}{100}+\frac{83\times 50}{100}=2270.8$$

$$T'=1.064+\frac{.045\times 21.1}{100}-\frac{.035\times 50}{100}=1.0560$$

$C=$ ....log 0.50076..................log 0.50076
$Z=2821.1$ .....log 3.45042
$\phi=1°\ 02'\ 24''$ ....tan 8.25894−10..sec 0.00007..cos 9.99993−10
$B'=$ ....log 0.09449
$u_\omega=2270.8$ ....log 3.35618
$T'=1.056$ ....log 0.02366

$X=8936.7$ .....log 3.95118

$\omega=1°\ 17'\ 34''$ ....tan 8.35343−10.............sec 0.00011

$T=3.3457$ ....log 0.52449

$v_\omega=2271$ ....log 3.35622

$X=2978.9$ yards. $T=3.3457$ seconds.
$\omega=1°\ 17'\ 34''$. $v_\omega=2271$ f. s.

179. Or, with perhaps no more labor, we may avoid the double interpolation necessary in the above solution by working the problem for $V=3100$ f. s. and then again for $V=3200$ f. s., and then get our final results by interpolation between those obtained for the two velocities. In this case, as $V=3150$, our final results should be half way between the results obtained for the two values of V with which we work. The value of C and that of A are of course the same as in the preceding problem, so starting from that point, with $A=.01146$ and $\log C=0.50076$, we have

For $V=3100$ f. s.

$Z=2751.9$ $\log B'=.09282$ $u_\omega=2248.5$ $T'=1.0428$

$C=$ ....log 0.50076..................log 0.50076
$Z=2751.9$ .....log 3.43963
$\phi=1°\ 02'\ 24''$ ....tan 8.25894−10..sec 0.00007..cos 9.99993−10
$B'=$ ....log 0.09282
$u_\omega=2248.5$ ....log 3.35190
$T'=1.0428$ ....log 0.01820

$X=8717.4$ .....log 3.94039

$\omega=1°\ 17'\ 16''$ ....tan 8.35176−10.............sec 0.00011

$T=3.3039$ ....log 0.51903

$v_\omega=2248.75$ ....log 3.35194

For $V=3200$ f. s.

$Z=2904$ $\log B'=.09674$ $u_\omega=2288.9$ $T'=1.0738$

$C=$ ....log 0.50076..................log 0.50076
$Z=2904$ ....log 3.46300
$\phi=1°\ 02'\ 24''$ ....tan 8.25894−10..sec 0.00007..cos 9.99993−10
$B'=$ ....log 0.09674
$u_\omega=2288.9$ ....log 3.35963
$T'=1.0738$ ....log 0.03092

$X=9199.4$ .....log 3.96376

$\omega=1°\ 17'\ 58''$ ....tan 8.35568−10.............sec 0.00011

$T=3.4021$ ....log 0.53175

$v_\omega=2289.1$ ....log 3.35967

Our results then are

	For $V=3100$ f. s.	For $V=3200$ f. s.	For $V=3150$ f. s. (By interpolation between the results obtained for 3100 and 3200 f. s.)
X	2905.8 yards.	3066.5 yards.	2986.1 yards.
ω	1° 17′ 16″.	1° 17′ 57″.	1° 17′ 37″.
T	3.3039 seconds.	3.4022 seconds.	3.3531 seconds.
v_ω	2248.75 f. s.	2289.1 f. s.	2268.9 f. s.

180. We will now take our standard problem, introduce the altitude factor, and solve. This for the 12″ gun, for which $V=2900$ f. s., $w=870$ pounds and $c=0.61$. For this problem we will take the angle of departure as 4° 13′ 14″, which we already know corresponds to a range of 10,000 yards, and will consider the atmospheric conditions as standard. Proceeding in a manner similar to that employed in originally computing the angle of departure, that is, by performing the work first without considering f until we have gone far enough to enable us to determine the value of f by a series of approximations, and then introducing it, we have, by the use of the formulæ employed in the preceding problem, and in addition of

$$Y=A''C\tan\phi \quad \text{and} \quad \log\log f=\log Y+5.01765-10$$

$C_1=K=$ (from Table VI)	colog	9.00417−10
$2\phi=8°\ 26'\ 28''$	sin	9.16670−10
$a_{0_1}'=.014821$	log	8.17087−10

$$A_1''=849+\frac{.000021\times 57}{.0012}=850$$

$A_1''=850$	log	2.92942
$C_1=$	log	0.99583
$\phi=4°\ 13'\ 14''$	tan	8.86803−10
$Y_1=$	log	2.79328
Constant	log	5.01765−10
$f_1=$ ... log 0.00647	loglog	7.81093−10
$C_1=$ ... log 0.99583		
$C_2=$ ... log 1.00230	colog	8.99770−10
$2\phi=8°\ 26'\ 28''$	sin	9.16670−10
$a_{0_2}'=.014602$	log	8.16440−10

$$A_2''=793+\frac{.000902\times 56}{.0011}=838.92$$

$A_2''=838.92$	log	2.92372
$C_2=$	log	1.00230
$\phi=4°\ 13'\ 14''$	tan	8.86803−10
$Y_2=$	log	2.79405
Constant	log	5.01765−10
$f_2=$ ... log 0.00648	loglog	7.81170−10
$C_1=$ ... log 0.99583		
$C_3=$ ... log 1.00231	colog	8.99769−10
$2\phi=8°\ 26'\ 28''$	sin	9.16670−10
$a_{0_3}'=.014601$	log	8.16439−10

$$A_3'' = 793 + \frac{.000901 \times 56}{.0011} = 838.87$$

$A_3'' = 838.87$		log 2.92370
$C_3 =$		log 1.00231
$\phi = 4°\ 13'\ 14''$		tan 8.86803 − 10
$Y_3 =$		log 2.79404
Constant		log 5.01765 − 10
$f_3 =$	log 0.00648	loglog 7.81169 − 10
$C_1 =$	log 0.99583	
$C_4 =$	log 1.00231	

and as $C_4 = C_3$, we see that we have reached the limit of accuracy in determining the value of C, and we therefore proceed with the work with $\log C = 1.00231$, $A = a_0'$ $= .014601$, $V = 2900$, and from Table II $Z = 2984$, $\log B' = .10371$, $T' = 1.2332$ and $u_\omega = 2026.2$. The further work then becomes

$C =$	log 1.00231		log 1.00231	
$Z = 2984$	log 3.47480			
$\phi = 4°\ 13'\ 14''$		tan 8.86803 − 10	sec 0.00118	cos 9.99882 − 10
$B' =$		log 0.10371		
$T' = 1.2332$			log 0.09103	
$u_\omega = 2026.2$				log 3.30668
$X = 29999$	log 4.47711			
$\omega = 5°\ 21'\ 11''$		tan 8.97174 − 10		sec 0.00190
$T = 12.431$			log 1.09452	
$v_\omega = 2029.55$				log 3.30740

A comparison between these results and those obtained in Chapter 8, where we computed the values of the same elements with V and X as the data, gives an interesting measure of the accuracy of the methods employed. Tabulating these results for comparison, we have:

	Value by work under	
Element.	Chapter 8.	This Chapter.
R	10,000 yards.	10,000 yards.
ω	5° 21′ 11″.	5° 21′ 11″.
T	12.43 seconds.	12.431 seconds.
v_ω	2029.0 foot-seconds.	2029.6 foot-seconds.

EXAMPLES.

1. Given the data contained in the following table, compute the values of R, ω, T and v_ω by Ingalls' methods, using Table II, and determining the value of f by successive approximations, and applying it to get the correct value of the ballistic coefficient.

Problem.	DATA. Projectile. *d.* In.	Projectile. *w.* Lbs.	Projectile. *c.*	Atmosphere. Bar. In.	Atmosphere. Ther. °F.	Velocity. f. s.	ϕ.			ANSWERS. Range. Yds.	ω.		*T.* Secs.	v_ω. f. s.
A.....	3	13	1.00	28.00	0	1150	7°	13′	36″	2564	8°	59′	8.22	816
B.....	3	13	1.00	28.10	5	2700	3	45	36	4072	7	18	8.22	988
C.....	4	33	0.67	28.50	10	2900	1	35	36	3547	2	09	4.61	1850
D.....	5	50	1.00	28.67	15	3150	2	02	42	4088	3	29	5.90	1412
E.....	5	50	0.61	29.00	20	3150	1	30	12	3934	2	02	4.71	2004
F.....	6	105	0.61	29.33	25	2600	12	30	06	13201	22	36	26.98	1067
G.....	6	105	1.00	29.75	35	2800	1	48	36	3646	2	30	5.01	1716
H.....	6	105	0.61	30.00	43	2800	1	00	00	2486	1	08	2.94	2306
I.....	7	165	1.00	30.20	47	2700	3	59	54	6189	6	28	10.06	1311
J.....	7	165	0.61	30.50	51	2700	3	00	24	5929	3	58	8.15	1781
K.....	8	260	0.61	30.75	58	2750	3	31	54	7214	4	39	9.73	1773
L.....	10	510	1.00	31.00	65	2700	6	17	48	9665	10	10	15.81	1313
M.....	10	510	0.61	30.45	75	2700	5	43	54	10806	7	50	15.34	1692
N.....	12	870	0.61	30.20	80	2900	10	45	00	19751	16	32	29.40	1516
O.....	13	1130	1.00	30.00	85	2000	10	12	24	9810	14	20	19.73	1205
P.....	13	1130	0.74	29.50	90	2000	10	40	48	11086	14	06	21.16	1315
Q.....	14	1400	0.70	29.00	95	2000	13	45	18	13838	18	17	27.01	1302
R.....	14	1400	0.70	28.67	100	2600	8	19	00	14553	11	14	21.44	1657

2. Given the data contained in the following table, compute the values of R, ω, T and v_ω by Ingalls' methods, using Table II, and correcting for f by the use of the maximum ordinate given in the table.

Problem.	DATA. Projectile. *d.* In.	Projectile. *w.* Lbs.	Projectile. *c.*	Atmosphere. Bar. In.	Atmosphere. Ther. °F.	Velocity. f. s.	ϕ.			Maximum ordinate. Feet.	ANSWERS. Range. Yds.	ω.		*T.* Secs.	v_ω. f. s.
A...	3	13	1.00	28.10	100	1150	5°	14′	18″	150	2042	6°	08′	6.14	900
B...	3	13	1.00	28.40	95	2700	2	09	24	115	3245	3	35	5.38	1263
C...	4	33	0.67	28.25	90	2900	1	06	06	43	2757	1	20	3.29	2179
D...	5	50	1.00	29.00	87	3150	1	27	42	79	3479	2	09	4.46	1759
E...	5	50	0.61	29.20	85	3150	1	02	24	45	3035	1	16	3.36	2333
F...	6	105	0.61	29.50	80	2600	10	55	18	2481	12755	19	16	24.58	1115
G...	6	105	1.00	29.75	77	2800	2	18	48	159	4447	3	20	6.32	1616
H...	6	105	0.61	30.00	73	2800	1	41	00	95	3912	2	03	4.86	2094
I...	7	165	1.00	30.10	70	2700	5	05	48	638	7298	8	42	12.50	1213
J...	7	165	0.61	30.20	60	2700	4	03	48	471	7449	5	43	10.79	1619
K...	8	260	0.61	31.00	50	2750	4	11	18	532	8132	5	46	11.38	1702
L...	10	510	1.00	30.50	40	2700	6	55	36	1214	10073	11	37	17.08	1245
M...	10	510	0.61	30.30	35	2700	5	18	24	824	9991	7	16	14.19	1685
N...	12	870	0.61	30.00	31	2900	13	44	18	5363	21989	22	52	35.96	1345
O...	13	1130	1.00	29.75	20	2000	9	54	12	1488	9220	14	13	18.94	1167
P...	13	1130	0.74	29.50	22	2000	9	45	12	1511	9978	13	05	19.24	1284
Q...	14	1400	0.70	29.00	20	2000	15	05	00	3450	14043	21	01	28.92	1219
R...	14	1400	0.70	28.50	10	2600	7	40	18	1569	13017	10	40	19.60	1585

CHAPTER 11.

THE DERIVATION AND USE OF SPECIAL FORMULÆ FOR FINDING THE ANGLE OF ELEVATION NECESSARY TO HIT A POINT ABOVE OR BELOW THE LEVEL OF THE GUN AND AT A GIVEN HORIZONTAL DISTANCE FROM THE GUN, AND THE TIME OF FLIGHT TO AND REMAINING VELOCITY AND STRIKING ANGLE AT THE TARGET; GIVEN THE INITIAL VELOCITY.

New Symbols Introduced.

ϕ_x.... Angle of departure for a horizontal distance x.

181. As we know, the secondary function a refers to the point (x, y) in the trajectory (A being its special value when $x=X$ and $y=0$); but since the pseudo velocity is independent of the height of this point, and dependent only on x, or the horizontal distance from the muzzle of the gun, we may consider x as the horizontal range of another trajectory having the same initial velocity, whose angle of departure may be designated by ϕ_x. For this case then, we have, from (115) **Transformation of formulæ.**

$$a=\frac{\sin 2\phi_x}{C} \tag{161}$$

as well as

$$A=\frac{\sin 2\phi}{C} \tag{162}$$

182. We have also derived, in (141), the expression

$$\frac{y}{x}=\frac{C}{2\cos^2\phi}(A-a) \tag{163}$$

183. Now substituting in (163) from (161) and (162), we get

$$\frac{y}{x}=\frac{C}{2\cos^2\phi}\left(\frac{\sin 2\phi}{C}-\frac{\sin 2\phi_x}{C}\right)$$

$$\frac{y}{x}=\frac{\sin 2\phi-\sin 2\phi_x}{2\cos^2\phi} \tag{164}$$

184. Now if p be the angle of position, we know that

$$\tan p=\frac{y}{x} \tag{165}$$

and combining (164) and (165) we get

$$\tan p=\frac{\sin 2\phi-\sin 2\phi_x}{2\cos^2\phi}$$

or

$$\sin 2\phi_x=\sin 2\phi-2\cos^2\phi\tan p \tag{166}$$

but as $2\cos^2\phi=1+\cos 2\phi$ (166) becomes

$$\sin 2\phi_x=\sin 2\phi-\tan p(1+\cos 2\phi)$$

or

$$\sin 2\phi-\cos 2\phi\tan p-\tan p=\sin 2\phi_x$$

Multiplying and dividing the first member by $\cos p$ gives

$$\frac{\sin 2\phi\cos p-\cos 2\phi\sin p-\sin p}{\cos p}=\sin 2\phi_x$$

or

$$\frac{\sin(2\phi-p)-\sin p}{\cos p}=\sin 2\phi_x$$

whence

$$\sin(2\phi-p)=\sin p+\cos p\sin 2\phi_x$$

or

$$\sin(2\phi-p)=\sin p(1+\cot p\sin 2\phi_x) \tag{167}$$

And we also know that $\psi=\phi-p$.

185. Now for any given point (x, y) we may compute the value of z from $z=\frac{x}{C}$, and then, with z and V as arguments, we may take the value of a from the A column of Table II.

186. We may then compute the value of $\sin 2\phi_\omega$ from $\sin 2\phi_\omega=aC$ and thence of ϕ from (167). Also, with the same arguments, we may take from Table II the values of a', u and t' for the point (x, y).

187. Assembling the formulæ deduced in this chapter, and also the other necessary formulæ previously deduced as given in (85), (113), (138) and (144), we have, for the solution of this problem,

$$C=\frac{fw}{\delta cd^2} \tag{168}$$

$$\tan p=\frac{y}{x} \tag{169}$$

$$z=\frac{x}{C} \tag{170}$$

$$\sin 2\phi_\omega=aC \tag{171}$$

$$\sin(2\phi-p)=\sin p(1+\cot p \sin 2\phi_\omega) \tag{172}$$

$$\psi=\phi-p \tag{173}$$

$$A=\frac{\sin 2\phi}{C} \tag{174}$$

$$\tan\theta=\frac{\tan\phi}{A}(A-a') \tag{175}$$

$$t=Ct'\sec\phi \tag{176}$$

$$v=u\cos\phi\sec\theta \tag{177}$$

Elevated target. **188.** Let us now compute these several elements for our standard problem 12″ gun, $V=2900$ f. s., $w=870$ pounds, $c=0.61$, for a target at a horizontal distance of 10,000 yards from the gun, and 1500 feet above the level of the gun, the barometer being at 29.00″ and the thermometer at 90° F. Also, instead of computing the altitude factor, we will take it from Table V as being sufficiently accurate for this purpose.

Taking the mean altitude as two-thirds of 1500 feet, that is, 1000 feet, Table V gives us that $f=1.026$. Taking K from Table VI.

$K=$		log 0.99583	
$f=1.026$		log 0.01115	
$\delta=.921$	log 9.96426−10....	colog 0.03574	
$C=$		log 1.04272....	colog 8.95728−10
$y=1500$	log 3.17609		
$x=30000$	log 4.47712........................		log 4.47712
$p=2°\ 51'\ 45''$	tan 8.69897−10		
$z=2719.0$			log 3.43440

From Table II

$a = .01299$ $a' = .0292$ $u = 2095.1$ $t' = 1.104$

$C =$ .... log 1.04272
$a = .01299$ .... log 8.11361−10

$2\phi_e =$ .... sin 9.15633−10
$p = 2°\ 51'\ 45''$ .... cot 1.30103

$\cot p \sin 2\phi_e = 2.8665$ .... log 0.45736
$1 + \cot p \sin 2\phi_e = 3.8665$ .... log 0.58732
$p = 2°\ 51'\ 45''$ ...... sin 8.69844−10

$2\phi - p = 11°\ 07'\ 59''$ ..... sin 9.28576−10
$p = 2°\ 51'\ 45''$ $\phi = 6°\ 59'\ 52''$

$2\phi = 13°\ 59'\ 44''$ $p = 2°\ 51'\ 45''$

$\phi = 6°\ 59'\ 52''$ $\psi = 4°\ 08'\ 07''$

$2\phi = 13°\ 59'\ 44''$ .... sin 9.38356−10
$C =$ .... colog 8.95728−10

$A = .02192$ .... log 8.34084−10
$a' = .02920$

$A - a' = (-).00728$ ..... (−)log 7.86213−10
$\phi = 6°\ 59'\ 52''$ .... tan 9.08908−10 .. sec 0.00324 ... cos 9.99676−10
$A = .02192$ .... colog 1.65916
$t' = 1.104$ .... log 0.04297
$u = 2095.1$ .... log 3.32120
$C =$ .... log 1.04272

$\theta = (-)2°\ 20'\ 05''$ .. (−)tan 8.61037−10 .... sec 0.00036

$t = 12.273$ .... log 1.08893

$v = 2081.2$ .... log 3.31832

189. Now suppose that, instead of the conditions worked out above, the gun had been in a battery on the hill and the ship had been the target, all other conditions being the same. The work would have been the same down to and including the determination of the values of a, a', u and t', except that y is negative, and therefore $p = (-)2°\ 51'\ 45''$. We then proceed as before, but with this negative value of p instead of the positive one employed before, and the subsequent work becomes: **Depressed target.**

$\cot p \sin 2\phi_e = (-)2.8665$
$1 + \cot p \sin 2\phi_e = (-)1.8665$ .... (−)log 0.27103
$p = (-)2°\ 51'\ 45''$ .... (−)sin 8.69844−10

$2\phi - p = 5°\ 19'\ 32''$ .... (+)sin 8.96947−10
$p = (-)2°\ 51'\ 45''$ $\phi = 1°\ 13'\ 54''$

$2\phi = 2°\ 27'\ 47''$ $p = (-)2°\ 51'\ 45''$

$\phi = 1°\ 13'\ 54''$ $\psi = 4°\ 05'\ 39''$

$2\phi = 2°\ 27'\ 47''$			sin 8.63321−10
$C =$			colog 8.95728−10
$A =$ .00390			log 7.59049−10
$a' =$ .02920			
$A - a' = (-).02530$	(−)log 8.40312−10		
$\phi = 1°\ 13'\ 54''$	tan 8.33243−10	sec 0.00010	cos 9.99990−10
$A = .0039$	colog 2.40951		
$t' = 1.104$		log 0.04297	
$u = 2095.1$			log 3.32120
$C =$		log 1.04272	
$\theta = (-)7°\ 57'\ 01''$	(−)tan 9.14506−10		sec 0.00419
$t = 12.184$		log 1.08579	
$v = 2114.9$			log 3.32529

190. Assembling the results of these last two problems for comparison, we have:

	Value for Ship attacking battery.	Value for Battery attacking ship.
ψ	4° 08′ 07″.	4° 05′ 39″.
θ	(−)2° 20′ 05″.	(−)7° 57′ 01″.
t	12.273 seconds.	12.184 seconds.
v	2081.2 f. s.	2114.9 f. s.

In working problems similar to the above, great care must be taken to carry through consistently the signs of the several quantities and logarithms.

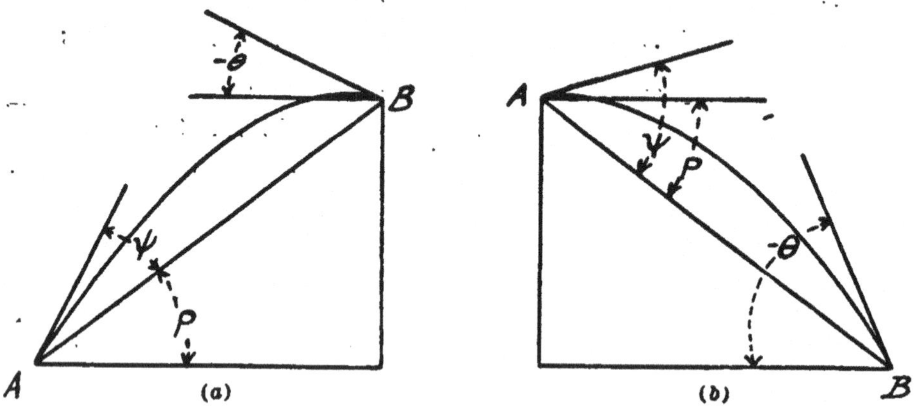

FIGURE 14.

191. From Figure 14, in which (*a*) represents the first case and (*b*) the second, we plainly see that in (*a*) the force of gravity acts to reduce the velocity of the projectile, and in (*b*) to increase it from what it would be in the horizontal trajectory. Therefore we would expect to find it necessary to give the gun a greater elevation relative to the line of sight in order to hit in (*a*) than in (*b*), and the results of the work show that such is the case.

192. Also, from the figures we can see that the angle of inclination of the curve to the horizontal at the point of impact would be greater in (*b*) than in (*a*), which is again shown by the work.

193. Also, as gravity in (a) reduces and in (b) increases the velocity, we would expect to have the remaining velocity less and the time of flight greater in (a) than in (b), and again the work shows this to be the case.

194. The angle of elevation resulting from the work is of course the angle at which the gun must be pointed above the target in either case, that is, above the line of sight AB. The sight drums are marked in yards, however, and not in degrees of elevation; so to practically set the sights we look in the range table of the gun and find in Column 2 an angle of departure equal to our found angle of elevation, and find in Column 1 the range in yards corresponding to that angle of departure. We then set our sights in range to that number of yards, and point the gun at the target, that is, bring the line of sight to coincide with the line AB of the figure. The gun is then elevated at the proper angle above the line AB, ψ from the work, and at an angle of departure above the horizontal of $\phi=\psi+p$.

195. In the problem shown in Figure 14(a), we have by a simple interpolation between Columns 1 and 2, that the range corresponding to an angle of departure of 4° 08′ 07″ is 9841 yards, which is the range at which the sight should be set.

196. Similarly, in Figure 14(b), the sight should be set for an angle of departure of 4° 05′ 39″, that is, at 9764 yards.

197. In Chapters 8, 9 and 10, and in this chapter, we have shown the methods and formulæ to be employed in solving certain of the more common and more important ballistic problems. Those selected for the purposes of this book are the ones most likely to be encountered in naval practice, but there are a large number of others that may arise under special circumstances, which may be solved by similar methods. Some of the more important of these are enumerated below, to show the scope of the methods that have been taught, for they are all solved in similar ways. In each case the solution consists of a preliminary transformation of the fundamental ballistic formulæ, in a manner similar to those shown in the preceding pages of this book, in order to fit them for use in the particular problem under consideration; and then the necessary computations may be made from the resultant equations. It should also be borne in mind that all our work has so far applied only to direct fire, as do also the problems enumerated below, and that when problems incident to mortar fire and other special classes of work are added, the number of problems that may present themselves becomes very large. Beside the problems already explained in these pages, some of the simpler direct fire problems that may be readily solved by similar methods are:

(a) Knowing X, C and v_ω; to compute V.
(b) Knowing V, C and v_ω; to compute X.
(c) Knowing V, X and C; to compute T.
(d) Knowing V, T and C; to compute v_ω.
(e) Knowing V, C and v_ω; to compute X, ϕ, ω and T.
(f) Knowing V, C and ω; to compute X, ϕ, T and v_ω.
(g) Knowing X, ϕ and C; to compute V.
(h) Knowing T, ϕ and C; to compute V.

EXAMPLE.

1. Given the data contained in the following table, compute the values of ψ, t, v and θ for the given values of x and y, both when y is positive and when it is negative; and, whenever the range tables available permit, tell how to set the sight in elevation in each case in order to hit. Correct for f from the data given.

Problem.	DATA.								
	Projectile.			Atmosphere.		Velocity. f. s.	Chart distance from gun to target. Yds.	Height of target above or below gun. Feet.	Maximum ordinate for trajectory of range x. Feet.
	d. In.	w. Lbs.	c.	Bar. In.	Ther. °F.				
A..........	3	13	1.00	31.00	5	1150	2500	± 200	252
B..........	3	13	1.00	30.90	10	2700	4000	± 350	251
C..........	4	33	0.67	30.75	20	2900	3300	± 400	70
D..........	5	50	1.00	30.33	27	3150	4200	± 450	144
E..........	5	50	0.61	30.00	33	3150	3700	± 475	75
F..........	6	105	0.61	29.80	37	2600	7300	± 600	522
G..........	6	105	1.00	29.50	32	2800	3800	± 500	109
H..........	6	105	0.61	29.25	30	2800	3100	± 460	57
I..........	7	165	1.00	29.00	40	2700	6800	± 750	518
J..........	7	165	0.61	28.50	50	2700	7200	± 800	424
K..........	8	260	0.61	28.25	55	2750	7800	± 825	456
L..........	10	510	1.00	28.00	60	2700	9700	± 850	995
M..........	10	510	0.61	28.10	75	2700	10800	± 900	952
N..........	12	870	0.61	28.07	80	2900	20500	±1500	3094
O..........	13	1130	1.00	29.00	83	2000	10500	±1100	1937
P..........	13	1130	0.74	29.15	87	2000	11000	±1000	1830
Q..........	14	1400	0.70	29.75	93	2000	13000	± 950	2637
R..........	14	1400	0.70	30.00	97	2600	13500	±1200	1630

Problem.	ANSWERS.									
	When y is positive.					When y is negative.				
	ψ.	Set sight at: Yds.	θ.	t. Secs.	v. f. s.	ψ.	Set sight at: Yds.	θ.	t. Secs.	v. f. s.
A......	7° 11.4′	.....	(—) 7° 34.4′	8.13	795	7° 08.8′	.....	(—) 10° 26.1′	8.07	807
B......	3 56.9	4308	(—) 6 09.4	8.38	948	3 56.0	4299	(—) 9 22.5	8.35	960
C......	1 28.3	3388	0 20.3	4.27	1866	1 28.1	3382	(—) 4 16.4	4.26	1875
D......	2 11.0	4364	(—) 1 48.3	6.24	1345	2 10.6	4358	(—) 5 51.3	6.22	1355
E......	1 23.3	3764	0 30.4	4.38	2059	1 22.9	3753	(—) 4 17.0	4.37	2069
F......	4 38.8	7452	(—) 5 25.1	11.60	1412	4 37.5	7429	(—) 8 27.0	11.55	1428
G......	1 54.9	3854	(—) 0 11.6	5.29	1670	1 54.6	3846	(—) 5 11.2	5.27	1691
H......	1 17.5	3117	1 18.5	3.77	2192	1 17.3	3114	(—) 4 20.6	3.76	2203
I......	4 36.0	6869	(—) 5 37.5	11.42	1244	4 34.4	6845	(—) 9 40.2	11.35	1263
J......	3 49.1	7170	(—) 3 07.8	10.23	1675	3 48.0	7145	(—) 7 17.2	10.18	1695
K......	3 49.0	7744	(—) 3 01.5	10.54	1815	3 47.9	7716	(—) 6 59.1	10.49	1835
L......	6 02.2	9543	(—) 7 46.7	15.40	1377	5 59.9	9505	(—) 10 55.3	15.31	1398
M......	5 35.5	10604	(—) 5 55.3	15.09	1741	5 33.6	10560	(—) 8 58.2	15.00	1763
N......	11 14.3	20180	(—) 16 02.3	30.72	1502	11 07.5	20046	(—) 18 16.0	30.41	1535
O......	11 15.6	10373	(—) 14 13.5	21.62	1169	11 05.8	10271	(—) 17 29.5	21.31	1206
P......	10 39.1	10879	(—) 12 30.4	21.12	1299	10 31.5	10786	(—) 15 27.7	20.87	1331
Q......	12 54.0	.....	(—) 15 57.0	25.39	1287	12 44.9	.....	(—) 18 07.7	25.09	1318
R......	7 42.8	13353	(—) 8 48.8	19.91	1645	7 39.0	13272	(—) 11 55.8	19.75	1675

CHAPTER 12.

THE EFFECT UPON THE RANGE OF VARIATIONS IN THE OTHER BALLISTIC ELEMENTS, WHICH INCLUDES THE DATA GIVEN IN COLUMNS 10, 11, 12 AND 19 OF THE RANGE TABLES.

New Symbols Introduced.

ΔX.... Variation in the range in feet.

ΔR.... Variation in the range in yards.

$\Delta(\sin 2\phi)$.... Variation in the sine of twice the angle of departure.

Δ_{VA}.... Quantity appearing in Table II, in the Δ_V column pertaining to A. With figures before the V it shows the amount of variation in V for which used. (Be careful not to confuse this symbol with ΔV or δV.)

δV.... Variation in the initial velocity. (Be careful not to confuse this symbol with Δ_{VA} or ΔV.)

ΔV.... Difference between V for two successive tables in Table II (Ingalls' table as originally computed; not the abridged tables reproduced for use with this text book) being either 50 f. s. or 100 f. s. (Be careful not to confuse this symbol with Δ_{VA} or δV.)

ΔV_w.... Variation in the initial velocity due to a variation in weight of projectile. Figures before the w show amount of variation in w in pounds.

ΔX_V.... Variation in the range in feet due to a variation in V. Figures before the V show the amount of variation in V in foot-seconds.

ΔR_V.... Variation in the range in yards due to a variation in V. Figures before the V show the amount of variation in V in foot-seconds.

ΔC.... Variation in the ballistic coefficient.

ΔX_C.... Variation in the range in feet due to a variation in C. Figures before the C show the percentage variation in that quantity.

ΔR_C.... Variation in the range in yards due to a variation in C. Figures before the C show the percentage variation in that quantity.

$\Delta\delta$.... Variation in the value of δ.

ΔX_δ.... Variation in the range in feet due to a variation in δ. Figures before the δ show the percentage variation in that quantity.

ΔR_δ.... Variation in the range in yards due to a variation in δ. Figures before the δ show the percentage variation in that quantity.

Δw.... Variation in w in pounds.

ΔX_w.... Variation in the range in feet due to a variation in w. Figures before the w show the amount of variation in that quantity in pounds.

$\Delta X_w'$.... That part of ΔX_w in feet which is due to the variation in initial velocity resulting from Δw.

$\Delta X_w''$.... That part of ΔX_w in feet which is due to Δw directly.

ΔR_w.... Variation in the range in yards due to a variation in w. Figures before the w show the amount of variation in that quantity in pounds.

$\Delta R_w'$.... That part of ΔR_w in yards which is due to the variation in initial velocity resulting from Δw.

$\Delta R_w''$.... That part of ΔR_w in yards which is due to Δw directly.

H.... Change in height of point of impact on vertical screen in feet, due to a change of ΔR in R. Figures as subscripts to the H show the change in range necessary to give that value of H.

Range tables.

198. The range tables are computed for standard conditions, but there are certain elements that are not always standard; for instance, the density of the atmosphere, which rarely is standard. The principal elements that may vary from standard are the initial velocity, variation in which may result from a variation of the temperature of the powder charge from standard or other causes; the density of the atmosphere and the weight of the projectile. In order that a satisfactory use may be made of the range tables, it is therefore necessary to include in them data showing the effect upon the trajectory of small variations from standard in the elements enumerated above. Columns 10, 11 and 12 of the range table therefore contain data showing the effect upon the range of small variations from standard in the initial velocity, in the weight of the projectile and in the density of the atmosphere, respectively. It is the province of this chapter to show how the data in these columns is derived, and also that in Column 19, which shows the effect upon the position of the point of impact in the vertical plane through the target of a small variation of the setting of the sight in range, or, as it was formerly called, the sight bar height.

199. Let us take the two principal equations of exterior ballistics, namely:

$$X = C(S_u - S_V) \tag{178}$$

$$\sin 2\phi = C\left(\frac{A_u - A_V}{S_u - S_V} - I_V\right) \tag{179}$$

These involve the range, X; the angle of departure, ϕ; the ballistic coefficient, C; and the initial velocity, V; either directly or through their functions as given in Table I. These four are the elements in which variations from standard may be expected, as indicated in the preceding paragraph; as a change in the density of the atmosphere involves a corresponding change in the value of C, and as a change in the weight of the projectile involves a corresponding change in both the initial velocity and ballistic coefficient, as will be explained later.

Formula for variations.

200. For our present purpose, therefore, we wish, if practicable, to derive from (178) and (179) a single differential equation in which all four of the quantities enumerated shall appear as variables. By a noteworthy series of mathematical combinations and differentiations, which need not be followed here, Colonel Ingalls has derived such an equation, his result being

$$\Delta(\sin 2\phi) = -C\Delta_{VA} - (B-A)\Delta C + BC\,\frac{\Delta X}{X} \tag{180}$$

In this equation the symbol Δ indicates a comparatively small difference in value or differential increment (either positive or negative) in the value of the quantity to which prefixed. C is the ballistic coefficient; ϕ is the angle of departure; A and B are Ingalls' secondary functions as they appear in Table II; and Δ_{VA} is the quantity contained in Table II in the Δ_V column pertaining to A, where Δ_{VA} is for ± 50 or ± 100 f. s. according to the table used. For 100 f. s. difference in velocity between successive tables, the solution of the above equation would give the proper result as it stands; but for 50 f. s. difference in velocity, fifty one-hundredths, or one-half, of the variation should be taken, as shown later. Great care must be exercised not to confuse the three quantities represented by the symbols Δ_{VA} as given above, δV, which represents a differential increment of the initial velocity and ΔV, which represents the difference in velocity between two successive tables in Table II. (Ingalls' tables as originally computed; not the abridged tables reprinted for use with this text book. The values of V given at the top of each table show the value of ΔV for that table.)*

201. Having the above general differential equation (180) involving all four variables with which we wish to deal, we now wish to apply it to the several cases at issue; and we will first consider the variation in range resulting from a small variation in the initial velocity; in other words, we will find out how to compute the data contained in Column 10 of the range table. For this case the initial velocity and the range are the only variables, and ΔC and Δ $(\sin 2\phi)$ therefore become zero. Equation (180) then becomes **For variation in initial velocity.**

$$\Delta X_V = \frac{\Delta_{VA}}{B} X \tag{181}$$

in which ΔX_V represents the change in range in feet resulting from a change of δV in initial velocity. To use this formula we must first compute the value of $Z = \frac{X}{C}$, and, then, from Table II, with V and Z as arguments, we may take the value of B.†

202. Suppose that we desire to compute the change in range at 10,000 yards resulting from a variation in the initial velocity of ± 50 foot-seconds from the standard, for our standard problem 12″ gun ($V = 2900$ f. s., $w = 870$ pounds, $c = 0.61$). In paragraph 157 we found that for this problem $Z = 2984.1$ and $\log C = 1.00231$. We desire our result in yards, and as there is no quantity appearing in the equation in

---

* In determining the value of Δ_{VA} from the table for use in the formula, the tabular value must be corrected by interpolation for the exact values of Z and V, as follows:

(a) Suppose we had $V = 2800$ f. s. and $Z = 3773.2$. The next lower tabular value of Δ_{VA} is .00149, and the difference between this and the next tabular value above it in value is $.00155 - .00149 = .00006$. Therefore our value for use in the formula would be

$$\Delta_{VA} = .00149 + \frac{.00006 \times 73.2}{100} = .0015339$$

which is carried out for the full limit of use with our log tables.

(b) Suppose we had $V = 2750$ f. s. and $Z = 3770.5$. The next lower tabular value of Δ_{VA} is .00167, and as in (a) the correction for Z would be $(.00173 - .00167)\frac{70.5}{100}$. The next lower tabular value of Δ_{VA}, as given above, is .00167, which is for $Z = 3700$; and turning to the table for $V = 2800$ f. s., we see that the value of Δ_{VA} for $Z = 3700$ f. s. is .00149. Therefore the variation in Δ_{VA} for 100 f. s. increase in V would be $.00149 - .00167 = -.00018$, and for 50 f. s. it would be half that. Our complete interpolation for this case would therefore be

$$\Delta_{VA} = .00167 + \frac{.00006 \times 70.5}{100} - \frac{.00018 \times 50}{100} = .0016223$$

(c) In the case of the 5″ gun for which $V = 3150$ f. s., this interpolation is further complicated by the fact that we have no table from which to determine the value of Δ_{VA} for $V = 3200$ f. s. The rate of change of Δ_{VA} at this point for an increase of 100 f. s. in initial velocity may be obtained with sufficient accuracy for every ordinary purpose as follows:

Suppose $V = 3150$ f. s. and $Z = 3770.5$
For $V = 2900$ f. s. and $Z = 3700$ we have $\Delta_{VA} = .00137$
For $V = 3100$ f. s. and $Z = 3700$ we have $\Delta_{VA} = .00111$

Therefore, for a change of V of 200 f. s. we here have a change in Δ_{VA} of $.00111 - .00137 = -.00026$. Assuming that the same rate of change continues for the next 100 f. s. increase in V, which assumption is not greatly in error, we would have that the change in the value of Δ_{VA} between $V = 3100$ f. s. and $V = 3200$ f. s. would be $\frac{1}{2}(-.00026) = -.00013$. Our interpolation would therefore become

$$\Delta_{VA} = .00111 + \frac{.00005 \times 70.5}{100} - \frac{.00013 \times 50}{100} = .0010803$$

† The convention employed in this chapter relative to the double sign ($\pm$) is that a positive sign in a result means an increase in range and a negative sign a decrease.

feet, we may use the range in yards, which will give a result also in yards. Also the difference Δ_{VA} at this point in the table is for a difference ΔV in velocity between two successive tables ($\Delta V=100$ f. s., between tables 2900 to 3000 f. s., and 3000 to 3100 f. s.), therefore we apply a factor of $\frac{\delta V}{\Delta V}\left(\frac{50}{100}\text{ in this case}\right)$. Therefore if we let ΔR_V represent the change in range in yards for a variation of $\delta V=50$ f. s. in the initial velocity, the expression becomes

$$\Delta R_V=\frac{\Delta_{VA}}{B}\times\frac{\delta V}{\Delta V}\times R$$

The work then becomes, from Table II:

$$\Delta_{VA}=.00099+\frac{.00004\times 84.1}{100}=.001024$$

$$B=.0178+\frac{.0009\times 84.1}{100}=.01856$$

$\Delta_{VA}=.001024$		log 7.01030−10
$\delta V=\pm 50$		±log 1.69897
$R=10000$		log 4.00000
$B=.01856$	log 8.26857−10	colog 1.73142
$\Delta V=100$	log 2.00000	colog 8.00000−10
$\Delta R_V=\pm 276$ yards		±log 2.44069

and the signs show that an increase in initial velocity will give an increase in range, and the reverse, which was of course to be expected.

For variation in density of atmosphere.

203. Again, suppose that the density of the air varies from standard, as it generally does, and we wish to determine the resultant effect upon the range. We know that $C=\frac{fw}{\delta c d^2}$, and in this case the only variables are X and δ, as ϕ, V and w are supposed to be constant. A change in the value of δ therefore causes a change of the same amount in the value of C, but as δ appears in the denominator of C, an increase of a certain per cent in the value of δ will cause a decrease of the same per cent in the value of C, that is, a $\pm\Delta\delta$ gives a $\mp\Delta C$. Equation (180) therefore becomes

$$BC\frac{\Delta X_C}{X}=-(B-A)\Delta C$$

or

$$\Delta X_C=-\frac{(B-A)X}{B}\times\frac{\Delta C}{C} \qquad (182)$$

204. As an example of the use of this formula, let us take the same data as in paragraph 202, and compute the change of range resulting from a variation from standard of ±10 per cent in the density of the atmosphere, letting $\Delta R_{10\delta}$ represent the desired result in yards, and again substituting R for X to get the result in yards. Equation (182) then becomes

$$\Delta R_\delta=-\frac{(B-A)R}{B}\times\frac{\Delta C}{C}=-\frac{(B-A)R}{B}\times\frac{\Delta\delta}{\delta}$$

$B=.018560$
$A=.014601$

$B-A=.003959$		log 7.59759−10
$R=10000$		log 4.00000
$B=.01856$	log 8.26857−10	colog 1.73143−10
$\frac{\Delta\delta}{\delta}=\pm .1$		±log 9.00000−10
$\Delta R_{10\delta}=\mp 213$ yards		±log 2.32902

Carrying through the signs shows that an increase in the density gives a decrease in the range, and the reverse, which was to be expected.

205. Again, suppose it is the weight of the projectile that varies, the other elements remaining fixed, and we wish to determine the resultant change in the range. This change is composed of two parts. As the charge which furnishes the propelling power for the projectile is supposed to remain fixed, a heavier projectile will leave the gun with a less initial velocity than a lighter one, which would result in a decrease in range, as already seen. The second part is the result of the change in weight affecting the flight after leaving the gun; and it will be seen that, of two shell of different weights leaving the gun with the same initial velocity, the heavier will have the greater momentum and therefore the greater range. The two effects are therefore of opposite sign, the heavier shell tending first to reduce the initial velocity with which the shell leaves the gun, but after so leaving tending to increase the range, through its greater momentum, over what would have been the range of a standard weight projectile leaving the gun with the same reduced initial velocity. This second part of the variation is represented by a change in the value of the ballistic coefficient, again, as was the case for a variation in atmospheric density, of the same per cent value as the per cent variation in the weight of the projectile, but this time with the same sign, as w appears in the numerator of the expression for the value of the ballistic coefficient. A change of $\pm \Delta w$ will therefore give a corresponding change of $\pm \Delta C$. **Effect of variation in weight of projectile.**

206. Let us now consider first the change in range due to the variation in the initial velocity resulting from the variation in the weight of the projectile. By a formula taken from interior ballistics, the derivation of which needs no inquiry here, we have **For variation in weight of projectile.**

$$\delta V = -M \frac{\Delta w}{w} V \tag{183}$$

in which $M = 0.36$ for guns $C, F, H, J, K, M, N, P, Q$ and R Other values of M were used in computing the range tables for other guns and projectiles given in the edition of the Range and Ballistic Tables published for use with this text book, but work under this head will here be confined to the guns enumerated above (for $M = 0.36$), and no inquiry into other values of M is necessary here.

And from (180)

$$\Delta X_V = \frac{\Delta_{VA}}{B} X \tag{184}$$

but Δ_{VA} is the difference for ΔV at that part of the table, and we must therefore introduce the factor $\frac{\delta V}{\Delta V}$; and we may also substitute R for X throughout, which gives us

$$\Delta R_w' = \frac{\Delta_{VA}}{B} \times \frac{\delta V}{\Delta V} \times R \tag{185}$$

in which Δ_{VA} in (184) and (185) is the quantity from Table II corresponding to the given value of Z.

207. Now for the second part of this change, that due to the variation in momentum resulting from the variation in weight, but acting only after the projectile has been expelled from the gun at the reduced initial velocity determined above, which is the part that affects the value of C. From what has already been explained we readily have for this

$$\Delta X_C = \frac{(B-A)X}{B} \times \frac{\Delta C}{C} = \frac{(B-A)X}{B} \times \frac{\Delta w}{w} \tag{186}$$

and substituting R for X to get the result in yards

$$\Delta R_w''=\frac{(B-A)R}{B}\times\frac{\Delta w}{w} \tag{187}$$

To combine the two results to get the total change in range resulting from both causes in yards, we would have

$$\Delta R_w=\Delta R_w'+\Delta R_w''=\frac{\Delta_{VA}}{B}\times\frac{\delta V}{\Delta V}\times R+\frac{(B-A)R}{B}\times\frac{\Delta w}{w} \tag{188}$$

the sign of the first term of the second member being inverted to make the last two terms of opposite sign and the final result of the proper sign.

208. As an illustration of the use of this formula, let us revert once more to our standard problem as given in paragraph 202, and compute the change in range in that case resulting from a variation from standard of ± 10 pounds in the weight of the projectile. Using the formulæ given in paragraphs 206 and 207 we have

$\Delta_{VA}=.001024$ $A=.014601$ $B=.018560$

$\Delta w=\pm 10$		$\pm$log 1.00000
$w=870$	log 2.93952	colog 7.06048−10
$V=2900$		log 3.46240
$M=.36$		log 9.55630−10
$\delta V=\mp 12$ f. s.		$\pm$log 1.07918
$\Delta_{VA}=.001024$		log 7.01030−10
$\delta V=\mp 12$		$\mp$log 1.07918
$R=10000$		log 4.00000
$B=.01856$	log 8.26857−10	colog 1.73143
$\Delta V=100$	log 2.00000	colog 8.00000−10
$\Delta R_w'=\mp 66.21$		$\mp$log 1.82091
$B=.018560$		
$A=.014601$		
$B-A=.003959$		log 7.59759−10
$R=10000$		log 4.00000
$B=.01856$	log 8.26857−10	colog 1.73143
$\Delta w=\pm 10$		$\pm$log 1.00000
$w=870$	log 2.93952	colog 7.06048−10
$\Delta R_w''=\pm 24.52$		$\pm$log 1.38950

$\Delta R_w=\mp 41.69$ **yards**

which shows that for this gun, at this range, an increase of 10 pounds above standard in the weight of the projectile decreases the range 41.6 yards, and the reverse. Note also that here a positive value of Δw gives a negative value of ΔR_w, but that in the range table there is no negative sign attached to the figures in the appropriate column. The above is of course the correct mathematical convention, but after the work is all done, as a decrease in range is the normal and general result of an increase in weight, in making up the range tables such a decrease is considered as positive and the signs in the tables are given accordingly.

Short method for variation in weight of projectile.

209. The above is the general method, but in actually computing the data for the range tables there is a short cut that may advantageously be used to reduce the amount of labor involved in the computations for Column 11. If we first compute the data for Columns 10 and 12, as is actually done in such computations and as we have already done here; that is, if we have already found, for the given range, the change in range resulting from a variation in the initial velocity of $\pm\delta V$, and also that resulting from a variation of $\pm\Delta C$ in the value of the ballistic coefficient which is the same as that due to a variation of $\mp\Delta\delta$ in the density of the air, we readily derive the following formulæ:

$$\Delta R_w' = \Delta R_V \times \frac{\delta V}{\delta V'} \tag{189}$$

$$\Delta R_w'' = \Delta R_\delta \times \frac{\Delta w}{w} \times \frac{\delta}{\Delta\delta} \tag{190}$$

$$\Delta R_w = \Delta R_w' + \Delta R_w'' = \Delta R_V \times \frac{\delta V}{\delta V'} + \Delta R_\delta \times \frac{\Delta w}{w} \times \frac{\delta}{\Delta\delta} \tag{191}$$

the two terms being combined with the proper signs.

For our given problem the work then becomes, after finding that $V=12$ f. s. in the same way that we did before

$\Delta R_V = 276$		log 2.44070
$\delta V = \mp 12$		$\mp$log 1.07918
$\delta V' = 50$	log 1.69897	colog 8.30103−10
$\Delta R_w' = \mp 66.21$		$\mp$log 1.82091
$\Delta R_\delta = 213$		log 2.32901
$\Delta w = \pm 10$		$\pm$log 1.00000
$w = 870$	log 2.93952	colog 7.06048−10
$\Delta\delta = 10$		log 1.00000
$\Delta R_w'' = \pm 24.52$		$\pm$log 1.38949
$\Delta R_w = \mp 41.62$ yards		

Note that the logarithms used above for 276 and 213 are not taken from the log table, but are the exact logarithms resulting from the previous work, as given in paragraphs 202 and 204.

The $\Delta\delta = 10$ in the last part of the above work comes in because the $\Delta R_\delta = 213$ is for 10 per cent variation in density; therefore for 100 per cent variation it would be $\Delta\delta \times \Delta R_\delta = 213 \times 10$, of which we take $\frac{\Delta w}{w} = \frac{10}{870}$.

210. We will now investigate the method of computing the data contained in Column 19 of the range tables; that is, of determining how much vertical displacement in the vertical plane through the target at the given range will result from an increase or decrease of a few yards in the setting of the sight in range; or, as it was formerly called, in the sight bar height. **Change of point of impact in vertical plane.**

211. Assuming that, for flat trajectories, when the point of fall is not far from the target as compared to the range, the portion of the trajectory between the target and the point of fall is practically a straight line, we see from Figure 15, in which $AB=\Delta X$, $AC=H$ and $ABC=\omega$, that, if we let H represent the vertical change of

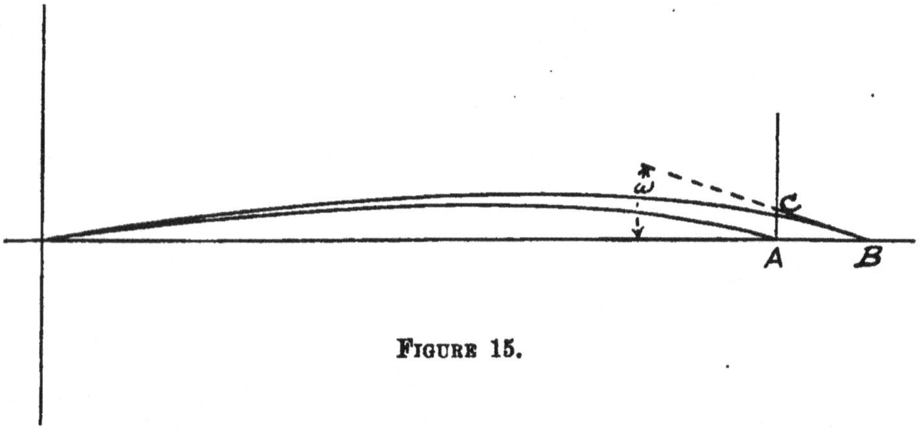

FIGURE 15.

point of impact in feet, and ΔX the change in range that will correspond, also in feet, we will have

$$\tan\omega=\frac{H}{\Delta X}, \text{ or } H=\Delta X\tan\omega \tag{192}$$

212. As an example, we will take our standard problem, for a range of 10,000 yards, and will find the change in the point of impact in the vertical plane through the target resulting from a change in sight setting of ±100 yards. By equation (192) the work becomes

$\Delta X=\pm300$	$\pm\log$ 2.47712
$\omega=5°\ 21'\ 11''$	tan 8.97174−10
$H_{100}=\pm28$ feet	$\pm\log$ 1.44886

The value of ω employed above is taken from paragraph 157 of Chapter 8, where we explained the opening work of computation relative to this particular trajectory.

EXAMPLES.

1. Require to be taken from the range tables the amount of change of range resulting from any reasonable:

(a) Variation from standard in the initial velocity.

(b) Variation from standard in the weight of the projectile.

(c) Variation from standard in the density of the atmosphere. The readings of barometer and thermometer should be given, and determination of change of range made by use of Table IV. Also exercise in the same problem, using Table III instead of Table IV.

(d) In addition to the above, call for the taking from the tables of the effect upon the range of two or more of the above variations combined.

(e) Also call for the determination from the tables of the change of the point of impact in the vertical plane resulting from a change in the setting of the sight in range, and *vice versa.*

2. Compute the change in range resulting from the variation from standard in the initial velocity given below, all other conditions being standard.

Problem.	DATA.							ANSWERS.
	Projectile.			Velocity. f. s.	Range. Yds.	Maximum. ordinate. Feet.	Variation in initial velocity. f. s.	Change in range. Yds.
	d. In.	*w.* Lbs.	*c.*					
A	3	13	1.00	1150	2000	150	+25	+ 49.8
B	3	13	1.00	2700	3600	180	—30	— 44.7
C	4	33	0.67	2900	3000	55	+50	+ 83.4
D	5	50	1.00	3150	4000	125	—60	— 08.4
E	5	50	0.61	3150	4000	90	+75	+144.8
F	6	105	0.61	2600	11500	1887	—45	—226.8
G	6	105	1.00	2800	4500	169	+50	+110.5
H	6	105	0.61	2800	3500	75	—40	— 82.9
I	7	165	1.00	2700	7000	563	+40	+127.4
J	7	165	0.61	2700	7000	395	—60	—227.9
K	8	260	0.61	2750	8000	485	+60	+260.7
L	10	510	1.00	2700	10000	1085	—45	—211.2
M	10	510	0.61	2700	11000	997	+45	+266.9
N	12	870	0.61	2900	21000	4218	—70	—647.2
O	13	1130	1.00	2000	10000	1701	+70	+460.7
P	13	1130	0.74	2000	11000	1830	—60	—467.3
Q	14	1400	0.70	2000	14000	3204	+45	+431.8
R	14	1400	0.70	2600	14000	1790	—45	—347.6

NOTE.—The above results vary slightly from those taken from the range tables. The reason for this is that the range table results are more accurately determined by using the corrected value of *C*, found by the methods of Chapter 8, Example 7; whereas in the above the value of *C* is determined by the use of a value of *f* determined by the use of the maximum ordinate given above and of Table V. The same variation from range table results will be found in all problems in which this latter process is employed.

3. Compute the change in range resulting from the variation from standard in the density of the atmosphere given below, other conditions being standard.

Problem.	DATA.							ANSWERS.
	Projectile.			Velocity. f. s.	Range. Yds.	Maximum ordinate. Feet.	Variation in density %.	Change in range. Yds.
	d. In.	*w.* Lbs	*c.*					
A	3	13	1.00	1150	1600	79	+ 5	— 10.9
B	3	13	1.00	2700	3000	104	— 7	+ 85.7
C	4	33	0.67	2000	3500	80	+10	— 83.7
D	5	50	1.00	3150	3000	57	—10	+ 90.9
E	5	50	0.61	3150	3000	45	+ 7	— 40.5
F	6	105	0.61	2600	13000	2725	— 5	+298.3
G	6	105	1.00	2800	3000	61	+ 6	— 30.7
H	6	105	0.61	2800	2500	35	— 6	+ 18.2
I	7	165	1.00	2700	6000	363	+ 8	—173.1
J	7	165	0.61	2700	6000	269	— 8	+113.3
K	8	260	0.61	2750	7000	350	+12	—190.3
L	10	510	1.00	2700	9000	807	—12	+384.3
M	10	510	0.61	2700	10000	784	+ 7	—177.8
N	12	870	0.61	2900	22000	4801	— 7	+617.5
O	13	1130	1.00	2000	9000	1292	+ 6	—155.7
P	13	1130	0.74	2000	10000	1438	— 6	+147.2
Q	14	1400	0.70	2000	13000	2637	+ 5	—176.1
R	14	1400	0.70	2600	13000	1480	— 5	+175.1

4. Compute the change in range resulting from the variation from standard in the weight of the projectile given below, other conditions being standard. Use the direct method, without the use of Columns 10 and 12 of the range tables.

Problem.	DATA. Projectile. d. In.	w. Lbs.	c.	Velocity. f. s.	Range. Yds.	Maximum ordinate. Feet.	Variation in weight. Lbs.	ANSWERS. Change in range. Yds.
C.	4	33	0.67	2900	3000	55	+ 1	—33.7
F.	6	105	0.61	2600	13600	3123	— 2	—22.2
H.	6	105	0.61	2800	2600	38	— 5	+62.0
J.	7	165	0.61	2700	6100	280	— 3	+34.1
K.	8	260	0.61	2750	7100	362	+ 4	—35.4
M	10	510	0.61	2700	10100	804	+ 5	—27.7
N.	12	870	0.61	2900	21000	4218	— 5	+ 8.3
P.	13	1130	0.74	2000	10100	1474	—15	+36.7
Q.	14	1400	0.70	2000	13100	2690	+12	—26.0
R.	14	1400	0.70	2600	13100	1509	—12	+28.4

NOTE.—The signs in the above results are mathematically correct; that is, a positive result means an increase in range. But remember the convention reversing these signs in the range tables, whereby a positive sign (or no sign) means a decrease in range, the normal and most common result of an increase in weight of projectile.

5. Compute the change in range resulting from the variation from standard in the weight of the projectile given below, other conditions being standard; using the data from Columns 10 and 12 of the range tables.

Problem.	DATA. Projectile. d. In.	w. Lbs.	c.	V. f. s.	Range. Yds.	Variation in weight. Lbs.	Col. 10. Change in range for var. of ±50 f. s. in *I. V.* Yds.	Col. 12 Change in range for var. of ±10% in density. Yds.	ANSWERS. Change in Range. Yds.
C	4	33	0.67	2900	4000	+ 1	103	109	—32.1
F	6	105	0.61	2600	12000	— 2	260	531	— 8.4
H	6	105	0.61	2800	3500	— 5	103	57	+71.7
J	7	165	0.61	2700	7000	— 5	190	188	+55.0
K	8	260	0.61	2750	8000	+ 7	217	204	—60.8
M	10	510	0.61	2700	11000	+ 8	296	300	—43.2
N	12	870	0.61	2900	18500	— 8	432	648	+23.4
P	13	1130	0.74	2000	11000	—12	391	286	+29.4
Q	14	1400	0.70	2000	14000	+12	484	392	—26.1
R	14	1400	0.70	2600	14000	—13	388	395	+30.8

NOTE.—See note to Example 4 about signs, which applies to this example also.

6. Compute the change in the position of the point of impact in the vertical plane through the target for the following variations in the setting of the sight in range, taking the values of the angle of fall from the range tables. Conditions standard.

Problem.	DATA.						ANSWERS.
	Projectile.			Velocity. f. s.	Range. Yds.	Variation in setting of sight in range. Yds. += incr'se. —= decr'se.	Change in point of impact. Ft. += raise. —= lower.
	d. In.	W. Lbs.	c.				
A	3	13	1.00	1150	2100	+ 50	+17.4
B	3	13	1.00	2700	3600	— 50	—13.5
C	4	33	0.67	2900	4000	+100	+13.2
D	5	50	1.00	3150	3600	—100	—12.9
E	5	50	0.61	3150	3600	+ 75	+ 6.6
F	6	105	0.61	2600	14000	— 75	—98.4
G	6	105	1.00	2800	3600	+ 60	+ 7.4
H	6	105	0.61	2800	3100	— 60	— 4.7
I	7	165	1.00	2700	6600	+ 80	+29.5
J	7	165	0.61	2700	6600	— 80	—19.2
K	8	260	0.61	2750	7600	+ 90	+23.2
L	10	510	1.00	2700	9600	— 90	—45.9
M	10	510	0.61	2700	10600	+110	+44.0
N	12	870	0.61	2900	17000	—110	—75.5
O	13	1130	1.00	2000	9600	+ 70	+53.1
P	13	1130	0.74	2000	10600	— 70	—51.0
Q	14	1400	0.70	2000	13600	+ 60	+61.4
R	14	1400	0.70	2600	13600	— 60	—34.6

PART III.

THE VARIATION OF THE TRAJECTORY FROM A PLANE CURVE.

INTRODUCTION TO PART III.

Having completed the consideration of the general trajectory in air for all velocities when considered as a plane curve, by means of the differential equations connected therewith, and having seen that for the purposes discussed in Parts I and II no material error is introduced into the results by such assumption that the trajectory is a plane curve, we now come to the question of how to hit a given spot with the projectile from a given gun, under given conditions, so far as the deflection of the projectile from the original plane of fire is concerned. Although such variation will not materially affect the results of computations of the values of the ranges, angles, velocities, times, etc., as already shown, it will at once be apparent that a variation of a very few yards from the original plane of fire will cause a miss, unless compensated for in the sighting of the gun. In Part III we therefore take up the study of the forces acting to deflect the projectile from the original plane of fire, thereby causing a miss unless compensated. These are drift, wind and motion of the gun or target; and expressions will be derived to determine the extent of the deflections arising from each cause, and methods will be devised for applying the necessary corrections in aiming to overcome these errors.

CHAPTER 13.

DRIFT AND THE THEORY OF SIGHTS, INCLUDING THE COMPUTATION OF THE DATA CONTAINED IN COLUMN 6 OF THE RANGE TABLES.

New Symbols Introduced.

$\mu = \frac{k^2}{R^2}$....In which k is the radius of gyration of the projectile about its longitudinal axis, and R is the radius of the projectile.

$\frac{\lambda}{h}$....A special ratio explained in the text.

n....Twist of the rifling at the muzzle.

D'....Ingalls' secondary function for drift.

D....Drift in yards.

l....Sight radius.

i....Permanent angle.

h....Sight bar height in inches.

D....Deflection in yards (used with R in yards).

213. Experience shows that the projectile from any rifled gun, when fired in still air, deviates from the plane of fire (a vertical plane through the axis of the gun) to an extent approximately proportional to the square of the time of flight, and in the direction towards which the upper surface of the projectile moves in its rotation. This deviation is called the "drift," and for all United States naval guns is to the right, since these guns are so rifled that their projectiles, viewed from the rear, rotate with the hands of a watch when in flight. **Drift.**

214. Since the drift increases more rapidly in proportion than does the range, the horizontal projection of the trajectory is really a curve convex to the horizontal trace of the plane of fire. Nevertheless, though the absolute value of the drift, especially at long ranges, is too great to be neglected in the practical use of guns, its relative value is always small enough to justify the assumption hitherto made that the trajectory is a plane curve, so far as the purposes for which we proceeded on that assumption are concerned. In other words, the actual trajectory differs so little from its projection upon the plane of fire that no appreciable error results from regarding them as coincident in taking account of the effect of the resistance of the atmosphere upon the range, time of flight, etc. When it comes to the question of hitting a given target, however, where a very few yards deviation from the original plane of fire will, if not compensated, make the difference between a hit and a miss, the case is far different, and the drift must therefore be taken into account in discussing the sighting of guns.

215. The cause of drift is that, soon after the projectile leaves the gun, the line of action of the air resistance ceases to coincide with the axis of the projectile, on account of the curvature of the trajectory; and, meeting that axis obliquely between the point of the projectile and the center of gravity, tends to raise the point; which action, combined with that of the rotation, causes the point to move first to one side (to the right for right-handed rotation) and then downward. This movement, by virtue of which the axis of the projectile tends to describe a cone about the tangent to the trajectory, is called the "precession," and its result, in combination with the angular motion of the tangent caused by the curvature of the trajectory, is to keep the point of the projectile always on that side of the plane of fire towards which it **Cause of drift.**

was first deflected. (The imprints of projectiles at their points of fall upon the ground at long ranges show this to be the case.) Therefore, with right-handed rifling, the projectile during its flight always points very slightly to the right of the direction of motion; and, as a result, the resistance of the air has a component normal to that direction, which carries the projectile bodily to the right with increasing velocity. (This applies only to direct fire. When the angle of departure exceeds 70°, as it sometimes does in mortar fire, the drift is reversed in direction. The reason for this appears to be that, at the vertex of the trajectory, the direction of the tangent changes so suddenly that the slow movement of precession is insufficient to cause the axis of the projectile to keep pace with it. The angle between the tangent and the axis of the projectile therefore becomes greater than 90°; the projectile moves approximately base first; the resistance of the air acts upon the opposite side of the projectile from that upon which it acted in the ascending branch of the curve; and the lateral movement to the right is speedily checked and reversed. With these very high angle trajectories the projectile always strikes base first.)

Computation of drift.

216. The precise experimental determination of the amount of drift is a matter of great difficulty, as its value is materially affected by lateral wind pressure and by unavoidable differences between different projectiles. For computing its value, Mayevski derived an approximate formula, which has been reduced by Ingalls to the form

$$D = \frac{\mu}{n} \times \frac{\lambda}{h} \times \frac{C^2 D'}{\cos^3 \phi} \qquad (193)$$

In which

$\mu = \frac{k^2}{R^2}$, where k is the radius of gyration of the projectile and R is its radius.

$\frac{\lambda}{h}$ = a quantity which depends upon the length of the projectile, the shape of the head, the angle which the resultant resistance makes with the axis and the distance of the center of pressure from the center of gravity.

n = the twist of the rifling in calibers at the muzzle, that is, the distance in calibers that the projectile advances along the trajectory at the muzzle while making one revolution.

C = the ballistic coefficient.

ϕ = the angle of departure.

D' = Ingalls' secondary function for drift, to be found in Table II, with V and Z as arguments.

D = drift in yards for the given range and angle of departure.

217. It has also been found necessary in some cases to multiply the results obtained by the use of the above formula by a certain empirical multiplier in order to get correct results. The data required for the drift computation is therefore:

Problem.	DATA.							
	Gun and projectile.			Velocity. f. s.	μ.	$\frac{\lambda}{h}$.	n.	Multiplier.
	d. In.	w. Lbs.	c.					
A	3	13	1.00	1150	0.53	0.32	25	1.0
B	3	13	1.00	2700	0.53	0.32	25	1.0
C	4	33	0.67	2900	0.53	0.32	25	1.0
D	5	50	1.00	3150	0.53	0.32	25	1.5
E	5	50	0.61	3150	0.53	0.32	25	1.5
F	6	105	0.61	2600	0.53	0.32	25	1.5
G	6	105	1.00	2800	0.53	0.32	25	1.0
H	6	105	0.61	2800	0.53	0.32	25	1.5
I	7	165	1.00	2700	0.53	0.32	25	1.0
J	7	165	0.61	2700	0.53	0.32	25	1.5
K	8	260	0.61	2750	0.53	0.32	25	1.5
L	10	510	1.00	2700	0.53	0.32	25	1.0
M	10	510	0.61	2700	0.53	0.32	25	1.5
N	12	870	0.61	2900	0.53	0.32	25	1.5
O	13	1130	1.00	2000	0.53	0.32	25	1.0
P	13	1130	0.74	2000	0.53	0.32	25	1.5
Q	14	1400	0.70	2000	0.53	0.32	25	1.5
R	14	1400	0.70	2600	0.53	0.32	25	1.5

218. Returning to our standard problem, we will compute the drift for the 12″ gun ($V=2900$ f. s., $w=870$ pounds, $c=0.61$) for a range of 10,000 yards, for which conditions we found in Chapter 8 that the angle of departure was 4° 13′ 14″, $Z=2984.1$ and $\log C=1.00231$. The computation then becomes

1.5		log 0.17609
$\mu=0.53$		log 9.72428−10
$\frac{\lambda}{h}=0.32$		log 9.50515−10
$n=25$	log 1.39794	colog 8.60206−10
$C=$	log 1.00231	2 log 2.00462
$D'=25.7$		log 1.40824
$\phi=4°\ 13'\ 14''$	sec 0.00118	3 sec 0.00354
$D=26.5$ yards		log 1.42398

219. Guns are usually, and naval guns always, pointed by directing what is called the "line of sight" at the target. Originally the upper surface of the gun itself was used as the line of sight; this was called "sighting by the line of metal," and resulted in giving to the gun an angular elevation corresponding to the difference in thickness of metal at the breech and at the muzzle. Later on, a piece of wood, called a "dispart," was secured to the muzzle, so as to give a line from breech to muzzle parallel to the axis of the gun. Such a line of sight had to be directed more or less above the target according to the range. Early in the last century came into use the method of having one fixed and one movable sight, so that the line between them, which is the line of sight, could be adjusted at any desired angle with the axis of the gun. The rear sight was usually the movable one. At the present time the most approved form of sight, and practically the only one in use in the navy, is that **Sights.**

in which a telescope has been substituted for the old pair of sights, front and rear. This telescope is so mounted that it is capable of being set at any desired angle with the axis of the gun, within necessary limits. The principles involved in the telescopic sight are the same as in the old bar sights, but in the former they are not so clearly apparent or so easily studied as in the latter. For this reason we will take up the theory of sights from the point of view of the old system of bar sights, rear sight adjustable, and the application of these theories to the telescopic sight will be plainly apparent.

Theory of bar sights.

220. The rear sight being movable, it is customary to graduate its bar in yards of range (and sometimes with the elevation in degrees corresponding to the range in yards), and sometimes there is added the time of flight in seconds corresponding to each range, this last information being for use in setting time fuses when using shrapnel, etc. This information is ordinarily not placed on the range scale of a telescopic sight, which shows only the range in yards; and if such information be wanted it must be taken from the range table for the gun which is now furnished to ships.

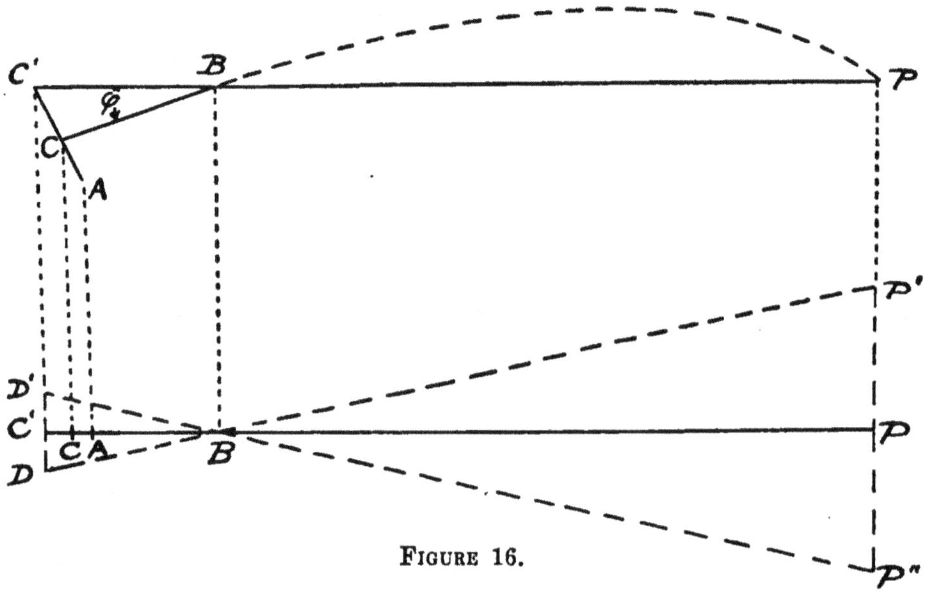

FIGURE 16.

Sight bar height.

221. Figure 16 represents the usual arrangement of bar sights, AC' being the movable graduated rear sight bar, at right angles to the axis of the gun, and B the fixed front sight. $C'B$ is the line of sight, being a line from the notch in the rear sight C' to the top of the front sight B, and CB is the position of the line of sight when it is parallel to the axis of the gun, the rear sight notch being then lowered to C, usually its lowest position. The distance $CB=l$ is called the "sight radius" of the gun, and the line CB is sometimes called the "natural line of sight." It will be seen that when the rear sight notch is raised to C', and the line of sight $C'B$ is directed at the target P, the axis of the gun, which is parallel to CB, is elevated at the angle $CBC'=\psi$, or the angle of elevation above the target. As we will deal only with horizontal trajectories, and disregard jump, the angle of departure will be equal to the angle of elevation, so $CBC'=\psi=\phi$. The distance $CC'=h$ is the "sight bar height" for the angle of departure ϕ, and it is evidently given by the equation

$$h=l \tan \phi \tag{194}$$

When the heights for the range graduations of the sight bar are to be computed the above formula is used.

222. In Figure 16 the trajectory is represented as though the axis of the gun coincided with the line of sight, instead of being, as it really is, offset from it by at least the radius of the breech of the gun. No appreciable error, however, results from making this assumption in the ordinary use of guns, except in the case of turret guns, where the pointers' sights may be located at a considerable distance from the axis of the gun, in the turret or in the pointers' hoods. In this case this distance must be allowed for in figuring on the fall of shot, and it is customary in bore sighting these guns to so adjust the sights that the line of sight of each of them will intersect the axis of the bore prolonged at the most probable fighting range. At the proving ground, where extreme accuracy is necessary, as in attacking armor plates, etc., it is customary to use bore sights in sighting the gun, thus eliminating the error due to the offset of the line of sight of the regular sights from the axis of the gun.

223. Besides the movement of the rear sight up and down to enable the gun to be pointed with the proper elevation, it is desirable to have some means of moving it sideways, so that the line of sight may be adjusted at any desired angle with the axis of the gun, within reasonable limits, in the horizontal plane as well as in the vertical. This is for the purpose of allowing for drift or other lateral deviations of the projectile, by causing the gun to point the proper amount to one side of the target at which the line of sight is directed. In the bar sight this is usually done by forming the rear sight notch in a "sliding leaf," a piece mounted on the head of the sight bar and movable by suitable mechanism at right angles to the sight bar and to the axis of the gun. **Sliding leaf.**

224. In Figure 16, D and D' represent two positions of the sliding leaf on opposite sides of the central position C'. Evidently, if the line of sight $D'B$ be directed at the target P'', and there be no deviation of the projectile in flight, the latter will fall at P; and so a movement $C'D'=d_1$ of the sliding leaf *to the left* will cause the projectile to fall $P''P=D_1$ *to the left* of the point aimed at P''. And, similarly, the moving of the sliding leaf $C'D=d_2$ *to the right* will cause the projectile to fall $P'P=D_2$ *to the right* of the point aimed at, P'. Therefore to correct for a deviation of the projectile due to drift, wind, motion of the gun or target, or any other cause, the sliding leaf is moved in the opposite direction to the deviation, and we have the general rule:

> *Move the sliding leaf (or rear, or eye end of the telescope) to the side towards which you wish the projectile to go.*

Also, for the relation between the motion, d, of the sliding leaf and the resulting deviation, D, of the projectile, we have from similar triangles

$$\frac{DC'}{C'B}=\frac{P'P}{PB} \quad \text{or} \quad \frac{d}{l \sec \phi}=\frac{D}{X}$$

whence

$$d=\frac{l \sec \phi}{X} D^{*} \qquad (195)$$

The error which results from putting $\sec \phi=1$ in (195) is inappreciable for the small angles of departure required in the ordinary use of modern guns, being only one-half of 1 per cent for $\phi=6°$; and, as it is only a little over 3 per cent for $\phi=15°$, the limit of elevation possible with our usual naval gun mounts; and, as the value of D to be allowed for is seldom as closely known as that, it is evident that in direct fire, under all ordinary circumstances, we may use

$$d=\frac{l}{X} D \qquad (196)$$

---

* D and X must be in the same units, either both feet or both yards, d will then come in the same units as l, usually inches.

Permanent angle.

225. It was common practice with naval guns and bar sights to correct for the greater part of the drift automatically by inclining the bar sight in a plane perpendicular to the axis of the bore of the gun, so as to make with the vertical an angle i called the "permanent angle." Referring to Figure 17, we see that the three points D, C and C' are in the same plane, which is perpendicular to the line CB, the angles $CC'D$ and $BC'D$ being right angles; the points B, C and C' are all three in the same plane, which is at right angles to DCC'; B, C' and D are in the same plane, which is at right angles to BCC'; and, similarly, for P, P' and Q. Then we have that

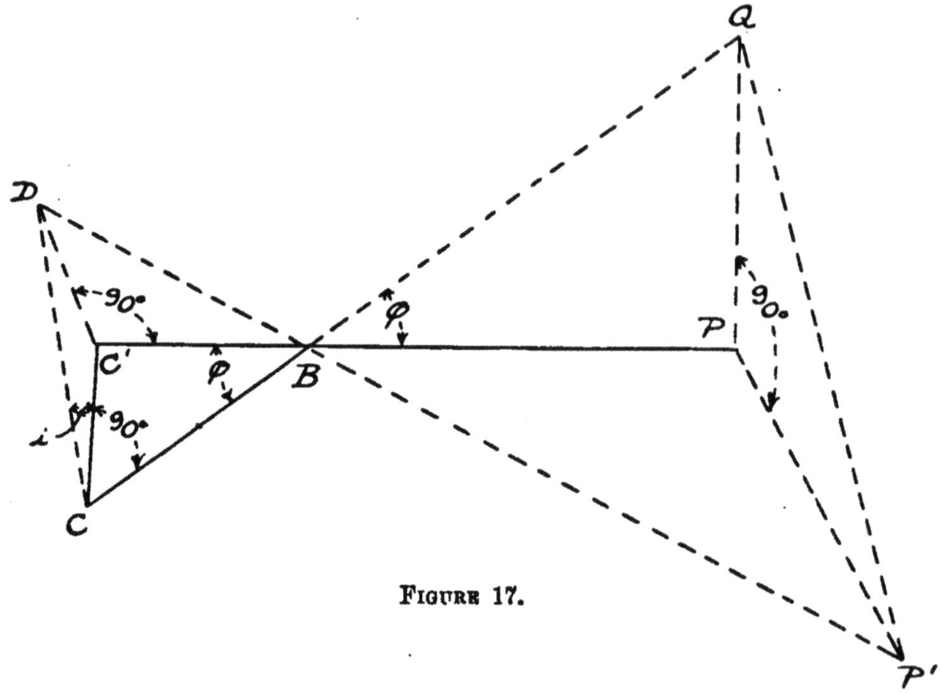

FIGURE 17.

$CB=l$, being the natural line of sight, and $CD=h$ is the sight bar height for the angle of departure ϕ, and is now given by

$$h=l \tan \phi \sec i \tag{197}$$

Then if PP' be the drift in yards, at the range R, from the similar triangles we have $\frac{DC'}{C'B} = \frac{D}{R}$; but $DC' = h \sin i = l \tan \phi \tan i$, and $C'B = l \sec \phi$. Therefore $\frac{\tan \phi \tan i}{\sec \phi} = \sin \phi \tan i = \frac{D}{R}$, whence we have

$$\tan i = \frac{D}{R \sin \phi}^{*} \tag{198}$$

226. If D were proportional to $X \sin \phi$, which it is not far from being, setting the sight bar at the permanent angle i given by (198) would exactly compensate for drift at all ranges. Actually, however, D increases a little more rapidly in proportion than $X \sin \phi$, and so the sight should be more inclined for long than for short ranges. In practice, when bar sights are used, it is customary to compute the value

* D and R must be in the same units. In the above equation they are both expressed in yards.

of i for an assumed average fighting range, and to set the bar at that permanent angle, leaving any uncompensated drift at other ranges to be corrected by setting the sliding leaf while using it to correct for deviations due to wind and speed.

227. The telescopic sight is now almost universally adopted, its great advantage being that with it the line of sight, which is the optical axis of the telescope, is much more clearly defined and can be directed with much greater accuracy than is the case with the old bar sight. Also, as the eye is held close to the telescope in pointing, which could not be done with the old sights, the parallactic errors, which it was formerly almost impossible to avoid, are now practically eliminated. The theory of the telescopic sight in no way differs from that of the bar sight as explained in the preceding paragraphs, however, but the mechanical features of the bar sight are such that the bar itself actually establishes the system of triangles with which we have been dealing and from which the mathematical relations are plainly apparent. With the telescopic sight, however, with both ranges and deflections marked on rotary drums, circular discs, etc., the motion of which is transferred to the telescope itself by gearing, or any similar devices ordinarily in use, the triangles are not readily apparent, although the relations arising from them of course still exist; the sight radius in the bar sight being replaced in the telescopic mounting by the distance from the pivot of the sight yoke to the circle of graduations on the sword arm, that is, by the radius of curvature of the scale on the sword arm. **Telescopic sights.**

228. In the telescopic sight the telescope is so mounted that it can be set at any desired vertical angle with the axis of the gun, within practical limits, thus enabling the gun to be pointed at the proper elevation, the elevating scale being marked in yards in range computed for the corresponding angle between the line of sight and the axis of the bore. The telescope can also be rotated, within reasonable limits, about its vertical axis, which corrects for deviation in the horizontal plane exactly as did setting over the sliding leaf of the bar sight; the rotation of the telescope about its vertical axis being recorded on the deflection scale, which is marked in "knots," the knots thus indicated corresponding to speed of target. The reasons for this graduation and the method of using it will be explained later, in the chapter describing the use of the range tables. Drift is not compensated for in the mounting of this sight, but as the gun is elevated the pointer on the deflection scale moves up or down over the scale, and the line on the scale for each knot setting of the sight in deflection, instead of being a straight line, is a curve so computed and laid on the scale that when the deflection pointer is on it the drift is compensated, no matter what the range may be. This system, while not automatic, gives perfect compensation for drift at all ranges, which the old permanent angle system did not, as we have already seen, and introduces no troubles or errors into the actual process of setting the sight which would not exist without it. (See Appendix C for a description of the system of arbitrary deflection scales now in use for turret guns.)

EXAMPLES.

1. Compute the drift in yards for the following conditions, taking the angle of departure and the maximum ordinate from the range tables. Conditions standard.

Problem.	DATA.					ANSWERS.
	Projectile.			Velocity. f. s.	Range. Yds.	Drift. Yds.
	d. In.	*w.* Lbs.	*c.*			
A	3	13	1.00	1150	2500	7.5
B	3	13	1.00	2700	4000	8.5
C	4	33	0.67	2900	3500	2.4
D	5	50	1.00	3150	4000	5.8
E	5	50	0.61	3150	3700	3.3
F	6	105	0.61	2600	10500	69.4
G	6	105	1.00	2800	3800	3.2
H	6	105	0.61	2800	3200	2.6
I	7	165	1.00	2700	7000	17.6
J	7	165	0.61	2700	6700	15.7
K	8	260	0.61	2750	8000	21.5
L	10	510	1.00	2700	10000	33.9
M	10	510	0.61	2700	11000	44.3
N	12	870	0.61	2900	22000	233.8
O	13	1130	1.00	2000	10000	52.1
P	13	1130	0.74	2000	11000	82.9
Q	14	1400	0.70	2000	14000	148.1
R	14	1400	0.70	2600	14500	89.3

2. Compute the sight bar heights in inches, and the distance in inches that the sliding leaf must be set over for the data given in the following table, conditions being standard.

Problem.	DATA.						ANSWERS.		
	Gun.		Range. Yds.	ϕ.	Sight radius or radius of curvature of sword arm. In.	Deflection to be compensated. Yds.	Sight bar height. In.	Set of sliding leaf.	
	Cal. In.	*I. V.* f. s.						Inches.	Right or left.
A	3	1150	1700	4° 19′ 06″	24.750	25 R.	1.869	0.365	Left
B	3	2700	3600	2 48 54	28.625	20 L.	1.408	0.159	Right
C	4	2900	3100	1 18 42	45.900	40 L.	1.051	0.592	Right
D	5	3150	4000	1 53 12	58.500	50 R.	1.927	0.732	Left
E	5	3150	4500	1 45 48	42.625	30 R.	1.312	0.284	Left
F	6	2600	13500	12 20 18	42.625	75 L.	9.324	0.242	Right
G	6	2800	4100	2 05 18	42.625	50 R.	1.554	0.520	Left
H	6	2800	3400	1 25 42	42.625	30 L.	1.063	0.376	Right
I	7	2700	7000	4 44 48	55.850	100 R.	4.637	0.801	Left
J	7	2700	6700	3 28 48	62.500	75 L.	3.801	0.701	Right
K	8	2750	7800	3 51 12	41.125	50 R.	2.770	0.264	Left
L	10	2700	9700	6 11 42	44.675	60 L.	4.849	0.278	Right
M	10	2700	10900	5 48 18	44.675	50 R.	4.542	0.206	Left
N	12	2900	23500	14 12 12	47.469	150 L.	12.014	0.313	Right
O	13	2000	9600	10 03 18	61.094	70 R.	10.833	0.452	Left
P	13	2000	10800	10 32 42	61.094	60 R.	11.373	0.345	Left
Q	14	2000	13600	13 54 00	36.219	50 L.	8.963	0.137	Right
R	14	2600	14000	8 14 06	36.219	75 L.	5.242	0.196	Right

NOTE.—The data given in the sight radius column is approximate only, and must not be accepted as reliable. The computed sight bar heights and the set of the sliding leaf are for the old bar sight. To use them for the telescopic sight they must be transformed as necessary into the proper distances for marking on sword arm scales or range or deflection scales, as the case may be. These supplementary computations have to do with the mechanical features of the sight only, and not with the principles of exterior ballistics, and are therefore not considered here.

CHAPTER 14.

THE EFFECT OF WIND UPON THE MOTION OF THE PROJECTILE. THE EFFECT OF MOTION OF THE GUN UPON THE MOTION OF THE PROJECTILE. THE EFFECT OF MOTION OF THE TARGET UPON THE MOTION OF THE PROJECTILE RELATIVE TO THE TARGET. THE EFFECT UPON THE MOTION OF THE PROJECTILE RELATIVE TO THE TARGET OF ALL THREE MOTIONS COMBINED. THE COMPUTATION OF THE DATA CONTAINED IN COLUMNS 13, 14, 15, 16, 17 AND 18 OF THE RANGE TABLES.

New Symbols Introduced.

W....Real wind, velocity in feet per second.
β....Angle between wind and line of fire.
W_x....Component of W in line of fire in feet per second.
W_{12x}....Wind component of 12 knots in line of fire in feet per second.
W_z....Component of W perpendicular to line of fire in feet per second.
W_{12z}....Wind component of 12 knots perpendicular to line of fire in feet per second.
X....Range in feet without considering wind.
X'....Range in feet considering wind.
V....Initial velocity in foot-seconds without considering wind.
V'....Initial velocity in foot-seconds considering wind.
ϕ....Angle of departure without considering wind.
ϕ'....Angle of departure considering wind.
T....Time of flight in seconds without considering wind.
T'....Time of flight in seconds considering wind.
ΔX_W....Variation in range in feet due to W_x.
ΔX_{12W}....Variation in range in feet due to a wind component of 12 knots in line of fire.
ΔR_W....Variation in range in yards due to W_x.
ΔR_{12W}....Variation in range in yards due to a wind component of 12 knots in line of fire.
γ....Angle between trajectories relative to air and relative to ground.
D_W....Deflection in yards due to wind component W_z perpendicular to line of fire.
D_{12W}....Deflection in yards due to wind component of 12 knots perpendicular to line of fire.
G....Motion of gun in feet per second.
G_x....Component of G in line of fire in feet per second.
G_{12x}....Motion of gun of 12 knots in line of fire in feet per second.
G_z....Component of G perpendicular to line of fire in feet per second.
G_{12z}....Motion of gun of 12 knots perpendicular to line of fire in feet per second.
ΔX_G....Variation in range in feet due to G_x.
ΔX_{12G}....Variation in range in feet due to a motion of gun in line of fire of 12 knots.
ΔR_G....Variation in range in yards due to G_x.
ΔR_{12G}....Variation in range in yards due to a motion of gun in line of fire of 12 knots.

D_G.... Deflection in yards due to a motion of gun of G_z perpendicular to line of fire.

D_{12G}.... Deflection in yards due to a motion of gun of 12 knots perpendicular to line of fire.

T.... Motion of target in feet per second.

T_x.... Motion of target in line of fire in feet per second.

T_{12x}.... Motion of target of 12 knots in line of fire in feet per second.

T_z.... Motion of target perpendicular to line of fire in feet per second.

T_{12z}.... Motion of target of 12 knots perpendicular to line of fire in feet per second.

ΔX_T.... Variation in range in feet due to T.

ΔX_{12T}.... Variation in range in feet due to a motion of target of 12 knots in line of fire.

ΔR_T.... Variation in range in yards due to T.

ΔR_{12T}.... Variation in range in yards due to a motion of target of 12 knots in line of fire.

D_T.... Deflection in yards due to a motion of target T_z perpendicular to line of fire.

D_{12T}.... Deflection in yards due to a motion of target of 12 knots perpendicular to line of fire.

a.... Angle of real wind with course of ship.

a'.... Angle of apparent wind with course of ship.

W_1.... Velocity of real wind in knots per hour.

W_2.... Velocity of apparent wind in knots per hour.

Section 1.—The Effect of Wind Upon the Motion of the Projectile.

229. In considering the effect of wind upon the flight of the projectile, we are obliged, for want of a better knowledge, to assume that the air moves horizontally only, and that its direction and velocity are the same throughout the trajectory as we observe them to be at the gun. Actually the wind is never steady, either in force or in direction; its velocity usually increases with the height above the gun, and its motion is not always confined to the horizontal plane. Moreover, lateral wind pressure alters the drift due to rotation.

230. It is for these reasons that the deviations caused by the wind can only be roughly approximated; and, consequently, that experiments for determining any of the ballistic constants, to be of value, must be made when it is calm or very nearly so.

Primary planes.

231. Let us denote by W the velocity of the wind in feet per second, and by W_x and W_z, respectively, the components of that velocity in and at right angles to the plane of fire. Also let us call W_x positive when it is with the flight of the projectile, and negative when it is against it. Let us also call W_z positive when it tends to carry the projectile from right to left of an observer looking from gun to target, and negative in the opposite case. In Figure 18 let us denote by β the angle between the direction from gun to target and the direction towards which the wind is blowing, measuring the angle to the left from the first direction around to the second.

Then in Figure 18(a), β is in the first quadrant, and W_x is blowing with the projectile and is positive, and W_z causes lateral motion to the left and is also positive. In Figure 18(b), β is in the second quadrant, and W_x is negative and W_z is positive. In Figure 18(c), β is in the third quadrant, and both W_x and W_z are negative. In Figure 18(d), β is in the fourth quadrant, and W_x is positive and W_z is negative. Note especially that, in the system of notation adopted, β is the angle between the plane of fire and the direction *towards* and not that *from* which the wind is blowing.

(In a later chapter dealing with practical service problems concerning the wind, it will be found that the wind is generally stated as *coming from* a given direction, but the reverse convention is used in this chapter. Bear the difference constantly in mind and do not be confused by it.)

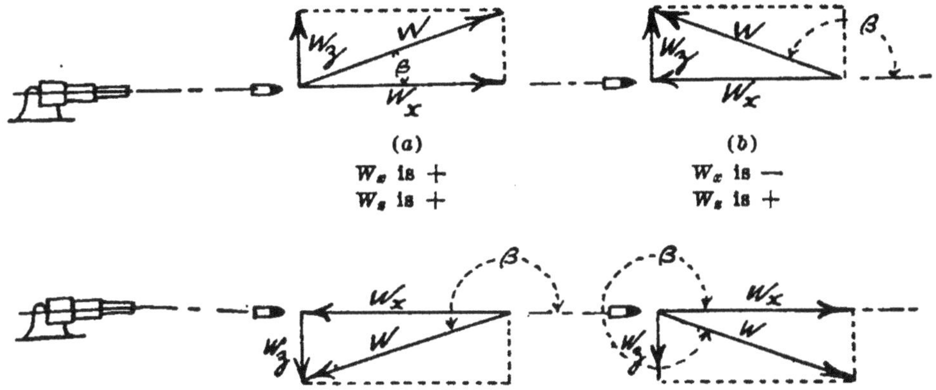

(a) W_x is + W_z is +

(b) W_x is − W_z is +

(c) W_x is − W_z is −

(d) W_x is + W_z is −

FIGURE 18.

232. By an examination of the figure we see that, no matter what the direction of the wind, we shall always have its components in the two primary reference planes given with their proper signs by the two expressions:

$$W_x = W \cos \beta \qquad (199)$$

$$W_z = W \sin \beta \qquad (200)$$

233. The respective values of the wind components being thus found, they are hereafter treated as though independent of each other, each producing its own effect in its own primary plane only.

234. To find the effect of the wind upon the range, let W_x be the wind component in the plane of fire in feet per second, positive when with the flight of the projectile and negative when against it; let V and ϕ be the initial velocity and angle of departure, respectively, *relative to still air or to the ground,* which is of course stationary; and let X be the range in feet for this initial velocity and angle of departure, that is, relative to the ground or to still air. **Effect in range.**

235. Let us now designate by X', V' and ϕ' the range, initial velocity and angle of departure, respectively, *relative to the moving air,* of a projectile fired with a range of X, initial velocity of V, and angle of departure of ϕ *relative to still air or to the ground,* and by dV and $d\phi$ the differences between V and V' and ϕ and ϕ', respectively. Let us designate by T' and T the corresponding times of flight. Now let us suppose that the wind component along the line of flight, W_x, is blowing with the flight of the projectile; in which case, while the projectile is in flight, the air through which it is traveling moves in the same direction, carrying the projectile with it a distance W_xT'. Then the total horizontal distance traveled by the projectile *relative to the ground or to still air* will be $X' + W_xT'$. As the normal range *relative to the ground* corresponding to V and ϕ is X, then the difference between the two ranges, or the change in range caused by the wind, would be

$$\Delta X = X' + W_xT' - X \qquad (201)$$

Force diagrams. 236. In order to use the above equation it is necessary to determine the values of X' and T', and we can do this by methods previously explained if we can determine the corresponding values of V' and ϕ'. This we can do if we can find the values of dV and $d\phi$. To do this let us draw the triangle of forces acting in this case (and also for a negative wind). We would have the results as shown in Figure 19.

Figure 19(a) is for a positive wind, for which W_x is positive (being drawn in the proper direction for constructing a triangle of forces with all parts of proper relation to one another), and from the diagram it will be seen that $OA = V$ combined with

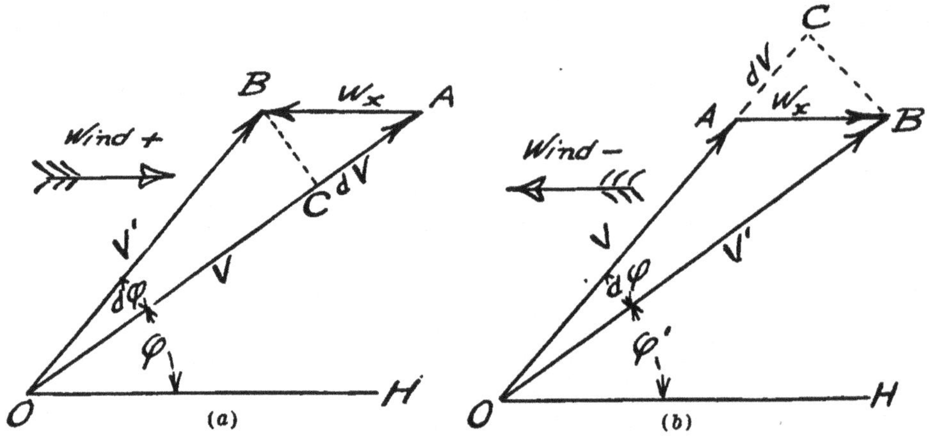

FIGURE 19.

$AB = W_x$ gives $OB = V'$, which is *less* than $OA = V$ by the amount $dV = AC = W_x \cos \phi$. Also the angle, $BOH = \phi'$ is *greater* than the angle $AOH = \phi$ by the angle

$$d\phi = AOB = \frac{BC}{OB} = \frac{W_x \sin \phi}{V'}$$

(assuming that for this small angle the sine and the circular measure of the angle are equal). In other words, the forces acting would produce a trajectory *relative to the moving air* for which the initial velocity is $V' = V - dV$ and the angle of departure is $\phi' = \phi + d\phi$. Similarly, from Figure 19(b), where W_x is negative or against the flight of the projectile, we would have V' *greater* than V by the amount $dV = W_x \cos \phi$, and ϕ' *less* than ϕ by the amount $d\phi = \frac{BC}{OB} = \frac{W_x \sin \phi}{V'}$. Thus, in both cases we can obtain the values of the changes in V and ϕ with their proper signs from the expressions

$$dV = -W_x \cos \phi \qquad (202)$$

$$d\phi = \frac{W_x \sin \phi}{V'} \qquad (203)$$

The negative sign is arbitrarily introduced into the second term of (202) to ensure that a positive value of W_x shall always produce a negative value of dV, and that a negative value of W_x shall always produce a positive value of dV, as is seen from the triangles of forces must always be the case.

237. To determine the effect of a wind W_x, therefore, we compute dV by (202) and $d\phi$ by (203); compute the range X given by V and ϕ by methods heretofore explained; compute the range X' and the time of flight T' given by $V' = V + dV$ and $\phi' = \phi + d\phi$ by methods heretofore explained, and then by (201) we can compute the change in range due to the wind.

238. An examination of Figure 20(a) and Figure 20(b) will help to reach a clear understanding of the foregoing method of determining the effect of wind upon the range. Let O represent the stationary gun and M the stationary target, which would be hit on a calm day at a range X by a projectile fired from O with an initial velocity of V and an angle of departure ϕ (Figure 20(a)).

If this same projectile were fired with the same V and the same ϕ on a day when a wind was blowing from the gun towards the target we know that the projectile will land at same point H', a distance ΔX, beyond M (Figure 20(a)).

This increase of range, due to the wind blowing with the projectile in flight, may be considered in two parts, as shown in Figure 20(*b*); first, an apparent shortening of the trajectory, due to an apparent decreased initial velocity; and second, a bodily carrying ahead of this same trajectory, due to the movement of the medium in which the projectile is fired.

In paragraph 236 we found that when considering the trajectory *relative to moving air*, the resultant velocity V', for a positive wind, is less than V. The resultant ϕ' is greater than ϕ, but since by formula (4), page 28, X varies as the square of the velocity, a change in velocity has greater effect than a change in the angle of departure. The trajectory, apparently shortened by a decreased in velocity, will be OSH, as shown in Figure 20(*b*), falling short of the target M by a distance HM.

Now the wind carries the projectile along in flight a distance W_xT', so that the trajectory OSH may be represented as taking up a new position $O'S'H'$, the projectile falling at H', a distance W_xT' ahead of point H. The distance beyond the target M will then be

$$\Delta X = X' + W_xT' - X$$

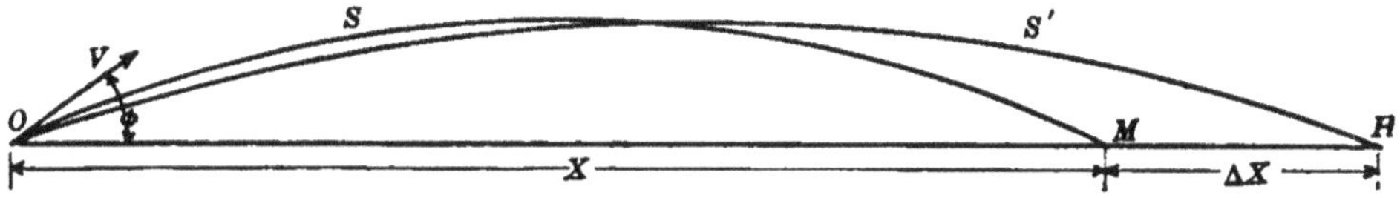

FIGURE 20(*a*)

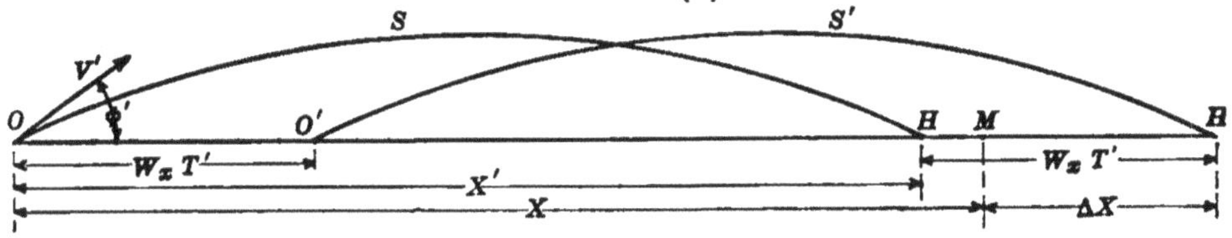

FIGURE 20(*b*)

If we had considered a negative wind, we would have obtained the same result in this form

$$-\Delta X = -X' - W_xT' + X$$

239. The process just explained is not only a somewhat lengthy and inconvenient one, but the methods of interpolation used with the ballistic tables were not devised with this particular process in view, and do not produce results sufficiently accurate to determine the small differences in range with the precision necessary in this class of problem.* A carrying out of the process just described may therefore not bring correct results, and it is desirable to reduce the formulæ, if possible, to some form more convenient for practical use and that will not involve the use of the ballistic tables. Although, as already stated, the above formulæ are not useful for obtaining practical results in this case, they are nevertheless theoretically correct, and from them will now be derived the formula that is actually used in practice in computing the data contained in Column 13 of the range tables. From Chapter 4 we see that (when $a=2$, which is sufficiently accurate for present purposes) the relation between the range in air and the angle of departure is

$$\sin 2\phi = \frac{gnX}{V^2} = \frac{gX}{V^2}\left(1+\tfrac{1}{3}kX\right) \qquad (204)$$

Taking logarithmic differentials of this expression, that is, differentiating and then dividing by the original equation, and considering ϕ and X as the only variables (the small angle 2ϕ being considered as having its natural sine equal to its circular measure) we get

$$\frac{2d\phi}{\tan 2\phi} = \frac{1+\frac{2}{3}kX}{1+\frac{1}{3}kX} \times \frac{dX}{X} \qquad (205)$$

* See foot-note to paragraph 153, Chapter 8. An effort to use the formulæ just derived for the value of the effects of wind upon the flight of the projectile, by the use of Ingalls' method, with the interpolation formulæ given in Chapter 8, will not be successful, because those interpolation formulæ neglect second and higher differences; and the limits of accuracy within which these results would have to be obtained in this case are too narrow to permit such higher differences than the first to be neglected in using Table II.

Now $1+\tfrac{1}{3}kX=n$; whence $1+\tfrac{2}{3}kX=2n-1$, and so (205) becomes

$$\frac{2d\phi}{\tan 2\phi}=\frac{2n-1}{n}\times\frac{dX}{X}$$

whence
$$\frac{dX}{X}=\frac{2n}{2n-1}\times\frac{d\phi}{\tan 2\phi} \tag{206}$$

240. In this and in similar expressions the value of $d\phi$ must of course be expressed in circular measure ($1'=.0002909$), but when the form is the ratio $\frac{d\phi}{\phi}$, the value is the same whether $d\phi$ and ϕ are expressed in minutes of arc or in circular measure. Now returning to (204) and writing it in the form

$$V^2 \sin 2\phi=gX(1+\tfrac{1}{3}kX)$$

and taking logarithmic differentials with regard to V and X as variables, we get

$$\frac{2dV}{V}=\frac{1+\tfrac{2}{3}kX}{1+\tfrac{1}{3}kX}\times\frac{dX}{X} \tag{207}$$

which, substituting n for $1+\tfrac{1}{3}kX$ and $2n-1$ for $1+\tfrac{2}{3}kX$, becomes

$$\frac{dX}{X}=\frac{2n}{2n-1}\times\frac{dV}{V} \tag{208}$$

241. We have found in (208) an expression for the variation in range due to a variation in initial velocity, and in (206) an expression for the variation in range due to a variation in the angle of departure; and we have already seen that the effect upon the range of a wind component in the plane of fire is to give, so far as results are concerned, an apparent variation in both V and ϕ. Therefore $X'-X$ is nothing but the change in range which would result from increasing V by dV and ϕ by $d\phi$, dV being determined by (202) and $d\phi$ by (203). Then by employing (208) and (206) we see that the change in X due to simultaneous changes $dV=-W_x\cos\phi$ and $d\phi=\frac{W_x\sin\phi}{V'}$ is given by the expression

$$\frac{X'-X}{X}=\frac{2n}{2n-1}\left(\frac{W_x\sin\phi}{V'\tan 2\phi}-\frac{W_x\cos\phi}{V}\right) \tag{209}$$

Now we may put V for V' in the preceding expression without material error, because dV is always very small compared with V, and the expression then reduces to

$$\frac{X'-X}{X}=\frac{2n}{2n-1}\times\frac{W_x}{V}\left(\frac{\sin\phi}{\tan 2\phi}-\cos\phi\right)$$

Now
$$\frac{\sin\phi}{\tan 2\phi}-\cos\phi=\cos\phi\left(\frac{\tan\phi}{\tan 2\phi}-1\right)$$

and
$$\tan 2\phi=\frac{\sin 2\phi}{\cos 2\phi}=\frac{2\sin\phi\cos\phi}{\cos^2\phi-\sin^2\phi}$$

whence
$$\cos\phi\left(\frac{\tan\phi}{\tan 2\phi}-1\right)=\cos\phi\left(\frac{\sin\phi}{\cos\phi}\times\frac{\cos^2\phi-\sin^2\phi}{2\sin\phi\cos\phi}-1\right)$$
$$=\cos\phi\left(\frac{\cos^2\phi-\sin^2\phi}{2\cos^2\phi}-1\right)$$
$$=\frac{\cos\phi}{2}(1-\tan^2\phi-2)$$

whence
$$\frac{\sin\phi}{\tan 2\phi}-\cos\phi=\frac{\cos\phi}{2}(-\tan^2\phi-1) \tag{210}$$

Therefore, from the above, we get

$$\frac{X'-X}{X} = \frac{n}{2n-1} \times \frac{W_x \cos\phi}{V}(-\tan^2\phi - 1)$$

whence, neglecting $\tan^2\phi$ in comparison with unity,

$$X'-X = -\frac{n}{2n-1} \times \frac{X\cos\phi}{V} W_x$$

and substituting this in (201) we finally get for the change in range due to the wind component W_x

$$\Delta X = W_x\left\{T - \left(\frac{n}{2n-1} \times \frac{X\cos\phi}{V}\right)\right\}^* \qquad (211)$$

In the above equation, T, although actually the time of flight for V' and ϕ', may be taken as the time of flight for the actual firing data, V and ϕ, without introducing any material errors. This formula is the one employed in computing the data in Column 13 of the range tables, giving the change in range resulting from a wind component of 12 knots in the plane of fire.

242. Now let us compute the data for that column for our standard problem, the 12″ gun, $V=2900$ f. s., $w=870$ pounds, $c=0.61$, $R=10{,}000$, $T=12.43$, and $\phi=4°\ 13'\ 14''$. We have the formula given in the preceding paragraph and

$$n = \frac{V^2\sin 2\phi}{gX} \text{ and } W_{12x} = \frac{12\times 6080}{60\times 60\times 3} \text{ yards per second}$$

$V=2900$	log 3.46239	2 log	6.92480
$2\phi=8°\ 26'\ 28''$		sin	9.16669 − 10
$g=32.2$	log 1.50786	colog	8.49214 − 10
$X=30000$	log 4.47712	colog	5.52288 − 10
$n=1.278$		log	0.10651
$2n=2.556$			
$2n-1=1.556$	log 0.19200	colog	9.80800 − 10
$n=1.278$		log	0.10651
$X=30000$		log	4.47712
$\phi=4°\ 13'\ 14''$		cos	9.99882 − 10
$V=2900$	log 3.46239	colog	6.53761 − 10
8.47		log	0.92806
$T=12.43$			
3.96		log	0.59770
12		log	1.07918
6080		log	3.78390
$60\times 60\times 3=10800$	log 4.03342	colog	5.96658 − 10
$\Delta R_{12W}=26.7$ yards		log	1.42736

* The above is the formula actually employed. There seems to be no good reason, however, for neglecting $\tan^2\phi$, for $\tan^2\phi + 1 \doteq \sec^2\phi$, and if we substitute this value, instead of dropping the $\tan^2\phi$, we would get as a final result

$$X = W_x\left(T - \frac{n}{2n-1} \times \frac{X}{V\cos\phi}\right)$$

which is equally easy for work, and is more in keeping with the form of the expression for determining the deflection due to wind given in equation (212). The difference in results is not material however.

Lateral deviation due to wind.

243. To determine the lateral deviation due to wind, let W_z be the lateral wind component in foot-seconds, positive when it blows from right to left across the line of fire, and negative when it blows in the reverse direction; let V and ϕ be the initial velocity and angle of departure *relative to still air or to the ground,* and X be the corresponding range, that is, the range *when there is no wind.* Then if we draw the triangle of forces for this case, we may obtain the initial velocity and direction of flight *relative to the moving air.* Thus referring to Figure 21 (*a*), which represents the case of a negative wind, the resultant of $OA=V$ with $OC=-W_z$ is $OB=V'$, which is very slightly greater than V; the angle $BOD=\phi'$, which V' makes with the horizontal, is very slightly less than $AOE=\phi$; and V' is inclined to the left so as to make with V the small angle BOA.

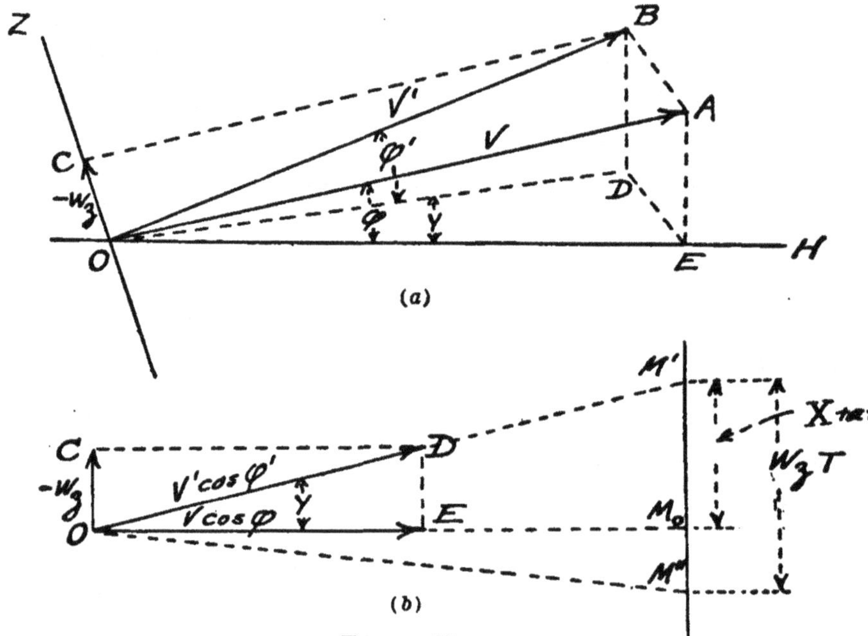

FIGURE 21.

244. Now since V' and ϕ' differ so little from V and ϕ, and since the effect of the increase in V is offset by that of the decrease in ϕ, we may take the range X' corresponding to V', ϕ', to be practically the same as the range X corresponding to V, ϕ. Therefore the only essential difference between the trajectory *relative to the moving air* and that *relative to the ground or still air* is that the plane of the former makes the angle $DOE=\gamma$ with the plane of the latter. Referring now to Figure 21 (*b*), in which O represents the gun and M_0 the target at the range $OM_0=X$, we see that $\tan\gamma=\dfrac{W_z}{V\cos\phi}$; and OM' is the horizontal trace of the trajectory *relative to the moving air.* But while the projectile moves through the air from O to M', the air itself has moved W_zT to the right, and so the projectile really strikes to the right of the target by the distance

$$M_0M''=W_zT-X\tan\gamma=W_z\left(T-\frac{X}{V\cos\phi}\right)$$

Thus the lateral deviation caused by the wind component W_z normal to the line of fire is given by the expression

$$D_W=W_z\left(T-\frac{X}{V\cos\phi}\right) \qquad (212)$$

in which T, though really the time of flight corresponding to V', ϕ', may without appreciable error be taken as the time of flight for the actual firing data.

245. Now let us return to our standard problem and find the data for Column 16 in the range table; deviation for lateral wind component of 12 knots; for our 12″ gun at 10,000 yards. We have the above formula, and also $W_{12z} = \frac{6080 \times 12}{60 \times 60 \times 3}$ yards per second.

$X = 30000$		log 4.47712
$V = 2900$	log 3.46240	colog 6.53760−10
$\phi = 4°\ 13'\ 14''$		sec 0.00118
10.37		log 1.01590
$T = 12.43$		
2.06		log 0.31387
12		log 1.07918
6080		log 3.78390
$60 \times 60 \times 3 = 10800$	log 4.03342	colog 5.96658−10
$D_{12W} = 13.9$ yards		log 1.14353

Section 2.—The Effect of Motion of the Gun Upon the Motion of the Projectile.

246. As in the case of the wind, we resolve the horizontal velocity of the gun due to the ship's motion into two components, G_x in the plane of fire, and G_z at right angles to that plane; and determine their effects separately, the first affecting the range only and the second the lateral deflection only.

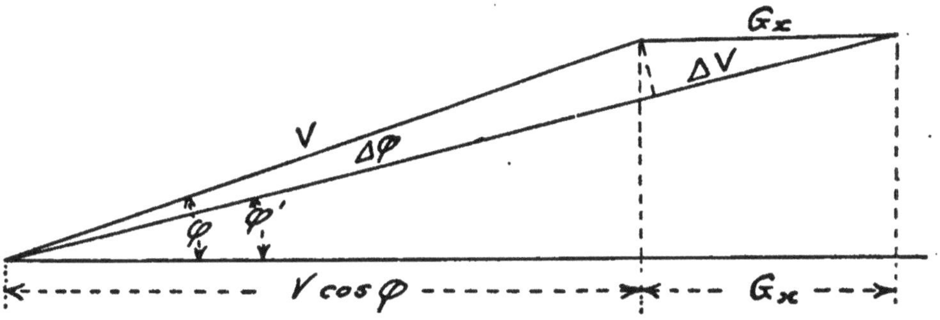

FIGURE 22.

247. Let G_x be the resolved part of the speed in the line of fire in foot-seconds, positive when with and negative when contrary to the flight of the projectile. Then evidently the true initial velocity of the projectile is the resultant of G_x and V, and, as shown in Figure 22, V receives the increment $\Delta V = G_x \cos\phi$, while ϕ is decreased by $\Delta\phi = \frac{G_x \sin\phi}{V}$. But by equations (208) and (206), these two changes in V and ϕ, respectively, will cause a change in range given by **Change in range due to motion of gun.**

$$\frac{\Delta X_G}{X} = \frac{2n}{2n-1}\left(\frac{G_x \cos\phi}{V} - \frac{G_x \sin\phi}{V \tan 2\phi}\right)$$

$$\frac{\Delta X_G}{X} = \frac{n}{2n-1} \times \frac{G_x \cos\phi}{V}\left(2 - \frac{2\tan\phi}{\tan 2\phi}\right)$$

Now as $$\tan 2\phi = \frac{2\tan\phi}{1-\tan^2\phi}$$

the above expression becomes

$$\frac{\Delta X_G}{X} = \frac{n}{2n-1} \times \frac{G_s \cos\phi}{V}(1+\tan^2\phi)$$

which, when ϕ is small enough to make $\tan^2\phi$ negligible in comparison to unity, reduces to

$$\frac{\Delta X_G}{X} = \frac{n}{2n-1} \times \frac{G_s \cos\phi}{V}$$

or $$\Delta X_G = \frac{n}{2n-1} \times \frac{X\cos\phi}{V} G_s \text{*} \tag{213}$$

248. As an illustration, let us return to our standard problem 12" gun, and compute for a range of 10,000 yards the data contained in Column 14 of the range table; change of range for motion of gun in plane of fire of 12 knots. We have the above formula and

$$n = \frac{V^2 \sin 2\phi}{gX} \qquad G_s = \frac{12\times 6080}{60\times 60\times 3} \text{ yards per second}$$

$V=2900$	log 3.46239	2 log	6.92478
$2\phi=8°\ 26'\ 28''$		sin	9.16669−10
$g=32.2$	log 1.50785	colog	8.49214−10
$X=30000$	log 4.47712	colog	5.52288−10
$n=1.278$		log	0.10649
$2n=2.556$			
$2n-1=1.556$	log 0.19200	colog	9.80800−10
$n=1.278$		log	0.10649
$X=30000$		log	4.47712
$\phi=4°\ 13'\ 14''$		cos	9.99882−10
$V=2900$	log 3.46239	colog	6.53761−10
12		log	1.07918
6080		log	3.78390
$60\times 60\times 3=10800$	log 4.03342	colog	5.96658−10
$\Delta R_{12G}=57$ yards		log	1.75770

Lateral deviation due to motion of gun. **249.** Now let G_s be the resolved part of the motion of the gun at right angles to the line of fire in foot-seconds. Then, in addition to the initial velocity V in the line of the axis of the gun, the projectile on leaving the gun has a lateral velocity G_z, and so, as may be seen from Figure 21(b), the real plane of departure makes an angle with the vertical plane of the gun's axis given by $\tan\gamma = \frac{G_s}{V\cos\phi}$, and the resultant deviation at range X is given by

$$D_G = X\tan\gamma \quad\text{or}\quad D_G = \frac{X}{V\cos\phi} G_s \tag{214}$$

* The above is the formula actually employed. There seems to be no good reason, however, for neglecting the $\tan^2\phi$, for $\tan^2\phi + 1 = \sec^2\phi$, and if we substitute this value, instead of dropping the $\tan^2\phi$, we would get as the final result

$$X_G = \frac{n}{2n-1} \times \frac{X}{V\cos\phi} \times G_s$$

which is equally easy for work, and more in keeping with the form of the expression for determining the deflection due to motion of the gun given in equation (214). The difference is not material however.

250. Taking our standard problem again, we have the above formula and $G_z = \frac{12 \times 6080}{60 \times 60 \times 3}$ yards per second.

$X=30000$		log	4.47712
$V=2900$	log 3.46240	colog	6.53760−10
$\phi=4°\ 13'\ 14''$		sec	0.00118
12		log	1.07918
6080		log	3.78390
$60\times 60\times 3=10800$	log 4.03342	colog	5.96658−10
$D_{12G}=70.1$ yards		log	1.84556

Section 3.—The Effect of the Motion of the Target Upon the Motion of the Projectile Relative to the Target.

251. Motion of the target evidently has no effect upon the actual flight of the projectile, but it is equally clear that it will affect the relative positions of the target and of the point of fall of the projectile, as the target has been in motion during the time of flight of the projectile.

Effect of motion of target.

252. Evidently, if the target be moving in the line of fire with the velocity T_x, in order to hit it the sight must be set for a range greater or less than the true range at the instant of firing by the distance which the target will traverse in the time of flight, or T_xT. So, also, if the speed of the target at right angles to the plane of fire be T_z, the shot will fall T_zT to one side of the target unless that much deviation is allowed for in pointing. Once more we consider the motion as resolved into two components, one in and the other normal to the plane of fire, and consider the two as producing results entirely independent of each other. And it is readily seen that, for the effect of the motion of the target we must correct the range and deviation by the quantities given by the expressions

$$\Delta X_T = T_x T \tag{215}$$

$$D_T = T_z T \tag{216}$$

253. For our standard 12" gun, again, for 10,000 yards, to compute the data in Columns 15 and 18 of the range tables, for 12 knots speed of target, the work would be

$$T_x = T_z = \frac{12 \times 6080}{60 \times 60 \times 3} \qquad X_{12T} = D_{12T} = T_{12x} \times T = T_{12z} \times T$$

$T=12.43$		log	1.09452
12		log	1.07918
6080		log	3.78390
$60\times 60\times 3=10800$	log 4.03342	colog	5.96658−10
$R_{12T}=D_{12T}=84$ yards		log	1.92418

Section 4.—The Effect Upon the Motion of the Projectile of All Three Motions Combined.

254. In the preceding sections we have discussed the effects upon the motion of the projectile of the wind and of the motions of the firing and target ships. The resultant combined effect of all three of these causes of error would of course be obtained by computing them separately and then performing the necessary algebraic additions, first for all range effects to get the total effect upon the range, and then of all deflection effects to get the total effect in deflection.

NOTE.—Professor Alger appends to this chapter the following foot-note:

The method herein adopted for the treatment of the problem of wind effect was first set forth, so far as I am aware, in General Didion's Traité de Ballistique though it has been generally accepted since. It is mathematically correct only for spherical projectiles, to the motion of which the air offers a resistance which is independent of the direction of motion. With elongated projectiles it will be seen that the initial motion *relative to the air* is not exactly in the line of the projectile's axis, so that we have no right to assume, as we do, that the flight *relative to the air* is the same when the air is moving as when it is still. It has been supposed by some writers that the lateral wind component produces the same pressure on the side of the moving projectile as it would if the projectile were stationary, and that the deviation can be computed upon that basis. If this were true, the deviation would be proportional to the square of the lateral wind component, whereas it is really much more nearly proportional to its first power. Actually the pressure is much greater when the projectile is moving at right angles to the wind current than when it is stationary, on account of the increased number of air particles which strike it.

EXAMPLES.

1. Compute the errors in range and in deflection caused by the wind components as given below.

Problem.	DATA.									ANSWERS.			
	Projectile.			*V.* f.s.	Range. Yds.	Wind component in knots per hour.				In line of fire.		Perpendicular to line of fire.	
						In line of fire.		Perpendicular to line of fire.					
	d. In.	*w.* Lbs.	*c.*			Knots.	With or against.	Knots.	To the right or left	Yards.	Short or over.	Yards.	To the right or left.
A..	3	13	1.00	1150	3000	8	With	6	Right	16.5	Over	6.3	Right
B..	3	13	1.00	2700	4500	10	Against	8	Left	34.5	Short	19.1	Left
C..	4	33	0.67	2900	4000	11	With	9	Right	12.7	Over	5.7	Right
D .	5	50	1.00	3150	4500	13	Against	11	Left	26.8	Short	14.4	Left
E..	5	50	0.61	3150	4500	14	With	13	Right	17.1	Over	8.8	Right
F..	6	105	0.61	2600	13600	15	Against	14	Left	146.9	Short	88.8	Left
G..	6	105	1.00	2800	4500	16	With	15	Right	25.9	Over	14.0	Right
H .	6	105	0.61	2800	4000	17	Against	16	Left	13.3	Short	6.4	Left
I . .	7	165	1.00	2700	7500	18	With	17	Right	74.2	Over	44.3	Right
J..	7	165	0.61	2700	7500	19	Against	18	Left	47.0	Short	24.8	Left
K .	8	260	0.61	2750	8500	20	With	19	Right	51.5	Over	26.9	Right
L..	10	510	1.00	2700	10500	19	Against	20	Left	100.4	Short	64.7	Left
M .	10	510	0.61	2700	11500	18	With	19	Right	69.0	Over	40.2	Right
N .	12	870	0.61	2900	19500	17	With	18	Left	141.5	Over	87.0	Left
O..	13	1130	1.00	2000	10500	16	Against	17	Right	93.3	Short	54.8	Right
P..	13	1130	0.74	2000	11500	15	With	16	Left	79.6	Over	44.4	Left
Q..	14	1400	0.70	2000	14500	14	Against	15	Right	105.6	Short	58.1	Right
R..	14	1400	0.70	2600	14000	13	With	14	Left	63.7	Over	37.3	Left

2. Compute the errors in range and in deflection caused by the motion of the gun as given below. Conditions standard.

Problem.	DATA.									ANSWERS.			
	Projectile.			V. f.s.	Range. Yds.	Speed component in knots per hour.				In line of fire.		Perpendicular to line of fire.	
						In line of fire.		Perpendicular to line of fire.					
	d. In.	w. Lbs.	c.			Knots.	With or against.	Knots.	To the right or left.	Yards.	Short or over.	Yards.	To the right or left.
A..	3	13	1.00	1150	2000	6	Against	8	Left	14.7	Short	23.6	Left
B..	3	13	1.00	2700	3500	7	With	8	Right	10.2	Over	17.5	Right
C..	4	33	0.67	2900	3000	8	Against	9	Left	11.5	Short	15.7	Left
D .	5	50	1.00	3150	3500	9	With	10	Right	12.4	Over	18.8	Right
E..	5	50	0.61	3150	3300	10	Against	11	Left	16.4	Short	22.4	Left
F..	6	105	0.61	2600	12600	11	With	13	Left	58.3	Over	108.4	Left
G..	6	105	1.00	2800	4000	13	Against	14	Right	24.1	Short	33.8	Right
H .	6	105	0.61	2800	3000	14	With	15	Left	22.2	Over	27.1	Left
I . .	7	165	1.00	2700	6500	15	Against	16	Right	43.1	Short	65.2	Right
J..	7	165	0.61	2700	6700	16	With	17	Left	52.8	Over	71.4	Left
K .	8	260	0.61	2750	7500	17	With	18	Right	62.6	Over	83.1	Right
L..	10	510	1.00	2700	9500	18	Against	19	Left	76.3	Short	113.5	Left
M.	10	510	0.61	2700	10500	19	With	20	Right	97.6	Over	132.0	Right
N .	12	870	0.61	2900	23000	20	Against	19	Left	182.3	Short	262.0	Left
O..	13	1130	1.00	2000	10000	19	With	18	Right	118.0	Over	154.7	Right
P..	13	1130	0.74	2000	11000	18	Against	17	Left	128.4	Short	160.8	Left
Q..	14	1400	0.70	2000	14000	17	With	16	Right	149.5	Over	195.4	Right
R..	14	1400	0.70	2600	13700	16	Against	15	Left	109.4	Short	134.8	Left

3. Compute the errors in range and in deflection caused by the motion of the target as given below. Conditions standard.

Problem.	DATA.									ANSWERS.			
	Projectile.			V. f.s.	Range. Yds.	Speed component in knots per hour.				In line of fire.		Perpendicular to line of fire.	
						In line of fire.		Perpendicular to line of fire.					
	d. In.	w. Lbs.	c.			Knots.	With or against.	Knots.	To the right or left.	Yards.	Short or over.	Yards.	To the right or left.
A..	3	13	1.00	1150	1800	7	With	8	Right	21.4	Short	24.4	Left
B..	3	13	1.00	2700	3300	8	Against	9	Left	26.2	Over	29.4	Right
C..	4	33	0.67	2900	2800	9	With	10	Right	17.3	Short	19.2	Left
D .	5	50	1.00	3150	3300	10	Against	11	Left	24.0	Over	26.4	Right
E..	5	50	0.61	3150	3400	11	With	13	Right	24.1	Short	28.5	Left
F..	6	105	0.61	2600	13800	13	With	14	Left	204.3	Short	220.1	Right
G..	6	105	1.00	2800	3800	14	Against	15	Right	41.1	Over	44.0	Left
H .	6	105	0.61	2800	2800	15	With	16	Left	28.1	Short	30.0	Right
I . .	7	165	1.00	2700	6300	16	Against	17	Right	91.1	Over	96.9	Left
J..	7	165	0.61	2700	6700	17	With	18	Left	89.5	Short	94.7	Right
K .	8	260	0.61	2750	7300	18	Against	19	Left	99.2	Over	104.6	Right
L..	10	510	1.00	2700	9300	19	With	20	Right	157.9	Short	166.2	Left
M.	10	510	0.61	2700	10300	20	Against	19	Left	162.7	Over	154.6	Right
N .	12	870	0.61	2900	20200	19	With	20	Right	326.7	Short	343.9	Left
O..	13	1130	1.00	2000	9300	18	Against	19	Left	188.6	Over	199.1	Right
P..	13	1130	0.74	2000	10300	17	With	18	Right	187.6	Short	198.6	Left
Q..	14	1400	0.70	2000	13300	16	Against	17	Left	236.8	Over	251.6	Right
R..	14	1400	0.70	2600	13700	15	With	16	Right	172.4	Short	184.5	Left

CHAPTER 15.

DETERMINATION OF JUMP. EXPERIMENTAL RANGING AND THE REDUCTION OF OBSERVED RANGES.

Jump. **255.** Primarily and in its narrowest sense, jump is the increase (algebraic, and generally positive) in the angle of elevation resulting from the angular motion of the gun in the vertical plane caused by the shock of discharge, as a result of which the projectile strikes above (for positive jump; below for negative) the point at which it theoretically should for the given angle of elevation. A definition which thus confines jump to the result of such angular motion is a narrow and restricted one, however, and other elements may enter to give similar results, all of which may be and are properly included in that resultant variation generally called jump. For instance, in the old gravity return mounts, the gun did not recoil directly in the line of its own axis, as it does in the most modern mounts, but rose up an inclined plane as it recoiled. As the projectile did not clear the muzzle until the gun had recoiled an appreciable distance, this upward motion of the gun imparted a similar upward motion to the projectile, which resulted in making the projectile strike slightly higher than it would otherwise have done. This small discrepancy, unimportant at battle ranges, but necessarily considered in such work as firing test shots at armor plate at close range, was properly included in the jump. Also most modern guns of any considerable length have what is known as "droop," that is, the muzzle of the gun sags a little, due to the length and weight of the gun, the axis of the gun being no longer a theoretical straight line; and this causes the projectile to strike slightly lower than it otherwise would, and introduces another slight error which may properly be included in the jump. Also it is probable that this droop causes the muzzle of the gun to move slightly in firing as the gun tends to straighten out under internal pressure, and perhaps this motion tends to produce another variation, "whip," in the motion of the projectile, which would modify the result of the droop. All these may therefore be properly included in the jump.

256. This matter has a direct bearing, under our present system of considering such matters, upon the factor of the ballistic coefficient which we have designated as the coefficient of form of the projectile, and which is supposed, under our previous definition, to be the ratio of the resistance the projectile meets in flight to the resistance that would be encountered in the same air, at the same velocity, by the standard projectile; that is, by a projectile about three calibers long and similar in all respects except in possessing a standard head, namely, one whose ogival has a two-caliber radius. Imagine that the gun jumps a little and increases the range in so doing. It gives the same range as a similar gun firing without jump a projectile exactly similar in all respects except in possessing a slightly lower coefficient of form. Suppose a gun droops and shoots lower. The coefficient of form calculated back from the range obtained by actual firing would work out a little large. And in practice we would probably have both jump and droop affecting the range, but by our method of determining the coefficient of form from actual firing, by comparing actual with computed ranges, all such effects are hidden in the found value of the coefficient of form.

Broader definition of coefficient of form. **257.** As a matter of fact, as intimated above, the value of the coefficient of form is determined by firing ranging shots, and then computing its value from the results.

This coefficient of form therefore includes not only the results of variations in form of projectiles, etc., but also variations in range resulting from jump, droop, whip, etc., In fact, in the sense in which we now use the term, coefficient of form might better be defined as "that value which, if substituted for c in the usual formulæ, will, for the given elevation, velocity, weight of projectile, etc., make the computed range come out in agreement with that actually attained in firing, after making all corrections to the firing results for atmospheric density, etc."

258. Thus a person looking over the range table computations for the first time would say off hand that jump, droop, etc., were neglected. Closer study, however, makes it evident that the adopted procedure amounts to taking jump, etc., into consideration as actually found to exist; not in assuming that it is zero, and, in fact, not greatly concerning ourselves as to just what its value really is (as we know it to be small), but still following a method that, for a given jump, etc., gives a correct computed result at a given range, and which checks well at all other ranges. If it be objected that different guns of the same type may jump, etc., differently, it may be answered that the coefficient of form used is an average of the values obtained in a great number of firings of different individual guns of the same type, and is really preferable to that obtained by a complete ranging of a single gun. As a matter of fact, variations in the value of the coefficient of form obtained do not seem to go with certain individual guns more than with others, so the range tables are equally good for all guns of the type. In other words, this method of procedure produces results that are within the limits of accuracy obtainable, and any errors that follow its use must necessarily be included in those inherent errors of the gun which must always exist, and which, after all possible precautions have been taken, will inevitably make it impossible to have all the shot from the same gun, when fired under exactly similar conditions, always strike in exactly the same spot.

259. Having explained how jump, etc., even if it exists, is looked out for by our methods, we may now go on and state that, as a matter of fact, it does not seem to exist to any extent appreciable in the service use of guns, and it may therefore be said that it is a matter which does not concern an officer afloat. He should, however, have a knowledge of the principles laid down in this chapter, in order that he may recognize unusual and abnormal conditions should they be found to exist under special conditions.

Practical determination of value of coefficient of form.

260. To determine the value of the coefficient of form for a projectile for our standard problem 12″ gun, the gun was mounted at the Proving Ground, and laid at an angle of elevation of 8°, using a gunner's quadrant. Correction for height of trunnions above the water level, for sphericity of the earth, etc., makes this angle the equivalent of an angle of elevation of 8° 04′. The gun, when fired at this elevation, at 2900 f. s. initial velocity, should range about 16,140 yards, from the range table, when the observed fall has been reduced to standard atmospheric conditions, but of course this is not perfectly obtained. Say the projectile falls 100 yards short of the computed range. It then remains to determine the value of the coefficient of form which produced this variation, and this may be done by calculating back by the methods that have already been explained in this book. In practice, at the Proving Ground, however, in order to avoid the constant repetition of tedious computations, the method actually employed is to work out a few ranges for different values of the coefficient of form, and to make a curve for the results. The curve is made for arguments "coefficient of form" and "error from corrected range table range," and one curve is needed for each caliber and service velocity. Having such curves and the results of ranging shots, it is a quick and easy matter to take from the proper curve the value of the coefficient of form for each projectile. These values are tabulated, and a running record is kept, so that a great number of results will be available as a cumulative check on the range table. For a new caliber, a curve of "corrected range" and "coefficient of form" is kept until enough data has been collected with which to start a range table. For rough work, the formula for change of range resulting from a variation in the value of the ballistic coefficient may be used in the absence of curves.

Computation of range tables.

261. Prior to the appearance of the present range tables, guns were ranged by firing experimental shots at a number of different angles of elevation, and a curve of angles and ranges was plotted. From these faired curves the angles corresponding to all ranges were taken and a range table was made up from the results. As more confidence in the mathematical process was acquired, through the accumulation of considerable data, we began to get our range tables by computation, gradually abandoning the old system of ranging by experimental firing; and the use of the value of the coefficient of form as unity, with the projectiles then in use, was found to give range tables that agreed with the results of experimental ranging. When different lots of projectiles are presented for acceptance, a few have to be tested for flight from each lot; and these are ranged at the Proving Ground at 8° elevation in all cases, in order to make comparisons possible. At this angle there are no dangerous ricochets, and variations in the coefficient of form and differences between different projectiles will show up best at these long ranges. With a coefficient of form accurately determined by firing at the longest practicable ranges, we can compute an extremely accurate range table extending down through the medium and short ranges. The method of ranging only at a single elevation was therefore adopted, an occasional check by firing at short ranges being made.

262. The process of experimental ranging, as formerly carried out, was to fire a number of shots at different angles of elevation. The results for these shots were reduced to standard conditions, and the reduced observed ranges were plotted as abscissæ, with the corresponding angles of elevation as ordinates. A fair curve was then drawn through these points, and from this curve the angle of elevation corresponding to any range could be obtained.

Reduction of observed ranges.

263. The process of reducing observed ranges to standard conditions was carried out in accordance with the principles and formulæ already explained in this book, and this still has to be done for every ranging shot fired; but as this process is one that pertains purely to Proving Ground work and has no bearing on the service use of the gun, it is not considered necessary to go into it at length here; nor is it considered necessary to further discuss the details of the methods used for determining the actual magnitude of the jump, etc.

PART IV.

RANGE TABLES; THEIR COMPUTATION AND USE.

INTRODUCTION TO PART IV.

Having completed the study of all computations connected with the trajectory in air, both as a plane curve and allowing for existing variations from that plane, we are now in a position to make use of our knowledge in a practical way. The practical and useful expression of the knowledge thus acquired takes the form of: first, the preparation of the range tables; and after that, second, their use. Part IV will be devoted to a consideration of the range tables from these two points of view: first, as to their preparation; and, second, as to their actual practical use in service. Each column in the tables will be considered separately, the method and computations by which the data contained in it is obtained will be indicated, and then consideration will be given to the practical use of this data by officers aboard ship in service.

CHAPTER 16.

THE COMPUTATION OF THE DATA CONTAINED IN THE RANGE TABLES IN GENERAL; AND THE COMPUTATION OF THE DATA CONTAINED IN COLUMN 9 OF THE RANGE TABLES.

New Symbols Introduced.

E_1.... Penetration, in inches, of Harveyized armor by capped projectiles.

E_2.... Penetration, in inches, of face-hardened armor by capped projectiles.

K.... Constant factor for face-hardened armor.

K'.... Constant factor for Harveyized armor.

264. With the single exception noted in the next paragraph, we have now considered in detail the formulæ and methods by which the data in each of the columns of the range table is computed. Summarized, this is as follows:

Column in Range Table No.	Data Contained	Chapter in this book in which explained
1	Range. This is the foundation column for which the data in the other columns is computed. There are therefore no computations in regard to it.	No explanation necessary.
2	Angle of departure	8
3	Angle of fall	8
4	Time of flight	8
5	Striking velocity	8
6	Drift	13
7	Danger space for a target 20 feet high	5
8	Maximum ordinate	8 and 9
9	Penetration of armor	This chapter
10	Change of range for variation of $\pm$ 50 foot-seconds initial velocity	12
11	Change of range for variation of $\pm\, dw$ pounds in weight of projectile	12
12	Change in range for variation of $\pm$ 10 per cent in density of air	12
13	Change in range for wind component in plane of fire of 12 knots	14
14	Change in range for motion of gun in plane of fire of 12 knots	14
15	Change in range for motion of target in plane of fire of 12 knots	14
16	Deviation for lateral wind component of 12 knots	14
17	Deviation for lateral motion of gun perpendicular to line of fire; speed 12 knots.	14
18	Deviation for lateral motion of target perpendicular to line of fire; speed 12 knots	14
19	Change of height of impact for variation of $\pm$ 100 yards in sight bar	12

265. The subject of penetration of armor is one which does not properly belong to the subject of exterior ballistics, but this text book is compiled from the special point of view of the computation and use of the range tables, and as Column 9 of each of these tables gives the penetration, the subject is covered here in a brief way, in order that the full range table computations may be covered together.

266. In the earlier range tables, the penetration of armor was given for Harveyized armor, and formulæ devised by Commander Cleland Davis, U. S. N., were employed in the computation. For later armor, the range tables give the penetration of face-hardened armor by capped projectiles, this data being computed by the use of De Marre's formula. The heading of the column in each range table shows which type of armor is referred to in that particular table. Given the penetration in Harveyized armor, the penetration for face-hardened armor may be approximately obtained by multiplying the known figure for Harveyized armor by 0.8. Davis's formulæ for Harveyized armor are: **Penetration formulæ.**

For projectiles without caps.

$$v=\frac{d^{0.5}E_1^{\,0.75}}{w^{0.5}}K \quad \text{or} \quad E_1^{\,0.75}=\frac{vw^{0.5}}{Kd^{0.5}} \tag{217}$$

in which E_1 = the penetration of Harveyized armor in inches.
v = the striking velocity in foot-seconds.
w = the weight of the projectile in pounds.
d = the diameter of the projectile in inches.
$\log K=3.34512$.

For capped projectiles.

$$v=\frac{d^{0.5}E_1^{\,0.8}}{w^{0.5}}K' \quad \text{or} \quad E_1^{\,0.8}=\frac{vw^{0.5}}{K'd^{0.5}} \tag{218}$$

in which $\log K'=3.25312$, and the other quantities are as before.

De Marre's formula for face-hardened armor is based on the following equation:

$$v=\frac{d^{0.75}E^{0.7}}{w^{0.5}}K \quad \text{or} \quad E^{0.7}=\frac{vw^{0.5}}{Kd^{0.75}} \tag{219}$$

in which $\log K=3.00945$, E = the penetration of oil tempered and annealed armor that has not been face hardened. For face-hardened armor (for the range tables accompanying this book and marked as C, F, H, K, M, N, P, Q and R), the results obtained by the use of the above formula must be divided by De Marre's coefficient, which has been found to be 1.5 for such purpose. (For the other range tables accompanying this book, the value of this coefficient was taken as unity.)

267. As an example of the work under Davis's formula, let us compute the penetration by a capped projectile of Harveyized armor by the 5″ gun; $V=3150$ f. s., $w=50$ pounds; for a range of 4000 yards, first for a projectile for which $c=1$, and next for a projectile whose coefficient of form is 0.61. For these two projectiles, the range tables give the remaining velocities at the given range as $v_1=1510$ f. s. for $c=1.00$ and $v_2=2048$ f. s. for $c=0.61$.

$w=50$	log 1.69897		0.5 log 0.84948
$K'=$	log 3.25312		colog 6.74688−10
$d=5$	log 0.69897	0.5 log 0.34948	0.5 colog 9.65052−10
		log 7.24688−10	log 7.24688−10
$v_1=1510$		log 3.17898	
$v_2=2048$			log 3.31133
$E^{0.8}$		log 0.42586	log 0.55821
		10	10
		8)4.25860	8)5.58210
$E_{1(c=1)}=3.4067''$		log 0.53233	
$E_{1(c=.61)}=4.9861''$			log 0.69776

Comparison of long and short pointed projectiles.

268. As the coefficient of form does not enter into the above equation, we see that the only thing that gives a long pointed projectile a greater penetration than a blunt pointed one at the same range is the fact that, at that range, the long pointed projectile will have a greater striking velocity than the blunt one. As a matter of fact, as far as their effect upon armor plate is concerned, the two projectiles are the same; for the main body of the projectile is the same in each case, the only difference between them being in the shape of the wind shield. In other words, that part of the projectile which really acts to penetrate armor is the same for both the standard and for the long pointed shell, but one has no wind shield and the other a sharply pointed one, the actual points of the two shells being equally efficient in their effect upon the penetration. No difference in penetration could therefore be expected for equal striking velocities.

269. Now let us take our standard problem and determine, by the use of De Marre's formula, the penetration of face-hardened armor at 10,000 yards, for the 12″ gun of the problem. The range table gives $v=2029$ f. s. for that range.

$$E^{0.7}=\frac{vw^{0.5}}{Kd^{0.75}} \text{ in which } \log K=3.00945$$

$v=2029$		log 3.30728
$w=870$	log 2.93952	0.5 log 1.46976
$K=$	log 3.00945	colog 6.99055−10
$d=12$	log 1.07918 . . . 0.75 log 0.80938	0.75 colog 9.19062−10
$E^{0.7}$		0.7 log 0.95821
$E_2\times 1.5=E$		log 1.36887
1.5	log 0.17609	colog 9.82391−10
$E_2=15.59''$		log 1.19278

270. Practical Computation of Range Tables.—Having learned how to compute the penetration of armor by a given projectile at a given range, we are now in a position to discuss the practical methods used in actually making the computations for a range table. The labor involved is of course very great, so much care has been taken to get up special forms, and these are printed and kept on hand for the work. These forms are given in the following pages, the figures given in them being for the problems that we have already worked out item by item. and shown here as they would appear in the work of preparing the 12″ range table with the data for which, at a single range only, we have been working. These forms therefore show only the computations involved for 10,000 yards range. In computing the actual table, the work is done first for 1000 yards, then for 1500 yards, etc., for each 500-yard increment in range, the values between the computed values being obtained by interpolations, which interpolations are not difficult, as in most cases the second and third differences are negligible. As the range table of the particular gun in question runs up to 24,000 yards, and as computations must be made for every 500 yards, it will be seen that the work must be repeated for every 500 yards from 1000 yards up, which will involve 47 complete computations like the one shown in the following forms. This will give some idea of the magnitude of the work involved, and of the necessity for having special forms prepared, and of otherwise reducing the labor and increasing the accuracy as much as possible. Therefore, if much of this kind of work is to be done, forms similar to the ones shown should be prepared before commencing it (if a supply of the printed forms be not at hand) ; but if only a single problem is to be worked, as will generally be the case in the instruction of midshipmen, then the forms given in the previous chapters of this book should be used, as showing more clearly the nature of the problems involved and the methods of solving them. In solving problems under this chapter the forms given below must be used.

271. The form given for determining the angle of departure for a given range provides space for only three approximations; if more approximations are necessary to get the correct result, the form is simply extended.

272. It is to be noted that, in order to get smooth curves on the deflection drums of the sights, it is necessary in some cases to fair the computed drift curve, and this produces, in some places, a small difference between the computed drift and that shown in the range tables. Thus the computed drift for our standard problem was 26.6 yards, while in the range tables it is given as 26.8 yards.

273. The problem before us then is to compute, for a range of 10,000 yards, the data for the columns of the range table for the 12″ gun for which $V=2900$ foot-seconds, $w=870$ pounds, and $c=0.61$. The forms and work follow.

STANDARD FORMS FOR COMPUTATION OF RANGE TABLE DATA.

Specific Problem.

Compute the data for all columns of the range table for a range of 10,000 yards for a 12" gun for which $V = 2900$ f. s., $w = 870$ pounds, and $c = 0.61$.

FORM No. 1.

For Computation of Angle of Departure.

Column 2.

Uncorrected value of C

$$C_1 = \frac{w}{cd^2} = 9.9045$$

log w	2	9	3	9	5	2	
colog c......	0	2	1	4	6	7	
colog d^2.....	7	8	4	1	6	4	
log C_1.......	0	9	9	5	8	3	

$$Z_1 = \frac{X}{C_1} = 3029$$

log X.......	4	4	7	7	1	2	
colog C_1.....	9	0	0	4	1	7	—10
log Z_1.......	3	4	8	1	2	9	

$A_1 = .01470 + .00063 \times 20 = .014882$

$\sin 2\phi_1 = A_1 C_1$

log A_1.......	8	1	7	2	6	6	—10
log C_1.......	0	9	9	5	8	3	
log sin $2\phi_1$..	9	1	6	8	4	9	—10

$2\phi_1 = 8° \ 28' \ 34''$

$\phi_1 = 4° \ 14' \ 17''$ first approximation

$A_1'' = 849 + \frac{.82 \times 57}{12} = 852.9$

$Z_2 = 2983.8$

$A_2 = .01408 + .838 \times .00062 = .014599$

log A_2.......	8	1	6	4	3	2	—10
log C_2.......	1	0	0	2	3	5	
log sin $2\phi_2$..	9	1	6	6	6	7	—10

$2\phi_2 = 8° \ 26' \ 26''$

$\phi_2 = 4° \ 13' \ 13''$ second approximation

$A_2'' = 793 + \frac{8.99 \times 56}{11} = 838.7$

$Z_3 = 2984.1$

$A_3 = .01408 + .00062 \times .841 = .014601$

log A_3.......	8	1	6	4	3	8	—10
log C_3.......	1	0	0	2	3	1	
log sin $2\phi_3$..	9	1	6	6	6	9	—10

$2\phi_3 = 8° \ 26' \ 28''$

$\phi_3 = 4° \ 13' \ 14''$ third approximation

$R = 10{,}000$ yards $X = 30{,}000$ feet.

$\log\log f = \log Y + 5.01765$

$Y = A''C \tan \phi$

log A''_1.....	2	9	3	0	9	0	
log C_1.......	0	9	9	5	8	3	
log tan ϕ_1...	8	8	6	9	8	3	—10
log constant.	5	0	1	7	6	5	—10
loglog f_1.....	7	8	1	4	2	1	—10
log f_1	0	0	0	6	5	2	
log C_1.......	0	9	9	5	8	3	
log C_2.......	1	0	0	2	3	5	
log X........	4	4	7	7	1	2	
log Z_2.......	3	4	7	4	7	7	

$Z_2 = 2983.8$

log A_2''	2	9	2	3	6	1	
log C_2.......	1	0	0	2	3	5	
log tan ϕ_2...	8	8	6	8	0	0	—10
log constant.	5	0	1	7	6	5	—10
loglog f_2.....	7	8	1	1	6	1	—10
log f_2	0	0	0	6	4	8	
log C_1.......	0	9	9	5	8	3	
log C_3.......	1	0	0	2	3	1	
log X	4	4	7	7	1	2	
log Z_3.......	3	4	7	4	8	1	

$Z_3 = 2984.1$

From the above work, we have for our final values:

$\phi = 4° \ 13' \ 14''$

$Z = 2984.1$

$\log C = 1.00231$

FORM No. 2.

For Computation of

Column 2. Angle of Departure (if C be already correctly known, and work on Form No. 1 is therefore unnecessary, except for Z).

Column 3. Angle of Fall. Column 4. Time of flight. Column 5. Striking velocity.
Column 6. Drift. Column 8. Maximum ordinate. Column 9. Penetration.

DATA.

$R = 10{,}000$ yards $\quad X = 30{,}000$ feet $\quad \log C = 1.00231 \quad Z = 2984.1$

$A = .01408 + .00062 \times .841 = .014601 \quad \log B' = .1006 + .0037 \times .841 = .10371$

$u = 2048 - 26 \times .841 = 2026.1 \quad T' = 1.192 + .049 \times .841 = 1.2332 \quad D' = 24 + 2 \times .841 = 25.9$

$B = .0178 + .0009 \times .841 = .01856$

$A'' = 793 + \dfrac{8.99 \times 56}{11} = 838.8 \quad \Delta_{v_A} = .00099 + .0004 \times .841 = .001024$

2. Angle of departure, $\phi = 4°\ 13'\ 14''$
$\sin 2\phi = AC$

log C........	1	0	0	2	3	1	
log A........	8	1	6	4	3	8	—10
log sin 2ϕ...	9	1	6	6	6	9	—10

$2\phi = 8°\ 26'\ 28''$

3. Angle of fall, $\omega = 5°\ 21'\ 11''$
$\tan \omega = B' \tan \phi$

log B'.......	0	1	0	3	7	1	
log tan ϕ....	8	8	6	8	0	3	—10
log tan ω....	8	9	7	1	7	4	—10

4. Time of flight, $T = 12.43$ seconds
$T = CT' \sec \phi$

log C........	1	0	0	2	3	1
log T'.......	0	0	0	1	0	3
log sec ϕ....	0	0	0	1	1	8
log T........	1	0	9	4	5	2

5. Striking velocity, $v_\omega = 2029$ f. s.
$v_\omega = u \cos \phi \sec \omega$

log u........	3	3	0	6	6	6	
log cos ϕ....	9	9	9	8	8	2	—10
log sec ω....	0	0	0	1	9	0	
log v_ω	3	3	0	7	3	8	

6. Drift, $D = 26.5$ yards

$D = \text{constant} \times \dfrac{C^2 D'}{\cos^2 \phi}$, where constant $= \dfrac{\mu\lambda}{nh}$

(See page 147)

log constant.	7	8	3	1	4	9	—10
log C^2.......	2	0	0	4	6	2	
log D'.......	1	4	0	8	2	4	
log sec² ϕ ...	0	0	0	3	5	4	
	1	2	4	7	8	9	
log 1.5	0	1	7	6	0	9	
log D	1	4	2	3	9	8	

As the value of $\dfrac{\mu\lambda}{nh}$ is constant for the same gun for all ranges, its value is computed first and then carried on as a constant through all the drift computations for the range table for the particular gun in question.

8. Maximum ordinate, $Y = 622$ feet
$Y = A''C \tan \phi$

log A''	2	9	2	3	6	6	
log C	1	0	0	2	3	1	
log tan ϕ....	8	8	6	8	0	3	—10
log Y	2	7	9	4	0	0	

9. Penetration of armor, $E = 15.59''$

$E^{0.7} = \dfrac{v w^{0.5}}{K d^{0.75}} = \text{constant} \times v$, where

$\text{constant} = \dfrac{w^{0.5}}{K d^{0.75}}$

log constant.	7	6	5	0	0	3	—10
log v........	3	3	0	7	3	8	
log $E^{0.7}$.....	0	9	5	8	3	1	
					1	0	
7)	0	5	8	3	1	0	
log ($E_2 \times 1.5$)	1	3	6	9	0	1	
colog 1.5....	9	8	2	3	9	1	—10
log E_2......	1	1	9	2	9	2	

1.5 is De Marre's coefficient for face-hardened armor as compared to simple oil tempered and annealed armor.

As the value of $\dfrac{w^{0.5}}{K d^{0.75}}$ is constant for the same gun for all ranges, its value is computed first and then carried through all the penetration computations for the entire range table for the particular gun in question.

NOTE—In forms Nos. 3 and 4, whenever it becomes necessary to use the logarithms of T, v_ω, etc., take the exact values of those logarithms correct to five decimal places from the work on this sheet, and *do not* use the approximate logarithms taken from the log tables for the values of the elements given here and correct only to two places as required for the range table.

FORM No. 3.

For Computation of

Column 7. Danger space for target 20 feet high.
Column 10. Change in range for variation of ± 50 f. s. in initial velocity.
Column 11. Change in range for variation of ± 10 pounds in weight of projectile.
Column 12. Change in range for variation of ± 10 per cent in density of air.

7. Danger space, $S_{20} = 72$ yards

$$S = \frac{h}{3}\cot\omega\left(1 + \frac{\frac{h}{3}\cot\omega}{R}\right)$$

$\log \frac{h}{3}$	0	8	2	3	9	1	
$\log \cot \omega$....	1	0	2	8	2	6	
$\log\left(\frac{h}{3}\cot\omega\right)$	1	8	5	2	1	7	
colog R.....	6	0	0	0	0	0	— 10
$\frac{h}{3} \times \frac{\cot\omega}{R} = .0071$ log	7	8	5	2	1	7	— 10

$1 + .0071 = 1.0071$

log (h cot ω)	1	8	5	2	1	7	
log 1.0071...	0	0	0	3	0	7	
log S_{20}......	1	8	5	5	2	4	

10. $\Delta R_{50V} = 276$ yards

$$\Delta R_{50V} = \frac{\Delta v_A R}{2B}$$

log Δv_A.....	7	0	1	0	3	0	— 10
log R........	4	0	0	0	0	0	
colog 2......	9	6	9	8	9	7	— 10
colog B......	1	7	3	1	4	2	
log ΔR_{50V}...	2	4	4	0	6	9	

12. $\Delta R_{10C} = 213$ yards

$$\Delta R_{10C} = \frac{B - A}{10B} R \qquad B - A = .003959 \qquad 10B = .1856$$

log ($B - A$).	7	5	9	7	5	9	— 10
log R........	4	0	0	0	0	0	
colog $10B$....	0	7	3	1	4	2	
log ΔR_{10C}...	2	3	2	9	0	1	

11. ΔR_w for ± 10 pounds in w,
$\Delta R_w = \pm 42$ yards

a. $\left\{ \delta V = 0.36 \frac{\Delta w}{w} V \quad \Delta R' = \Delta R_{50V} \times \frac{12}{50} \right\}$ For change in initial velocity.

b. $\Delta R'' = \Delta R_{50C} \times \frac{10}{87}$ } For change in weight.
c. $\Delta R_w = \Delta R' + \Delta R''$

(See page 1[illegible].)

log 0.36.... .	9	5	5	6	3	0	— 10
log Δw......	1	0	0	0	0	0	
colog w.....	7	0	6	0	4	8	— 10
log V.......	3	4	6	2	4	0	
log δV......	1	0	7	9	1	8	

$\delta V = 12$ f. s., $\Delta v_A = .001024$

log ΔR_{50V}...	2	4	4	0	7	0	
log 12.......	1	0	7	9	1	8	
colog 50.....	8	3	0	1	0	3	— 10
log $\Delta R'$......	1	8	2	0	9	1	

$\Delta R' = 66.21$

log ΔR_{10C}....	2	3	2	9	0	1	
log 10.......	1	0	0	0	0	0	
colog 87.....	8	0	6	0	4	8	— 10
log $\Delta R''$.....	1	3	8	9	4	9	

$\Delta R'' = 24.52$

$\Delta R' = 66.21$
$\Delta R'' = 24.52$

$\Delta R_{10w} = 41.62$

Determination of n, $n = \frac{V^2 \sin 2\phi}{gX}$

log V^2.......	6	9	2	4	8	0	
log sin 2ϕ...	9	1	6	6	6	9	— 10
colog g......	8	4	9	2	1	4	— 10
colog X.....	5	5	2	2	8	8	— 10
log n........	0	1	0	6	5	1	

$n = 1.278$
$2n = 2.556$
$2n - 1 = 1.556$ log $(2n - 1) = 0.19201$
$R = 10000$ log $R = 4.00000$
$X = 30000$ log $X = 4.47712$

FORM No. 4.

For Computation of

Column 13. Wind effect in range.
Column 14. Gun motion in range.
Columns 15 and 18. Target motion effect in range and deflection.
Column 16. Wind effect in deflection.
Column 17. Gun motion effect in deflection.
Column 19. Change in height of impact for variation of ± 100 yards in sight bar.

.13. Wind effect in range,
$\Delta R_{w} = 26.7$ yards.

$$\Delta X_W = W_{12x}\left(T - \frac{n}{2n-1} \times \frac{X \cos \phi}{V}\right)$$

$$W_{126} = W_{128} = G_{12x} = G_{128} = T_{120} = T_{126}$$

$$= \frac{12 \times 6080}{60 \times 60 \times 3} = 6.7556$$

log n........	0	1	0	6	5	1	
log X........	4	4	7	7	1	2	
log cos ϕ....	9	9	9	8	8	2	—10
colog $(2n-1)$	9	8	0	7	9	9	—10
colog V.....	6	5	3	7	6	0	—10.
log $\frac{nX \cos \phi}{(2n-1) V}$	0	9	2	8	0	4	

$$\frac{nX \cos \phi}{(2n-1) V} = 8.47$$
$$T = 12.43$$
$$3.96$$

log W_{12x}.....	0	8	2	9	6	7
log 3.96.....	0	5	9	7	7	0
log ΔR_W....	1	4	2	7	3	7

14. Gun motion effect in range,
$\Delta R_G = 57$ yards

$$\Delta X_G = \frac{nX \cos \phi}{(2n-1) V} G_{128}$$

log $\frac{nX \cos \phi}{(2n-1) V}$	0	9	2	8	0	4
log G_{128}.....	0	8	2	9	6	7
log ΔR_G....	1	7	5	7	7	1

15 and 18. Target motion effect in range and deflection,
$\Delta R_T = D_T = T_{126} T = T_{12x} T = 84$ yards

log T_{128} = log T_{126}.	0	8	2	9	6	7
log T........	1	0	9	4	5	2
log ΔR_T = log D_T..	1	9	2	4	1	9

16. Wind effect in deflection,
$D_W = 13.9$ yards

$$D_W = W_{128}\left(T - \frac{X}{V \cos \phi}\right)$$

log X........	4	4	7	7	1	2	
colog V.....	6	5	3	7	6	0	—10
log sec ϕ....	0	0	0	1	1	8	
log $\frac{X}{V \cos \phi}$	1	0	1	5	9	0	

$$\frac{X}{V \cos \phi} = 10.37$$
$$T = 12.43$$
$$2.06$$

log W_{128}.....	0	8	2	9	6	7
log 2.06......	0	3	1	3	8	7
log D_W.....	1	1	4	3	5	4

17. Gun motion effect in deflection,
$D_G = 70.1$ yards

$$D_G = \frac{X}{V \cos \phi} G_{128}$$

log G_{12x}.....	0	8	2	9	6	7
log $\frac{X}{V \cos \phi}$...	1	0	1	5	9	0
log D_G.....	1	8	4	5	5	7

19. Change in height of impact for variation of ± 100 yards in sight bar, $H = 28$ feet
$H = \Delta X \tan \omega$ $\Delta X = 300$ feet

log ΔX......	2	4	7	7	1	2	
log tan ω....	8	9	7	1	7	4	—10
log H_{100}.....	1	4	4	8	8	6	

EXAMPLES.

1. For examples in determining the angle of departure corresponding to any given range, the data in the range tables may be used, computing for standard atmospheric condition, and proceeding to determine the true value of the ballistic coefficient by successive approximations. (See also Examples in Chapter 8.)

2. As the process of successive approximations is somewhat long for section room work, the following are given. Given the data contained in the following table, compute the corresponding values of ϕ, ω, T and v_ω of the drift, of the maximum ordinate, and of the penetration of armor by capped projectiles (Harveyized armor, by Davis's formula for guns *A, B, D, E, G, I, J, L* and *O*; face-hardened armor, by De Marre's formula for guns *C, F, H, K, M, N, P, Q* and *R*. De Marre's coefficient $=1.5$). Atmosphere standard.

Problem.	DATA.							ANSWERS.							
	Projectile.			Value of *f*.	*V*. f.s.	Range. Yds.	Multiplier for drift.	ϕ.	ω.	*T*. Secs.	v_ω. f.s.	Drift. Yds.	Maximum ordinate. Ft.	Penetration.	
	d. In.	*w*. Lbs.	*c*.											Harv. In.	F.H. In.
A...	3	13	1.00	1.0044	1150	2500	1.0	6° 53.1′	8° 26′	7.89	837	7.5	253	0.96	....
B...	3	13	1.00	1.0034	2700	3600	1.0	2 48.9	5 10	6.61	1094	5.9	181	1.30	....
C...	4	33	0.67	1.0011	2900	3000	1.0	1 15.3	1 35	3.71	2043	1.6	55	....	4.9
D...	5	50	1.00	1.0025	3150	4000	1.5	1 53.4	3 05	5.57	1511	5.8	126	3.40	....
E...	5	50	0.61	1.0024	3150	4500	1.5	1 45.7	2 26	5.49	1932	5.4	122	4.6	....
F...	6	105	0.61	1.0605	2600	14000	1.5	13 27.3	24 17	28.88	1070	183.0	3513	....	2.9
G...	6	105	1.00	1.0022	2800	3800	1.0	1 52.6	2 35	5.21	1729	3.2	109	5.7	....
H..	6	105	0.61	1.0015	2800	3500	1.5	1 28.6	1 46	4.29	2153	3.0	74	....	7.9
I...	7	165	1.00	1.0095	2700	7000	1.0	4 45.6	7 59	11.78	1243	17.6	566	4.6	....
J...	7	165	0.61	1.0083	2700	7500	1.5	4 04.1	5 42	10.82	1631	20.9	473	6.4	....
K..	8	260	0.61	1.0085	2750	8000	1.5	3 59.8	5 21	10.96	1771	21.5	484	....	8.4
L...	10	510	1.00	1.0141	2700	9000	1.0	5 31.6	8 33	14.14	1401	24.6	811	8.6	....
M..	10	510	0.61	1.0137	2700	10000	1.5	5 10.5	6 55	13.95	1744	34.5	785	....	10.4
N..	12	870	0.61	1.1130	2900	24000	1.5	15 07.7	25 01	39.51	1359	309.9	6358	....	8.8
O...	13	1130	1.00	1.0337	2000	10500	1.0	11 32.4	16 40	21.90	1157	59.9	1955	9.4	....
P...	13	1130	0.74	1.0316	2000	11000	1.5	10 52.1	14 37	21.36	1279	82.9	1845	....	8.9
Q...	14	1400	0.70	1.0571	2000	14000	1.5	14 37.1	20 02	28.28	1246	148.4	3246	....	9.3
R...	14	1400	0.70	1.0342	2600	14500	1.5	8 41.7	12 13	22.10	1560	89.3	1975	.....	12.8

3. Given the data and results contained in Example 2, compute the corresponding values of:

1. Danger space for a target 20 feet high.
2. Change in range resulting from a variation from standard of ± 50 f. s. in the initial velocity.
3. Change in range resulting from a variation from standard of ± 10 per cent in the density of the atmosphere.
4. Change in range resulting from a variation from standard as given below in the weight of the projectile:

Gun *C* .... ± 1 pound.
Guns *F* and *H*............... ± 3 pounds.
Gun *J* .... ± 4 pounds.
Gun *K* .... ± 5 pounds.
Guns *M, N, P, Q* and *R*........ ±10 pounds.

ANSWERS.

Problem.	Danger space. Yds.	Change in range for variation in V. Yds.	Change in range for variation in density. Yds.	Change in range for variation in w. Yds.
A.	45.8	± 114.5	∓ 46.3	......
B.	75.2	± 74.4	∓ 163.9	......
C.	260.6	± 83.2	∓ 63.0	∓ 33.6
D.	127.3	± 82.3	∓ 154.7	......
E.	162.4	± 104.4	∓ 125.6	......
F.	14.8	± 279.8	∓ 656.4	± 37.9
G.	153.5	± 99.0	∓ 104.7	......
H.	229.5	± 103.2	∓ 56.8	∓ 43.2
I.	47.9	± 159.1	∓ 284.4	......
J.	67.4	± 199.9	∓ 214.7	∓ 42.2
K.	71.8	± 217.4	∓ 204.3	∓ 41.6
L.	44.6	± 220.4	∓ 319.9	......
M.	55.3	± 275.9	∓ 253.9	∓ 55.4
N.	14.3	± 522.0	∓ 1010.3	∓ 9.2
O.	22.3	± 339.9	∓ 333.7	......
P.	25.6	± 389.5	∓ 290.0	∓ 24.0
Q.	18.3	± 479.8	∓ 399.0	∓ 20.9
R.	30.9	± 395.4	∓ 425.2	∓ 22.5

4. Given the data and results contained in Example 2, compute the corresponding values of (atmospheric conditions being standard):

1. n.
2. Effect in range and deflection of wind components of 12 knots.
3. Effect in range and deflection of a speed of gun of 12 knots.
4. Effect in range and deflection of a speed of target of 12 knots.
5. Change in position of point of impact in the vertical plane through the target for a variation of ±100 yards in the setting of the sight in range.

ANSWERS.

Problem.	Value of n.	Wind.		Speed of gun.		Speed of target.	Change of point of impact in vertical plane. Ft.
		Range. Yds.	Deflection. Yds.	Range. Yds.	Deflection. Yds.	Range and deflection. Yds.	
A.	1.3032	17.8	8.9	35.5	44.4	53.3	± 44.5
B.	2.0577	26.8	17.6	17.8	27.1	44.7	± 27.1
C.	1.2709	7.8	4.1	17.3	21.0	25.1	± 8.3
D.	1.6929	19.4	11.9	18.3	25.7	37.6	± 16.2
E.	1.4028	14.6	8.1	22.5	29.0	37.1	± 12.7
F.	2.2622	126.9	82.9	68.1	112.1	195.1	± 135.4
G.	1.3981	13.8	7.7	21.4	27.5	35.2	± 13.5
H.	1.1947	7.2	3.6	21.8	25.3	29.0	± 9.3
I.	1.7830	43.2	26.9	36.4	52.7	79.6	± 42.1
J.	1.4241	29.8	16.7	43.3	56.4	73.1	± 29.9
K.	1.3609	27.6	14.0	46.5	59.1	74.0	± 28.1
L.	1.6075	46.7	27.7	48.8	67.9	95.5	± 45.1
M.	1.3558	35.0	18.9	59.2	75.4	94.2	± 36.4
N.	1.8278	155.4	93.2	111.5	173.7	266.9	± 140.0
O.	1.5459	70.9	39.4	77.0	108.6	147.9	± 89.8
P.	1.3941	59.0	30.8	85.3	113.5	144.0	± 78.2
Q.	1.4446	86.1	44.4	105.0	140.6	191.1	± 109.4
R.	1.4424	63.8	35.0	85.5	114.3	149.3	± 65.0

CHAPTER 17.

THE PRACTICAL USE OF THE RANGE TABLES.

Range tables. **274.** A range table should be so constructed as to supply all the data necessary to enable the gun for which it is computed to be properly and promptly laid in such a manner that its projectiles may hit a target whose distance from the gun is known. This condition is fulfilled by the official range table computed and issued by the Bureau of Ordnance for each of our naval guns. In its simplest form, such a range table consists of a tabular statement of the values of the elements of a series of computed trajectories pertaining to successive horizontal ranges, within the possible limits of elevation of the gun as mounted, which is generally about 15° for naval guns, but is increased in late mounts, with such ranges taken as arguments and with the ranges and corresponding data disposed in regular order for ready reference, so that any desired range may be quickly found in the table, and from it all the corresponding elements of the required trajectory. In other words, complete and accurate knowledge of all the elements of the trajectory for each range is essential to the efficient use of the gun, and to this must be added complete data as to the effect upon the range of any reasonable variations in such of the ballistic elements as are liable to differ in service from those standard values for which the table is computed. There must also be added the necessary data to show the variations in range and deflection resulting from the velocity of the wind and from motion of the gun and target. We have seen in the preceding chapters how to compute all this data.

Constants and their variations. **275.** The constants upon which a range table is based we have seen to be the caliber, weight and coefficient of form of the projectile, that is, the factors from which the value of the ballistic coefficient is computed; the initial velocity; and the jump, this last being habitually considered as practically non-existent in service unless there is reason to believe to the contrary in special cases. The initial velocity, as well as the characteristics of the projectile, constitute features of the original design of each particular type of gun; and, although the values of some of them may be somewhat modified as the result of preliminary experimental firings, they are fixed quantities when the question of sight graduations and of range table data is under consideration. Of course the initial velocity and weight of projectile may vary somewhat from their assigned standard values, the amount of variation from round to round depending upon the regularity of the powder, the care taken in the manufacture and inspection of the ammunition and in putting up the charges, etc. Two very possible and important causes of variation in the initial velocity are variations from standard in the temperature of the powder, and drying out of the volatiles from the powder. Both of these causes have a very marked effect upon the initial velocity, and to overcome them efforts are made to keep the magazines at a steady temperature and all at the same temperature; while each charge is kept in an air-tight case in order to prevent evaporation of the solvent remaining in the powder when it is issued to service. It may be pointed out that it is more important that all magazine temperatures shall be kept the same throughout the ship than that they should be kept at the standard temperature. If the charges for all guns are at the same temperature, then, so far as that point is concerned, the guns will all shoot alike if the battery has been properly calibrated; and the spotter can readily allow for variations from standard; but if one magazine is at a high temperature and another at a low, then the guns involved will have different errors resulting from this cause, and the spotter cannot hope to get the salvos bunched when the sights of the several guns are set for the same range.

276. The sights are marked and the range table computed for the mean initial velocity and the mean weight of projectile, and these are made identical with the fixed standard values as given in the range table. In preparing projectiles for issue to the service great care is exercised to bring the weight of each one to standard so that this cause of variation in range may not appear. **Sight markings.**

277. Up to within the past few years (that is, up to the adoption of the long pointed projectile) the value of the coefficient of form was taken as unity. This was its value, for which the ballistic tables were computed, for the type of projectile then standard in service, as described in the preceding chapters of this book. With the adoption of the long pointed projectile, however, the value of the coefficient of form has dropped below unity, and for the several guns and projectiles covered by the Range and Ballistic Tables published for use with this text book, its value ranges from 1.00 for blunt pointed projectiles (radius of ogival of 2.5 calibers) to from 0.74 to 0.61 for long pointed projectiles (radius of ogival of 7 calibers). Its value, whatever it is, must be used in computing the value of the ballistic coefficient, so long as the present ballistic tables are used. Perhaps it may be advisable some day to recompute the ballistic tables with the long pointed projectile as the standard projectile of the tables, in which case the coefficient of form of such a projectile would then become unity for computations with the new tables; and a coefficient of form whose value is greater than unity would have to be used for computations involving the blunt-nosed projectiles. Such recomputation of the tables has not yet been made, however, and it is unlikely that it will be done unless progress in the development of ordnance makes recomputation necessary by raising service initial velocities above the present upper limit of the ballistic tables. **Standard projectiles.**

278. To show the results obtained by the adoption of the long pointed projectile, let us compare the range tables for the 7″ gun of 2700 f. s. initial velocity, weight of projectile 165 pounds, for a range of 7000 yards, for each of the two values of the coefficient of form. The two range tables give:

Value of c.	Range for an angle of elevation of about 15°. Yards.	Time of flight. Secs.	Striking velocity. f. s.	Danger space for target 20′ high. Yards.	Maximum ordinate. Feet.	Penetration in Harveyized armor. Inches.
1.00	13100	11.76	1247	48	563	4.6
0.61	16900	9.89	1690	76	395	6.7

From what has been studied in the preceding chapters, a glance at the above figures will show at once how vastly improved the performance of the gun has been in every particular by the introduction of the long pointed projectile.

279. After the preceding preliminary remarks it is possible to proceed to a careful consideration of the uses to which the range tables may be put in service, and this will now be done, column by column.

280. Explanatory Notes.—The explanatory notes at the beginning of each range table are in general a statement of the standard conditions for which the data in the columns is computed, and of the methods by which it is computed. There is one item given therein which is used in practical computations aboard ship, however, and that is the information in regard to the effect upon the initial velocity of variations in the temperature of the powder. The note in every case gives the standard temperature of the powder, which is generally taken as 90° F.; and then states that a variation from this standard temperature of $\pm 10°$ causes a variation in initial velocity of about ± 35 foot-seconds in the initial velocity in most cases, although in some cases the variation in initial velocity for that amount of variation in temperature is ± 20 foot- **Explanatory notes to range tables.**

seconds instead of ± 35 foot-seconds. For instance, with our standard problem 12" gun, we see that the variation in initial velocity for a variation of $\pm 10°$ from standard is ± 35 foot-seconds. Therefore, if the temperature of the charge were 80° F., our initial velocity would be 2865 foot-seconds and not 2900 foot-seconds. If the temperature of the charge were 100° F., the initial velocity would be 2935 foot-seconds. A variation of $\pm 5°$ in the temperature of the charge gives a proportionate change in the initial velocity, that is, $\pm \frac{35}{10} \times 5 = \pm 17.5$ foot-seconds; and if the temperature of the charge were 77° F., we would have a resultant initial velocity of

$$2900 - \frac{35 \times 13}{10} = 2854.5 \text{ foot-seconds}$$

and similarly for other variations. (See note after paragraph 303.)

Col. 1, range.

281. Column 1. Range.—As already explained, this is the argument column of the table. The data in the other columns is obtained by computation for ranges beginning at one thousand yards and increasing by five-hundred yard increments, and that for intermediate ranges by interpolation from the computed results (using second or higher differences where such use would affect the results). Therefore, to obtain the value of any element corresponding to a range lying between the tabulated ranges as given in Column 1, proceed by interpolation by the ordinary rules of proportion.

Col. 2, ϕ.

282. Column 2. Angle of Departure = Angle of Elevation + Jump.—As has been said, although jump must be watched for and considered in any special case where it may be suspected or found to exist, still it is normally practically nonexistent in service, and the angle of departure and angle of elevation coincide for horizontal trajectories.

To lay gun at given angle of elevation.

283. To lay the gun at any desired angle of elevation, the sights being marked in yards and not in degrees; find the angle of elevation in Column 2, and the corresponding range from Column 1. Set the sight at this range, point at the target, and the gun will then be elevated at the desired angle. An example of this kind is given in paragraphs 188, 189, 190 and 191 of Chapter 11. As there seen, this process is necessary when shooting at an object that is materially elevated or depressed relative to the horizontal plane through the gun.

Let us now see how correctly the range tables may be used to determine the proper angle of elevation to be used to hit an elevated target; assuming the theory of the rigidity of the trajectory as true within the angular limits probable with naval gun mounts. For this purpose we will consider the problem solved in paragraph 188 of Chapter 11, which was for the 12" gun; $V=2900$ f. s.; $w=870$ pounds; $c=0.61$; horizontal distance $=10,000$ yards; elevation of the target $=1500$ feet above the gun; barometer $=29.00''$; thermometer $=90°$ F. In paragraph 188 we computed that the correct angle of elevation for this case is 4° 08.1′.

Now let us use Column 12 and correct for atmospheric conditions, for which, from Table IV, the multiplier is $+0.79$; from which we have that for a sight setting of 10,000 yards the shell would range $10000 + (215 \times .79) = 10169.85$ yards. Therefore in order to make the shell travel 10,000 yards we must set the sight in range for 9830.15 yards. From the range table, by interpolation, the proper angle of departure for this range is 4° 07.9′. If we use this for the angle of elevation desired (instead of the computed value of 4° 08.1′) we will have an error of 2′, that is, of about 7 yards short.

Now if we solve the triangle to determine the actual distance from the gun to the target in a straight line, we will find it to be 9857.8 yards (by use of traverse tables), using the horizontal distance corrected for atmospheric conditions as the base. From the range table, the angle of departure for this range is 4° 08.6′. If we use this as the desired angle of elevation we will have an error of 5′ in elevation, or of about 17 yards over.

The above processes show, for this individual case, the degree of inaccuracy that would enter from the use of the range table for this purpose; and the errors introduced above are not great enough to prevent the first shot from falling within reasonable spotting distance. That this will be the case under all circumstances cannot be predicted, and each individual case must be considered on its own merits. For instance, it is evident that the horizontal distance could not be used in attacking an aeroplane at a high angle with a gun so mounted as to enable such angles to be used.

It is to be noted that, when we use the range table as described above, assuming that the trajectory be rigid, we get the same results whether the target be elevated above or depressed below the horizontal plane of the gun. This shows at once that the method is not theoretically perfect.

284. For subcaliber practice a one-pounder gun is mounted in or on a turret gun, the axes of the two guns being parallel; and it is desired to point the pair, using the sights of the turret gun, so that the one-pounder projectile will hit a target at a known range. A combination range table for this purpose is given on page 34 of the Gunnery Instructions, 1913, but if this be not available we may proceed as follows (and this is the method by which the table referred to was prepared) for our standard problem 12″ gun: Suppose that our subcaliber target is 1750 yards away. Look in the range table for the one-pounder gun that is to be used, and it will be found that the angle of departure for that gun for 1750 yards is 4° 13′. The problem then becomes similar to that stated in the preceding paragraph. Look in the 12″ range tables and it will be seen that for that gun the angle of departure of 4° 13′ corresponds to a range of 10,000 yards. Set the 12″ sights at 10,000 yards, point at the target with those sights, and the guns will then be so elevated that the one-pounder shell should hit at 1750 yards. **Subcaliber sighting.**

285. A problem that has come up a number of times in our service has been to use the sights marked for the initial velocity due to a full charge when firing with reduced charges and correspondingly reduced initial velocities. Suppose, for instance, we have our standard problem 12″ gun and are to fire it with the reduced charge which gives 2100 f. s. initial velocity instead of the regular 2900 f. s. given by the full charge. Proceeding by the methods already explained, we would compute the angles of departure necessary to give the desired ranges with the reduced velocity. Having tabulated the results, suppose we find that, for a given range A, the proper angle of departure is 6° 08′ 42″. Looking in the range tables for 2900 f. s., we find that the proper range at which to set the sights in order to get this angle of departure is 13,300 yards, and if we set the full charge sights for that range we should hit at A yards with the reduced charge. The results should be tabulated for all probable ranges, and the resulting table used by the spotter; or else paper sight scales may be prepared for the reduced velocity and pasted on the sights over the old scales. **Use of same sights for varying initial velocities.**

286. If the range tables for the reduced velocity are at hand, the angle of departure for the given range may be found in the tables, and the work proceeds as in Example 13 of this chapter. If, however, no range tables for the reduced velocity are to be had, the angle of departure must be computed, as in Example 14. It will be noted in this example that the value of f is picked out for two-thirds of the maximum ordinate of the full velocity trajectory, which ordinate is necessarily less than that of the real trajectory, but this error is so small as not greatly to affect the results.

287. Knowing the possible angle of elevation resulting from the mechanical features of the mount, Column 2 will also show what degree of roll will necessarily **Roll as limiting fire.**

throw the line of sight off the target at, say, the bottom of the roll. We have seen that, with our standard problem 12″ gun at 10,000 yards, we must have an angle of departure of 4° 13′. Most turret guns cannot be elevated more than 15°, therefore when a ship has rolled so as to depress her guns 10° the total angle of elevation required of the mount at the bottom of the roll would be 10°+4° 13′=14° 13′, which is so near the limit of elevation of 15° as to show that it would probably be impossible to fire on the bottom of the roll under these conditions.

Col. 3, ω. **288. Column 3. Angle of Fall.**—This column will give information as to the angle of inclination of the axis of the projectile to the face of the target at any given range which is known as the "angle of impact"; and, also, its inclination to the surface of the water at the point of fall, and hence of the probability of a ricochet.

289. It is also used for computing the value of the danger space by the use of the formulæ given in Chapter 5.

Col. 4, T. **290. Column 4. Time of Flight.**—This column gives one of the elements that enter into the time interval necessary between successive shots from the same gun, that is, between salvos. For instance, with our standard problem 12″ gun at 10,000 yards, we see that the time of flight is 12.43 seconds. The time that must elapse between salvos is therefore 13 seconds plus the additional time it takes to spot the shot and get ready for the next one. It will be seen from this that the longer the range the longer must be the interval between salvos, provided they be properly spotted. At the longer ranges ordinarily used the time between two successive salvos as determined above is ample for loading, so that the loading interval does not enter under those conditions in determining the time between salvos. At short ranges, however, the loading interval might be greater than the time as determined above, and in such cases the loading interval would necessarily determine the salvo interval.

291. The information contained in this column is also necessary to determine the setting for time fuses when using shrapnel. In order to have this information readily available at the gun, the range scales of the sights generally bear corresponding time scales showing the time of flight in seconds corresponding to any given range.

292. When guns of different calibers are being fired together at the same target, or when different ships are firing together at the same target, the information contained in this column aids the spotter to identify the splashes of the shot which he is spotting. An assistant should start a stop watch at the instant the guns in question are fired, and then the shot that splash at the end of the tabulated time of flight are in all probability the ones in which the spotter is interested.

Col. 5, v_ω. **293. Column 5. Striking Velocity.**—The only practical use of this column is to enable a judgment to be formed of the effect of the projectile at any given range, and hence as to the advisability of using a given gun for a given purpose of attack at a given range.

Col. 6, drift. **294. Column 6. Drift.**—The drift being accurately compensated in sight setting with all modern telescopic sights, at all ranges, the data in this column is of no special value with modern guns, but of general interest only. With the old bar sights, however, in which the drift compensation was made by inclining the sight bar at a permanent angle, the compensation for drift was correct at a single range only, and at all other ranges the uncompensated portion of the drift had to be allowed for by the use of the sliding leaf. In such a case, if the accurate compensation be at 7000 yards, we would have to know the amount of drift compensated by the permanent angle at any other range at which we wish to shoot, say 10,000 yards, and the difference between that and the tabulated value of the drift at 10,000 yards would have to be compensated by the use of the sliding leaf.

Col. 7, danger space. **295. Column 7. Danger Space for a Target 20 Feet High.**—This column is very frequently used. In the first place, it gives us a quick general idea of the probability of making a hit, for the greater the danger space the greater the chance of success.

It also shows us the "danger range" or "point blank range"; that is, the maximum range for which the projectile never rises higher than the top of the target. (Compare with the same information as given in Column 8.) For our standard problem 12″ gun we see that this is the case up to and including 2100 yards, at which range the maximum ordinate is 20 feet. For targets of other heights than 20 feet, the danger space may be determined within reasonable limits of height by a simple proportion from the data contained in this column. Thus, for our standard problem 12″ gun, at 10,000 yards, the danger space for a target 30 feet high would be about $72 \times \frac{30}{20} = 108$ yards. If the height be so great that these results are not sufficiently accurate, then the new danger space must be computed by the formulæ given, the shorter one, $S = h \cot \omega$, being ordinarily sufficiently accurate.

A wrong conception of the danger space is often acquired, namely, that it may be defined as the distance from the target to the point of fall of a projectile that just touches the top of the target. This conception may apply fairly well at long ranges, but a reference to Column 7 of the range table for short ranges will show that it does not fit the data given in that column. Considering Column 19 of the range table, which gives the change in the height of the point of impact in the vertical plane through the target resulting from a variation of 100 yards in the setting of the sight in range, for long ranges the height of the target divided by the figures given in Column 19 gives the same result as the danger space given in Column 7, but this is not the case for short ranges. Bearing in mind that the danger space is the distance that the target can be moved from the point of fall directly toward the gun at the given range, and still be hit, it will be seen that, as the range is reduced, as soon as the maximum ordinate becomes equal to the height of the target, then the target may be moved all the way to the gun and still have the trajectory pierce the screen, so that the danger space is then equal to the range, and at the point where this happens we have the danger range. As a matter of fact Column 19 should be used for all practical computations, but there should be no confusion of thought as to the relation existing between Columns 7 and 19.

296. At long ranges a knowledge of the danger space shows immediately how far beyond the target a shot will fall that just touches the top of the target screen.

297. Column 8. Maximum Ordinate.—This column is valuable for use in determining the value of the altitude factor, f, in making ballistic computations to obtain approximate solutions. Col. 8, Y

298. Column 9. Penetration of Armor (Harveyized or Face Hardened) with Capped Projectiles.—The data in this column is of value only in determining the probable efficiency of attack upon armor at different ranges. The figures given in the column are for normal impact, and the angle of fall (as given in Column 3) must be taken into account in considering this subject in order to determine the angle of impact, the "angle of impact" against any surface being that angle less than 90° between the axis of the projectile at the moment of impact and the surface in question. Thus, for a vertical armor plate at the same level as the gun, the angle of impact is the complement of the angle of fall. For elevated or depressed targets the angle of inclination at the striking point must be used instead of the angle of fall given in the table. Up to a certain critical angle we get penetration in the usual manner, although a pronounced increase in the angle of impact probably reduces the efficiency of penetration. The critical angle referred to is that at which the point of the projectile ceases to bite, and we no longer have the penetrative effect due to the shape of the point but simply the smashing effect due to the momentum, which effect is of course Col. 9, E_1 and E_2.

small as compared to penetration proper. This subject is not particularly well understood up to the present time.

299. The tables which give the penetration in Harveyized armor were computed before the present form of face-hardened armor came into general use. A rough approximation to the penetration of face-hardened armor may be obtained from those tables by multiplying the penetration in Harveyized armor by 0.8.

300. For our standard problem 12″ gun, at 10,000 yards range, the angle of fall, as given by the range table, is 5° 21′. The angle of impact against a vertical side armor plate would therefore be 84° 39′. The angle of impact against a protective deck plate inclined to the horizontal at an angle of 15° would be 20° 21′, which is probably very near or less than the biting angle, and little if any penetrative effect could be expected; in other words, the protective deck would probably deflect the projectile, thus fulfilling the purpose for which it was designed. If, however, the ships being on parallel courses, the target ship were rolled 10° towards the gun at the moment of impact, the angle of impact against the vertical side armor would be 74° 39′; and that against the protective deck plate would be 30° 21′.

301. For an elevated target, a vertical armor plate, taking the problem given in paragraph 188 of Chapter 11, the angle of inclination to the horizontal at the target is $\theta = 2° \; 20.1'$, and the angle of impact would therefore be 87° 39.9′. For the problem given in paragraph 189 of Chapter 11, the angle of impact against the vertical plate would similarly be 82° 03′, as we have $\theta = (-) 7° \; 57'$ in this case.

Col. 10. $\Delta R_{50 f.}$ **302. Column 10. Change of Range for a Variation of ± 50 Foot-Seconds Initial Velocity.**—A number of causes tend to produce variations in initial velocity, one being a variation in the temperature of the charge, which has already been discussed. The volatiles in the powder may dry out, giving a resultant quicker burning powder, with an increase in both pressure and initial velocity. A damp powder will burn more slowly and give a reduced initial velocity. Slight deterioration in the powder not sufficient in amount or of a character to cause danger may reduce the initial velocity (any deterioration that causes an increase in the initial velocity will cause increased pressure, and should be looked upon as dangerous). There is no means of determining the amount of variation of initial velocity due to these last two causes except experimental firing. Firing at a given range under known conditions, with all known causes of variation eliminated, as will hereafter be explained in the discussion of calibration practice, and a comparison of the resulting actual range with that given in the range tables for the given angle of elevation, would give an approximate idea of any such change in initial velocity, by working backwards in this column.

303. For our standard problem 12″ gun, suppose we know that our charge was at a temperature of 100° F.; that the solvent had dried out enough to cause an increase in initial velocity of 15 f. s., and that deterioration of the non-dangerous kind had reduced the initial velocity by 20 f. s. Our final initial velocity would then be:

Standard initial velocity		2900 f. s.
Variation due to temperature of charge	+35 f. s.	
Variation due to drying out of volatiles	+15 f. s.	
Variation due to deterioration of powder	−20 f. s.	
Total variation	+30 f. s.	30 f. s.
Actual initial velocity		2930 f. s.

And at 10,000 yards range, this variation in initial velocity would give us, from Column 10, a resulting actual range of $10000 + \frac{277}{50} \times 30 = 10166$ yards, or the gun would shoot 166 yards over the target unless allowance was made for this variation by setting the sight at 9834 yards.

The figure of 35 foot-seconds due to the variation in temperature has recently (July, 1911) been the subject of experimentation, which indicates that this value is too high, and that for each 10° variation in temperature of the powder the change in initial velocity is only 20 foot-seconds.

It is well to appreciate this fact, as the curve on the Farnsworth gun error computer has been drawn for it, and it should be used in actual work in the fleet. However, in order to obtain the answers given to the wind and speed problems in this book, the value of 35 foot-seconds will have to be used.

304. These figures show the importance of keeping all powder charges at a constant temperature, and all the charges in the ship, particularly for guns of the same caliber, at the same temperature; and also for keeping the volatiles from drying out and for keeping the powder from becoming damp; as well as for using care to prevent deterioration, even if not of the dangerous kind. They also show how seriously results may be affected by keeping a powder charge in a hot gun before being fired long enough to let the temperature of the gun materially raise that of the charge; it being particularly necessary to look out for this point when carrying on a calibration practice.

305. Working back with the problem given above, suppose the gun had been fired at an angle of elevation of 4° 13′ 14″, that is, sighted for 10,000 yards, and that the point of fall had been accurately determined by triangulation; and, that, after the observed results had been reduced to standard conditions, the data showed an actual range of 10,100 yards, or 100 yards in excess of normal. This would tend to show that a drying out of volatiles had taken place sufficient to give an increase in initial velocity of $\frac{50\times100}{277}=18$ f. s. If this work be deemed reliable, we could then figure on an initial velocity of 2918 f. s. for further firing.

306. Column 11. Change of Range for a Variation of $\pm\Delta w$ Pounds in Weight of Projectile.—All projectiles, before issue to service, should be brought to standard weight, and it will be found that this has usually been done, and that there is ordinarily little use for the data contained in this column. However, if for calibration or for any other form of experimental firing, we find that the projectiles are not of standard weight, and that it is not practicable or convenient to make them so, we can reduce the results to standard by the use of this column. (The regular service projectile for the 14″ gun is subject to a tolerance of ±4 pounds in weight; that is, these projectiles may weigh anywhere from 1396 to 1404 pounds. For ordinary firing this small variation in weight is considered as immaterial.) Col. 11, ΔR_w.

307. It is important to note that, where there is no sign prefixed to the entry in this column, an increase in the weight of the projectile causes a decrease in range and the reverse; but if the entry in the column carries a negative sign (as is the case in some parts of the table for the 6″ gun for which $V=2600$, $w=105$, and $c=0.61$), then an increase in weight causes an increase in range at all ranges for which the negative sign appears in this column.

308. With our standard problem 12″ gun at 10,000 yards, a projectile weighing 877 pounds would travel $10000-\frac{42\times7}{10}=9970$ yards.

309. With the 6″ gun, for which $V=2600$ f. s., $w=105$ pounds, and $c=0.61$, if the shell weighed 110 pounds, for a set range of 12,400 yards, the travel would actually be $12400+\frac{18\times5}{3}=12430$ yards.

310. The physical reason why, under some conditions, an increase in weight of projectile gives a decrease in range at one range and an increase at another may be readily understood if we remember that the effect upon the range of an increase in the weight of the projectile is the result of two entirely independent causes. The first acts entirely before the projectile leaves the gun, and an increase of weight thus acting always causes a decrease in the initial velocity, and hence, so far as this part of the effect alone is concerned, an increase in weight would always cause a decrease in range. The second part of the effect, however, which acts entirely outside the gun, is that due to the momentum stored in the moving projectile; that is, it depends upon the weight. As the weight is a factor in Mayevski's expression for retardation, we see that an increase in weight increases the power of the projectile to overcome the atmospheric resistance, and hence increases the range. Therefore of two similar projectiles, differing somewhat in weight but leaving the gun with the same initial velocity, the heavier would travel the further; and, so far as this part of the effect alone is concerned, an increase in weight of the projectile would always give an increase in the range. We do not have equal initial velocities in the case under consideration, however, and the increase in the weight of the projectile acts first to decrease the initial velocity, and then, after leaving the gun, to make the projectile travel further than would one of standard weight if fired with the same reduced initial velocity. It can readily be conceived from this line of reasoning that, under some conditions, this second effect might more than balance that due to loss of initial velocity, and in all such cases an increase in the weight of the shell will increase the range. The proper sign for the data in Column 11 is determined by a careful consideration of the relative values of the two parts in the formulæ from which the data is derived.

311. An inspection of the range table for the 6″ gun referred to in paragraph 309 above will show that for ranges from 1000 yards to 10,800 yards an increase in the weight of the projectile will cause a decrease in the range; at 10,900 yards it will cause no change in the range; and from 11,000 yards up an increase in range will result.

312. For the standard problem 12″ gun, through the entire table, from 1000 to 24,000 yards, it will be seen that increase in weight of projectile causes decrease in range. It is of interest to note, however, that from 1000 yards to about 12,000 yards this decrease in range increases with the range from a minimum of 8 yards at 1000 yards to a maximum of 42 yards at about 12,000 yards; and that from about 12,000 yards up the variation decreases until, at the highest point of the table, 24,000 yards, the decrease in range, due to an overweight of 10 pounds in the projectile, is only 12 yards. Apparently there is some theoretical point beyond the upper limit of the range table at which this quantity would change sign, and beyond which an increase of 10 pounds in the weight of the projectile would cause an increase in range, in a manner similar to that discussed above in regard to the 6″ gun. This point is of course of no practical value in connection with the 12″ gun, whereas it must necessarily be taken into account in dealing with the 6″ gun.

Col. 12, ΔR_{10c}. **313. Column 12. Change of Range for a Variation of Density of Air of ±10 Per Cent.**—As has been stated, the range tables have been computed for a standard atmosphere of half-saturated air, for 59° F. (15° C.) and 29.53″ (750 mm.) barometric height. Of course this exact atmospheric condition will rarely exist in actual firing, and the data in this column has been computed to enable allowance to be made for variations from standard density. It is of course easier for a projectile to travel through a less dense than through a more dense medium; and if the air be below the standard density the range will therefore be greater than the standard range, etc.

314. For our standard problem 12" gun, range 10,000 yards, suppose the barometer stood at 31.00" and the thermometer at 50° F. From Table III of the Ballistic Tables, for those conditions, the value of δ is 1.069, or the air is 6.9 per cent above the standard density, and our actual range would be $10000-\frac{215\times 6.9}{10}=9852$ yards. If the barometer stood at 29.00" and the thermometer at 96° F., the value of δ would be 0.910, that is, the air would be 9 per cent below standard density, and the actual range would be $10000+\frac{215\times 9}{10}=10194$ yards.

315. Or for the same problem, using Table IV of the Ballistic Tables, in the first case the actual range would be $10000-215\times 0.69=9852$ yards, and in the second case it would be $10000+215\times 0.9=10194$ yards; which process is shorter but cannot be understood unless the first and longer method has first been comprehended.

316. This column is designated as referring to variations in the density of the air, this factor (δ) being the one going to make up the value of the ballistic coefficient that is most apt to vary. If we remember that the formula for the value of the ballistic coefficient is $C=\frac{fw}{\delta c d^2}$, we can see that a variation of any given per cent in any one of the factors gives the same numerical percentage change in the value of C, remembering that an increase in f or w gives an increase in C, and an increase in δ, c or d^2 gives a decrease in C. Changes in w cannot be handled in this way, owing to the resultant change in initial velocity already explained. Changes in f are not often known in such shape as to make it convenient to handle them by this method, that is, by the use of the data given in this column, although it could of course be done in this way were the percentage variation in the value of f known. Also c and d are ordinarily constant, thus leaving δ as the only one of the factors of the ballistic coefficient that would ordinarily be considered from this point of view. From the range table for this gun computed for $c=1.00$, for 3000 yards range, we have an entry of 84 yards in Column 12. If now the value of c becomes 0.95, we have a decrease of 5 per cent in the value of c, and therefore our range would increase to $3000+\frac{84\times 5}{10}=3042$ yards. Now, similarly, if we use the table for the same gun, but with $c=0.61$, we have in Column 12 of that table, for a range of 3000 yards, the data 66 yards. Now if the value of c increases from 0.61 to 0.66, we have an increase of $\frac{5}{61}=.082$, or 8.2 per cent; and the decreased range resulting from this change would be

$$3000-\frac{66\times 8.2}{10}=2945.88$$

Theoretically we should be able, starting at a given range in the table for $c=1.00$, to reduce the range by the correction from Column 12 for a variation of 39 per cent, and thus get the range for a projectile for which $c=0.61$ that would correspond to the range of 3000 yards for the projectile for which $c=1.00$. Then starting with this new range in the table for which $c=0.61$, and applying the correction from Column 12 for a variation of $\frac{39}{61}=.64$, or 64 per cent, we should get the original range from which we started as the corresponding range for the projectile for which $c=1.00$. This will not work out very closely, however, because the percentage change in such a case is too large to be handled by the use of data such as that contained in Column 12, which is computed by the use of a formula based on differential increments. 39 per cent and 64 per cent manifestly cannot be considered as such increments.

Col. 13, wind in range.

317. Column 13. Change of Range for Wind Component in Plane of Fire of 12 Knots.—This column is constantly used. For our standard problem 12" gun, at 10,000 yards, a wind blowing directly from the target to the gun with a velocity of 12 knots would decrease the actual range 27 yards, and would increase it the same

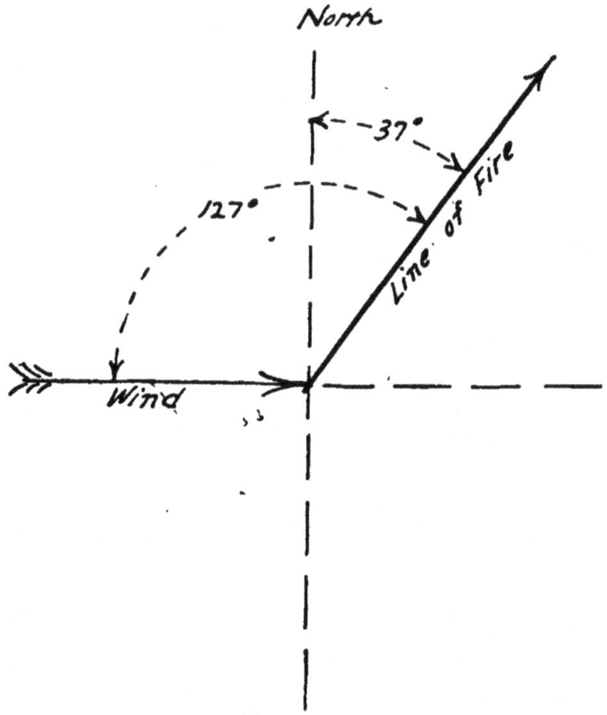

FIGURE 23.

amount if blowing the other way. Suppose the line of fire were 37° true, and the wind were blowing from 270° true with a velocity of 25 knots. Then the wind component in the line of fire would be 25 cos 53°, or (by use of the traverse tables) 15 knots, and the range would be increased $\frac{27\times 15}{12}=34$ yards by this component.

318. Column 14. Change of Range for Motion of Gun in Plane of Fire of 12 Knots.—This column is also constantly used. For our standard problem 12″ gun, at 10,000 yards, if the gun be moving at 12 knots directly towards the target, it will overshoot 57 yards unless the motion of the gun be allowed for in pointing; and if **Col. 14, gun motion in range.**

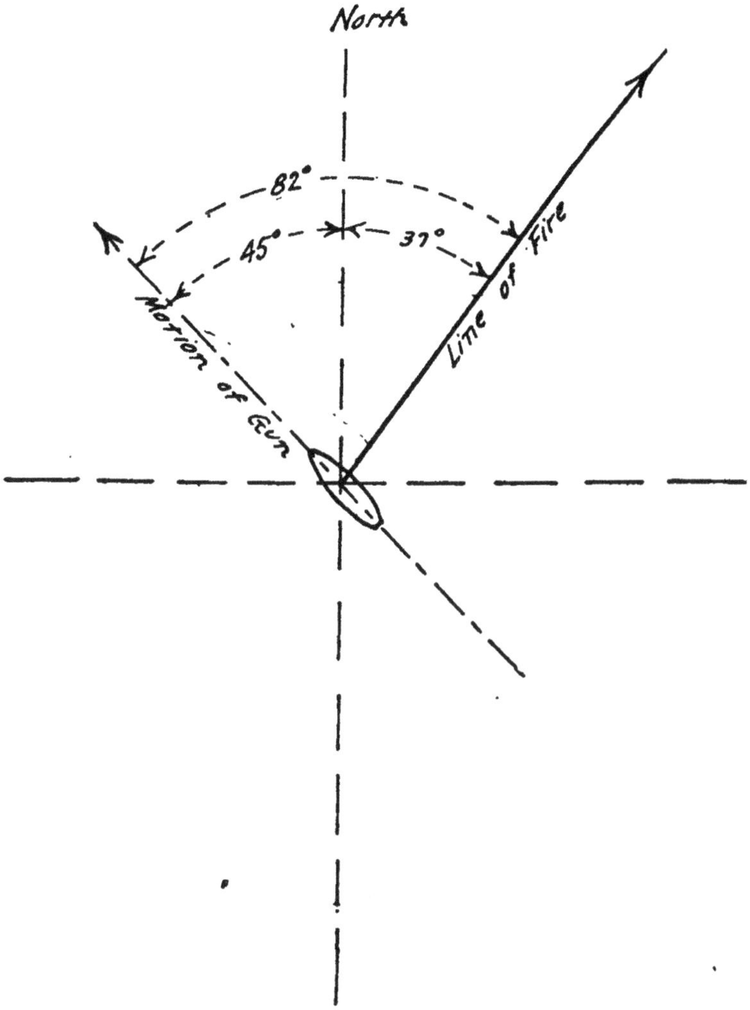

FIGURE 24.

moving in the opposite direction it would undershoot by the same amount. If the line of fire be 37° true, and the firing ship be steaming 315° true at 20 knots, the component speed in the line of fire would be 20 cos 82°, or (by the use of the traverse tables) 2.8 knots towards the target, and the gun would overshoot $\frac{57\times 2.8}{12}=13.3$ yards.

Col. 15, target motion in range.

319. Column 15. Change of Range for Motion of Target in Plane of Fire of 12 Knots.—This column is also constantly used. For our standard problem 12″ gun at 10,000 yards, if the target be steaming directly towards the gun at 12 knots, the gun would overshoot the mark 84 yards unless the motion were allowed for in pointing; and if it were steaming at the same rate in the opposite direction it would under-

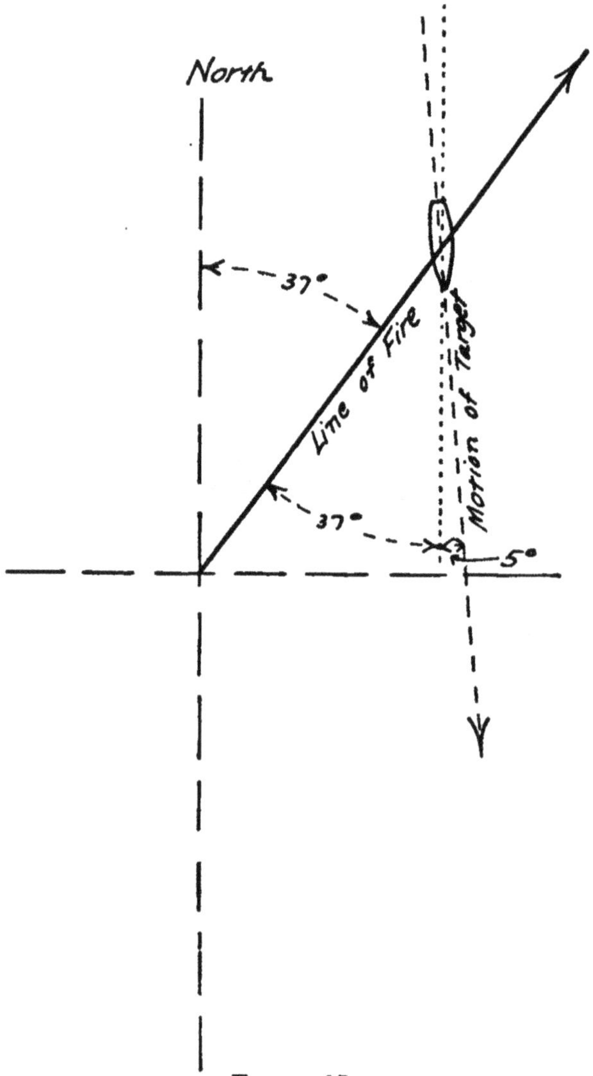

FIGURE 25.

shoot by the same amount. If the line of fire were 37° true, and the target were steaming 175° true at 23 knots, the component of motion in the line of fire would be 23 cos 42°, or (by the use of the traverse tables) 17.1 knots toward the gun, and the gun would overshoot $\frac{84\times 17.1}{12}=143.6$ yards.

320. Column 16. Deviation for Lateral Wind Component of 12 Knots.—This column is also constantly used. For our standard problem 12" gun at 10,000 yards, if the wind were blowing perpendicular to the line of fire and across it from right to left, with a velocity of 12 knots, the shot would fall 14 yards to the left of the target **Col. 16, wind in deflection.**

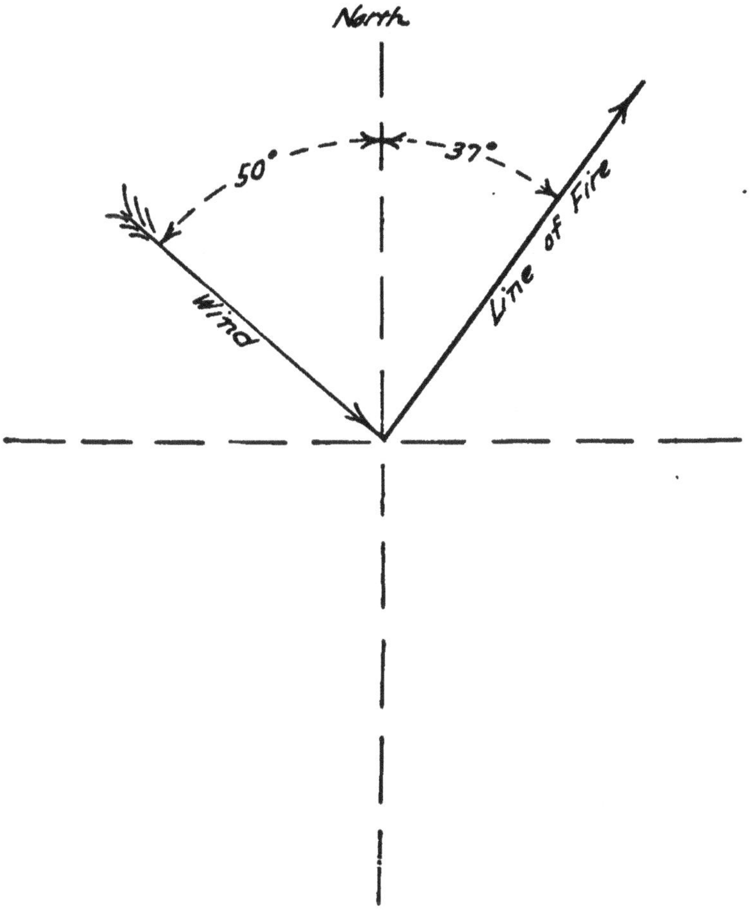

FIGURE 26.

unless the effect of the wind were allowed for in pointing. If the line of fire be 37° true, and the wind be blowing from 310° true at 23 knots, the wind component perpendicular to the line of fire would be 23 sin 87°, or (by the use of the traverse tables) 23 knots, and the shot would fall $\frac{14\times 23}{12}=27$ yards to the right of the target.

Col. 17, gun motion in deflection.

321. Column 17. Deviation for Lateral Motion of Gun Perpendicular to Line of Fire, Speed 12 Knots.—This column is also constantly used. For our standard problem 12" gun, at 10,000 yards, if the gun be moving at 12 knots perpendicular to the line of fire, and from right to left, the shot would fall 70 yards to the left of the

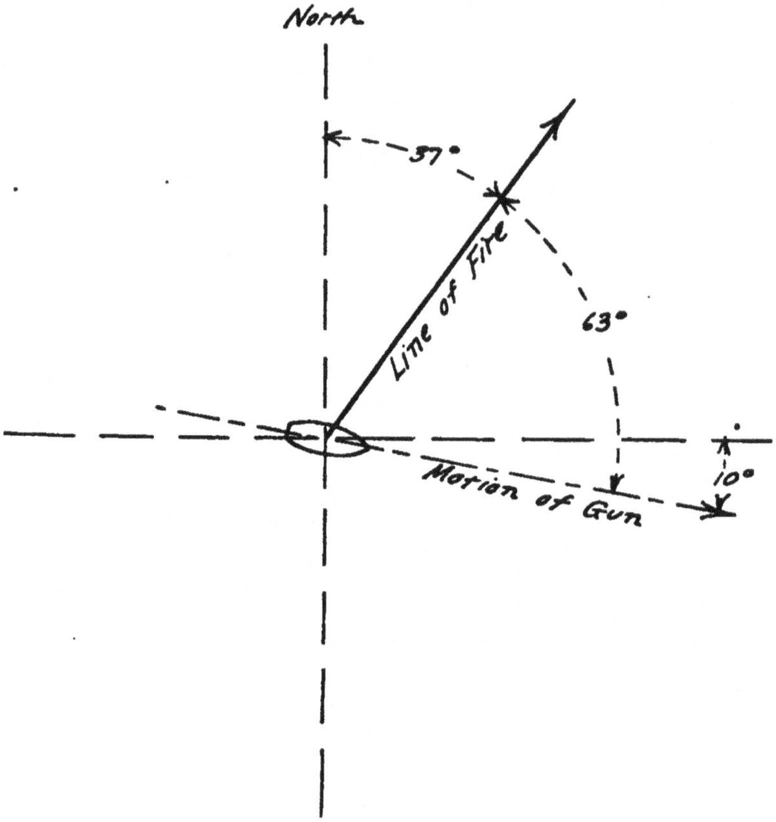

FIGURE 27.

target unless the motion were allowed for in pointing. If the line of fire be 37° true, and the firing ship be steaming 100° true at 21 knots, the component of this motion perpendicular to the line of fire would be 21 sin 63°, or (by use of the traverse tables) 18.7 knots to the right, and the shot would fall $\frac{18.7 \times 70}{12} = 109$ yards to the right.

322. Column 18. Deviation for Lateral Motion of Target Perpendicular to Line of Fire, Speed 12 Knots.—This column is also constantly used. Note that the change of range in yards for the given speed when the target is moving in the line of fire is always the same numerically as the deviation in yards for the same speed when the motion is perpendicular to the line of fire. This is manifestly correct, as the motion of the target, unlike any of the other motions considered, has no effect upon the actual motion of the projectile relative to the ground. This motion of the target simply removes the target from the point aimed at by an amount equal to the dis- Col. 18, target motion in deflection.

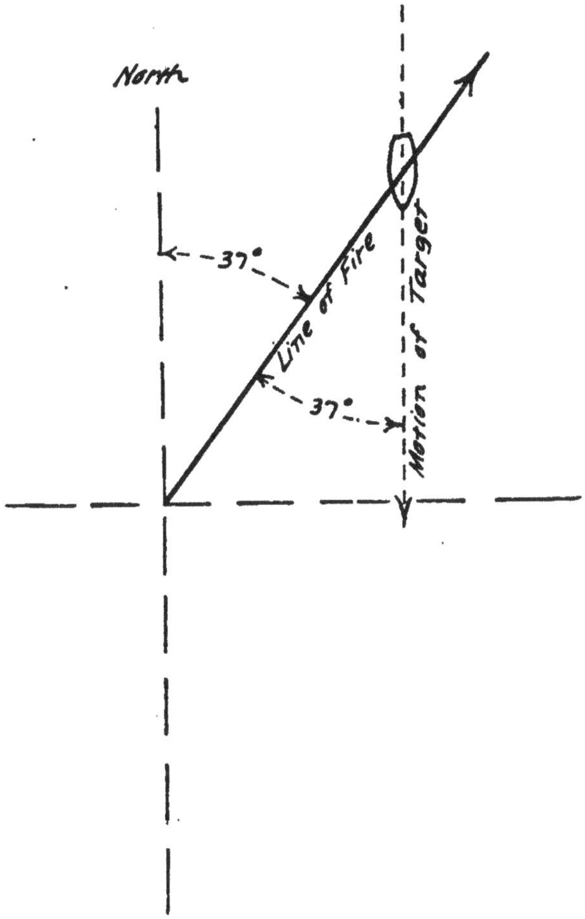

FIGURE 28.

tance traveled by it during the time of flight. For our standard problem 12″ gun at 10,000 yards, if the target be moving at 12 knots perpendicular to the line of fire, from right to left, the shot would fall 84 yards astern of, that is, to the right of the target unless allowance were made for this motion in pointing. If the line of fire be 37° true, and the target be steaming 180° true at 20 knots, then the component of motion perpendicular to the line of fire would be 20 sin 37°, or (by the use of the traverse tables), 12 knots to the left, and the shot would fall $\frac{84 \times 12}{12} = 84$ yards to the left.

Relation between deflection in yards and in knots.

323. There is another most important use to which the data contained in this column is constantly put, and that is the determination of the point at which to set the deflection scale of the sight to compensate for any known deviation in yards. Deflection scales could just as properly be marked in any units, say parts of an inch motion of the sliding leaf either way from the central position, or simply in arbitrary divisions of convenient size; and some such method was formerly employed before the present more scientific and accurate methods of pointing were introduced. Whatever the system of marking the deflection scales, the essential point is that there must be some simple and convenient means of determining quickly how many divisions change in the set of the deflection scale is necessary to correct a deviation of a known number of yards at any given range. It has therefore been found most convenient to mark the deflection scale in "knots," meaning "knots speed of target," and to make the size of the divisions such that setting the scale over by 12 knots, that is, by 12 of the divisions, will produce at any given range the number of yards deviation shown in Column 18 for that range. Our telescopic sights have their deflection scales marked in this way. To avoid the confusion that was found to arise from the necessity for using the words "right" and "left" in giving orders for sight setting, the mark of zero deflection for the sight is now commonly marked as "50 knots," and to shift the point of fall of the shot to the left we lower the reading of the deflection scale ("left" and "lower" both begin with the letter *l*), and to shift the point of fall of the shot to the right we raise the reading of the deflection scale ("right" and "raise" both begin with the letter *r*). For our standard problem 12″ gun, at 10,000 yards, if we wish to correct a deflection of 84 yards left, we wish to shift the point of fall of the shot that distance to the right, and we accordingly set the deflection scale at 62 knots. To correct a deflection of 84 yards right, we would similarly set the scale at 38 knots. If the deflection had been 25 yards, we would have set the deflection scale over $\frac{25 \times 12}{84} = 3.6$ knots, say 4 knots; and if we were correcting an error to the right (the original deflection setting having been 50), we would set the sight on 46 knots on the deflection scale; whereas had the original error been to the left the setting would be 54 knots.*

Col. 19, vertical position of point of impact.

324. Column 19. Change in Height of Impact for Variation of ±100 Yards in Sight Bar.—This column is also frequently used. For our standard problem 12″ gun, at 10,000 yards, suppose the shot were striking at an estimated distance of 50 feet above the target, and we want to know how much to change the setting of the sight in range to hit. Manifestly, we would lower the sight in range by $\frac{50 \times 100}{28} = 172$ yards.

The above is of value in shooting at objects on shore, where it is in some cases easier to estimate the vertical distance of the point of impact from the target than it is the error in range; and also in direct flight spotting where the shot can be seen to pass over the screen.

325. We also see that, by the use of Column 19, a change, with our standard problem 12″ gun of $\frac{20 \times 100}{28} = 72$ yards in range will change the vertical position of the point of impact 20 feet, at 10,000 yards range, that is, from the top to the bottom, or *vice versa*, of a target screen 20 feet high, which is the danger space at that range for such a target, and corresponds with the danger space as given in Column 7.

---

* See Appendix C for a description of the arbitrary deflection scale for sights, which has recently been adopted for service use.

326. If we were shooting at 10,000 yards on the sight bar, with the same gun, and gave a spot of "up 200," this would raise the position of the point of impact on the target screen, or rather in the vertical plane through it, a distance of $\frac{28\times 200}{100}=56$ feet.

327. In all wind and speed problems, draw roughly separate diagrams for gun, target and wind. Draw in each diagram a heavy line in the proper direction, to show the line of fire. For the gun and for the target, put the ship at the center, heading correctly, and draw a dotted line in the proper direction for the course of the gun or the target. For the wind draw a dotted line through the center with an arrow pointing in the direction towards which the wind is blowing. Find the angle, less than 90°, between course of gun or target or direction of wind, and line of fine. The cosine **Real wind and speed problem.**

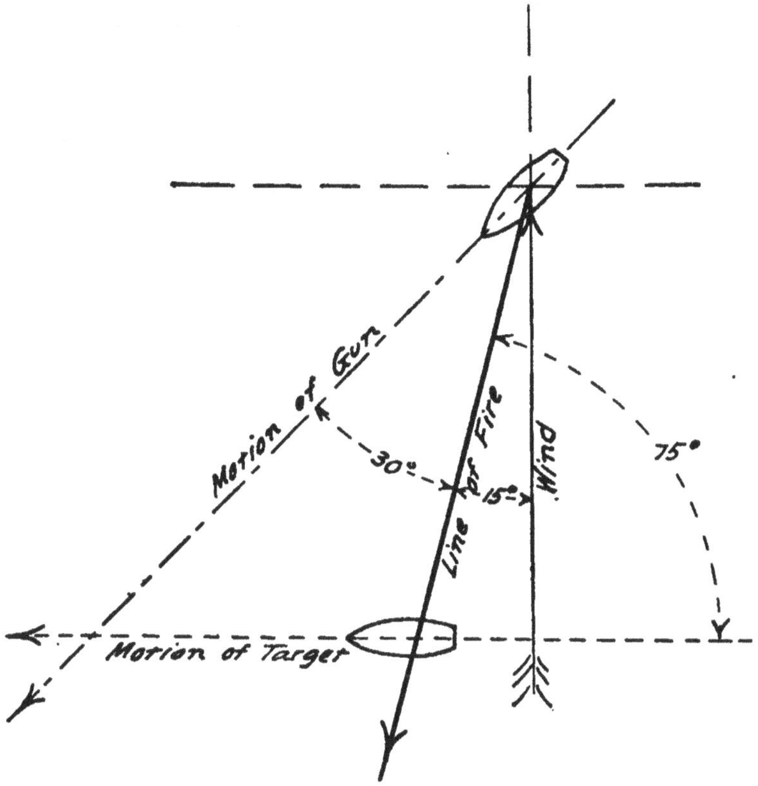

FIGURE 29

of that angle represents change in range, and the sine, change in deflection. We are now in a position to proceed to the solution of some every-day practical problems by the use of the range tables, and for the first one we will take a ship steaming southwest at 18 knots, which wishes to fire a 12″ gun ($V=2900$ f. s., $w=870$ pounds, $c=0.61$) at another ship that is 8000 yards distant and bears 30° off the port bow of the firing ship at the moment of firing. The target ship is steaming west at 22 knots, and the real wind is blowing from the south at 20 knots. The barometer is at 29.67″ and the thermometer at 20° F. The temperature of the powder is 70° F. Drying out of volatiles has raised the initial velocity of 25 f. s., and dampness of powder has reduced it 10 f. s. The shell weighs 875 pounds. How must the sights be set to hit? *

* See Appendix B for a description of the Farnsworth Gun Error Computer, by the use of which these problems may be solved mechanically.

For given atmospheric conditions $\delta=1.089$, that is, the air is 8.9 per cent over standard density.

Use traverse tables for all resolutions of speeds.

Powder is 20° below standard, reducing V by $\frac{35}{10}\times20$ .... -70 f. s.

Drying out of volatiles increases V by .... $+25$ f. s.

Dampness of powder reduces V by .... -10 f. s.

Total variation of initial velocity from standard .... -55 f. s.

Cause of variation. Speed of or variation in—	Affects.	Formulæ.	Range. Short. Yds.	Range. Over. Yds.	Deflection. Right. Yds.	Deflection. Left. Yds.
Gun	Range	$18\cos 30\times\frac{47}{12}=15.6\times\frac{47}{12}$	....	61.1	....	....
	Deflection	$18\sin 30\times\frac{56}{12}=9\times\frac{56}{12}$	....	....	42.0	....
Target	Range	$22\cos 75\times\frac{65}{12}=5.7\times\frac{65}{12}$	30.9	....	....	....
	Deflection	$22\sin 75\times\frac{65}{12}=21.3\times\frac{65}{12}$	....	....	....	115.4
Wind	Range	$20\cos 15\times\frac{17}{12}=19.3\times\frac{17}{12}$	27.3	....	....	....
	Deflection	$20\sin 15\times\frac{8}{12}=5.2\times\frac{8}{12}$	....	....	3.5	....
Initial velocity	Range	$55\times\frac{229}{50}$	251.9	....	....	....
w	Range	$5\times\frac{39}{10}$	19.5	....	....	....
δ	Range	$8.9\times\frac{136}{10}$	121.0	....	....	....
			450.6 61.1	61.1	45.5	115.4 45.5
Point of fall of shot if uncorrected			389.5 yards short.			69.9 yards left.

To correct a deflection of 69.9 yards, set deflection scale to right $\frac{69.9\times12}{65}=12.9$ knots of scale. Therefore to point correctly, set sights at

In range .... 8389.5 yards
In deflection .... 62.9 knots

or, to nearest graduations of sight scales, remembering to shoot short rather than over,

In range .... 8350 yards
In deflection .... 63 knots

Real wind and speed problem. **328.** A 12″ gun ($V=2900$ f. s., $w=870$ pounds, $c=0.61$) mounted on board a ship steaming 45° (magnetic) at 18 knots, is to be fired at a target ship on the starboard bow of the firing ship and steaming 315° (magnetic) at 14 knots, at the moment when the firing ship is 9530 yards from the point of intersection of the two courses, and the target ship is 5500 yards from the same point. The barometer is at 28.25″ and the thermometer at 80° F. The temperature of the powder is 105° F. Dampness of the powder has reduced the initial velocity, at standard temperature, to 2875 f. s. The shell is 7.5 pounds over weight. There is a real wind blowing from 260° by compass (Dev. 10° E.) at 20 knots. How should the sights be set to hit?

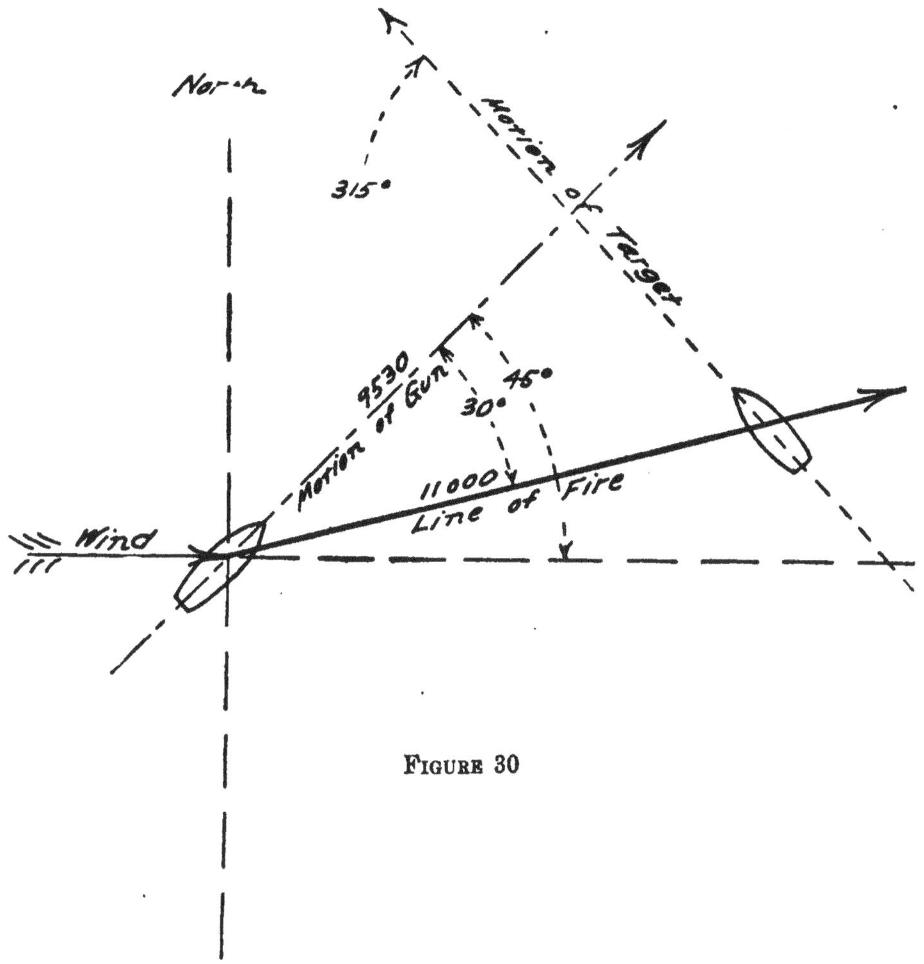

FIGURE 30

By use of the traverse tables, at the moment of firing, the target will be 30° on the starboard bow of the firing ship, distant 11,000 yards.

Temperature of powder $35 \times \frac{15}{10}$	+52.5 f. s.
Dampness	−25.0 f. s.
Total variation in initial velocity	+27.5 f. s.

For the given atmospheric conditions, $\delta = 0.916$, and the air is therefore 8.4 per cent below standard density.

Use the traverse tables for all resolutions of speeds.

Cause of error. Variation in or speed of—	Affects.	Formulæ.	Range.		Deflection.	
			Short. Yds.	Over. Yds.	Right. Yds.	Left. Yds.
Gun	Range	$18 \cos 30 \times \frac{62}{12} = 93 \cos 30$	....	80.5	....	....
	Deflection	$18 \sin 30 \times \frac{77}{12} = 115.5 \sin 30$	....	....	....	57.8
Target	Range	$14 \cos 60 \times \frac{94}{12} = 109.7 \cos 60$	....	54.8	....	....
	Deflection	$14 \sin 60 \times \frac{94}{12} = 109.7 \sin 60$	....	....	95.0	....
Wind	Range	$20 \cos 15 \times \frac{32}{12} = 53.3 \cos 15$	....	51.5	....	....
	Deflection	$20 \sin 15 \times \frac{17}{12} = 28.3 \sin 15$	....	....	7.3	....
Initial velocity	Range	$27.5 \times \frac{297}{50}$	....	163.4	....	....
w	Range	$7.5 \times \frac{42}{10}$	31.5	....	....	....
δ	Range	$8.4 \times \frac{256}{10}$	....	215.0	....	....
			31.5	565.2 31.5	102.3 57.8	57.8
Point of fall of shot if uncorrected			......	533.7 yards over.	44.5 yards right.	

To correct for a deflection of 44.5 yards, set deflection scale to left by

$$\frac{12}{94} \times 44.5 = 5.7 \text{ knots}$$

Therefore to point correctly, set the sights

In range for................10466.3 yards
In deflection for............. 44.3 knots

or, to nearest graduations of scales, remembering to shoot short rather than over,

In range for.................10450 yards
In deflection .... 44 knots

329. In all the preceding discussions relative to the wind, both in Chapter 14 and in this chapter, we have dealt with the *real* wind, and it is now time to take up the discussion of the *apparent* wind. The difference between the two must always be clearly borne in mind. The *real wind* is the wind that is actually blowing; that is, as it would be recorded by a stationary observer; while the *apparent wind* is the wind that appears to be blowing to an observer on board a moving ship. Thus, in Figure 31, let W be the velocity of the *real* wind, blowing at an angle $\alpha°$ with the direction of motion of the ship, and let G be the motion of the ship (in the same units as W).

Then, if the figure be drawn to scale, W' will represent the velocity of the *apparent wind*, and α'° its direction. Or the solution may be made by the ordinary rules of plane trigonometry.

FIGURE 31.

330. Columns 13 and 16 of the range tables are computed for real wind, and equations (211) and (212) were therefore used for the purpose, and these columns were therefore primarily computed for use in correcting for the effects of a known *real* wind. The same columns may be used, under some circumstances, for correcting for the effects of an *apparent* wind, as will now be explained.

331. Equations (213) and (214) give the total effect upon the range and deviation of G_x and G_z, respectively, but instead of using them (that is, Columns 14 and 17 of the range table), we may proceed in another way. The horizontal velocity of the ship, which is added to the projectile's proper velocity, would add to the range the distance G_xT, in which T is the time of flight, if it were not for the retardation caused by the resistance of the air. But the reduction of this added distance by air resistance is exactly equal to the change of range that would be caused by a wind component of G_x. The reasoning is similar for deflection. Consequently if, in determining the wind effect, we take account of the direction and velocity of the wind *relative to the moving ship,* that is, of the *apparent* wind instead of the *real* wind, in so doing we are including part of the effect of the ship's motion, and the remaining effect of that motion must be found, not by (213) and (214), but by

$$\Delta X_G = G_xT \qquad (220)$$

$$D_G = G_zT \qquad (221)$$

Observe that the change of range due to the *apparent* wind which results from the motion of the ship, G_x, is by (211)

$$-G_x\left(T - \frac{n}{2n-1} \times \frac{X \cos\phi}{V}\right)$$

so that, if we take account of this apparent wind, we must use G_xT to correct the range for the motion G_x in order that the sum of the two corrections may be the true effect of the motion given by (213); and similarly for the lateral motion.

332. The change in range and the lateral deviation due to wind, as given in Columns 13 and 16 of the range tables are those for an actual or real wind, and the values in those columns are computed for the condition that both gun and target are stationary in the water. Column 13 shows the number of yards a shot would have its range, as given in Column 1, increased or decreased by a real wind of 12 knots an hour blowing directly with or directly against its flight. Column 16 shows the number of yards the shell would be driven to the right or left, with the wind, by a real wind of 12 knots an hour blowing perpendicular to the line of fire during the time the shell is in the air traveling from the gun to the point of fall, that is, during the time of flight as given in Column 4, for the corresponding range as given in Column 1. **Real and apparent wind.**

333. If our standard problem 12″ gun be fired abeam, at a stationary target 10,000 yards away, on a calm day, while the ship is steaming at 12 knots an hour, the time of flight would be (from Column 4) 12.43 seconds, but the shell would not advance during its flight as far in the direction of the course of the ship as would the ship herself, because the initial sideways motion of the shell due to the motion of the gun in that direction would be retarded by the resistance of the air to such sideways motion of the shell after leaving the gun. In its sideways motion the shell has to overcome this air resistance. For example, for the above gun and conditions, the ship, during the time of flight, would travel 84 yards perpendicular to the line of fire (Column 18), but a wind effect equal to the speed of the ship, but in the opposite direction, would reduce the sideways motion of the shell in space by 14 yards (Column 16). Therefore the sideways motion of the shell in space due to the speed of the ship would be $84-14=70$ yards, which is the figure given in Column 17.

334. Again, if both ship and target were stationary, the other conditions being as given above, except that a real wind of 12 knots is blowing directly across the line of fire; we would then see, from Column 16, that the shell would be blown sideways during flight, or deflected, by 14 yards in the direction in which the wind is blowing, and this is the same amount as the difference between the travel of the ship and the travel of the shell in the direction of the course as given in the preceding paragraph. It will thus be seen that Column 17 in the range table allows for that portion of the apparent wind which is produced by the speed of the ship through still air. Hence to use Columns 13 and 16 for an apparent wind, which is the algebraic sum of the speed of the ship and of the velocity of the real wind, and Columns 14 and 17 for the motion of the gun, would be to correct twice for that portion of the apparent wind which is produced by the ship steaming in still air. The practical method of using the tables for apparent wind is further discussed in paragraph 338 of this chapter.

335. As an example of the above, an inspection of the range table for our standard problem 12″ gun for 10,000 yards shows the following data:

	Error in Yards.
(a) Gun fired in vacuum as far as resistance of air is concerned, ship steaming at 12 knots towards or away from target (Col. 15)..	84 Over or Short
(b) Gun fired in vacuum as far as resistance of air is concerned, ship steaming at 12 knots perpendicular to line of fire (Col. 18)...	84 R. or L.
(c) Calm day, shot fired in air, ship steaming at 12 knots towards or away from target (Col. 14)................................	57 Over or Short
(d) Calm day, shot fired in air, ship steaming at 12 knots perpendicular to line of fire (Col. 17)............................	70 R. or L.
(e) Ship stationary, 12-knot breeze blowing from ship to target, or the reverse (Col. 13)	27 Over or Short
(f) Ship stationary, 12-knot breeze blowing perpendicular to the line of fire (Col. 16)..	14 R. or L.
(g) Ship steaming east at 12 knots, real wind from west of 12 knots, target abeam to starboard (Cols. 16 and 17 combined).......	84 Left
(h) Ship steaming east at 12 knots, real wind from east of 12 knots, target abeam to starboard (Cols. 16 and 17 combined).......	56 Left

336. In the above the target is considered as stationary in every case; if it be not stationary, then the errors introduced by its motion must be added algebraically from Columns 15 and 18. If motions be not in or perpendicular to the line of fire, then their resolved components in those two directions must be taken.

337. From what has already been said, the combined effects of the wind and of the motions of the firing and target ships may therefore be analyzed as follows:

Given a wind blowing, and both ship and target in motion, there are really four corrections that must be applied to correct for the combined errors produced by these three causes, although the columns of the range tables give separately corrections for only three causes. They are as follows:

A. Correction for *real* wind. (The corrections for this are computed and given in Columns 13 and 16.)

B. Correction for the wind caused by the motion of the gun. (Not given by itself in any columns.)

[A and B:] These two corrections if combined correct for *apparent* wind, by using Columns 13 and 16.

C. Correction for the motion of the gun itself, disregarding the effect of the wind created by such motion; that is, the distance the ship will travel during the time of flight, T seconds. (Given in Columns 15 and 18.)

[B and C:] These two corrections if combined correct for the total effect of the motion of the gun, including effect of the wind created by the motion of the gun, by using Columns 14 and 17.

D. Correction for the motion of the target; that is, the distance the target ship will travel during the time of flight, T seconds. (Given in Columns 15 and 18.)

338. From the above tabular statement we see at once that if we use the *real* wind in our computations we must:

(1) Correct for A by the use of Columns 13 and 16.
(2) Correct for B and C combined by the use of Columns 14 and 17.
(3) Correct for D by the use of Columns 15 and 18.

If we wish to use the *apparent* wind we must:

(1) Correct for A and B combined by the use of Columns 13 and 16.
(2) Correct for C by the use of Columns 15 and 18.
(3) Correct for D by the use of Columns 15 and 18.

339. In other words, it is merely a question of how it is preferred to consider the wind effect created by the motion of the gun (B); whether as a part of the wind (A), or as a part of the motion of the gun (C). If it be considered as a part of C the conditions are those for which the range tables are computed and the process is to correct for:

(1) *Real* wind by Columns 13 and 16.
(2) Motion of gun by Columns 14 and 17.
(3) Motion of target by Columns 15 and 18.

If, however, B be considered as a part of A, we are then dealing with an *apparent wind,* and must not use Columns 14 and 17 at all, but must correct for:

(1) *Apparent* wind by Columns 13 and 16.
(2) Motion of the gun by Columns 15 and 18.
(3) Motion of target by Columns 15 and 18.

340. Let us now take our standard problem 12″ gun, for 10,000 yards. If the ship be steaming 90° at 20 knots, and there be an apparent wind blowing from 62.5° at 32 knots an hour, if the target bears 45° at the moment of firing, we have from the above rules, the target being stationary:

Cause of error.	Affects.	Formulæ.	Range.		Deflection.	
			Short. Yds.	Over. Yds.	Right. Yds.	Left. Yds.
Motion of gun. Cols. 15 and 18.	Range.....	$20 \cos 45 \times \frac{84}{12} = 14.1 \times \frac{84}{12}$	....	98.7	....	....
	Deflection..	$20 \sin 45 \times \frac{84}{12} = 14.1 \times \frac{84}{12}$	....	....	98.7	....
Apparent wind. Cols. 13 and 16.	Range.....	$32 \cos 17.5 \times \frac{27}{12} = 30.5 \times \frac{27}{12}$	68.625	....	....	....
	Deflection..	$32 \sin 17.5 \times \frac{14}{12} = 9.65 \times \frac{14}{12}$	....	....	....	11.258
			68.625	98.7 68.625	98.7 11.258	11.258
				30.075 yards over.	87.442 yards right.	

These are the combined errors caused by the motion of the gun and of the apparent wind.

341. If we plot the above speed of ship and apparent wind to scale, which is sufficiently accurate and much simpler and quicker than solving the oblique triangle mathematically, we will find that the corresponding real wind was blowing from 30° with a velocity of 17 knots an hour. Let us now compute the results by using the speed of the ship and the real wind by the methods originally explained, and compare them with the results obtained in the preceding paragraph by using the apparent wind. The work becomes:

Cause of error.	Affects.	Formulæ.	Range.		Deflection.	
			Short. Yds.	Over. Yds.	Right. Yds.	Left. Yds.
Motion of gun. Cols. 14 and 17.	Range.....	$20 \cos 45 \times \frac{57}{12} = 14.1 \times \frac{57}{12}$	....	66.975	....	....
	Deflection..	$20 \sin 45 \times \frac{70}{12} = 14.1 \times \frac{70}{12}$	....	....	82.25	....
Real wind. Cols. 13 and 16......	Range.....	$17 \cos 15 \times \frac{27}{12} = 16.4 \times \frac{27}{12}$	36.9	....	....	....
	Deflection..	$17 \sin 45 \times \frac{14}{12} = 4.4 \times \frac{14}{12}$	....	....	5.133	....
			36.9	66.975 36.9	87.383 yards right.	....
				30.075 yards over.		

The above are therefore the errors produced by the motion of the gun and real wind combined, and we see that the results are the same (within decimal limits) as those obtained in the preceding paragraph where we worked with the motion of the gun and the apparent instead of the real wind.

EXAMPLES.

1. Find the actual range for each gun given in the following table for the actual initial velocity given, by the use of Column 10 of the range table.

Problem.	DATA.						ANSWERS.
	Gun.			Initial velocity.		Range under standard conditions. Yds.	Range for actual initial velocity. Yds.
	Cal. In.	w. Lbs.	c.	Standard. f. s.	Actual. f. s.		
A	3	13	1.00	1150	1175	2467	2523.5
B	3	13	1.00	2700	2600	4050	3893.0
C	4	33	0.67	2900	2930	3250	3302.8
D	5	50	1.00	3150	3100	3675	3597.3
E	5	50	0.61	3150	3182	3130	3183.5
F	6	105	0.61	2600	2532	14525	14131.3
G	6	105	1.00	2800	2871	4250	4399.8
H	6	105	0.61	2800	2757	2950	2873.0
I	7	165	1.00	2700	2731	7350	7451.7
J	7	165	0.61	2700	2685	7450	7390.3
K	8	260	0.61	2750	2800	8450	8676.0
L	10	510	1.00	2700	2630	10430	10092.2
M	10	510	0.61	2700	2747	11425	11712.2
N	12	870	0.61	2900	2837	23975	23323.0
O	13	1130	1.00	2000	2100	10100	10764.0
P	13	1130	0.74	2000	1900	11500	10692.0
Q	14	1400	0.70	2000	1950	14400	13906.0
R	14	1400	0.70	2600	2683	14400	15057.4

2. Find the actual range of the guns given in the following table for the weights of projectile given, by the use of Column 11 of the range tables.

Problem.	DATA.						ANSWERS.
	Gun.			Standard initial velocity. f. s.	Standard range. Yds.	Actual weight of projectile. Lbs.	Actual range. Yds.
	Cal. In.	w. Lbs.	c.				
C	4	33	0.67	2900	3100	30	3199.0
D	5	50	1.00	3150	3600	54	3500.0
E	5	50	0.61	3150	4000	47	4099.0
F	6	105	0.61	2600	14600	110	14666.7
G	6	105	1.00	2800	4050	101	4114.3
H	6	105	0.61	2800	3600	107	3571.3
I	7	165	1.00	2700	7000	167	6981.4
J	7	165	0.61	2700	7000	160	7063.8
K	8	260	0.61	2750	8100	267	8041.2
L	10	510	1.00	2700	9600	515	9574.0
M	10	510	0.61	2700	11100	507	11116.2
N	12	870	0.61	2900	20800	875	20789.0
O	13	1130	1.00	2000	9000	1125	9015.9
P	13	1130	0.74	2000	11300	1135	11288.0
Q	14	1400	0.70	2000	13500	1413	13470.1
R	14	1400	0.70	2600	14200	1391	14220.7

3. Find the actual range of the guns given in the following table for the given atmospheric conditions by the use of Table IV of the Ballistic Tables and of Column 12 of the range tables.

Problem.	DATA. Gun Cal. In.	w. Lbs.	c.	Standard initial velocity. f. s.	Standard range. Yds.	Atmosphere. Bar. In.	Ther. °F.	ANSWERS. Actual range. Yds.
A	3	13	1.00	1150	2000	28.10	5	1979.6
B	3	13	1.00	2700	3400	28.50	10	3296.5
C	4	33	0.67	2900	3500	29.00	15	3435.1
D	5	50	1.00	3150	4100	29.50	20	3973.0
E	5	50	0.61	3150	4500	30.00	25	4372.4
F	6	105	0.61	2600	13400	30.33	30	12844.7
G	6	105	1.00	2800	4300	30.75	35	4176.3
H	6	105	0.61	2800	3750	31.00	40	3690.7
I	7	165	1.00	2700	7300	30.50	50	7141.9
J	7	165	0.61	2700	7500	30.00	60	7470.0
K	8	260	0.61	2750	8200	29.50	70	8250.3
L	10	510	1.00	2700	10100	29.00	75	10295.0
M	10	510	0.61	2700	11200	28.50	80	11434.1
N	12	870	0.61	2000	19000	28.00	85	19684.8
O	13	1130	1.00	2000	9700	28.25	90	10000.8
P	13	1130	0.74	2000	11300	29.00	95	11564.0
Q	14	1400	0.70	2000	14000	30.00	100	14262.6
R	14	1400	0.70	2600	14500	31.00	97	14621.8

4. Find the errors in range and deflection caused by the *real* wind in the problems given below, using the traverse tables and Columns 13 and 16 of the range tables.

Problem.	DATA. Gun. Cal. In.	w. Lbs.	c.	Initial velocity. f. s.	Range. Yds.	Line of fire. °True.	Real wind. From. °True.	Velocity. Knots.	ANSWERS. Errors due to wind. In range. Yds. Short or over.	In deflection. Yds. Right or left.
A	3	13	1.00	1150	2600	35	22	15	21.9 short	2.7 right
B	3	13	1.00	2700	4000	150	37	18	19.3 over	30.4 right
C	4	33	0.67	2900	3800	200	45	20	19.6 over	5.0 right
D	5	50	1.00	3150	4100	270	0	21	0.0	21.7 left
E	5	50	0.61	3150	3500	300	350	17	7.3 short	4.3 left
F	6	105	0.61	2600	13000	23	170	25	187.3 over	78.2 left
G	6	105	1.00	2800	3900	70	280	30	31.4 over	10.1 right
H	6	105	0.61	2800	4000	90	90	13	9.75 short	0.0
I	7	165	1.00	2700	7300	225	100	20	44.9 over	40.2 right
J	7	165	0.61	2700	6600	260	240	18	32.4 short	6.2 right
K	8	260	0.61	2750	8400	45	180	16	28.2 over	16.0 left
L	10	510	1.00	2700	10400	225	300	4	5.0 short	12.3 left
M	10	510	0.61	2700	11400	70	200	23	55.5 over	36.6 left
N	12	870	0.61	2900	24000	33	95	30	175.0 short	194.3 left
O	13	1130	1.00	2000	10000	330	115	20	87.1 over	33.6 left
P	13	1130	0.74	2000	11000	80	210	15	46.4 over	28.8 left
Q	14	1400	0.70	2000	14200	350	23	27	162.0 short	53.9 left
R	14	1400	0.70	2600	14000	37	105	19	34.9 short	47.0 left

5. Find the errors in range and deflection caused by the motion of the gun in the problems given below, using traverse tables and Columns 14 and 17 of the range tables.

Problem.	DATA.								ANSWERS.	
	Gun.			Initial velocity. f. s.	Range. Yds.	Line of fire. °True.	Course of ship. °True.	Speed of ship. Knots.	Errors due to speed of firing ship.	
	Cal. In.	w. Lbs.	c.						In range. Yds. Short or over.	In deflection. Yds. Right or left.
A........	3	13	1.00	1150	2100	37	0	10	20.0 over	18.6 left
B........	3	13	1.00	2700	3700	40	100	15	11.3 over	30.1 right
C........	4	33	0.67	2900	3400	200	135	20	13.5 over	36.2 left
D........	5	50	1.00	3150	4200	205	340	25	28.0 short	39.8 right
E........	5	50	0.61	3150	3900	75	280	30	43.1 short	25.4 right
F........	6	105	0.61	2600	13500	270	60	27	130.6 short	121.5 right
G........	6	105	1.00	2800	3100	145	145	25	38.2 over	0.0
H........	6	105	0.61	2800	2700	270	90	22	31.2 short	0.0
I........	7	165	1.00	2700	7200	210	120	20	0.0	90.3 left
J........	7	165	0.61	2700	6900	250	340	19	0.0	80.8 right
K........	8	260	0.61	2750	8400	300	160	17	53.1 short	56.3 left
L........	10	510	1.00	2700	10200	240	27	15	56.7 short	52.7 right
M........	10	510	0.61	2700	11300	247	215	15	69.0 over	55.9 left
N........	12	870	0.61	2900	19600	199	160	30	188.3 over	220.5 left
O........	13	1130	1.00	2000	10300	275	32	20	57.8 short	157.8 right
P........	13	1130	0.74	2000	11100	105	223	8	27.6 short	68.0 right
Q........	14	1400	0.70	2000	14100	247	330	27	29.2 over	328.3 right
R........	14	1400	0.70	2600	13600	303	162	23	120.8 short	129.3 left

6. Find the errors in range and in deflection caused by the motion of the target in the problems given below, using the traverse tables and Columns 15 and 18 of the range tables; giving also the setting of the sight in deflection to compensate for the deflection.

Problem.	DATA.								ANSWERS.		
	Gun.			Initial velocity. f. s.	Range. Yds.	Line of fire. °True.	Course of target. °True.	Speed of target. Knots.	Errors due to motion of target.		Set sight for deflection at knots of scale.
	Cal. In.	w. Lbs.	c.						Range. Yds. Short or over.	Deflection. Yds. Right or left.	
A........	3	13	1.00	1150	2000	220	90	8	17.0 over	20.3 right	43.9
B........	3	13	1.00	2700	4100	155	32	35	86.4 over	133.0 right	20.6
C........	4	33	0.67	2900	3700	110	157	32	58.1 short	62.4 left	73.4
D........	5	50	1.00	3150	4200	320	287	37	103.3 short	67.3 right	29.8
E........	5	50	0.61	3150	4400	242	311	33	35.4 short	92.4 left	80.8
F........	6	105	0.61	2600	13700	73	201	30	288.3 over	367.8 left	73.6
G........	6	105	1.00	2800	3800	73	73	28	81.9 short	0.0	50.0
H........	6	105	0.61	2800	3600	332	152	27	67.5 over	0.0	50.0
I........	7	165	1.00	2700	7000	143	53	26	0.0	172.0 right	24.0
J........	7	165	0.61	2700	7400	343	73	25	0.0	147.9 left	75.0
K........	8	260	0.61	2750	8300	135	0	22	101.4 over	101.4 right	34.4
L........	10	510	1.00	2700	10200	250	270	20	177.0 short	64.0 left	56.8
M........	10	510	0.61	2700	11400	320	10	19	112.8 short	135.1 left	64.6
N........	12	870	0.61	2900	22000	67	300	18	208.8 over	278.4 right	35.6
O........	13	1130	1.00	2000	10300	313	47	16	13.2 over	191.6 left	66.0
P........	13	1130	0.74	2000	11500	137	37	15	32.9 over	187.5 right	35.2
Q........	14	1400	0.70	2000	14300	57	330	20	16.3 short	325.0 right	30.0
R........	14	1400	0.70	2600	13700	45	180	23	187.4 over	187.4 left	66.3

7. Given the *apparent* wind, the motions of the gun and target, and the actual range and bearing of the target from the gun, as shown in the following table, compute the errors in range and in deflection resulting from those causes, and tell how to set the sights in range and in deflection in order to hit.

DATA.

Problem.	Gun.			Initial veloc-ity. f. s.	Actual range Yds.	Bearing of target. °True.	Gun.		Target.		Apparent wind.	
	Cal. In.	*w*. Lbs.	*c*.				Course. °True.	Speed. Knots.	Course. °True.	Speed. Knots.	From. °True.	Veloc-ity. Knots.
A.	3	13	1.00	1150	2300	15	45	6	80	10	180	10
B.	3	13	1.00	2700	3800	260	315	35	200	30	290	52
C..	4	33	0.67	2900	3400	45	220	22	260	25	48	15
D.	5	50	1.00	3150	4000	153	153	25	153	30	300	25
E.	5	50	0.61	3150	4100	75	67	25	80	32	10	42
F..	6	105	0.61	2600	11600	300	110	20	130	25	270	15
G.	6	105	1.00	2800	4000	45	180	20	90	20	315	18
H.	6	105	0.61	2800	3400	27	305	22	350	24	120	10
I..	7	165	1.00	2700	6600	265	37	18	190	19	15	37
J..	7	165	0.61	2700	6300	170	135	20	170	35	340	12
K.	8	260	0.61	2750	8100	260	220	21	315	30	300	30
L..	10	510	1.00	2700	9700	110	275	15	275	20	52	20
M.	10	510	0.61	2700	10700	270	330	18	330	25	190	35
N.	12	870	0.61	2900	20600	22	15	22	30	20	330	45
O..	13	1130	1.00	2000	10200	345	103	15	120	20	355	15
P..	13	1130	0.74	2000	10900	60	227	12	80	15	240	30
Q..	14	1400	0.70	2000	13800	320	340	21	165	19	300	25
R..	14	1400	0.70	2600	14200	125	17	21	23	17	325	20

ANSWERS.

Problem.	Combined errors		Set sights at—	
	Range. Yds. Short or over.	Deflection. Yds. Right or left.	Range. Yds.	Deflection. Knots.
A.	16.0 over	25.5 left	2284.0	56.5
B.	91.2 short	178.1 right	3891.2	6.0
C.	15.9 short	38.8 right	3415.9	34.0
D	19.6 over	13.3 left	3980.4	54.3
E.	37.2 short	1.8 right	4137.2	49.4
F.	32.8 short	130.0 right	11632.8	39.4
G.	88.2 short	12.9 right	4088.2	45.9
H	37.3 short	19.8 left	3437.3	58.5
I.	62.4 short	125.8 right	6662.4	29.3
J.	69.1 short	57.5 left	6369.1	61.9
K.	62.5 short	262.3 left	8162.5	92.0
L.	4.8 short	34.6 right	9704.8	46.0
M.	50.1 short	11.3 right	10750.1	48.7
N	220.9 short	95.1 right	20820.9	44.6
O.	2.2 over	18.5 left	10197.8	51.6
P.	162.9 short	28.4 left	11062.9	52.4
Q.	413.4 over	265.7 right	13386.6	32.9
R.	59.4 over	22.4 left	14140.6	51.9

8. Given the data contained in the following table, find how the sights must be set in range and deflection in order to hit. Use traverse tables for all resolutions of forces.

	C.	E.	H.	J.	K.	M.	N.	P.	R.
Caliber of gun....	4	5	6	7	8	10	12	13	14
Standard initial velocity.........	2900	3150	2800	2700	2750	2700	2900	2000	2600
Standard weight of projectile....	33	50	105	165	260	510	870	1130	1400
Coefficient of form.	0.67	0.61	0.61	0.61	0.61	0.61	0.61	0.74	0.70
Course of firing ship, °true......	90	300	75	200	25	330	230	115	27
Speed of firing ship, knots...........	15	19	17	25	18	22	20	18	15
Course of enemy, °true...........	180	200	110	200	25	60	10	70	350
Speed of enemy, knots...........	28	21	19	20	30	20	15	22	18
Bearing of enemy at moment of firing, °true.......	135	260	165	20	25	330	90	80	70
Distance of enemy at moment of firing, yards.......	3400	4300	4000	7500	7000	10500	20000	11000	14500
Direction from which real wind is blowing, °true.	315	25	300	225	90	150	330	200	10
Velocity of real wind, knots.....	30	19	25	18	16	21	18	20	15
Barometer, inches.	30.70	30.00	30.50	30.25	30.00	29.50	29.00	29.33	30.15
Temperature of air, °F.........	50	25	75	80	30	15	80	90	40
Temperature of powder, °F......	80	65	95	97	75	70	95	100	60
Actual weight of projectile.......	30	52	107	160	267	500	877	1122	1415

ANSWERS.

	C.	E.	H.	J.	K.	M.	N.	P.	R.
Total error in range, yards....	10.0†	356.3§	6.6§	272.1†	496.0§	427.4§	487.1†	264.6†	1125.8§
Total error in deflection, yards...	69.1*	71.5‡	4.3*	10.1‡	13.3*	166.7*	483.6‡	100.2‡	160.8‡
Exact setting in range, yards....	3390.0	4656.3	4006.6	7227.9	7496.0	10927.4	19512.9	10735.4	15625.8
Exact setting in deflection, knots.	78.6	25.5	51.5	48.3	52.5	70.0	21.6	41.6	37.1
Actual setting in range, yards....	3350	4650	4000	7200	7450 or 7500	10900	19500	10700	15600
Actual setting in deflection, knots.	79	25 or 26	51 or 52	48	52 or 53	70	22	42	37

* = left, † = over, ‡ = right, § = short.

9. Given the data contained in the following tables, find how the sights should be set to hit. Use traverse tables for all resolutions of forces.

	C.	D.	F.	I.	K.	L.	N.	O.	Q.
Caliber of gun....	4	5	6	7	8	10	12	13	14
Standard initial velocity.........	2900	3150	2600	2700	2750	2700	2900	2000	2000
Standard weight of projectile....	33	50	105	165	260	510	870	1130	1400
Coefficient of form.	0.67	1.00	0.61	1.00	0.61	1.00	0.61	1.00	0.70
Course of firing ship, °true......	33	115	213	302	350	265	171	105	77
Speed of firing ship, knots......	35	27	25	20	20	19	16	18	23
Course of enemy, °true...........	357	307	245	45	135	0	180	81	349
Speed of enemy, knots...........	32	30	28	15	20	21	23	25	19
Bearing of enemy at moment of firing, °true.....	67	345	23	180	287	111	351	265	223
Distance of enemy at moment of firing, yards.....	3600	3400	13000	6800	7700	9300	16200	9700	14000
Direction from which apparent wind is blowing, °true...........	21	97	165	237	300	7	214	165	107
Apparent velocity of wind, knots..	52	43	38	28	27	5	25	22	30
Barometer, inches.	28.00	29.00	30.00	31.00	30.00	29.00	29.00	28.00	30.00
Temperature of air, °F.........	15	40	50	60	70	80	90	85	95
Temperature of powder, °F......	60	70	75	80	85	95	99	97	100
Actual weight of projectile.......	35	48	107	162	268	507	876	1123	1408

ANSWERS.

Total error in range, yards....	204.1 §	159.2 §	265.5 §	261.3 §	30.1 §	219.8 †	829.6 †	582.9 †	366.7 †
Total error in deflection, yards...	45.9 ‡	71.2 ‡	73.0 ‡	126.5 ‡	151.6 ‡	242.3 ‡	101.2 ‡	28.0 *	351.3 *
Exact setting in range, yards....	3804.1	3559.2	13265.5	7061.3	7730.1	9080.2	15370.4	9117.1	13633.3
Exact setting in deflection, knots.	32.2	21.5	44.9	30.1	24.0	20.6	42.1	52.5	72.2
Actual setting in range, yards....	3800	3550	13250	7050	7700	9050	15350	9100	13600
Actual setting in deflection, knots.	32	21 or 22	45	30	24	21	42	52 or 53	72

* = left, † = over, ‡ = right, § = short.

10. A ship steaming on a course N. W. (p. c.) at 20 knots, wishes to fire a 14″ gun ($V=2000$ f. s., $w=1400$ pounds, $c=0.70$) at a target ship which bears off the port bow of the firing ship and is steaming N. E. (p. c.) at 18 knots. The gun is to be fired at the moment when the firing ship and target ship are 12,010 and 6380 yards, respectively, from the point of intersection of their two courses. A real wind is blowing from 100° (p. c.) with a velocity of 30 knots. The deviation is 3° W. The barometer is at 28.13″ and the thermometer at 90.5° F. The temperature of the powder charge is 99° F. The powder has suffered a loss of volatiles which increases the initial velocity 22 f. s., and has become damp enough to reduce the initial velocity 11 f. s. The actual weight of the projectile is 1385 pounds. The sight is out of adjustment an amount which is known to cause the shot, at the range given by the above conditions, to strike 25 feet above the point aimed at and 50 yards to the left of it. How must the sight be set in order that the shot may strike the point aimed at on the enemy's hull?

Answers. Total errors......Range 1216.4 yards over; deflection 193.9 yards left.
Exact setting.....Range 12383.6 yards; deflection 62.6 knots.
Actual setting....Range 12350 yards; deflection 63 knots.

11. A ship steaming on a course 293° true, at 17 knots, wishes to fire a 6″ gun ($V=2600$ f. s., $w=105$ pounds, $c=0.61$) at a torpedo-boat bearing 300° true and distant 9132 yards at the moment of firing. The torpedo-boat is steaming on a course 320° true, at 35 knots. The barometer is at 29.00″ and the thermometer at 10° F. The temperature of the powder is 50° F. The shell weighs 109 pounds. A real wind is blowing from 74° true at 21 knots. How must the sights be set to hit? All work must be correct to two decimal places.

Answers. Total errors.....Range 1104.1 yards short; deflection 157.8 yards left.
Exact setting....Range 10236.1 yards; deflection 68.2 knots.
Actual setting...Range 10200 yards; deflection 68 knots.

12. A ship steaming 0° true at 18 knots, desires to fire a 6″ gun ($V=2600$ f. s., $w=105$ pounds, $c=0.61$) at a torpedo-boat distant 13,600 yards, and bearing 90° true, and steaming on a course 0° true at 32 knots. A real wind is blowing from 180° true with a velocity of 20 knots. The barometer is at 29.00″ and the thermometer at 80° F. The temperature of the powder is 80° F. The shell weighs 110 pounds. How must the sights be set to hit?

Answers. Total errors.....Range 225.2 yards over; deflection 203.1 yards right.
Exact setting....Range 13374.8 yards; deflection 36.8 knots.
Actual setting...Range 13350 yards; deflection 37 knots.

13. The 6″ gun ($V=2800$ f. s., $w=105$ pounds, $c=.61$) is to fire with a reduced charge giving an initial velocity of 2600 f. s., at a range of 3500 yards. Compute the correct setting of the 2800 f. s. sight in range to hit the target, under standard atmospheric conditions.

14. With the data of Example 13, find the correct setting in range to hit the target, using the reduced velocity range table "F."

PART V.

THE CALIBRATION OF SINGLE GUNS AND OF A SHIP'S BATTERY.

INTRODUCTION TO PART V.

The calibration of a ship's battery means, in brief, the process of adjusting the sights so that all the guns of the same caliber will shoot together when the sights are set alike, and so that the salvos will therefore be well bunched. Formerly it was considered necessary for every ship to calibrate her battery upon first going into commission, but now we find the work of manufacture and installation is ordinarily so well done that calibration practice is not considered necessary unless there are indications to the contrary. If the guns persistently scatter their salvos, and the reason for such a performance is not apparent, then it may become necessary to calibrate the battery; and, in any event, this form of test is so clearly illustrative of the principles involved in directing gun fire, that it should be thoroughly understood by every naval officer. Part V deals with this subject.

CHAPTER 18.

THE CALIBRATION OF A SINGLE GUN.

New Symbols Introduced.

α..., β..., γ... Angles for plotting the point of fall of the shot.

a, a'..., b, b'..., c, c'..., d, d'... Coordinates of point of fall of shot.

h.... Height of center of bull's eye above water.

S_h.... Danger space for height h.

342. Calibration may be defined as the process of firing singly each gun of a ship's battery, noting carefully the position of the point of fall of each shot, finding the average point of fall for each gun of the battery, and then adjusting the sight scales of each gun so that all the shots fired from all the guns will fall at the same average distance from the ship when all sight bars are set to the same reading; and similarly in deflection.* **Definition.**

343. As will be realized from what follows, the process of holding a calibration practice involves considerable time, labor and expense. It is evident that, if accurate salvo firing is to be carried on, all sight scales must be so adjusted that, if the guns be properly pointed, the shot from them will all fall well bunched, if the sights be all set alike; and the method of adjusting the sights to accomplish this by holding a calibration practice will now be described, as illuminative of the principles involved.

344. Like human beings, and like all other kinds of machinery, each particular gun has its own individual peculiarities. With its own sights properly adjusted it may shoot consistently and regularly, the shot falling in a well-grouped bunch; but this bunch may not coincide with the bunch of shot fired from another gun of the same battery in another part of the ship, even if the latter also has its sights theoretically perfectly adjusted, and set for the same range and deflection as the first. Also the bunches of shot from these two guns may neither of them coincide with that from still another gun. Thus each gun may work well individually, and yet the battery may not be doing proper team work. And yet, with our modern method of fire control and firing by salvos, it is of the utmost importance that, when the spotter causes all the sights of a battery to be set alike, the shots of all the guns, if fired together, shall strike as nearly together as the inherent errors of the guns themselves will permit. It is to accomplish this that calibration practice is held. It must be noted that, in this discussion, it is supposed that all preventable errors in pointing, etc., have been eliminated; nothing can be well done as long as any of these remain. **Peculiarities of individual guns.**

---

* If there be any question in the mind of the student as to the meaning of any of the terms used in this chapter relative to the mean point of impact, deviations, deflections, etc., reference should be made to the definitions given in the opening paragraphs of Chapter 20; and those definitions are to be considered as included in the lesson covering the present chapter so far as they may be necessary to a clear understanding of the subject of calibration.

345. There are many causes which may operate to produce the condition in which one well-adjusted and well-pointed gun lands its shot at a point quite widely separated from the point of fall of the shot from another equally well-adjusted and well-pointed gun; as, for example, the fact that there is more give to the deck under one of the guns than under the other, etc.

Mean point of impact.

346. If a great number of shot be fired from a gun, under as nearly as possible the same conditions, it will be found that the impacts are grouped closely together around one point, which point we will call the "mean point of impact." This point is in reality the mathematical center of gravity of all the impacts; and, with reference to the target (at the range for which the gun is pointed) this mean point of impact may be either on, short of, or over the target; and either on, to the right, or to the left of the target.

Mean dispersion.

347. The point of fall of each individual shot is situated at a greater or less distance from the mean point of impact; and the arithmetical average of these distances from the mean point of impact for all the shots from the gun is called the "mean deviation from the mean point of impact" or the "mean dispersion" of the

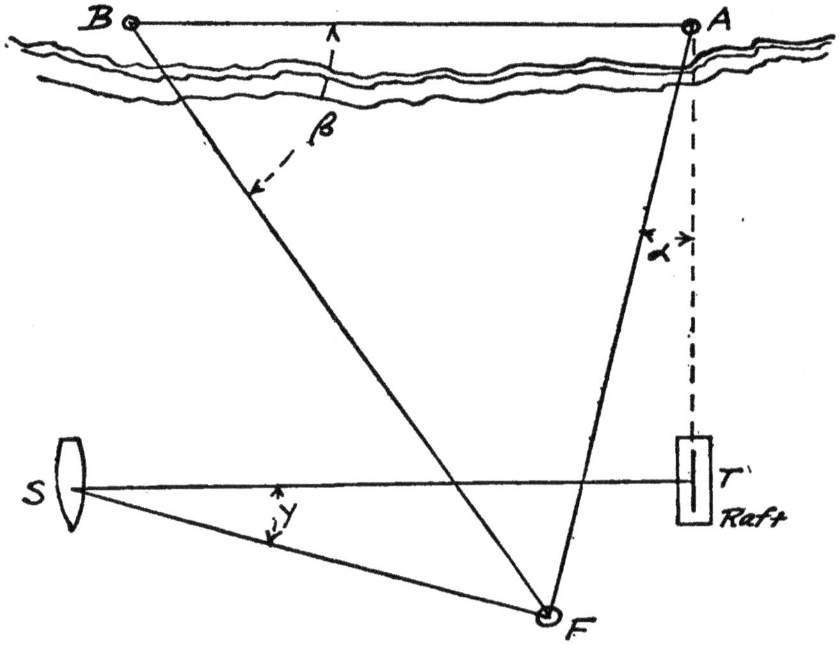

FIGURE 32.

gun. In dealing with these quantities it is customary to consider deviations or errors in range separately from those in deflection; so we would speak of the "mean deviation (or error) in range from the mean point of impact," and similarly for deflection. These quantities are also called the "mean errors" of the gun in range and in deflection.

Calibration range.

348. The general plan of a calibration range is shown in Figure 32. A raft carrying a vertical target screen is moored in such a position that one or more observing stations, preferably two, may be established on shore, as shown at *A* and *B*. The ship is then moored at *S*, broadside to the target; and the screen of the latter should be as nearly as possible parallel to the keel of the ship. The angle *STA* should be as nearly a right angle as possible.

349. The base line *AB* must then be measured or determined by surveying methods; and then the positions of the ship, target, etc., must be accurately plotted, and their distance apart accurately determined.

350. Having found the distance, *ST*, from the gun to the target, the sights of the gun to be calibrated are set to that range, and a string (usually of four) carefully aimed shots is fired at the target. (It is usual to set the sights a small known distance off in deflection, to prevent damage to the target and consequent frequent delays in completing practice.) Let us suppose that the first shot fell at *F*. By the use of sextants, plane tables or their equivalents (preferably plane tables), the angles α, β and γ should be observed, and the point of fall should be plotted on the drawing board. This process should be repeated for each shot, and the results tabulated for the gun, the errors in range and in deflection being measured from the drawing board for each shot. This process is repeated for each gun of the battery, and in doing this it is well to fire one shot from each gun in turn instead of having one gun fire its whole allowance at once, as more uniform conditions for firing the battery as a whole are obtained in this way, especially in regard to the temperature of the guns. A gun is not loaded until immediately before it is fired, for a number of reasons, among which is the fact that otherwise the temperature of the charge would be changed by contact with the heated walls of the powder chamber.

351. It is most desirable in calibration practice that the conditions of weather should be good, and should be uniform for the firing of all guns of the same caliber. The weather should be uniform for the whole firing, if practicable. If the weather be not uniform throughout the firing for one caliber, then it is necessary that the data for each shot be reduced to standard conditions individually before any combination of the results of different shots is made. The complete practice should be finished in one day if possible; as it is bad practice to have part of the firing on the afternoon of one day and the remainder on the forenoon of the next, for instance, as the weather conditions may be entirely different on the two days, and misleading results may follow such a course. **Weather conditions.**

352. The greater the number of shots fired the more reliable are the results. Four shots are usually fired from each gun, which is a small number; but the cost of the ammunition so expended is not small and limits the practice to that allowed by a reasonable economy, to say nothing of the wear on the guns, especially on those of large caliber. **Number of shot.**

353. During the practice, for each shot, the observers at each shore station should record: **Observations.**

(a) The time of flash.

(b) The consecutive number of the shot.

(c) The angle between the point of fall and the center of the target.

(d) The force and direction of the wind.

354. The observers on board ship, in addition to the above, should record the following for each shot:

(e) Time of shot (in place of time of flash).

(f) Consecutive number of shot (should be same as (b)).

(g) Number of gun from which fired.

(h) Whether or not the cross wires of the telescope were on the center of the bull's eye at the instant the gun was fired; and, if not, how much they were off in each direction (estimated in feet on the target screen; lines painted on the screen should assist in making this estimate).

(i) Direction and force of the wind in knots per hour.

(j) Barometer.

(k) Temperature of the air.

(l) Temperature of the charge (assumed as the same as the temperature of the magazine, from which the charge should not be removed until it is actually needed for the firing).

(m) Weight of the shell.

(n) Any other information that may be desirable.

((i), (j) and (k) need only be recorded when a change occurs, but the record must be such that the conditions at the beginning and at the end of the practice, and at the moment when any individual shot is fired may be readily and accurately obtained from it.)

Necessity for care.

355. The members of the observing parties should realize the necessity for accurate observations and records. Nothing is more disastrous than carelessness in regard to details, as inaccuracy in any one of the apparently minor points may easily result in rendering the results of the whole practice entirely worthless. Such inaccuracies may readily be of such a nature that they cannot be detected, and might lead to confident entry into battle or target practice with a battery with which it is impossible to do good work owing to the undiscovered carelessness or inaccuracy of some person charged with some of the duties in regard to the observations taken during the calibration practice.

Plotting of observed points of fall.

356. Suppose we have four shots fired from a single gun, which fell as follows relative to the foot of the perpendicular from the center of the bull's eye upon the water:

No. 1..........*a* yards over..........*a'* yards to the right.
No. 2..........*b* yards short.........*b'* yards to the left.
No. 3..........*c* yards over..........*c'* yards to the right.
No. 4..........*d* yards short.........*d'* yards to the left.

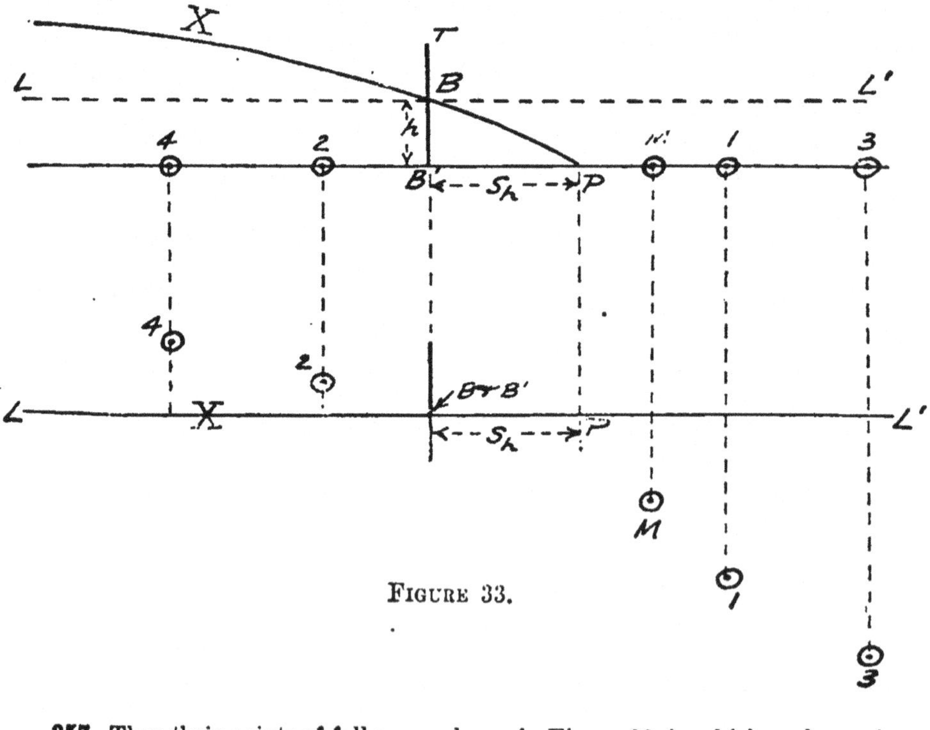

FIGURE 33.

357. Then their points of fall are as shown in Figure 33, in which we have given a projection in the vertical plane through the line of fire and the center of the bull's eye, and also the corresponding projection upon the horizontal plane of the water. *T* is the target, the center of the bull's eye being at *B*, which is *h* feet above the water. *LL'* is the line of sight such that the gun pointer looking along it sees the cross wires of the telescope on the center of the bull's eye. Now if the gun were in perfect adjustment when fired, its shot would travel along the trajectory X, pierce the bull's eye at B and strike the water at P. Note that the recorded errors are actually observed from the point B' on the surface of the water vertically below B. Therefore we have to reduce our observations to the point P, by subtracting for overs in range, the distance $B'P$ from the recorded range, and by adding the same distance for shorts; and $B'P$ may therefore be considered as a constant error affecting all shots alike.

358. The distance S_h is the danger space for a target h feet high at a range equal to the distance from the gun to the target plus the danger space. For practical purposes, however, when the range is considerable, this danger space may be taken from the range tables for the height h for a range equal to the distance from the gun to the target. The amount of correction to be applied because of the height h should also be taken from Column 19 of the range table. It sometimes happens, also, that the point of sight may not be exactly on the center of the bull's eye at the moment of firing, but may, by the check telescope, be determined to have been a certain distance above or below the proper point of aim; in which case h would have to be modified accordingly. To work out the observed data:

1. Take a large drawing board, and plot on it to scale (scale sufficiently large to give accurate results) the positions of the observing parties, gun and center of the target.

2. Using the observed data, plot the point of fall of each shot, and measure the distance from the foot of the perpendicular through the center of the bull's eye on the water, in range and in deflection, recording the results.

3. From the results obtained by (2), find the location of the mean point of impact in range and in deflection with reference to the perpendicular noted in (2), which for range will be $\frac{+a+(-b)+c+(-d)}{4}$ yards from the foot of the perpendicular; a, b, c and d being taken with their proper algebraic signs, + for an over and − for a short; the sign + on the result showing that the point is over and − that it is short.

4. For the mean point of impact in deflection, by similar methods. the distance from the line of sight will be $\frac{+a'+(-b')+c'+(-d')}{4}$; a', b', c' and d' being taken with their proper algebraic signs, + for a deviation to the right and − to the left; a + sign on the result will show that the mean point of impact is to the right of the line of fire and a − sign that it is to the left. It is equally as good, and sometimes more convenient, instead of using the + and − signs in this work, to keep to the nomenclature of "short" and "over," etc.; using the letters "S" and "O" to represent them and "R" and "L" to represent "rights" and "lefts"; thus a shot might be "155 S and 25 L."

359. Having obtained from these plotted positions for the particular group of shots under consideration the mean distances in range and in deflection from the foot of the perpendicular on the water through the bull's eye, it is now necessary to reduce those distances, first to the point P as an origin, and then from firing to standard conditions. The method of doing this is simply an application of methods that have already been studied in this book, and it may be best understood from the solution of a problem. **Reduction to standard conditions.**

Calibration problem.

360. Let us suppose that six shots were fired on a calibration practice from a 12″ gun ($V=2900$ f. s., $w=870$ pounds, $c=0.61$) under the following conditions:

Actual distance of target from gun ....8000 yards.
Sights set in range for ....8000 yards.
Sights set in deflection at.......................38 knots.
Center of bull's eye above the water..............12 feet.
Bearing of target from ship.......................45° true.
Wind blowing from.................................270° true.
Wind blowing with a velocity of...................18 knots.
Barometer ....30.00″.
Temperature of the air............................75° F.
Temperature of the powder.........................94° F.
Weight of projectile..............................875 pounds.

Measured from the foot of the perpendicular upon the water through the center of the bull's eye, the shot fell.

No. 1..200 yards short; 90 yards left.
No. 2..150 yards short; 95 yards left.
No. 3..100 yards short; 95 yards left.
No. 4..150 yards short; 85 yards left.
No. 5..100 yards short; 75 yards left.
No. 6.. 50 yards short; 70 yards left.

Find the true mean errors in range and in deflection under standard conditions, and adjust the sight scales in range and in deflection in order to have the sights properly set; that is, under standard conditions, to have the mean point of impact at the point P when the sight is set for 8000 yards in range and for 50 knots on the deflection scale.

No. of shot.	Range. Short. Yds.	Deflection. Left. Yds.
1	200	90
2	150	95
3	100	95
4	150	85
5	100	75
6	50	70
Mean errors on foot of perpendicular through bull's eye.	6|750 125 yards short.	6|510 85 yards left.

The error in range due to the fact that the point of aim is at the bull's eye and not at the water line of the target is the correction that should be applied to the observed distance from the foot of the perpendicular on the water through the bull's eye in order to refer it to the point P as an origin. By Column 19 of the range tables, this would be $12\times\frac{100}{20}=60$ yards.

The error in deflection intentionally introduced in order to avoid wrecking the target, by setting the sight off in deflection, would be, by Column 18 of the range table, $(50-38)\times\frac{65}{12}=65$ yards left.

Now to bring the observed errors to their true values under standard conditions, we proceed as follows:

Temperature of the powder is 4° above the standard, therefore the initial velocity is $4 \times \frac{35}{10} = 14$ f. s. above standard. From Table IV, the multiplier for Column 12 is +.18.

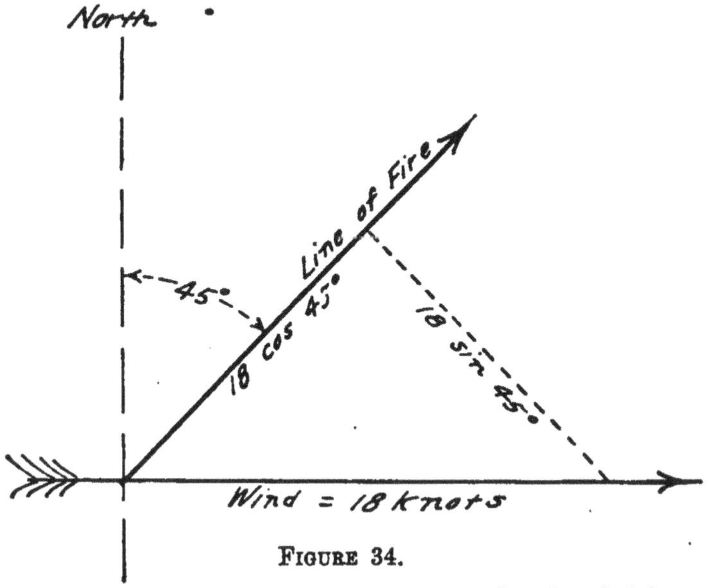

FIGURE 34.

Therefore we have, using the traverse tables to resolve the wind forces:

Cause of error.	Affects.	Formulæ.	Range. Short. Yds.	Range. Over. Yds.	Deflection. Right. Yds.	Deflection. Left. Yds.
Wind	Range.....	$18 \cos 45° \times \frac{17}{12} = \frac{12.7 \times 17}{12}$	....	18.0	....	....
	Deflection..	$18 \sin 45° \times \frac{8}{12} = \frac{12.7 \times 8}{12}$	....	....	8.5	....
w................	Range.....	$5 \times \frac{39}{10}$	19.5	....	....	....
Atmosphere.......	Range.....	$.18 \times 136$	....	24.5	....	....
Velocity..........	Range.....	$14 \times \frac{229}{50}$	....	64.1	....	....
Height of bull's eye	Range.....	$12 \times \frac{100}{20}$	....	60.0	....	....
Intentional deflection.	Deflection..	$12 \times \frac{65}{12}$	....	....	....	65.0
			19.5	166.6 19.5	8.5	65.0 8.5
Errors on point P as an origin for standard conditions........				147.1 over		56.5 left.

Observed distance from target in range.............................125.0 yds. short
Error (where shot should have fallen)...........................147.1 yds. over

True mean error in range under standard conditions.............272.1 yds. short

Observed distance from line of fire through bull's eye in deflection.. 85.0 yds. left
Error (where shot should have fallen)........................... 56.5 yds. left

True mean error in deflection under standard conditions......... 28.5 yds. left

That is, under standard conditions, the mean point of impact of this gun is 272.1 yards short of and 28.5 yards to the left of the point of fall (P) of the perfect trajectory of the gun through the bull's eye. We want to so adjust the sight scales as to bring the mean actual trajectory of the gun into coincidence with the perfect trajectory of the gun; that is, to shift the mean point of impact of the gun to its proper theoretical position, that is, to the point P. To do this we:

1. Run up the sight in range until the pointer indicates 8272.1 yards. Then slide the scale under the pointer until the pointer is over 8000 yards on the scale. Then clamp the scale in this position.

2. From Column 18 of the range table, we see that 28.5 yards deflection at 8000 yards range corresponds to a movement of $28.5 \times \frac{12}{65} = 5.3$ knots on the deflection scale. Therefore set the sight in deflection at 55.3 knots. Then slide the deflection scale under the pointer until the pointer is over 50 knots on the scale. Then clamp the scale in that position.*

When the above process has been completed, the gun should shoot, under standard conditions, so that the mean point of impact will fall at P.

361. With the sights adjusted as described above, under standard conditions, the shot should fall at the range and with the deflection given by the sight setting; that is, the shot should all fall at the mean point of impact. And any variation from standard conditions should cause the errors indicated for such variations in the range tables; and such errors could be easily handled by the spotter. Of course this statement, if taken literally, means that all errors have been eliminated from the gun, and that all shots fired from it under the same conditions will strike in the same place, that place being the mean point of impact for those conditions. It is of course never possible to actually accomplish this, owing first to the inherent errors of the gun, and second to unavoidable inaccuracies in the work. If the work be well done, however, the result will be to come as near as is humanly possible to that most desirable perfect condition.

Mean dispersion.

362. If the distance of the point of fall of each shot from the mean point of impact be found for every shot fired, and the arithmetical mean of these distances be found, we have a distance which is called the "mean dispersion from the mean point of impact." This information is desirable because it gives an idea of the accuracy and of the consistency of shooting of the gun. For example, one gun of a battery may have its mean point of impact with reference to a certain target at a distance, say, of 100 yards over and 25 yards to the right, but all of its shot may fall at, say, a mean distance of only 10 yards from the mean point of impact; that is, its shot will all be well bunched and closely grouped around the mean point of impact. Its mean dispersion from mean point of impact is small, and it is a good gun; for the spotter can readily bring its shot on the target, and when he has done this they will all fall there. If, on the contrary, with another gun, the mean point of impact be, say, only 10 yards over and 10 yards to the right of the target, but the mean dispersion from the mean point of impact be, say, 75 yards, the shot will fall scattered, the spotter will have difficulty in bringing the mean point of impact on the target and in keeping it there, and after he has done so the percentage of hits will be much smaller than

* For setting the sights preparatory to adjusting the scales, given the true mean errors, we may readily figure out the following rules:

Range.......	If the error be "short," add it to the standard range. If the error be "over," subtract it from the standard range.
Deflection ...	If the error be "right," subtract its equivalent in knots from 50. If the error be "left," add its equivalent in knots to 50.

with the first gun. Comparing the two guns, we would say that the second gun was a poor one compared to the first.

363. All that the spotter can hope to do, with a single gun, is to bring the mean point of impact on the target and hold it there; then if the gun shoots closely he will make the maximum possible number of hits. If, however, the gun does not shoot closely, there is nothing that can be done to increase the number of hits; he is simply doing the best that he can with an inferior weapon. Similarly, with salvo shooting, in which the spotter tries to bring the mean point of impact of all the guns (that is, the mean point of impact of all the mean points of impact of all the individual guns) on the target (or slightly in front of it) and keep it there. After he has done this the result depends upon the mean dispersion of each gun from its own mean point of impact, and upon the accuracy with which the work of calibration has brought the mean points of impact of all the guns into coincidence for the same setting of the sights. **Power of spotter.**

364. As an example of the mean dispersion from the mean point of impact, we will now determine that quantity for the 12″ gun already calibrated.

No. of shot.	In range.			In deflection.		
	Fall relative to target. Short or over. Yds.	Position of mean point of impact relative to target. Short or over. Yds.	Variation of each shot from mean point of impact. Short or over. Yds.	Fall relative to target. Right or left. Yds.	Position of mean point of impact relative to target. Right or left. Yds.	Variation of each shot from mean point of impact. Right or left. Yds.
1.....	200 short	125 short	75 short	90 left	85 left	5 left
2.....	150 short	125 short	25 short	95 left	85 left	10 left
3.....	100 short	125 short	25 over	95 left	85 left	10 left
4.....	150 short	125 short	25 short	85 left	85 left	0
5.....	100 short	125 short	25 over	75 left	85 left	10 right
6.....	50 short	125 short	75 over	70 left	85 left	15 right
			6|250 41.7 yards in range.			6|50 8.3 yards in deflection.

Therefore the mean dispersion of this gun from the mean point of impact is:

In range ....42 yards.
In deflection .... 8 yards.

365. Note that in finding the position of the mean point of impact we combined the errors of the several shots with their proper algebraic signs, because we were finding the mathematical center of gravity of the group of points of fall; but in computing the mean dispersion from the mean point of impact we were simply trying to find the average distance at which the shot fell from that point, without regard to direction, and so we discard the algebraic signs and simply take the arithmetical mean. It is to be noted that all corrections applied to the original data change all the shot alike, and therefore do not change their position *relative to each other.* We may therefore find the dispersion by using the original data before correction, as was done above. Or we could correct each shot separately and then find the dispersion from the results, but the former process is of course the shorter and simpler. Corrections to the original data do of course change the positions of the shot relative to any fixed outside point, such as the target or the point P, and therefore we have the process previously employed for finding errors, etc. **Mean point of impact and mean dispersion.**

EXAMPLES.

1. For the following results of different calibration practices, compute the true mean errors under standard conditions and the mean dispersion from mean point of impact; and tell how to adjust the sight scales in each case in range and deflection to make the gun shoot as pointed when all conditions are standard.

14″ gun; $V=2600$ f. s.; $w=1400$ pounds; $c=0.70$.

	1.	2.	3.	4.	5.	6.	7.	8.
Actual distance of target from gun, yds.	13000	13500	14000	14500	13300	13700	14200	14400
Sights set in range for, yds.	13000	13500	14000	14500	13300	13700	14200	14400
Sights set in deflection for, knots	35	40	30	42	60	65	70	63
Center of bull's eye above water, feet	4	3	5	6	4	5	6	4
Bearing of target from ship, °true	45	180	80	315	270	250	345	0
Wind blowing from, °true	180	225	0	90	180	250	165	270
Wind blowing with a velocity of, knots.	12	15	18	20	25	15	18	22
Barometer, inches	28.50	29.00	29.50	30.00	30.50	31.00	30.25	29.75
Temperature of air, °F	60	65	70	75	80	85	90	83
Temperature of powder, °F	80	85	95	100	97	82	75	80
Weight of shell, pounds	1395	1390	1405	1410	1407	1393	1397	1404
Number of shots fired	4	4	4	4	4	4	4	4
Fall of—								
Shot No. 1	25	100	150	75	150	200	100	20
	S.	S.	Ov.	S.	S.	Ov.	S.	Ov.
	75	70	200	20	15	30	100	50
	L.	L.	L.	L.	R.	R.	R.	R.
Shot No. 2	50	75	200	90	100	250	75	25
	S.	S.	Ov.	S.	S.	Ov	S.	Ov.
	100	75	150	10	20	35	80	55
	L.	L.	L.	L.	R.	R.	R.	R.
Shot No. 3	100	50	175	20	125	275	50	30
	S.	S.	Ov.	Ov.	S.	Ov.	S.	Ov.
	150	50	175	15	30	50	110	60
	L.	L.	L	L.	R.	R.	R.	R.
Shot No. 4	75	25	150	10	110	225	0	22
	S.	Ov.	Ov.	Ov.	S.	Ov.		Ov.
	80	50	150	20	25	40	90	50
	L.	L.	L.	L.	R.	R.	R.	R.

ANSWERS.

	True mean errors.		Mean dispersion from M. P. of I.		Set sights for.		Clamp scales at.	
	Range. Yds.	Deflection. Yds.	Range. Yds.	Deflection. Yds.	Range. Yds.	Deflection. Knots.	Range. Yds.	Deflection. Knots.
1.	11.7 Ov.	79.0 R.	25.0	24.4	12988.3	42.6	13000	50
2.	8.4 S.	78.5 R.	37.5	11.3	13508.4	43.1	13500	50
3.	41.2 S.	20.7 R.	18.75	18.75	14041.2	48.5	14000	50
4.	449.4 S.	124.0 R.	48.75	3.75	14949.4	40.0	14500	50
5	332.9 S.	148.7 L.	16.25	5.00	13632.9	63.4	13300	50
6.	479.2 Ov.	133.7 L.	25.0	6.25	13220.8	61.6	13700	50
7.	89.2 Ov.	146,7 L.	31.25	10.0	14110.8	62.1	14200	50
8.	134.1 Ov.	168.8 L.	3.25	3.75	14265.0	63.7	14400	50

2. For the following results of different calibration practices, compute the true mean errors under standard conditions and the mean dispersion from mean point of impact; and tell how to adjust the sight scales in range and deflection in each case to make the gun shoot as pointed under standard conditions.

7″ gun; $V=2700$ f. s.; $w=165$ pounds; $c=0.61$.

	1.	2.	3.	4.	5.	6.	7.	8.
Actual distance of target from gun, yds.	6000	6200	6500	6700	7000	7200	7500	7300
Sights set in range for, yds.	6000	6200	6500	0700	7000	7200	7500	7300
Sights set in deflection at, knots	70	65	63	60	55	45	43	40
Center of bull's eye above water, feet	6	5	4	3	4	5	6	5
Bearing of target from ship, °true	0	180	90	180	350	220	160	225
Wind blowing from, °true	180	180	180	90	220	350	30	270
Wind blowing with velocity of, knots	13	17	12	20	25	18	30	22
Barometer, inches	30.50	30.25	30.00	29.33	29.67	29.00	29.10	28.90
Temperature of air, °F	50	55	60	65	70	75	80	85
Temperature of powder, °F	95	97	100	98	93	87	85	80
Weight of shell, pounds	170	172	168	162	160	161	164	169
Number of shots fired	4	4	4	4	4	4	4	4
Fall of—								
Shot No. 1	50	75	75	200	150	100	250	100
	Ov.	Ov.	S.	Ov.	S.	Ov.	Ov.	S.
	150	100	95	75	5	5	20	25
	R.	R.	R.	R.	R.	R.	L.	L.
Shot No. 2	75	50	55	250	125	110	275	125
	Ov.	Ov.	S.	Ov.	S.	Ov.	Ov.	S.
	165	95	90	50	10	10	25	30
	R.	R.	R.	R.	R.	L.	L.	L.
Shot No. 3	70	25	70	200	100	125	300	130
	Ov.	Ov.	S.	Ov.	S.	Ov.	Ov.	S.
	155	70	85	25	0	25	30	35
	R.	R.	R.	R.		L.	L.	L.
Shot No. 4	65	25	75	175	130	117	280	135
	Ov.	S.	S.	Ov.	S.	Ov.	Ov.	S.
	150	75	90	10	5	20	27	40
	R.	R.	R.	L.	L.	L.	L.	L.

ANSWERS.

	True mean errors.		Mean Dispersion from M. P. of I.		Set sights at.		Clamp scales at.	
	Range. Yds.	Deflection. Yds.	Range. Yds.	Deflection. Yds.	Range. Yds.	Deflection. Knots.	Range. Yds.	Deflection. Knots.
1.	91.8 Ov.	63.3 R.	7.5	5.0	5908.2	36.2	6000	50
2.	88.7 Ov.	13.7 R.	31.25	12.5	6111.3	47.1	6200	50
3.	150.4 S.	35.9 R.	6.85	2.5	6641.7	43.0	6500	50
4.	19.2 Ov.	39.2 L.	21.9	27.5	6680.8	57.5	6700	50
5.	312.5 S.	47.8 L.	13.75	6.25	7312.5	58.6	7000	50
6.	39.9 S.	33.6 R.	8.0	10.0	7239.9	44.2	7200	50
7.	142.1 Ov.	13.6 L.	16.25	3.0	7357.9	52.2	7500	50
8.	63.7 S.	45.3 R.	11.25	5.0	7363.7	42.2	7300	50

CHAPTER 19.

THE CALIBRATION OF A SHIP'S BATTERY.

Reasons for calibrating battery. **366.** In the preceding chapter we have seen how a single gun is calibrated and the sights so adjusted that, so far as the inherent errors of the gun, etc., will permit, the gun will shoot, under standard conditions, as the sights indicate. It was stated that it is not possible to accomplish this result with absolute accuracy. If it were, we could adjust the sights of each gun of the battery separately, and then, if they were all mechanically just alike, we would have all the shot from each gun falling at its mean point of impact (within the limits of inherent errors), and the mean points of impact of all the guns would be the same. As a matter of fact, however, the mean points of impact of the several guns would not coincide, if this method were followed, and of course all the shot from any one gun would not all fall at its mean point of impact. Some remarks were made in the last chapter relative to the necessity for getting the guns so calibrated that the shot from all of them will fall together for the same sight setting, and, as a matter of fact, this is more important than it is to get them so that actual and sight-bar ranges coincide under standard conditions. Conditions are almost never standard during firing, and even if they were there are many other factors which prevent the actual and the sight-bar ranges from being the same. But if the mean points of impact of the several guns for the same sight setting can be brought very nearly into coincidence, then any variation of the resultant point from the target (that is of difference between actual and sight-bar ranges) can be readily handled by the spotter. This means that if the salvos are well bunched the spotter can control the fire successfully, but if the shots are scattered he cannot. We will now proceed with an entire battery to bring all guns to shoot together.

Standard gun. **367.** Having calibrated each gun separately, as described in the preceding chapter, we now proceed to select a gun as the "standard gun," to the shooting of which we propose to make that of all the others conform, providing the performance of any one gun is good enough to justify selecting it for the purpose. From what we have seen in the preceding chapter we would naturally select one whose mean dispersion from mean point of impact is small, that is, one that bunches its shots; and, other things being equal, if we have one whose sights are very nearly in adjustment, we will use that one without changing the sight adjustment. Any gun may of course be selected as the standard, and the sights of the others brought to correspond to it, but the considerations set forth above would naturally govern, as a matter of common sense. If no gun be sufficiently accurate, or if none has its sights sufficiently well adjusted to justify its selection as a standard gun, then we must correct all guns to the mean point of impact. The practical method of bringing the sights of a number of guns to correspond is best shown by an actual problem.

368. The results of the individual calibration of a battery of eight 12″ guns ($V=2900$ f. s., $w=870$ pounds, $c=0.61$), at an actual range of 8000 yards, were as follows: **Calibration problem.**

Number of gun.	True mean errors under standard conditions. Yards.			
	In range.		In deflection.	
	Short. Yards.	Over. Yards.	Right. Yards.	Left. Yards.
1	100	....	....	15
2	75	....	20	....
3	....	40	15	....
4	....	90	10	....
5	80	....	....	15
6	25	....	....	20
7	5	....	5	....
8	....	125	....	20

It is desired to calibrate the above battery. From an examination of the above results, assuming that the eight guns are equally good in the absence of any knowledge to the contrary, we will select No. 7 as the standard gun; and, as its sights are very slightly out, we will leave them unchanged and bring the sights of the other guns to correspond with them.

The work, which is best expressed in tabular form, then becomes (all guns were fired with sights set at 8000 yards in range and 50 knots in deflection):

Number of gun.	With reference to standard gun, each gun shot.			To bring all sights together set them for each gun as follows:	
	In range. Yds.	In deflection.		In range. Yds.	In deflection. Knots.
		Yards.	Knots.*		
1	95 short	20 left	3.7 left	8095	53.7
2	70 short	15 right	2.8 right	8070	47.2
3	45 over	10 right	1.9 right	7955	48.1
4	95 over	5 right	1.0 right	7905	49.0
5	75 short	20 left	3.7 left	8075	53.7
6	20 short	25 left	4.6 left	8020	54.6
7	Standard	Standard	Standard	Standard	Standard.
8	130 over	25 left	4.6 left	7870	54.6

* From the range table, at 8000 yards, one yard in deflection corresponds to $\frac{12}{65}$ knots on the deflection scale.

After the sights have been set as indicated in the two right-hand columns of the above table, move the sight scales under the pointers until the pointers are over the 8000-yard mark in range and the 50-knot mark in deflection in each case, and then clamp the scales in those positions. The guns are then calibrated to shoot together. It will be noted that, theoretically, we should have set the range scales for the 5 yards short in range and the deflection scales for the 5 yards right in deflection of the standard gun, to be absolutely accurate; but, as the sight scales are graduated to 50-yard increments in range only, it is impracticable to go any closer in range. It would perhaps be well to adjust each deflection scale to 51 knots instead of 50, in order to allow for the 5 yards right deflection of the standard gun.

Different batteries. **369.** When we wish to calibrate a ship's battery that is composed of separate batteries of different calibers, we calibrate each caliber by itself, as already described. The difference between the mean points of impact of the standard guns of the different calibers will be the difference between the centers of impact of the salvos from the several calibers, and this must be allowed for in firing all calibers together. To attempt to calibrate the sights of all calibers together by a readjustment of the sight scales would not be wise; for if they could be brought to shoot together at one range in this way, it would necessarily ensure dispersion of the several salvos at all other ranges. Therefore the only practical way of handling this proposition is to determine the error of each caliber at the range in use and apply it properly in sending the ranges to the guns; which means send different ranges to the guns of different calibers, so related that the results will bring the mean points of impact of the several calibers together at the range in use. As far as possible, these differences in ranges should be tabulated for different ranges. As the fire-control system is arranged, as a rule, to permit the control of each caliber battery independently of the others, this method presents no difficulties other than a little care on the part of the spotter group.

370. For instance, suppose that we have a ship with a mixed battery of 7″, 8″ and 12″ guns; that each of these calibers has been calibrated at 8000 yards; and has had the mean point of impact of its salvos located with reference to the target as follows:

7″ battery........100 yards over........3 knots right.
8″ battery........ 50 yards short.......3 knots left.
12″ battery........150 yards over........2 knots left.

Then if we wish to fire broadside salvos from this entire battery, the ranges and deflections should be sent to the guns as follows, for 8000 yards:

To the 7″........7900 yards........47 knots deflection.
To the 8″........8050 yards........53 knots.
To the 12″........7850 yards........52 knots.

If these errors have not been corrected by shifting scales on bore-sighting, they can only be overcome by the spotter's corrections.

EXAMPLES.

1. Having determined the true mean errors of guns under standard conditions, by calibration practice, to be as given in the following table; how should the sights of each caliber be adjusted to make all the guns of that caliber shoot together? (Six separate problems.)

Number of gun.	True mean errors of guns under standard conditions.											
	6"—G.		7"—J.		8"—K.		12"—N.		13"—P.		14"—R.	
	Errors at range of 4500 yards.		Errors at range of 6500 yards.		Errors at range of 8500 yards.		Errors at range of 10000 yards.		Errors at range of 11000 yards.		Errors at range of 13000 yards.	
	Range. Yds.	Defl. Yds.	Range. Yds.	Defl. Yds.	Range. Yds.	Defl. Yds.	Range. Yds.	Defl. Yds.	Range. Yds.	Defl. Yds.	Range. Yds.	Defl. Yds.
1..	25 S.	20 R.	50 Ov.	30 L.	100 S.	5 R.	100 Ov.	15 L.	125 Ov.	25 L.	75 S.	15 L.
2..	50 Ov.	30 R.	75 Ov.	40 L.	120 S.	15 L.	75 Ov.	10 L.	100 Ov.	30 L.	100 Ov.	15 R.
3..	75 Ov.	35 L.	100 Ov.	25 R.	90 Ov.	20 L.	50 Ov.	20 R.	75 Ov.	25 R.	75 Ov.	20 R.
4..	5 S.	5 L.	75 S.	15 L.	75 Ov.	25 R.	0	5 R.	100 S.	30 R.	50 S.	20 L.
5..	30 Ov.	30 R.	125 S.	10 L.	100 Ov.	20 R.	100 S.	25 R.	....	....	100 S.	25 L.
6..	50 S.	25 L.	10 S.	70 R.	80 S.	10 L.	90 S.	15 R.	....	....	100 Ov.	30 R.
7..	100 S.	40 R.	100 Ov.	25 R.	70 S.	25 R.	75 Ov.	30 L.	....	....	75 Ov.	20 R.
8..	100 Ov.	40 L.	90 S.	20 L.	70 Ov.	30 L.	100 S.	30 R.	....	....	70 S.	15 L.

ANSWERS.

Number of gun.	To bring all sights together for each caliber, set the sights for that caliber as given below, and then slide scales to standard readings and clamp.											
	6"—G.		7"—J.		8"—K.		12"—N.		13"—P.		14"—R.	
	Range. Yds.	Defl. Kts.	Range. Yds.	Defl. Kts.	Range. Yds.	Defl. Kts.	Range. Yds.	Defl. Kts.	Range. Yds.	Defl. Kts.	Range. Yds.	Defl. Kts.
1..	4520	43.0	6450	56.0	8600	49.25	9900	52.8	10875	52.0	13075	51.35
2..	4445	40.2	6425	58.0	8620	52.25	9925	52.1	10900	52.4	12900	48.65
3..	4420	58.4	6400	45.0	8410	53.00	9950	47.9	10925	48.0	12925	48.20
4..	Standard.		6575	53.0	8425	46.25	Standard.		11100	47.6	13050	51.80
5..	4465	40.2	6625	52.0	8400	47.00	10100	47.2	....	....	13100	52.25
6..	4545	55.6	6510	36.0	8580	51.50	10090	48.6	....	....	12900	47.30
7..	4595	37.4	6400	45.0	8570	46.25	9925	54.9	....	....	12925	48.20
8..	4395	59.8	6590	54.0	8430	54.50	10100	46.5	....	....	13070	51.35

PART VI.

THE ACCURACY AND PROBABILITY OF GUN FIRE AND THE MEAN ERRORS OF GUNS.

INTRODUCTION TO PART VI.

We have now learned all that mathematical theory can teach us with certainty about the flight of a projectile in air, about the errors that may be introduced into such flight by known causes, and about the methods of compensating for such errors. After all this has been done there must, in the nature of things, remain certain errors that cannot be either eliminated or covered by strict mathematical theories, and such errors are known as the inherent errors of the gun. It is the purpose of Part VI to discuss the general nature of these errors, their methods of manifesting themselves, and their probable effect upon the accuracy of fire.

CHAPTER 20.

THE ERRORS OF GUNS AND THE MEAN POINT OF IMPACT. THE EQUATION OF PROBABILITY AS APPLIED TO GUN FIRE WHEN THE MEAN POINT OF IMPACT IS AT THE CENTER OF THE TARGET.

New Symbols Introduced.

X.... Axis of; axis of coordinates lying along range, for points over or short of the target.

Y.... Axis of; axis of coordinates in vertical plane through target, for points above or below the center of the target.

Z.... Axis of; axis of coordinates in vertical plane through target, for points to right or left of center of the target.

(z_1, y_1, etc.).... Coordinates of points of impact in vertical plane through target.

Σz.... Summation of z_1, z_2, etc.

Σy.... Summation of y_1, y_2, etc.

n.... Number of shots.

γ_x.... Mean error in range.

γ_y.... Mean vertical error.

γ_z.... Mean lateral error.

371. Before proceeding to the discussion of the accuracy and probability of gun fire, it is wise to collect and consider certain definitions and descriptions of which a full understanding is necessary in order to clearly understand what is to follow.

372. There are three general classes of errors which enter into gun fire, and the distinction between which must be clearly comprehended. They may be stated as follows: **Classes of errors.**

1. **Errors Resulting from Mistakes or Accidents.**—As examples of these may be mentioned mistakes in estimating ranges or deflections, mistakes in sight setting, mistakes in pointing, etc. These are matters that pertain to the training of the personnel, and of course have no place in any discussion of the principles of ballistics, etc., for no theory can be developed unless all such causes of error are first eliminated. Such mistakes of course cause poor shooting, but they have no place in any theoretical investigation of the performance of the gun. **Mistakes.**

2. **Preventable Errors.**—These are errors arising from causes which must necessarily exist, but in regard to which the theories are well understood, and for which it is possible to compensate by a practical application of such theories. Examples of this class are the errors due to wind, to variation in the temperature of the powder, etc. One of the principal provinces of the science of exterior ballistics is to teach the principles governing such errors, and to show how they may be overcome. In general, it may be said that it is the principal duty of the spotter to discover the magnitude and direction of these errors and to give the instructions necessary to compensate for them. **Preventable.**

3. **Unpreventable Errors.**—These may be generally classified as the inherent errors of the gun. That is, they are the result of the very many elements entering into the shooting which cause variations in successive shots even when most carefully fired under as nearly as possible the same physical conditions, and which therefore ensure that any considerable number of shots from the same gun will have their **Unpreventable.**

successive points of impact more or less scattered about within a certain area. These causes are probably very numerous, it not even being certain that we have yet been able to recognize them all, and no satisfactory laws governing them have as yet been discovered, nor is it probable that such laws ever will be determined.

Summary. **373.** To summarize, it may be said that before entering on any theoretical investigation of the subject of gunnery we must first throw out all errors resulting from mistakes. We may then, by the study of exterior ballistics, learn certain principles governing the errors produced by certain known causes, and in consequence may learn how to eliminate such errors from our shooting. When all this has been done, however, we necessarily have left certain other causes of error which, although not great as compared with the others, are still sufficient to cause a scattering of the points of impact of successive shots from the same gun, even when fired under similar physical conditions. We manifestly cannot hope to eliminate these inherent errors, and therefore we must accept them as they are; all that we can do in regard to them is to investigate their probable effect upon the results of our shooting. It is this investigation that is to be undertaken in the last two chapters of this book, and it is to be noted that here we cannot speak of anything as a certainty, even in a theoretical and mathematical way, but can only say that, mathematically, it is probable or improbable that a certain thing will happen, and in addition attempt to measure the degree of probability or improbability which attaches to a certain effort.

Mean point of impact. **374. Mean Point of Impact.**—Let us suppose that all errors except the inherent errors of the gun have been eliminated, and that a large number of shots be fired, under as nearly the same physical conditions as possible, at a vertical target screen of sufficient size to receive all the shot under such conditions. Manifestly, if there were no errors of any kind whatsoever, all these shot would describe the same trajectory and strike the target at the same point. Of course this result can never be attained in practice, and the many causes of inherent error tend to scatter the several shot about the target, and only a certain percentage of absolute efficiency can be secured, no matter how skillfully the gun may be handled. The point which is at the geometrical center of all the points of impact on the screen is known as the "mean point of impact," and is of course the center of gravity of the group of points of impact. We may also speak of the mean point of impact in the horizontal plane as well as in the vertical plane as given above.

Mean trajectory. **375. Mean Trajectory.**—The mean trajectory of the gun for these conditions is the trajectory from the gun to the mean point of impact. It is manifestly the trajectory over which all the shot would travel were there no errors of any kind whatsoever.

Deviation or deflection. **376. Deviation or Deflection.**—Suppose Figure 35 to represent the vertical target screen, the point O at the center being the point aimed at. Suppose the shot struck at the point P. Then the deviation or deflection of the shot from the point aimed at is the distance OP in the direction shown. So considered, however, for manifest reasons, this information is not useful, so it is usual to speak of the horizontal deviation or deflection, which is a, and of the vertical deviation or deflection of the shot, which is b. And algebraic signs are assigned to these deviations or deflections, $+$ being above or to the right and $-$ below or to the left. Thus the deviations or deflections of the four points of impact shown in Figure 35 would be:

For P ....$+a$ and $+b$. For P'' ....$-a''$ and $-b''$.
For P' ....$-a'$ and $+b'$. For P'''....$+a'''$ and $-b'''$.

In place of the signs we might speak of horizontal deviations as being to the right or to the left, and of vertical deviations as being above or below. In addition to the above we may consider the deviation (the term "deflection" is not ordinarily used in this connection) in range, as the shot falls short of or beyond the target. These are denoted by the + sign for a shot that goes beyond and by a − sign for one that falls short, but usually the words "short" and "over" are used instead of the algebraic signs, and such shots are spoken of as "shorts" or "overs," as the case may be.

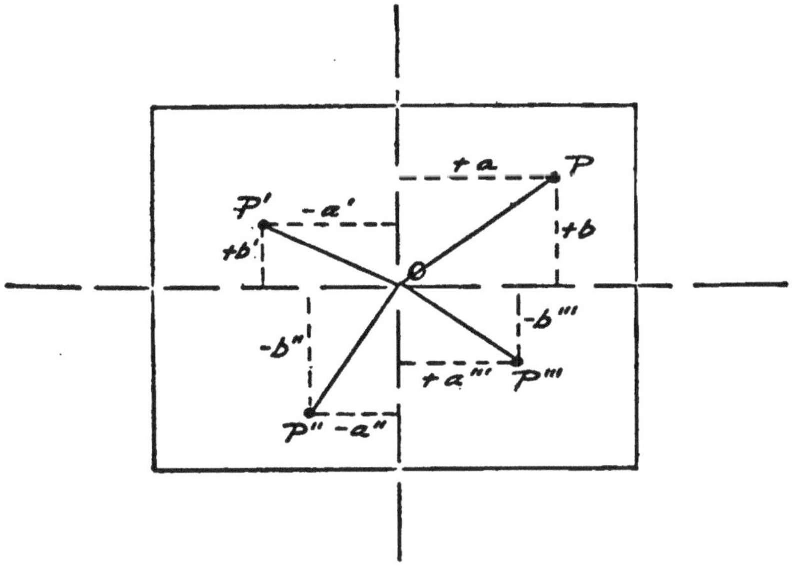

FIGURE 35.

377. Deviation or Deflection from Mean Point of Impact.—In the preceding paragraph we explained deviation or deflection from any given point of aim; the results giving the actual amount by which the shot missed the point aimed at. In theoretical consideration of the accuracy of a gun, however, it is customary to assume that the point of reference or origin of coordinates is the mean point of impact, rather than any given point of aim, and our results are then the "deviations or deflections from the mean point of impact." As the mean point of impact is, by definition, the center of gravity of the group of impacts caused by a large number of shot, it is evident that the summation of all the deviations from the mean point of impact must be equal to zero. **Deviation from mean point of impact.**

378. Dispersion.—Now suppose that, in Figure 35, we had disregarded the algebraic signs, and considered only the actual distances of the points of impact from the point aimed at. The distance OP in this case would be the "dispersion" for the single shot; but again it is customary to separate the distance in the two directions, and we would have a "horizontal dispersion" of a and a "vertical dispersion" of b; although it is not customary or appropriate to speak of the "dispersion" of a single shot, the word being collective in its nature. The "mean dispersion" of the four shots shown in Figure 35 from the point aimed at would be: **Dispersion.**

$$\text{Mean lateral dispersion } \frac{a+a'+a''+a'''}{4}$$

$$\text{Mean vertical dispersion } \frac{b+b'+b''+b'''}{4}$$

We may also have "dispersion in range" as well as in the vertical plane.

Mean dispersion from mean point of impact.

379. Mean Dispersion from Mean Point of Impact.—Suppose we again consider our dispersions from the mean point of impact as an origin. Then it is evident that the "mean dispersion from mean point of impact," or "mean dispersion" as it is usually called, is the average distance or arithmetical mean of the distances of the points of impact of all the shot from the mean point of impact. Now as this latter point is the one at which every theoretically perfect shot should strike, it is evident that the mean dispersion from mean point of impact gives us a measure of the accuracy of the gun, that is, of the extent to which its shooting is affected by its inherent errors.

380. It must be said in regard to the above definitions, that the terms defined are often very loosely and more or less interchangeably used in service. The term "deflection" is ordinarily used only to represent lateral displacement, in either the vertical or the horizontal planes; and the term "deviation" is used for either vertical or lateral displacement or for displacement in range, in which case the terms "vertical deviation," "lateral deviation" or "deviation in range" are customarily used. There is also confusion in the use of the terms as to whether deviation or deflection from the point aimed at or from the mean point of impact is meant. The term "dispersion" is fairly regularly used as defined above, but even here the point as to whether dispersion from the point aimed at or from the mean point of impact is meant is often left obscure. The context of the conversation or written matter will usually show what is meant. In this book the terms will be used strictly as defined.

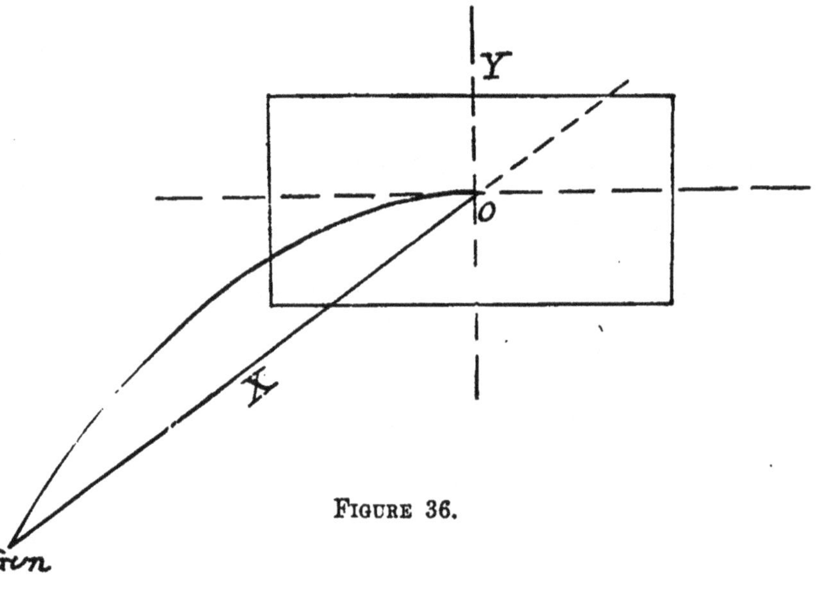

FIGURE 36.

System of coordinates.

381. For use in these last two chapters we will also introduce a special system of coordinates, as shown in Figure 36. This figure represents a perspective view of a vertical target screen of which O at the center is the mean point of impact in the vertical plane. The axis of X is the line from the muzzle of the gun to O, the mean trajectory being shown. Z is the horizontal axis and Y the vertical axis through the center of the target. It will be noted that in this system the axes of X and Z are interchanged from what they ordinarily are in geometry of three dimensions; and this is done in this particular subject to preserve the convention that has been consistently used throughout, that X and all functions thereof represent quantities pertaining to the range. In this system of coordinates it will be seen that, the mean point of impact at the center of the screen being considered as the origin, coordinates (z, y) will definitely locate any point of impact on the screen, while coordinates (x, z) will definitely locate any point of impact on the horizontal plane through O. And here it may be stated that it rarely becomes necessary to consider hits in the vertical and in the horizontal plane together. Therefore for hits in the vertical plane we use as an origin the mean point of impact in the vertical plane, and for hits in the horizontal plane we use as an origin the mean point of impact on the surface of the water. In Figure 36, O being the mean point of impact in the vertical target screen, the mean point of impact in the horizontal plane of the water would lie behind the target at the point where the mean trajectory through O strikes the surface of the water.

382. Having cleared up these preliminary matters, and bearing in mind that all errors have been eliminated except the inherent errors of the gun, it may now be stated that it becomes important, under these conditions, to be able to answer certain questions in regard to the probability of securing hits under given conditions. For instance, with a properly directed fire from which all avoidable errors have been removed, what are the chances of hitting a given target at a given range; what proportion of the total number of shot fired at it may reasonably be expected to hit it, etc.?

383. In other words, the preceding chapters having taught us the methods to be followed in eliminating all possible sources of error or of compensating for their effects, we now wish to conduct an investigation that will enable us to determine what are our chances of hitting under given conditions. From the results of this investigation, applied to any particular case, we can tell how much of a drain it would probably be upon our total ammunition supply to make an effective attack under given conditions, and hence whether or not we can afford to make the attempt. To arrive at answers to such questions we must fall back upon the theory of probability.

384. It will be readily understood from what has been said that the deviations of projectiles from their mean point of impact are closely analogous to what are called "accidental errors" in the text books on the subjects of probability and least squares; such, for example, as errors that are made in the direct measurement of a magnitude of any kind; and they obey the same laws. Small deviations are more frequent than large ones; positive and negative deviations are equally probable and therefore equally frequent, if the number of shot be great; very large deviations are not to be expected at all (if one occur it must be the result of some mistake or some avoidable error). **Deviations are "accidental errors."**

385. Suppose that we have as the point of aim the center, O, of the vertical target screen shown in Figure 37, and suppose we had n points of impact as shown (18 are shown) of which the coordinates are (z_1, y_1), (z_2, y_2), (z_n, y_n), each with its proper algebraic sign. Then manifestly the coordinates of the mean point of impact referred to O as an origin are $\left(\frac{\Sigma z}{n}, \frac{\Sigma y}{n}\right)$, which for the 18 shot shown on the figure would place the mean point of impact somewhere near the point P. Of course the larger we can make n, the more accurately is the position of the mean point of impact determined. Then, the origin being shifted to P, we get new values of the coordinates z and y, from which we know the deviations of each shot from the mean point of impact, both horizontal and vertical. The same process is resorted to in the horizontal plane, with coordinates x and z to determine the position of the mean

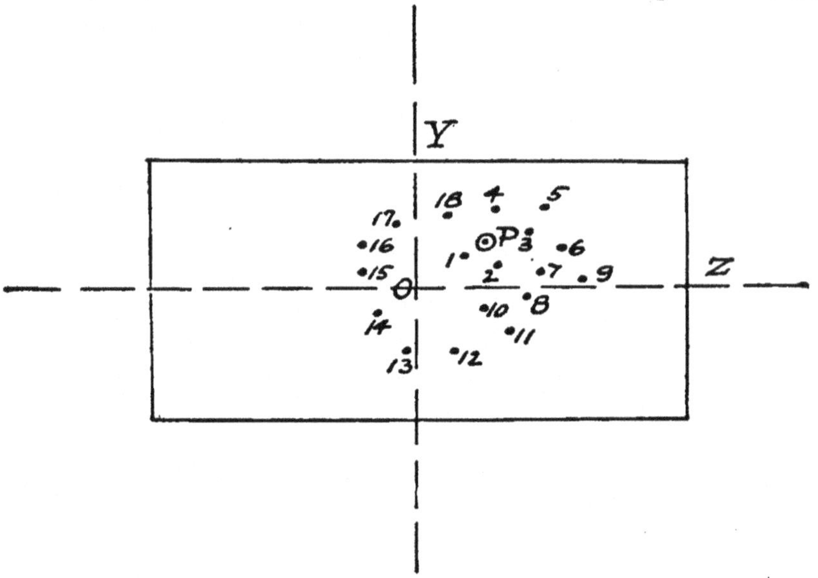

FIGURE 37.

point of impact in that plane, and thence the deviations of the several shots in that plane.

386. Having found the position of the mean point of impact as described above, and the coordinates of the several points of impact in relation to it, we then get the mean dispersion from mean point of impact in the lateral and in the vertical directions by taking the *arithmetical* mean (all signs positive) of all the z coordinates for the one and of all the y coordinates for the other, taking the mean point of impact as an origin. The mean dispersion from mean point of impact in the horizontal plane is determined in a similar way.

Probability. **387.** The probability of a future event is the numerical measure of our reasonable expectation that it will happen. Thus, knowing no reason to the contrary, we assign an equal probability to the turning up of each of the six different faces of a die at any throw, and we may say that the probability that an ace, for example, will turn up on any single throw is measured by the fraction $\frac{1}{6}$. This does not mean that we should expect an ace to turn up once and once only in every six times, but merely that in a great number of throws, n, we may reasonably expect very nearly $\frac{n}{6}$ aces to be thrown, and that the greater n is the more likely it is that the result will agree with the expectation.

388. If an event may happen in a ways and fail in b ways, each of the $a+b$ ways being equally likely to occur, the probability that it will happen is $\frac{a}{a+b}$ and the probability that it will fail is $\frac{b}{a+b}$, and the sum of these two fractions, unity, represents the certainty that the event will either happen or fail. Thus, if the probability that an event will happen be P, then the probability that it will not happen must be $1-P$. For example, since of the 52 different cards which may be drawn from a pack, 13 are spades, the probability that a single card drawn from a pack will be a spade is $\frac{13}{52}=\frac{1}{4}$, while the chance that it will not be a spade is $1-\frac{13}{52}=\frac{39}{52}=\frac{3}{4}$.

389. If the probability that one event will happen be P, and that another independent event will happen be Q, then the probability that both events will happen will be the product of P and Q. For example, the probability that a single card drawn from a pack will be a face card (king, queen or knave) is $\frac{12}{52}$, and the chance that it will be a spade is $\frac{13}{52}$; therefore the chance that it will be either the king, queen or knave of spades is $\frac{12}{52}\times\frac{13}{52}=\frac{3}{52}$.

390. It will be noted in the preceding discussion of the laws of probability that we have been dealing with cases in which one or more of a fixed number of events in question must either happen or fail; that is, with definite numbers of equally probable events. When we consider the deviations of projectiles this is no longer the case, for we are then dealing with values which may be anything whatever between certain limits. We cannot assign any finite measure to the probability that a deviation shall have a definite value because the number of values that it may have is unlimited. With a single throw of a die there are just six things that *may* happen and one of the six *must* happen. With the fire of a gun, however, within the limits which we are considering, there are an infinite number of points at which the shot may strike, and therefore no such definite fraction as $\frac{1}{6}$ can be assigned, as was done with the die. We can, however, measure the probability that the deviation of a certain shot will lie within certain limits, or that it will be greater or less than an assigned quantity. Suppose, for example, that a very large number, n, of shots have been fired, and that, their lateral deviations having been measured, it is found that m of these deviations are between 2 feet and 3 feet, either plus or minus; then we could say that, in any future trial under similar circumstances, the probability that a single shot will have a lateral deviation between 2 and 3 feet is $\frac{m}{n}$. Or if, of the n impacts, q were less than 4 feet to one side or the other of the mean point of impact, we could say that the probability that the lateral deviation of any single shot would be less than 4 feet is $\frac{q}{n}$. The actual case given in the following paragraph will serve as an illustration, although n is not really as large as it should be.

391. On December 17, 1880, at Krupp's proving ground, at Meppen, 50 shots were fired from a 12-centimeter gun at 5° elevation, giving a mean range of 2894.3 meters. The points of fall were marked on the ground and the position of the mean point of impact was determined (note that this is in the horizontal plane). Measur- **Observed results.**

ing the lateral deviations from this mean point of impact, the following results were obtained:

Limits	Number of shot	
	To the right	To the left
Between 0 and 1 meter............	14	13
Between 1 and 2 meters...........	8	8
Between 2 and 3 meters...........	2	5
	—	—
	24	26

The mean lateral deviation was found to be 1.07 meter. Taking horizontal and vertical axes through the mean point of impact (assuming that the lateral deviations are the same in the horizontal and in the vertical plane, which is very nearly the case), laying off equal spaces to left and to right of the origin, each representing one meter, and constructing on each space a rectangle whose height represents, on any

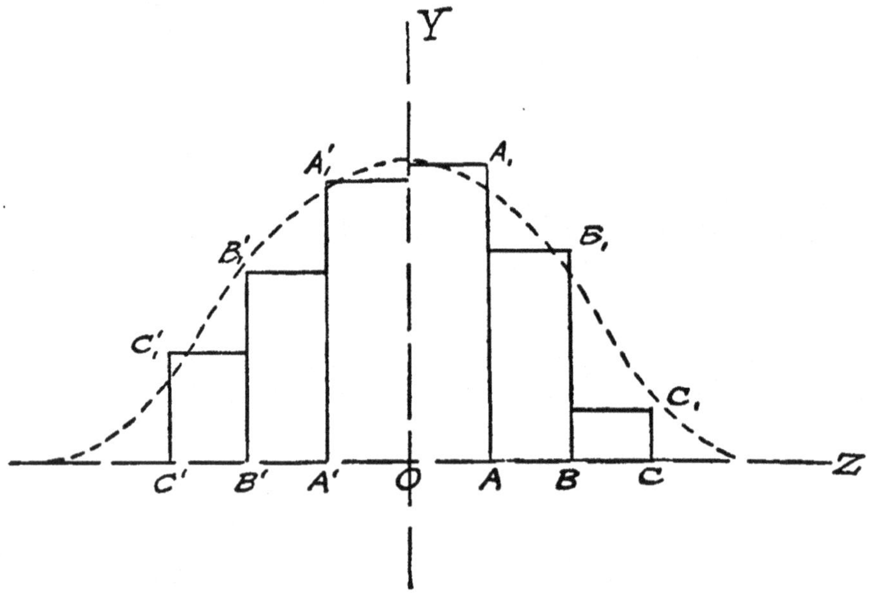

FIGURE 38.

convenient scale, the number of shots whose lateral deviations were within the limits corresponding to the space, we obtain Figure 38.

392. It will be seen that the distribution of the deviations is fairly symmetrical to the axis of Y, there being 26 to the left and 24 to the right; also that the maximum does not exceed three times the mean deviation; also that the area of each rectangle divided by the whole area of the figure is the measure of the probability (as defined) that any single deviation will fall within the limits represented by its base. Thus, the area $OAA_1=14$, divided by the total area, 50, is the probability, $\frac{14}{50}$, that any single deviation will lie between 0 and +1 meter, the area $OAA_1A_1'A'=27$, divided by the total area is the probability, $\frac{27}{50}$, that any single deviation will lie between +1 meter and −1 meter; and the total area divided by itself, $\frac{50}{50}=1=$certainty, is the probability that no deviation will exceed 3 meters.

393. Now if the number of shot be increased, while the width of the horizontal spaces be diminished in the same proportion, the area of each rectangle divided by the whole area of the figure will continue to measure, with increasing accuracy, the probability that any one deviation will fall within the limits represented by its base. At the limit, when the number of shot is infinite and the width of the horizontal spaces has been reduced to the infinitesimal dz, the height, y, of each rectangle will still be finite; the upper contour of the figure will become a curve approximately like that shown in the figure; the area of each rectangle now becomes the elementary area ydz and the whole area under the curve now becomes $\int_{-Z}^{Z} ydz$, and the quotient of the first by the second will still measure the probability that any one shot will fall between the limits represented by the base of the rectangle, that is, between z and $z+dz$. The area between any two ordinates of the curve, that is, $\int_{b}^{a} ydz$, divided by the whole area, will still measure the probability that any one deviation will lie between a and b. **Mathematical theory.**

394. The curve just described is the probability curve for the lateral deviations of the projectiles from the particular gun considered, under the given conditions, and while the probability curve for the vertical deviations for the same case, or for either lateral or vertical deviations or for deviations in range in the case of other guns or other conditions would differ from the particular curve shown in Figure 38, they would all present the following general features:

1. Since plus and minus deviations are equally likely to occur, the curve must be symmetrical to the right and to the left of the origin, which is the mean point of impact.

2. Since the deviations are made up of elemental deviations which, as they may have either direction, tend to cancel one another, small deviations are more frequent than large ones, so the maximum ordinate occurs at the origin.

3. Since large deviations can only result when most of the elemental deviations have the same directions and their greatest magnitudes, such large deviations must be rare, and deviations beyond a certain limit do not occur at all. Therefore the curve must rapidly approach the horizontal axis, both to the right and to the left of the origin, so that the ordinate, which can never be negative, practically vanishes at a certain distance from the origin.

395. If $y=F(z)$ be the equation to the probability curve, the general features stated in the preceding paragraph require that: **Conditions existing.**

1. $F(z)$ shall be an even function; that is, a function of z^2.

2. $F(0)$ shall be its maximum value.

3. It shall be a decreasing function of z^2 and shall practically vanish when z is large. Since it is impracticable to so select the function F that $F(z)$ shall be constantly equal to zero when z exceeds a certain limit, this last condition requires that the curve shall have the axis of Z for an asymptote; in other words, we must have $F(\pm\infty)=0$.

396. The foregoing characteristics being thus established, and taking as a basis the axiom that the arithmetical mean of the observed values (made under similar circumstances and with equal care) of any quantity is its most probable value, the theory of accidental errors deduces as the equation to the probability curve **Probability curve.**

$$y=\frac{1}{\pi\gamma}\epsilon^{-\frac{z^2}{\pi\gamma^2}} \qquad (222)$$

in which γ is the mean error, or in our case the mean deviation from mean point of impact, $\pi=3.1416$, and $\epsilon=2.7183$, and the factor $\frac{1}{\pi\gamma}$ has been introduced to make the whole area under the curve equal to unity

$$\left(\int_{-\infty}^{+\infty} \epsilon^{-\frac{z^2}{\pi\gamma^2}} dz = \pi\gamma\right)$$

thus obviating the necessity for dividing the partial area by the whole area whenever a probability is to be computed.

397. Figure 39 represents the probability curve for the Krupp 12-centimeter siege gun, taking its mean error to be 1.07 meter, as given by the 50 shots previously described. There is also shown in dotted lines, for comparison, the probability curve

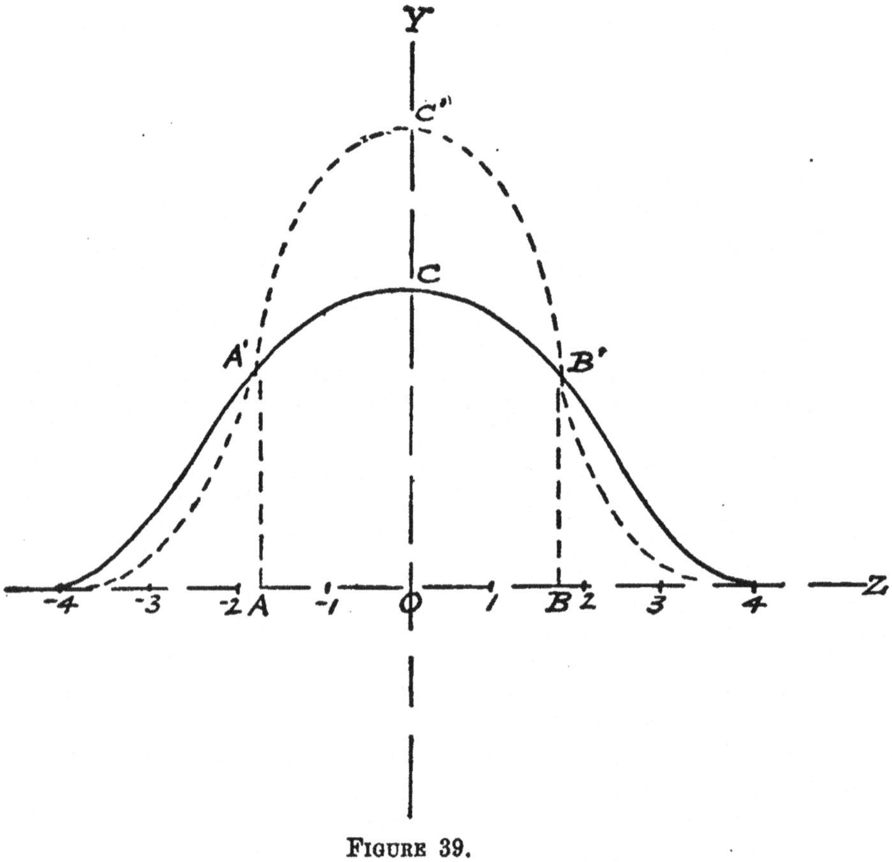

FIGURE 39.

for a gun whose mean error is three-quarters that of the 12-centimeter gun. In both cases the ordinates are exaggerated ten times as compared with the abscissæ.

398. The maximum ordinate being the value of y when $z=0$, is therefore inversely proportional to the mean deviation, that is, $y\Big]_{z=0} = \frac{1}{\pi\gamma}$; the probability that any one deviation will be less than $OB=OA$ is the numerical value of the area $AA'CB'B$ in the one case, and of the area $AA'C'B'B$ in the other; the probability that any one deviation will exceed $OB=OA$ is the area under that part of the curve which is to the left of AA' and to the right of BB'; the whole area under the curve has the numerical value of unity. It will be seen how very small is the probability that any deviation will exceed three times the mean deviation.

399. The probability, P, that the deviation of any single shot will be numerically less than a given quantity, a, being measured by the area between the ordinates of the probability curve at $z = \pm a$, and that curve being symmetrical to the axis of Y, we have

$$P = \frac{2}{\pi\gamma}\int_0^a \epsilon^{-\frac{z^2}{\pi\gamma^2}} dz \qquad (223)$$

400. In order to avoid repeated integrations, the following table gives the value of P, calculated from the above equation, but arranged for convenient use with the ratio $\frac{a}{\gamma}$ as an argument. Knowing the mean deviation of a gun, γ, to find the probability of a shot striking within a given distance of the mean point of impact, it is only necessary to take from the table the value of P which corresponds to $\frac{a}{\gamma}$. It is to be noted that if a and γ relate to lateral errors on a vertical screen, we get, by the use of this table, the probability that any one shot will strike between the two vertical lines on the screen distant a to the right and left, respectively, of the mean point of impact on the vertical screen; that if a and γ relate to vertical errors on a vertical screen, we get the probability that any one shot will strike between two horizontal lines distant a above or below the mean point of impact, respectively; if a and γ relate to the point of impact in the horizontal plane and to lateral deflections, we get the probability that any single shot will fall between two lines drawn on the surface of the water parallel to the horizontal trace of the vertical plane of the mean trajectory and distant a to the right and left, respectively, from the mean point of impact; and if a and γ relate to the point of impact in the horizontal plane and to deviations in range, we get the probability that any single shot will fall between two lines drawn on the surface of the water perpendicular to the horizontal trace of the vertical plane of the mean trajectory and a short of or beyond the mean point of impact. Each one of these four cases is of use under proper conditions.

PROBABILITY OF A DEVIATION LESS THAN a IN TERMS OF THE RATIO $\frac{a}{\gamma}$.

$\frac{a}{\gamma}$.	P.	$\frac{a}{\gamma}$.	P.	$\frac{a}{\gamma}$.	P.	$\frac{a}{\gamma}$.	P.
0.1	.064	1.1	.620	2.1	.906	3.1	.987
0.2	.127	1.2	.662	2.2	.921	3.2	.990
0.3	.189	1.3	.700	2.3	.934	3.3	.992
0.4	.250	1.4	.735	2.4	.945	3.4	.994
0.5	.310	1.5	.768	2.5	.954	3.5	.995
0.6	.368	1.6	.798	2.6	.962	3.6	.996
0.7	.424	1.7	.825	2.7	.969	3.7	.997
0.8	.477	1.8	.849	2.8	.974	3.8	.998
0.9	.527	1.9	.870	2.9	.979	3.9	.998
1.0	.575	2.0	.889	3.0	.983	4.0	.999

401. As an illustration of the use of the above table, we will find the probability of a deviation not exceeding 1 meter and 2 meters in the case of a gun whose mean lateral deviation is 1.07 meter, and will compare our results with those given by the actual firing of 50 shots from the Krupp 12-centimeter gun. Taking $a = 1$ meter, we have $\frac{a}{\gamma} = \frac{1}{1.07} = .935$, and from the table $P = .544$. The probability that the lateral deviation will not exceed 1 meter is therefore .544; therefore of 50 shots 27 should fall within 1 meter on either side of the mean point of impact, and actually 27 did so fall. Taking $a = 2$ meters, we have $\frac{a}{\gamma} = \frac{2}{1.07} = 1.87$, whence $P = .864$, which is the probability that the lateral deviation of any one shot will not exceed 2 meters. Therefore of 50 shots 43 should fall within 2 meters on either side of the mean point of impact, and actually 43 did so fall.

402. If P be the probability that the deviation of any single shot will not be greater than a, then evidently $100P$ will be the probable number of shots out of 100 which will fall within the limits $\pm a$; in other words, $100P$ is the percentage of hits to be expected upon a band $2a$ wide with its center at the mean point of impact. Thus we see from the table that the half width of the band which will probably receive 25 per cent of the shot is 0.4γ, while the half width of the band that will probably receive 50 per cent of the shot is 0.846γ. These facts are usually expressed by saying that the width of the 25 per cent rectangle is 0.80 and of the 50 per cent rectangle is 1.69 times the mean error.

403. The half width of the 50 per cent rectangle is known as the "probable error," or in our case the "probable deviation," since it is the error or deviation which is just as liable to be exceeded as it is not to be exceeded.

404. If we wish to find the probability of hitting an area whose width is $2b$ and whose height is $2h$, since the lateral and vertical deviations are independent of each other, the probability is the product of the two values of P taken from the table with the arguments $\frac{b}{\gamma_z}$ and $\frac{h}{\gamma_y}$, where γ_z and γ_y are the mean lateral and mean vertical deviations, respectively. Thus, supposing γ_z to be 4 feet and γ_y to be 5 feet, the probability of hitting with a single shot a 20-foot square with its center at the mean point of impact is $P_1P_2=.954\times.889=.848$, $P_1=.954$ being the value of P for $\frac{b}{\gamma_z}=\frac{10}{4}=2.5$ and $P_2=.889$ being the value of P for $\frac{h}{\gamma_y}=\frac{10}{5}=2$.

EXAMPLES.

1. The coordinates (z, y) of 10 hits made by a 6-pounder gun on a vertical target at 2000 yards range, axes at center of target, were as follows, in feet:

$$(-10, +13)\quad(+11, +9)\quad(+4, -2)\quad(-1, +1)$$
$$(-4, +2)\quad(+2, +1)\quad(-1, -2)\quad(0, -4)$$
$$(-1, -3)\quad(-4, -4)$$

Find the mean point of impact and the mean vertical and lateral deviations.

Answers. $z_0=-0.4$; $y_0=+1.1$; $\gamma_y=4.14$; $\gamma_z=3.72$.

2. The coordinates of 8 hits made by a 28-centimeter gun on a vertical target at 4019 meters range, axes at center of target, were as follows, in centimeters:

$$(-80, -90)\quad(-10, +210)\quad(+30, -70)\quad(-70, +355)$$
$$(+30, +40)\quad(-220, -150)\quad(-40, +40)\quad(-65, +90)$$

Find the mean point of impact and the mean vertical and lateral deviations.

Answers. $z_0=-53$; $y_0=+53$; $\gamma_y=123.9$; $\gamma_z=55.7$

3. The following ranges and lateral deflections from the plane of fire, in meters, were given by 10 shots from a 28-centimeter gun at 8° 30′ elevation:

Range.	Deflection left.	Range.	Deflection left.
6285	18	6204	16
6228	21	6141	17
6187	15	6200	19
6187	12	6256	15
6192	17	6205	18

Find the mean point of impact, the mean lateral deviation and the mean deviation in range.

Answers. Mean range 6208.5 meters $\gamma_s = 28.7$ meters.
Mean lateral deflection 16.8 meters $\gamma_s = 1.8$ meters.

4. *A* and *B* shoot alternately at a mark. If *A* can hit once in n trials and *B* once in $n-1$ trials, show that their chances are equal for making the first hit. What are the odds in favor of *B* after *A* has missed the first shot?

Answer. n to $n-2$.

5. What is the probability of throwing an ace with a single die in two trials?

Answer. $\frac{11}{36}$.

6. Taking the mean vertical error given from Example 1, and supposing the mean point of impact to be at the center of a vertical target, what would be the percentage of hits on targets of unlimited width and of heights, respectively, of 8 feet, 12 feet, 16 feet, 20 feet and 24 feet?

Answers. 55.9%; 75.1%; 87.6%; 94.6%; 97.9%.

7. Taking the mean errors given from Example 1, what percentage of shot would enter a gun port 4 feet square, supposing the mean point of impact to be at the center of the port? What would be the percentage if the port were 3 feet high by 5 feet wide? *Answers.* 9.9%; 9.2%.

8. What would be the probability of a single shot from the 28-centimeter gun of Example 2 hitting a turret 2 meters high and 8 meters in diameter at the range for which the mean errors are given, supposing the fire to be accurately regulated?

Answer. 0.48.

9. If a zone of a certain width receives 20% of hits, how many times as wide is the zone which receives 80% of hits? *Answer.* 5.05 times.

10. At Bucharest, in 1886, 94 shots were fired from a Krupp 21-centimeter rifled mortar at a Gruson turret, distant 2510 meters, without hitting it. The mean deviations were 33.27 meters in range and 9.90 meters laterally, and the mean point of impact practically coincided with the center of the turret. What was the probability of hitting, supposing the target to have been a 6-meter square (it was really a circle of 6 meters diameter)? *Answer.* 0.011.

11. How many of the 94 shots of Example 10 would probably have struck a rectangle 80 meters by 16 meters, with the longer axis in the plane of fire?

Answer. 31.8%.

CHAPTER 21.

THE PROBABILITY OF HITTING WHEN THE MEAN POINT OF IMPACT IS NOT AT THE CENTER OF THE TARGET. THE MEAN ERRORS OF GUNS. THE EFFECT UPON THE TOTAL AMMUNITION SUPPLY OF EFFORTS TO SECURE A GIVEN NUMBER OF HITS UPON A GIVEN TARGET UNDER GIVEN CONDITIONS. SPOTTING SALVOS BY KEEPING A CERTAIN PROPORTIONATE NUMBER OF SHOTS AS "SHORTS."

Mean point of impact not at center of target.

405. In the preceding chapter we considered only the chance of hitting when the mean point of impact is at the center of the target, but this is far from being an attainable condition in the service use of guns, especially of naval guns. In fact to bring the mean point of impact upon the target is the main object to be attained in gunnery, for, from what has already been said, if the mean point of impact be brought into coincidence with the center of the target and kept there, we will get the maximum number of hits possible, and it is to the accomplishment of this that the spotter gives his efforts. Even with a stationary target, at a known range, however, it is difficult to so regulate the fire as to bring about and maintain this coincidence of center of target and mean point of impact; and when the target is moving with a speed and in a direction that are only approximately known; when the range is not accurately known; when there is a wind blowing which may vary in force and direction at different points between the gun and the target; when the density of the air may vary at different points between the gun and the target; and when the firing ship is also in motion, etc.; even the most expert regulation of the fire by the observation of successive points of fall can do no more than keep the mean point of impact in the neighborhood of the object attacked. All this applies to a single gun, and in salvo firing we have the additional trouble that the mean points of impact of the several guns cannot be brought into coincidence. This makes it necessary for the spotter to estimate the position of the mean point of impact of the whole salvo, that is, the mean position of the mean points of impact of all the guns, and it is this combined mean point of impact of all the guns that the spotter must determine in his own mind and endeavor to bring upon the target and keep there. The difficulties attending this process are manifest.

406. In Figure 40, let O be the mean point of impact of a single gun, and let $ABCD$ be the target at any moment, and let the coordinates of the center of $ABCD$, with reference to the horizontal and vertical axes through O be z_0 and y_0; also let the mean lateral and vertical deviations of the gun be γ_z and γ_y, respectively, and let the dimensions of the target be $2b$ and $2h$. Then the probability that a shot will fall between the vertical lines Cc and $C'c'$ is the tabular value of P for the argument $\frac{z_0+b}{\gamma_y}$, which we will call $P_z(z_0+b)$; and the probability that a shot will fall between Dd and $D'd'$ is the tabular value of P for the argument $\frac{z_0-b}{\gamma_z}$, which we will call $P_z(z_0-b)$. Therefore the probability that a shot will fall between Cc and Dd is one-half the difference of the two preceding probabilities, or

$$\tfrac{1}{2}[P_z(z_0+b)-P_z(z_0-b)] \tag{224}$$

Similarly, the probability that a shot will fall between the horizontal lines $C'C$ and $B'B$ is

$$\tfrac{1}{2}[P_y(y_0+h)-P_y(y_0-h)] \tag{225}$$

Hence the probability of hitting $ABCD$ is the product of the two expressions given in (224) and (225), or

$$\tfrac{1}{4}[P_z(z_0+b)-P_z(z_0-b)]\times[P_y(y_0+h)-P_y(y_0-h)] \qquad (226)$$

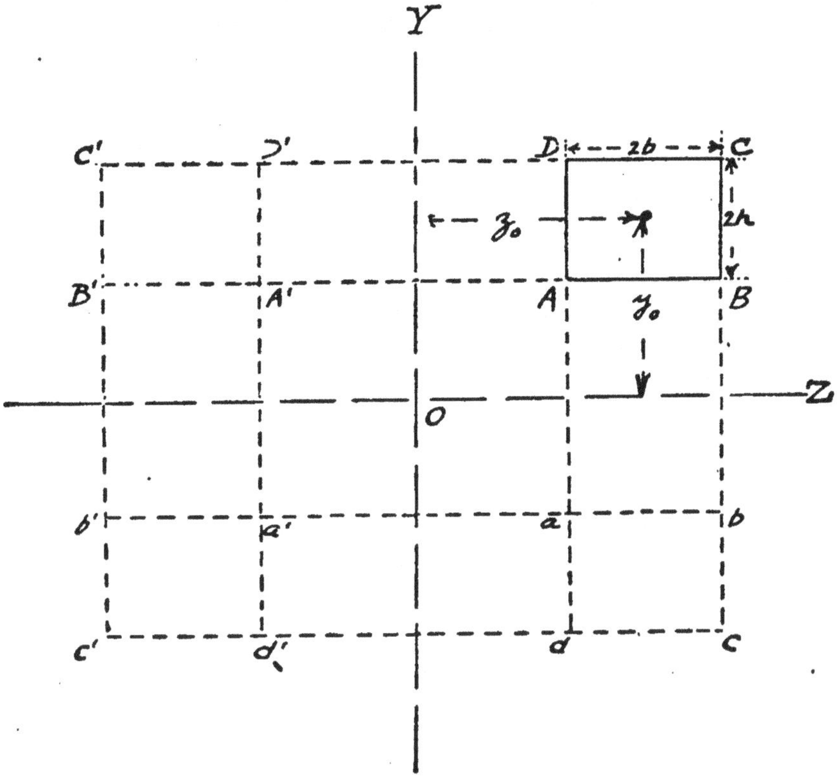

FIGURE 40.

407. To illustrate, suppose we wish to find the probable percentage of hits on a gun port 4 feet square, if the mean point of impact be 3 feet to one side of and 4 feet below the center of the port, the value of γ_z being 3.72 feet and of γ_y being 4.14 feet. Here we have:

$$P_z(z_0+b)=P_z(5)=.717 \qquad P_y(y_0+h)=P_y(6)=.751$$
$$P_z(z_0-b)=P_z(1)=.170 \qquad P_y(y_0-h)=P_y(2)=.298$$
$$P_z(5)-P_z(1)=.547 \qquad P_y(6)-P_y(2)=.453$$

From which we have $\quad P=\tfrac{1}{4}\times.547\times.453=.062$

Therefore the percentage of hits under the given conditions would be 6.2 per cent. Under the same conditions, but with the mean point of impact at the center of the port, the percentage of hits would be 9.9 per cent.

408. From what has been said it is evident that the less the mean errors of the gun, the more important it becomes to accurately regulate the fire; for if the distance of the mean point of impact from the target be more than three times the mean error of the gun we would get practically no hits at all. Therefore a reduction in the mean error of the gun renders imperative a corresponding reduction in the distance within which the spotter must keep the mean point of impact from the target if hits are to be made. Therefore, unless good control of the fire be secured, a gun with a small mean error will make fewer hits than one with a larger mean error, and this has sometimes been used as an argument in favor of guns that do not

Bearing of mean errors upon fire control.

shoot too closely. Conversely, however, if good control be secured—that is, if the spotter be competent and careful—the close-shooting gun will secure more hits than the other. Therefore the scientific method of securing hits is to have a competent spotter and a close-shooting gun; the other process is a discarding of science and knowledge and a falling back upon luck, which cannot but meet with disaster in the face of an enemy using proper and scientific methods.

409. To illustrate the statements contained in the preceding paragraph, we will take the case of a 6″ gun firing at a turret 25 feet high by 32 feet in diameter, and 3000 yards distant. Suppose the mean vertical and lateral deviations each to be 10 feet; if the mean point of impact coincides with the center of the target, the probable percentage of hits will be 54.3 per cent; but if the sights be set for a range of 10 per cent more or less than the true distance the mean point of impact will be raised or lowered about 43 feet (this is one of the older 6″ guns; not the one given in the accompanying range tables), and the percentage of hits will be reduced to 0.7 per cent. If, on the other hand, the mean errors of the gun were each 20 feet, or double the first assumption, while the percentage of hits with perfect regulation of fire (that is, with the mean point of impact at the center of the target) would be reduced to 18.2 per cent, that with sight setting for a range 10 per cent in error would be 4.7 per cent. Thus we see that if the fire be not accurately regulated a gun will be severely handicapped by its own accuracy if the range be not known within 10 per cent.

410. The work for the problem in the preceding paragraph is as follows:

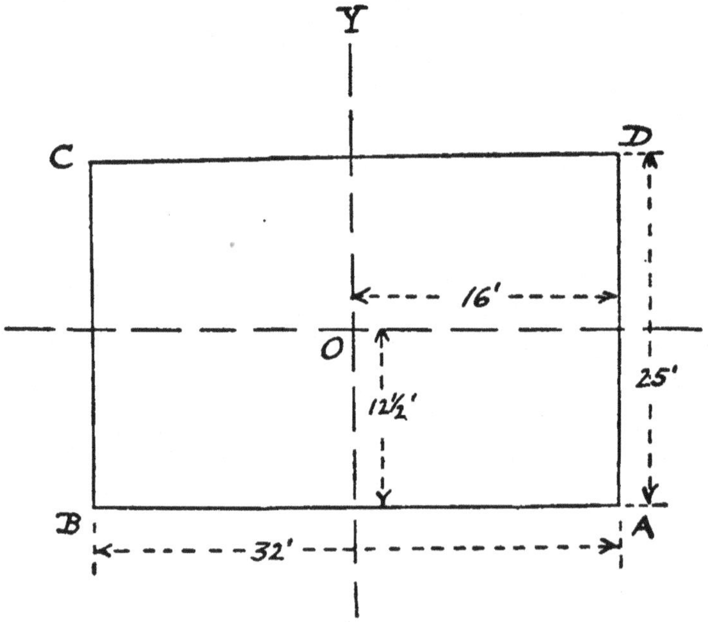

FIGURE 41.

Case 1. Mean deviation 10 feet. Mean point of impact at O (Figure 41).

$$\frac{a_1}{\gamma_x} = \frac{16}{10} = 1.6 \qquad P_x = .798$$

$$\frac{a_2}{\gamma_y} = \frac{12.5}{10} = 1.25 \qquad P_y = .681$$

$$P_x \times P_y = .543438$$

Therefore the percentage of hits is 54.3 per cent.

Case 2. Mean deviation 10 feet. Mean point of impact at O (Figure 42). Chances of hitting between $A'D$ and $B'C$.

$$P_z(z_0+16)-P_z(z_0-16)=P_z(16)-P_z(-16) \qquad =1.596$$

$$z_0=0 \qquad \frac{a_1}{\gamma_z}=\frac{16}{10}=1.6 \qquad P_z(16)=.798$$

Chances of hitting between AB and CD.

$$P_y(y_0+12.5)-P_y(y_0-12.5)=P_y(55.5)-P_y(30.5) \qquad = .0168$$

$$y_0=43\ \frac{a_2}{\gamma_y}=\frac{55.5}{10}=5.55 \quad P_y(55.5)=1.0000 \qquad 4\,\lfloor\, .026208 \qquad .0065$$

$$\frac{a_2}{\gamma_y}=\frac{30.5}{10}=3.05 \quad P_y(30.5)=\ .9832$$

$$.0168$$

Percentage of hits is 0.7 of 1 per cent.

Case 3. Mean deviation 20 feet. Mean point of impact at O (Figure 41).

$$\frac{a_1}{\gamma_z}=\frac{16}{20}=0.8 \qquad P_z=.477$$

$$\frac{a_2}{\gamma_y}=\frac{12.5}{20}=\ .625 \qquad P_y=.382$$

$$P_z\times P_y=.182214$$

Percentage of hits is 18.2 per cent.

Case 4. Mean deviation 20 feet. Mean point of impact at O (Figure 42).

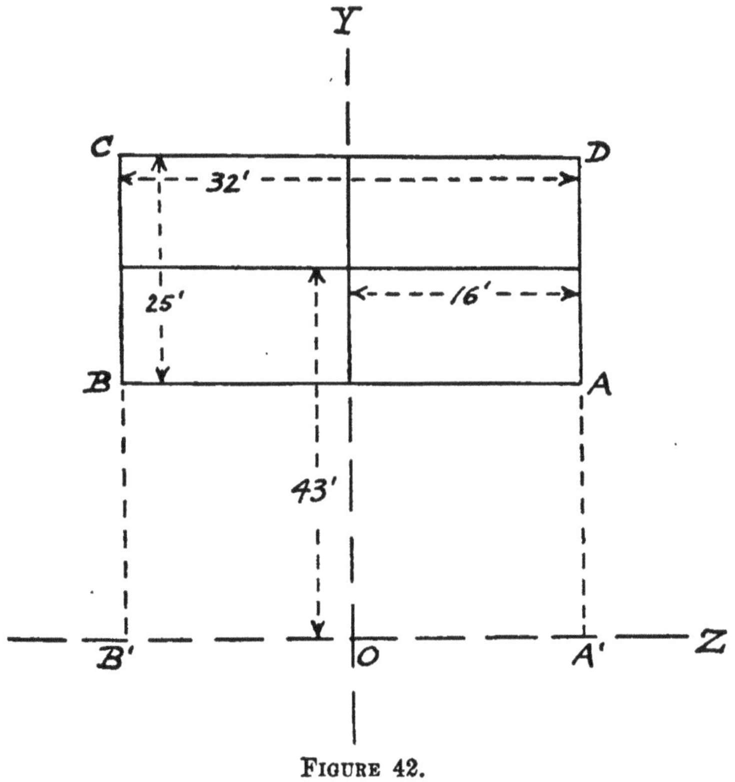

FIGURE 42.

Chances of hitting between $A'D$ and $B'C$.

$$P_z(z_0+16)-P_z(z_0-16)=P_z(16)-P_z(-16)= \qquad .954$$

$$\frac{a_1}{\gamma_z}=\frac{16}{20}=.8$$

Chances of hitting between *AB* and *CD*.

$$P_y(y_0+12.5)-P_y(y_0-12.5)=P_y(55.5)-P_y(30.5)=$$

$$\frac{a_3}{\gamma_y}=\frac{55.5}{20}=2.775 \quad P_y(55.5)=.97275$$

$$\frac{a_3}{\gamma_y}=\frac{30.5}{20}=1.525 \quad P_y(30.5)=.77550$$

$$P_y(55.5)-P_y(30.5)=.19725$$

$$\begin{array}{r} .19725 \\ 4\,\underline{|\,.1881765} \\ .047 \end{array}$$

Percentage of hits is 4.7 per cent.

411. If we know the percentage of hits at a given range on a target of given size, we can make a rough estimate of the mean errors of the gun by assuming that the mean point of impact was at the center of the target, and the greater the number of rounds fired the more nearly correct will this determination probably be. For example, on a certain occasion, the eighty 6" gun of certain British ships, firing separately, made 295 hits out of 650 rounds fired; that is, 45.4 per cent of hits; on a target 15 feet high by 20 feet wide, at a mean range of 1500 yards. Here we have given that the product

$$P_z\left(\frac{10}{\gamma_z}\right)\times P_y\left(\frac{7.5}{\gamma_y}\right)=.454$$

Assuming that $\gamma_z=\gamma_y$, we may solve the above by a process of trial and error, that is, by assuming successive integral values of γ, and by this process we see that when $\gamma=7$ we have

$$P_z\left(\frac{10}{7}\right)\times P_y\left(\frac{7.5}{7}\right)=.745\times .581=.432$$

and as .432 is very nearly .454, we can say that the mean deviations are slightly less than 7 feet; and we could go on and determine the solution of the equation more accurately by trying 6.9 feet instead of 7 feet as the value of γ. This would probably not make the result any nearer the truth, however, as any correction resulting therefrom would probably be less than the error caused by the assumption that the mean point of impact was at the center of the target.

412. The number of rounds necessary to make at least one hit may be determined by the following method: Let p be the probability of hitting with a single shot; then $1-p$ is the probability that a single shot will miss; and $(1-p)^n$ is the probability that all of n shots will miss. Therefore the probability of hitting at least once with n shots is $P=1-(1-p)^n$. Solving this equation for n, we get

$$\log(1-P)=n\log(1-p)$$

$$n=\frac{\log(1-P)}{\log(1-p)} \qquad (227)$$

and by giving P a value near unity we can find the value of n which will make one hit as nearly certain as we wish.

413. As an example, taking a case in which 94 shots were fired from a mortar at a turret, and in which the calculated probability of a hit with a single shot was .011, let us see how many rounds would have to be fired to make the probability of at least one hit .95. In that case, $p=.011$, and so we have, from (227),

$$n=\frac{\log(1-.95)}{\log(1-.011)}=\frac{\log .05}{\log .989}=\frac{8.69897-10}{9.99520-10}=\frac{-1.30103}{-0.00480}=271$$

Therefore 271 shots must be fired to make the odds 19 to 1 that there will be at least one hit. The probability of at least one hit with the 94 shots fired was

$$P=1-(1-p)^{94}=1-.354=.646$$

414. The deviations of the projectiles fired from a gun on a steady platform, the mean of which we will call the mean error of the gun, lateral or vertical as the case may be, are principally caused by:

1. Errors of the gun pointer in sighting the gun, but bear in mind that this does not include "mistakes," which are supposed to have been eliminated, but only accidental errors that must necessarily ensue even when the pointer is working as accurately as it is humanly possible to do.

2. An initial angular deviation of the projectile; that is, when the projectile does not leave the muzzle in a path in line with the axis of the gun.

3. Variations in initial velocity between successive rounds.

4. Differences between projectiles existing even after all possible differences have been eliminated.

415. With open sights the most expert gun pointers make a considerable angular error (this is an angular error in sighting, not to be confused with the angular deviation described in 2 of the preceding paragraph), which varies from round to round, when the gun is pointed by directing the line of sight at a target. With telescopic sights this error is greatly reduced but still exists. There is also always an error in setting the sights (we suppose the range to be unchanged from shot to shot, but that the sights are reset for each round). The mean angular error of sighting can only be estimated.

416. The initial angular deviation results from the projectile not leaving the gun in the exact line of the axis of the latter. This deviation, which occurs indifferently in all directions, was quite large with smooth-bore guns and with some of the earlier rifles, but with modern guns, using projectiles rotated by forced bands, it is undoubtedly much less.

417. With all powders the muzzle velocity varies somewhat from round to round, no matter what care be taken to insure uniformity in the charges. With the nitrocellulose powder now used in our navy, if the charges have been made up with proper care, and if the projectiles are all of the same weight, the average difference between the velocities given by successive rounds and the mean velocity of all the rounds fired on any one occasion will probably not be great. If a large number of rounds be fired, and the velocity for no one round differs a f. s. from the average, then somewhat more than half the velocities will be within $\frac{a}{3}$ f. s. of the average, a not being large.

418. The projectiles of any gun differ among themselves, but when they all have the same form of head and are not of greatly different lengths, the resulting deviations are not so important as those caused by variations in the weight.

419. Of course the only correct way of determining the mean errors of a given gun is by actually firing a large number of rounds at a target and measuring the deviations. That the errors are very small under favorable circumstances is illustrated in Figure 43, which represents a target made at Meppen on June 1, 1882, with a 28-centimeter gun, the distance of the target from the gun being 2026 meters (2215 yards). The dotted cross is the mean point of impact, whose coordinates referred to the horizontal and vertical axes at the center of the target are $z=32.4$ inches and $y=-11.6$ inches. The mean lateral deviation is 9.5 inches, and the mean vertical deviation is 11.6 inches. These actual deviations are considerably less than those encountered in service, which may be plausibly ascribed to the fact that in proving

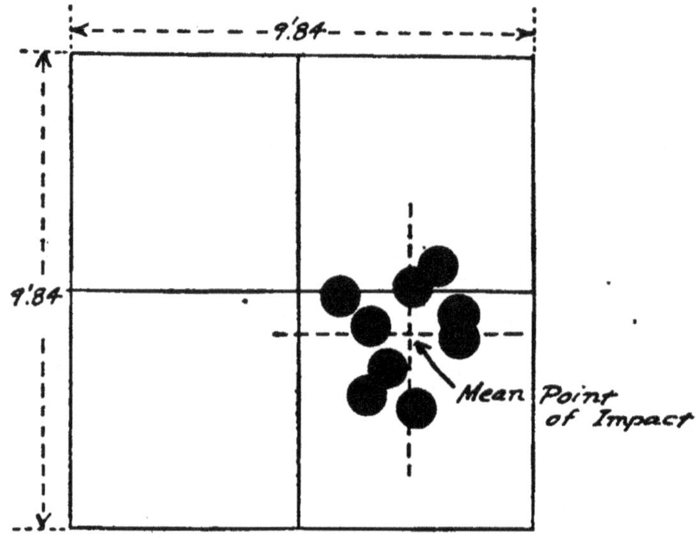

FIGURE 43.

ground firings greater care can be taken in pointing than is usually practicable under service conditions.

Effect of rolling, pitching and yawing.

420. The three angular motions of a ship's deck, caused by the rolling, pitching and yawing, greatly increase the actual mean errors of naval guns in service, but their effects depend so much upon the skill of the gun pointer, as well as upon the state of the sea and the characteristics of the particular ship and gun mounting, that only the roughest estimates of their values can be made. Many naval guns are mounted in broadside and only train from bow to quarter, and even those mounted on the midships line are likely to be most used in broadside; thus the roll, which is the greatest and most rapid of a ship's motions, has its largest component in the plane of fire, and acts principally to increase the vertical deviations. The principal effect of pitching, on the other hand, is to increase the lateral deviations by causing the plane of the sights to be more or less inclined, now to one side and now to the other of the plane of fire. Motion in azimuth, yawing, mostly due to unsteady steering, affects the lateral deviations only.

Motion of target.

421. If the target be in motion, the person controlling the fire of the gun must of course estimate its speed and direction in order to direct the fire at the point where the target will be when the projectile strikes, and his corrections must always vary in accuracy from round to round, thus increasing both the lateral and the vertical deviations. Furthermore, variations in the accuracy of the estimated corrections for the speed of the firing ship and for the effect of the wind must occur from round to round, which will also affect the lateral and the vertical deviations. Moreover, the changing direction of the target will cause the angle between the direction of the wind and the plane of fire to vary, thus necessitating a variable allowance for wind effect and again increasing the deviations of projectiles.

422. Taking everything into account, probably a fair estimate of the mean vertical deviation of modern naval guns of medium and large caliber, at 2000 yards range, with skilled fire-control personnel and gun pointers, and under average conditions, would be 5 feet. The mean lateral deviation, which for guns on steady platforms, is from two-thirds to three-fourths the mean vertical deviation, may be taken to be the same as the mean vertical deviation in the case of naval guns, without any great error. Both vertical and lateral deviations may be taken to be proportional to the range, at least up to 4000 or 5000 yards range, though the former really increases somewhat more rapidly than the range. For ranges greater than those given, the increase in the deviations will be at a greater rate.

423. It will be noticed that, in the earlier part of the discussion of the subject, we referred to the "accidental deviations" of a gun as being due to the "inherent errors" of the gun, but we have now seen that there are "accidental errors" that are not really inherent in the gun itself, although their results are similar. The angular deviation resulting from the fact that the shell does not leave the gun exactly in the axis of the gun is strictly an inherent error of the gun; but the angular error in pointing due to the fact that even the most perfectly trained and most skillful pointer cannot point twice exactly alike is an error that does not pertain to the gun itself but to its manipulation. The results, as stated, are similar, however, and may therefore be considered together, as making up the sum of the accidental errors that cause the deviations. To recapitulate, we have first deviations due to mistakes, which we eliminate from consideration. Then we have deviations resulting from known causes, which we also eliminate by the methods of exterior ballistics. When these two sources of error have been eliminated, we have remaining two sources of error, those pertaining to the imperfections of the gun itself and those pertaining to the inherent imperfections of even the most perfect personnel handling the gun. It is these last two only that may be considered under the theory of probability. And bear in mind the difference between a mistake and an accidental error. A mistake is the result of bad judgment, and may cause a large error, as, say, a mistaken estimate of two points in the direction of the wind; and an accidental error is that small error which must necessarily be made even by a thoroughly trained judgment. Accidental errors are necessarily small, and are necessarily as likely to occur on one side as on the other.

Inherent errors.

424. Although the targets of naval guns are generally vertical, the fire of such guns must, as a rule, be regulated by the observation of points of fall in the horizontal plane. The lateral deviations are practically the same whether measured on the vertical plane perpendicular to the line of fire, or on the horizontal plane, provided the error of the shot in range be not too great. The deviations in range, however, differ very greatly from the vertical deviations, the ratio between them being the cotangent of the angle of fall.

425. Since the mean deviation in range, γ_x, is related to the mean vertical deviation, γ_y, by the formula $\gamma_x = \gamma_y \cot \omega$, and since the angle of fall increases and its cotangent correspondingly decreases with increase of range at about the same rate as the mean vertical deviation, it will be seen that the mean deviation in range remains nearly the same for widely different ranges. Thus, for example, while the estimated mean vertical deviation of the 12″ gun of 2800 f. s. initial velocity increases from 2.5 feet at 1000 yards range to 10.5 feet at 4000 yards range, the corresponding deviation in range only changes from 119 yards to 104 yards; and while in the case of smaller guns the mean deviation in range decreases more rapidly, still the change is always very much less proportionately than the change in range itself.

426. The principal use of knowledge of the mean deviation in range is in the regulation of gun fire by observation of the points of fall. Suppose the axis of Z, in Figure 44, represents the water-line of the target, the axis of X being the horizontal trace of the vertical plane of the mean trajectory, and let the distance from the axis of Z to the dotted lines *aa*, *a′a′*, *bb*, *b′b′*, *cc*, *c′c′*, *dd*, *d′d′*, etc., represent the mean deviation in range, γ_x, of the gun. Then if the point of impact be on the axis of Z, that is, on the water-line, half of all the shot will fall short; if it be on *a′a′* the percent-

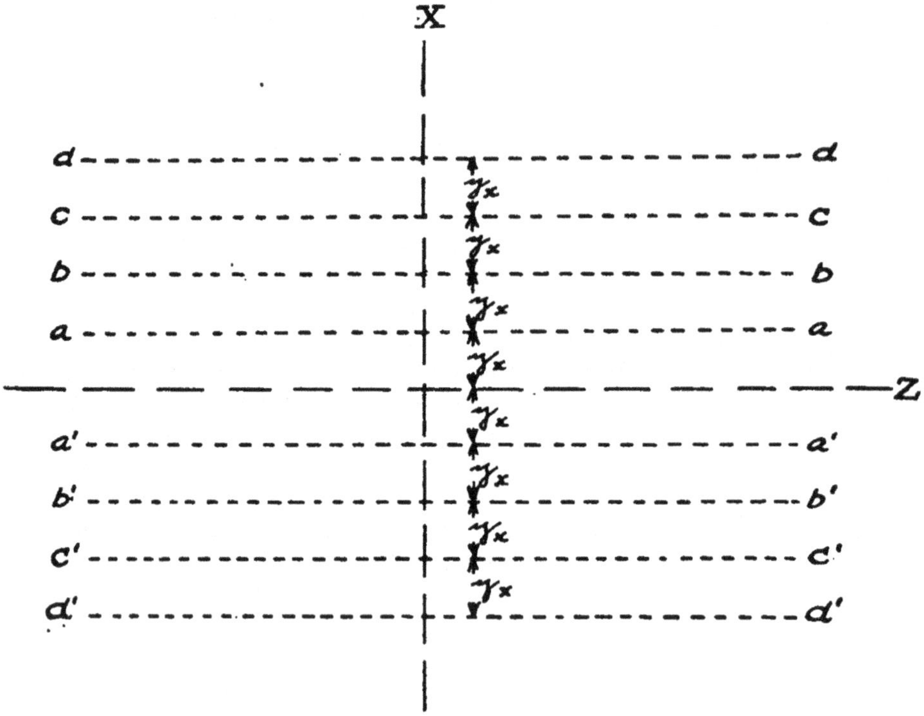

FIGURE 44.

age of shot that will fall short will be increased by the number which fall between the axis of Z and *a′a′*, or, from the table of probabilities, it will be $50+\frac{57.5}{2}=79$ per cent. If the mean range be still further short, so that the mean point of impact falls on *b′b′*, the percentage of shorts will be $50+\frac{88.9}{2}=94$ per cent; and, finally, if the mean point of impact be three or more times the mean deviation short, then practically all the shot will fall short. The same reasoning shows that if no shot strike short of the axis of Z, the mean point of impact is three or more times the mean deviation in range beyond the axis of Z; if about 6 per cent strike short, the mean point of impact is about twice the mean deviation in range beyond the axis of Z; and if about 21 per cent are short, it is about the mean deviation in range beyond the axis of Z. Thus, by observation of the percentage of shot which strike short it is possible to determine with some degree of accuracy how much the setting of the sight in range should be increased or decreased to bring the mean point of impact on the target.

427. Let us now suppose that we are going to fire salvos from a battery of 12″ guns, for which $V=2900$ f. s., $w=870$ pounds and $c=0.61$. Let us also assume that we have a vertical target 30 feet high and wide enough to eliminate the necessity for considering lateral deviations due to accidental errors. Let us take the mean errors of the gun in range, first as 40 yards, next as 60 yards, and then again as 80 yards; and also that they are approximately the same at all ranges. Let us also assume that the mean point of impact is at the center of the water-line of the target, in which case, as we have already seen, 50 per cent of the shot will fall short. Let us also assume that the three mean deviations correspond to total deviations of 150, 200 and 300 yards, respectively. Now let us see what percentage of the shot in each salvo will probably hit, at a range of 7000 yards, at which range the danger space for a target 30 feet high is, by the range table, 180 yards. **Method of "shorts."**

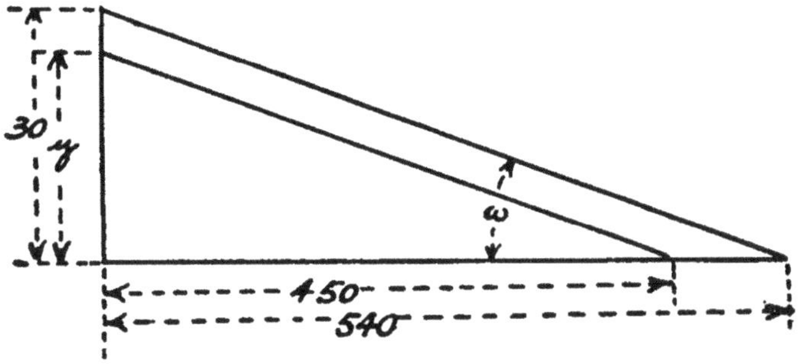

FIGURE 45.

1. Mean dispersion in range 40 yards; maximum dispersion in range 150 yards (Figure 45).

$$\tan \omega = \frac{30}{540} = \frac{1}{18}$$

$$\frac{y}{450} = \frac{1}{18} \quad y=25 \text{ feet}$$

That is, for a maximum dispersion of 150 yards, or 450 feet, no shot would pass more than 25 feet above the water-line of the target, and all shots that do not fall short would hit. Therefore, by our assumption, we would have 50 per cent of shorts and 50 per cent of hits.

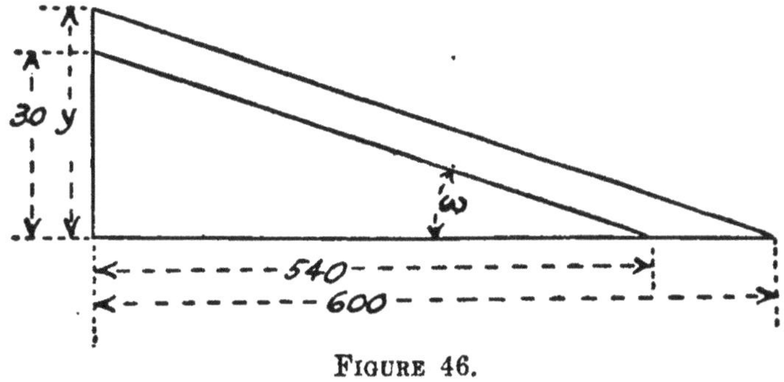

FIGURE 46.

2. Mean dispersion in range of 60 yards; maximum dispersion in range of 200 yards (Figure 46).

$$\frac{y}{600} = \frac{1}{18} \quad y=33\tfrac{1}{3} \text{ feet}$$

Also the mean dispersion in range is 180 feet, therefore the mean vertical dispersion is

$$\gamma_y = 180 \tan \omega = \frac{180}{18} = 10 \text{ feet}$$

Our problem therefore becomes to find how many shot will pass between the top of the target and a line parallel to it and $3\frac{1}{3}$ feet above it, knowing that 50 per cent of the shot fired will fall short, and the other 50 per cent will pass between the waterline of the target and a horizontal line $33\frac{1}{3}$ feet above it. As we have already taken out the 50 per cent of the shot that fall short, the $\frac{1}{2}$ disappears from the formula, and we have

$$P_y(33) - P_y(30) = .009$$

$$\frac{a_1}{\gamma} = \frac{33}{10} = 3.3 \qquad P_y(33) = .992$$

$$\frac{a_2}{\gamma} = \frac{30}{10} = 3.0 \qquad P_y(30) = \underline{.983}$$

$$.009$$

That is, .9 of 1 per cent of the shot that do not fall short will pass over the top of the target, leaving 99.1 per cent of them as hits. Therefore, of the 100 per cent of shot fired, 50 per cent will fall short; 99.1 per cent of 50, or 49 per cent of them, will hit; and 1 per cent of them all will go over.

3. Mean dispersion in range 80 yards; maximum dispersion in range 300 yards.

$$\frac{y}{900} = \frac{1}{18} \; y = 50 \text{ feet} \qquad \gamma_y = 240 \times \frac{1}{18} = \frac{40}{3} \text{ feet}$$

and in the same manner as in 2, to find the number of shot that will pass between the top of the target and a horizontal line 50 feet above the water-line, we have

$$P_y(50) - P_y(30) = .035$$

$$\frac{a_1}{\gamma} = \frac{50 \times 3}{40} = 3.75 \qquad P_y(50) = .9975$$

$$\frac{a_2}{\gamma} = \frac{30 \times 3}{40} = 2.25 \qquad P_y(30) = \underline{.9275}$$

$$.07$$

Therefore 7 per cent will go over, and 93 per cent will hit out of the 50 per cent that do not fall short. Therefore we have that there will be 50 per cent of shorts, 46 per cent of hits and 4 per cent of overs. Proceeding similarly for other ranges, we can make up a table like the following:

Range. Yds.	Mean point of impact at water-line. Mean dispersion in range of— 40 yards. Percentage of—			60 yards. Percentage of—			80 yards. Percentage of—			Danger space. Yds.
	Shorts.	Hits.	Overs.	Shorts.	Hits.	Overs.	Shorts.	Hits.	Overs.	
7000	50	50	0	50	49	1	50	46	4	180
10000	50	49	1	50	42	8	50	35	15	108
13000	50	42	8	50	32	18	50	25	25	70
15000	50	36	14	50	27	23	50	21	29	55
18000	50	28	22	50	20	30	50	15	35	39

The above mean dispersions are less than have been experienced at recent target practices.

The above chances of hitting are based only on vertical errors; if the target be short they will be materially reduced by the lateral errors.

428. For the above problem let us now suppose that the mean point of impact had been at the center of the danger space, instead of at the water-line, and we had desired to tabulate the same data as before. Let us start with the range of 7000 yards, for which the danger space is 180 yards, and compute the results for a mean dispersion in range of 40 yards, corresponding to a total dispersion of 150 yards.

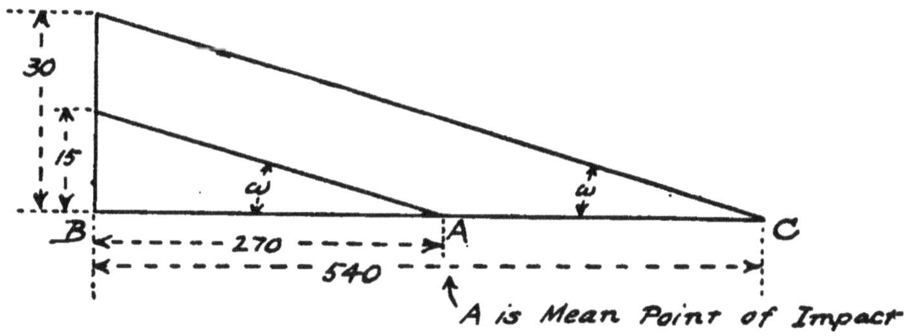

FIGURE 47.

All shot that fall less than 270 feet short of the mean point of impact are hits. For space between mean point of impact and target,

$$\frac{a}{\gamma}=\frac{270}{120}=\frac{9}{4}=2.25 \qquad P=.9275$$

Therefore, for those short of the mean point of impact, 92.75 per cent will hit and 7.25 per cent will fall short. But only 50 per cent of the total number of shot fired fall shot of the mean point of impact, therefore the above percentages become, of the total,

Hits ....46.375 per cent
Shorts .... 3.625 per cent

For the space between A and C, which is 270 feet, we know that any shot that falls between A and C hits, and any that falls beyond C is over. Therefore the work is the same as the above, and we have

Hits ....46.375 per cent
Overs .... 3.625 per cent

Therefore the total is

Shorts .... 3.625 per cent
Hits ....92.750 per cent
Overs .... 3.625 per cent

Working out similar data for the other ranges and dispersions gives us the following table:

Range. Yds.	Mean point of impact at center of danger space. Mean dispersion in range of— 40 yards. Percentage of— Shorts.	Hits.	Overs.	60 yards. Percentage of— Shorts.	Hits.	Overs.	80 yards. Percentage of— Shorts.	Hits.	Overs.	Danger space. Yds.
7000	4	93	3	12	77	11	19	63	18	180
10000	14	72	14	24	53	23	30	40	30	108
13000	25	49	26	32	36	32	37	27	36	70
15000	29	42	29	36	29	35	40	21	39	55
18000	35	31	34	40	21	39	42	16	42	30

429. From the tables given in the two preceding paragraphs, if we assume the mean point of impact on the target, we see that, as the mean dispersion increases, the percentage of hits decreases very rapidly.

430. It will also be seen that, to get the greatest possible number of hits, a greater percentage of shorts is necessary at long ranges than at short ranges.

431. It will also be seen that, where the mean point of impact in range is at some distance from the target, an increase in dispersion gives an increase in the number of hits, which is in accord with the principles previously enunciated. It may be shown mathematically that the mean dispersion for maximum efficiency is equal to 80 per cent of the distance from the mean point of impact in range to the center of the danger space.

432. From what has been said, it will readily be seen that, in controlling the firing of salvos from a battery of similar guns, we desire to keep a certain proportion of the shot striking short of the target in order to get the maximum number of hits. There are also other good reasons for so keeping a number of the shot striking short. From what we have seen, we may determine certain general rules which will govern the spotter in thus controlling salvo firing. This question, however, is one that may more appropriately be considered at length in the study of another branch of gunnery, so there will be no further discussion of it in this book.

433. It will be interesting to compare the results of actual firing with the computed results in some one case, to see how closely the two agree, and to get some idea of the correctness for service purposes of percentages determined mathematically. Such results are given in the following table taken from Helie's well-known Traité de Balistique. It represents the results of about 500 shots fired at Gavre from a 16.5-centimeter rifle at various angles of elevation:

	Probability that the lateral deviations will not exceed— $\frac{\gamma_z}{4}$.	$\frac{\gamma_z}{2}$.	γ_z.	$2\gamma_z$.	$3\gamma_z$.
By table..........	0.158	0.310	0.575	0.889	0.983
By firing..........	0.176	0.300	0.592	0.885	0.988

EXAMPLES.

1. Supposing a row of gun ports, each 4 feet high by 6 feet wide, are spaced 18 feet between centers; show by comparing the percentages of shot which would enter a port that it would be better to aim a gun whose mean vertical and lateral errors are each 5 feet at the center of a port than half way between two ports.

Answer. 9.5 per cent to 7.0 per cent.

2. Compare the percentages of hits on ports in the two cases of Example 1 if the mean errors of the gun were 7.5 feet instead of 5 feet.

Answer. 5.8 per cent to 5.8 per cent.

3. The 12″ guns of a certain ship made 69 per cent of hits on a target 15 feet high by 20 feet wide at 1700 yards range. Supposing the mean vertical and lateral deviations to have been equal, what was their approximate value? Supposing through ignorance of the range the sights had been set for 1870 yards, thus raising the mean point of impact 9 feet, what would the percentage of hits have been?

Answers. 5 feet; 35.7 per cent.

4. The mean errors, laterally and in range, of a rifled mortar are 3.5 yards and 53 yards, respectively, at a mean range of 3357 yards. What is the chance of hitting a ship's deck (taking its equivalent area to be a rectangle 300 feet by 60 feet) when she is end on; (1) if the mean point of impact be at one corner of the rectangle; (2) if it be at the center of the rectangle? *Answers.* .217; .555.

5. What are the chances of hitting under the same circumstances as in Example 4, excepting that the ship is broadside on? *Answers* ..059; .120.

6. At a range at which the mean vertical error of the guns equals the freeboard of the enemy, what is the ratio of the respective probabilities of hitting her when you aim at her water-line and when you aim at her middle height, suppose the fire to be accurately regulated in each case? What is the same ratio at a range at which the mean vertical error is only half the freeboard?

Answers. .288 to .310; .445 to .575.

7. A torpedo-boat steaming directly for a ship at 24 knots is discovered and fire is opened on her at 1500 yards range. If the probability of a single 3″ shot striking her is .02, and there are eight 3″ guns each firing 12 rounds a minute at her, what is the chance that she will be struck at least once before she is within 500 yards? What is the chance of her being hit at least twice? *Answers.* .911; .694.

8. At 4000 yards, a ship with 30 feet freeboard gives a danger space of 90 yards for the 3″ gun ($V=2800$ f. s.) and the mean error in range of the same gun at 4000 yards is 30 yards (estimated). How closely must the range of such a ship be known to make the probable percentage of hits as great as 0.5 per cent, supposing the guns to be pointed at the middle of the freeboard? *Answer.* 141 yards.

9. The mean error in range of the 12″ gun ($V=2800$ f. s.) at 4000 yards range is 100 yards (estimated), and its danger space for 30 feet freeboard is 300 yards. How closely must the range be known to make the probable percentage of hits as great as 0.5 per cent, supposing the guns to be pointed at the middle height of the freeboard? *Answer.* 470 yards.

10. Fire is opened with eight 3″ guns on a torpedo-boat coming head on when she is at 1500 yards range. She covers 100 yards every 7.5 seconds, and each gun fires once every 7.5 seconds. The mean lateral and vertical deviations are each 6 feet, and the target offered is 6 feet high by 15 feet wide. If an error of 100 yards in the sight setting displaces the mean point of impact 3 feet vertically, and the sights are all set for 1000 yards range, what is the probable number of hits while the boat advances to 500 yards range? *Answer.* 10+.

11. The turrets of a monitor steaming obliquely to the line of fire present a vertical target consisting of two rectangles, each 24 feet wide by 12 feet high, and 36 feet from center to center. If the mean errors of a gun be 12 yards laterally and 8 yards vertically, would it be better to aim at a turret or half way between them?
Answers. 1st case, $P=.057$; 2d case, $P=.061$.

12. A gun has 30 shell, one of which, if landed in a certain gun position, would silence the gun contained therein. The gun pit is 10 yards in diameter, and the probability of hitting it with the gun in question is .05. What would be the probability of silencing the gun, using all the ammunition? *Answer.* $P=.785$.

13. The 12″ guns of a ship made 68 per cent of hits on a target 15 feet high by 20 feet wide at 1700 yards range. What was the probable value of the mean deviations, vertical and lateral? Supposing the mean deviation to be proportional to the range, what percentage of hits would the same guns make on the same target at 3400 and at 5100 yards? *Answers.* 5 feet; 25.9 per cent; 12.6 per cent.

14. If the probability of hitting a target with a single shot is .05, what will be the probability of making at least two hits with 50 shots? *Answer.* .721.

15. What is the greatest value of the mean deviation of a gun consistent with a probability equal to .90 of its making at least one hit in a hundred shots on a gun port 2 feet wide by 4 feet high? *Answer.* 5.95 feet.

16. Compute the data for 10,000 yards contained in paragraph 427.
17. Compute the data for 13,000 yards contained in paragraph 427.
18. Compute the data for 15,000 yards contained in paragraph 427.
19. Compute the data for 18,000 yards contained in paragraph 427.
20. Compute the data for 10,000 yards contained in paragraph 428.
21. Compute the data for 13,000 yards contained in paragraph 428.
22. Compute the data for 15,000 yards contained in paragraph 428.
23. Compute the data for 18,000 yards contained in paragraph 428.

APPENDIX A.

FORMS TO BE EMPLOYED IN THE SOLUTION OF THE PRINCIPAL EXAMPLES GIVEN IN THIS TEXT BOOK.

NOTES.

1. In preparing these forms the problem taken has been the 8″ gun (gun *K* in the tables) for which $V=2750$ f. s., $w=260$ pounds, $c=0.61$, generally for a range of 19,000 yards. More specific data is given at the head of each form.

2. In the problems under standard conditions, which should give the exact results contained in the range tables, it should be borne in mind that the latter are given, for the angle of departure to the nearest tenth of a minute, for the angle of fall to the nearest minute, for the time of flight to the nearest hundredth of a second, etc., only. Also that results given in the range tables are entered after the results of the computations have been plotted as a curve, and the faired results are those contained in the tables. Small discrepancies between the computed results and those given in the tables may therefore sometimes be expected.

3. Also, results obtained by direct computation are of course more accurate than those obtained by taking multiples of quantities given in the range tables, and small discrepancies may be expected in some such cases between computed results and those taken from the range tables.

INDEX TO FORMS IN APPENDIX A.

Form No.	Chapter No.	Example No.	Nature of Example.
1	8	7	Computing ϕ, etc., for a given range, by Ingalls' method of successive approximations.
2	8	8	Computing ϕ, etc., for a given range, by Ingalls' method, knowing f.
3	8	9	Computing ϕ, etc., for a given range, by Alger's method of successive approximations.
4	9	1	Computing the elements of the vertex for a given R and ϕ, by successive approximations.
5	9	2	Computing the elements of the vertex for a given R and ϕ, knowing f.
6	9	3	Deriving special formulæ for y and $\tan \theta$ for a given trajectory.
7	9	4	Computing values of y and θ for given abscissæ in a given trajectory.
8	10	1	Computing R, etc., for a given ϕ, by successive approximations.
9	10	2	Computing R, etc., for a given ϕ, knowing f.
10A, 10B	11	1	Computing ϕ, ψ, θ, t and v for an elevated or depressed target.
11	12	2	Computing change in range resulting from a variation in initial velocity.
12	12	3	Computing change in range resulting from a variation in atmospheric density.
13	12	4	Computing change in range resulting from a variation in weight of projectile: method by direct computation.
14	12	5	Computing change in range resulting from a variation in weight of projectile; method by using Columns 10 and 12 of range table.
15	12	6	Computing change in position of point of impact in vertical plane through target resulting from a variation in the setting of the sight in range.
16	13	1	Computing the drift at a given range.
17	13	2	Computing sight-bar height and set of sliding leaf for a given range and deflection.
18	14	1	Computing the effect of wind.
19	14	2	Computing the effect of motion of the gun.
20	14	3	Computing the effect of motion of the target.
21	16	—	Computing the penetration of armor.
22	16	2	Range table computations, ϕ, etc.
23	16	3	Range table computations.
24	16	4	Range table computations.
25A, 25B	17	8	Wind and speed problems. Real wind.
26	17	9	Wind and speed problems. Apparent wind.
27A	17	13	Reduced velocity by range tables.
27B	17	14	Reduced velocity by computation
28	18	1 and 2	The calibration of a single gun.
29	19	1	The calibration of a ship's battery.

Form No. 1.

CHAPTER 8—EXAMPLE 7.

FORM FOR THE COMPUTATION OF THE DATA CONTAINED IN COLUMNS 2, 3, 4 AND 5 OF THE RANGE TABLES; THAT IS, FOR THE VALUES OF THE ANGLE OF DEPARTURE (ϕ), ANGLE OF FALL (ω), TIME OF FLIGHT (T) AND STRIKING VELOCITY (v_ω) FOR A GIVEN RANGE, CORRECTING FOR ALTITUDE BY A SERIES OF SUCCESSIVE APPROXIMATIONS, THE ATMOSPHERE BEING CONSIDERED AS OF STANDARD DENSITY—INGALLS' METHOD.

FORMULÆ.

$C_1=K=\frac{w}{cd^2}$; $Z=\frac{X}{C}$; $\sin 2\phi=AC$; $Y-A''C \tan\phi$; $\log\log f=\log Y+5.01765-10$; $\tan\omega=B'\tan\phi$; $T=CT'\sec\phi$; $v_\omega=u_\omega\cos\phi\sec\omega$

PROBLEM.

Cal.=8″; V=2750 f. s.; w=260 pounds; c=0.61; Range=19,000 yds.=57,000 ft.

$C_1=K=$ (from Table VI) .... colog 9.17654−10
$X=57000$ .... log 4.75587

$Z_1=8558.75$ .... log 3.93241

$$A_1=.08673+\frac{.00198\times 58.75}{100}-\frac{.00644\times 50}{100}=.084673 \text{ (from Table II)}$$

$A_1=.084673$ .... log 8.92775−10
$C_1=$ .... log 0.82346

$2\phi_1=34°\ 19'\ 36''$ .... sin 9.75121−10
$\phi_1=17°\ 09'\ 48''$ (first approximation, disregarding f)

$$A_1''=2948-\frac{50}{100}\times\frac{(-.0064)\times 71}{.0031}+\frac{50\times 0}{100}+\frac{.000273\times 71}{.0031}=3027.5 \text{ (Table II)}$$

$A_1''=3027.5$ .... log 3.48109
$C_1=$ .... log 0.82346
$\phi_1=17°\ 09'\ 48''$ .... tan 9.48974−10

$Y_1=$ .... log 3.79429
Constant .... log 5.01765−10

$f_1=$ .... log 0.06485 .... loglog 8.81194−10
$C_1=$ .... log 0.82346

$C_2=$ .... log 0.88831 .... colog 9.11169−10
$X=57000$ .... log 4.75587

$Z_2=7371.5$ .... log 3.86756

$$A_2=.06520+\frac{.00164\times 71.5}{100}-\frac{.00497\times 50}{100}=.0638876$$

$A_2=.0638876$ .... log 8.80542−10
$C_2=$ .... log 0.88831

$2\phi_2=29°\ 36'\ 14''$ .... sin 9.69373−10
$\phi_2=14°\ 48'\ 07''$ (second approximation)

$$A_2''=2398-\frac{50}{100}\times\frac{(-.0046)\times 67}{.0025}+\frac{50\times 0}{100}+\frac{.001488\times 67}{.0025}=2499.5$$

$A_2''=2499.5$ .... log 3.39786
$C_2=$ .... log 0.88831
$\phi_2=14°\ 48'\ 07''$ .... tan 9.42201 − 10

$Y_2=$ .... log 3.70818
Constant .... log 5.01765 − 10

$f_2=$ .... log 0.05319 .... loglog 8.72583 − 10
$C_1=$ .... log 0.82346

$C_3=$ .... log 0.87665 .... colog 9.12335 − 10
$X=57000$ .... log 4.75587

$Z_3=7572.15$ .... log 3.87922

$$A_3=.06851+\frac{.00170\times 72.15}{100}-\frac{.00520\times 50}{100}=.067137$$

$A_3=.067137$ .... log 8.82696 − 10
$C_3=$ .... log 0.87665

$2\phi_3=30°\ 21'\ 22''$ .... sin 9.70361 − 10
$\phi_3=15°\ 10'\ 41''$ (third approximation)

$$A_3''=2465-\frac{50}{100}\times\frac{(-.0048)\times 68}{.0025}+\frac{50\times 0}{100}+\frac{.002237\times 68}{.0025}=2591.1$$

$A_3''=2591.1$ .... log 3.41349
$C_3=$ .... log 0.87665
$\phi_3=15°\ 10'\ 41''$ .... tan 9.43342 − 10

$Y_3=$ .... log 3.72356
Constant .... log 5.01765 − 10

$f_3=$ .... log 0.05511 .... loglog 8.74121 − 10
$C_1=$ .... log 0.82346

$C_4=$ .... log 0.87857 .... colog 9.12143 − 10
$X=57000$ .... log 4.75587

$Z_4=7538.75$ .... log 3.87730

$$A_4=.06851+\frac{.00170\times 38.75}{100}-\frac{.00520\times 50}{100}=.066569$$

$A_4=.066569$ .... log 8.82327 − 10
$C_4=$ .... log 0.87857

$2\phi_4=30°\ 13'\ 10''$ .... sin 9.70184 − 10
$\phi_4=15°\ 06'\ 35''$ (fourth approximation)

$$A_4''=2465-\frac{50}{100}\times\frac{(-.0048)\times 68}{.0025}+\frac{50\times 0}{100}+\frac{.001669\times 68}{.0025}=2575.6768$$

$A_4''=2575.7$ .... log 3.41090
$C_4=$ .... log 0.87857
$\phi_4=15°\ 06'\ 35''$ .... tan 9.43137 − 10

$Y_4=$ .... log 3.72084
Constant .... log 5.01765 − 10

$f_4=$ .... log 0.05476 .... loglog 8.73849 − 10
$C_1=$ .... log 0.82346

$C_5=$ .... log 0.87822 .... colog 9.12178 − 10
$X=57000$ .... log 4.75587

$Z_5=7544.85$ .... log 3.87765

$$A_5=.06851+\frac{.00170\times 44.85}{100}-\frac{.00520\times 50}{100}=.06667245$$

$A_5 = .06667245$ ....log 8.82395−10
$C_5 =$ ....log 0.87822

$2\phi_5 = 30°\ 14'\ 42''$ ....sin 9.70217−10
$\phi_5 = 15°\ 07'\ 27''$ (fifth approximation)

$$A_5'' = 2465 - \frac{50}{100} \times \frac{(-.0048)\times 68}{.0025} + \frac{50\times 0}{100} + \frac{.001773\times 68}{.0025} = 2578.5$$

$A_5'' = 2578.5$ ....log 3.41137
$C_5 =$ ....log 0.87822
$\phi_5 = 15°\ 07'\ 27''$ ....tan 9.43175−10

$Y_5 =$ ....log 3.72134
Constant ....log 5.01765−10

$f_5 =$ ....log 0.05483..........loglog 8.73899−10
$C_1 =$ ....log 0.82346

$C_6 =$ ....log 0.87829.......... colog 9.12171−10
$X = 57000$ .... log 4.75587

$Z_6 = 7543.65$ .... log 3.87758

$$A_6 = .06851 + \frac{.00170\times 43.65}{100} - \frac{.00520\times 50}{100} = .066652$$

$A_6 = .066652$ ....log 8.82381−10
$C_6 =$ ....log 0.87829

$2\phi_6 = 30°\ 14'\ 21''$ ....sin 9.70210−10
$\phi_6 = 15°\ 07'\ 10''$ (sixth approximation)

$$A_6'' = 2465 - \frac{50}{100} \times \frac{(-.0048)\times 68}{.0025} + \frac{50\times 0}{100} + \frac{.001752\times 68}{.0025} = 2577.9$$

$A_6'' = 2577.9$ ....log 3.41126
$C_6 =$ ....log 0.87829
$\phi_6 = 15°\ 07'\ 10''$ ....tan 9.43166−10

$Y_6 =$ ....log 3.72121
Constant ....log 5.01765−10

$f_6 =$ ....log 0.05481..........loglog 8.73886−10
$C_1 =$ ....log 0.82346

$C_7 =$ ....log 0.87827.......... colog 9.12173−10
$X = 57000$ .... log 4.75587

$Z_7 = 7544.0$ .... log 3.87760

$$A_7 = .06851 + \frac{.00170\times 44}{100} - \frac{.00520\times 50}{100} = .066658$$

$A_7 = .066658$ ....log 8.82386−10
$C_7 =$ ....log 0.87827

$2\phi_7 = 30°\ 14'\ 30''$ ....sin 9.70213−10
$\phi_7 = 15°\ 07'\ 15''$ (seventh approximation)

$$A_7'' = 2465 - \frac{50}{100} \times \frac{(-.0048)\times 68}{.0025} + \frac{50\times 0}{100} + \frac{.001758\times 68}{.0025} = 2578.1$$

$A_7''=2578.1$ ....log 3.41130
$C_7=$ ....log 0.87827
$\phi_7=15°\ 07'\ 15''$ ....tan 9.43170−10

$Y_7=$ ....log 3.72127
Constant ....log 5.01765−10

$f_7=$ ....log 0.05481..............loglog 8.73892−10
$C_1=$ ....log 0.82346

$C_8=$........................log 0.87827

As $C_8=C_7$, the limit of accuracy has been reached and the work of approximation can be carried no further.

By the preceding work we have derived the following data for the remainder of the problem:

$$\phi=15°\ 07'\ 15'' \qquad Z=7544.0 \qquad \log C=0.87827$$

From Table II, with the above value of Z,

$$\log B'=.2652+\frac{.0023\times 44}{100}+\frac{.0026\times 50}{100}=.26751$$

$$T'=4.600+\frac{.092\times 44}{100}-\frac{.173\times 50}{100}=4.5540$$

$$u_\omega=1086-\frac{9\times 44}{100}+\frac{30\times 50}{100}=1097.0$$

$B'=$ ....log 0.26751
$C=$ ....log 0.87827
$\phi=15°\ 07'\ 15''$ ....tan 9.43170−10..sec 0.01530......cos 9.98470−10
$T'=4.554$ ....log 0.65839
$u_\omega=1097$ ....log 3.04021

$\omega=26°\ 34'\ 40''$ ....tan 9.69921−10..................sec 0.04850

$T=35.642$ ....log 1.55196

$v_\omega=1184.2$ ....log 3.07341

RESULTS.

	By above computations.	As given in range table.
ϕ	15° 07′ 15″	15° 07′ 00″
ω	26° 34′ 50″	26° 35′ 00″
T	35.642 seconds	35.64 seconds
v_ω	1184.2 foot-seconds	1184 foot-seconds

Note to Form No. 1.—The number of approximations necessary to secure correct results increases with the range, therefore problems for shorter ranges will not involve so much labor as the one worked out on this form.

Form No. 2.

CHAPTER 8—EXAMPLE 8.

FORM FOR THE COMPUTATION OF THE VALUES OF THE ANGLE OF DEPARTURE (ϕ), ANGLE OF FALL (ω), TIME OF FLIGHT (T) AND STRIKING VELOCITY (v_ω) FOR A GIVEN RANGE, MAXIMUM ORDINATE AND ATMOSPHERIC CONDITION.

FORMULÆ.

$$C=\frac{f}{\delta}K;\ Z=\frac{X}{C};\ \sin 2\phi=AC;\ \tan\omega=B'\tan\phi;\ T=CT'\sec\phi;\ v_\omega=u_\omega\cos\phi\sec\omega$$

PROBLEM.

Cal.=8″; V=2750 f. s.; w=260 pounds; c=0.61; Range=19,000 yards=57,000 feet; Barometer=28.33″; Thermometer=82.7° F.; Maximum ordinate=5261 feet.

From Table III, δ=.91396; $\frac{2}{3}Y$=3507′, hence f=1.0962 from Table V.

K=(from Table VI)	log 0.82346		
f=1.0962	log 0.03989		
δ=.91396 ....log 9.96093−10..colog	0.03907		
C=	log 0.90242	......colog	9.09758−10
X=57000		log	4.75587
Z=7136.0		log	3.85345

From Table II.

$$A=.06201+\frac{.00158\times 36}{100}-\frac{.00475\times 50}{100}=.060204$$

$$\log B'=.2551+\frac{.0027\times 36}{100}+\frac{.0014\times 50}{100}=.25677$$

$$T'=4.238+\frac{.089\times 36}{100}-\frac{.163\times 50}{100}=4.1885$$

$$u_\omega=1124-\frac{10\times 36}{100}+\frac{34\times 50}{100}=1137.4$$

$A=.060204$	log 8.77963−10			
$B'=$		log 0.25677		
$T'=4.1885$			log 0.62206	
$u_\omega=1137.4$				log 3.05591
$C=$	log 0.90242		log 0.90242	
$2\phi=28°\ 44'\ 38''$	sin 9.68205−10			
$\phi=14°\ 22'\ 19''$		tan 9.40864−10	sec 0.01381	cos 9.98619−10
$\omega=24°\ 50'\ 08''$		tan 9.66541−10		sec 0.04215
$T=34.537$			log 1.53829	
$v_\omega=1214.1$				log 3.08425

RESULTS.

ϕ.........14° 22′ 19″.
ω.........24° 50′ 08″.
T.........34.537 seconds.
v_ω.........1214.1 foot-seconds.

Note to Form No. 2.—To solve the above problem with strict accuracy the maximum ordinate should not be used, but the approximation method should be employed as in Form No. 1, starting with a value of $C_1=\frac{K}{\delta}$, and proceeding as shown on Form No. 1. In order to get a series of shorter problems for section room work, an approximately correct value of the maximum ordinate is given in the above data, from which, by the use of the value of f obtained from Table V, an approximately correct value of C may be determined without employing the longer method of Form No. 1. The results are sufficiently accurate to enable the process to be used for the purpose of instruction in the use of the formulæ subsequently employed.

Form No. 3.

CHAPTER 8—EXAMPLE 9.

FORM FOR THE COMPUTATION OF THE VALUES OF THE ANGLE OF DEPARTURE (ϕ), ANGLE OF FALL (ω), TIME OF FLIGHT (T) AND STRIKING VELOCITY (v_ω) FOR A GIVEN RANGE, CORRECTING FOR ALTITUDE BY A SERIES OF SUCCESSIVE APPROXIMATIONS, FOR GIVEN ATMOSPHERIC CONDITIONS—ALGER'S METHOD; NOT USING TABLE II.

FORMULÆ.

$$C=\frac{fw}{\delta cd^2}\ ;\ S_{u_\omega}=S_V+\frac{X}{C}\ ;\ \sin 2\phi=C\left(\frac{A_{u_\omega}-A_V}{S_{u_\omega}-S_V}-I_V\right)\ ;\ T=C\sec\phi(T_{u_\omega}-T_V)\ ;$$

$$\tan\omega=\frac{C^{\prime\prime}}{2\cos^2\phi}\left(I_{u_\omega}-\frac{A_{u_\omega}-A_V}{S_{u_\omega}-S_V}\right);\ v_\omega=u_\omega\cos\phi\sec\omega;\ Y=\frac{gT^2}{8}$$

PROBLEM.

Cal.=8″; $V=2750$ f. s.; $w=260$ pounds; $c=0.61$; Range=19,000 yards=57,000 feet; Variation in V due to wind=-25 f. s.; Effective initial velocity=2725 f. s.; Barometer=30.50″; Thermometer=10° F.

$w=260$ .... log 2.41497
$\delta=1.144$ ......log 0.05843......colog 9.94157−10
$c=0.61$ ....log 9.78533−10..colog 0.21467
$d^2=64$ ....log 1.80618......colog 8.19382−10

$C_1=$ .... log 0.76503......colog 9.23497−10
$X=57000$ .... log 4.75587

$\frac{X}{C}=S_{u_\omega}-S_V=\Delta S_1=$ 9791.2 .... log 3.99084

	$S_V=$ 2565.2		From Table I.	
	$S_{u_\omega}=12356.4$	$A_{u_\omega}=1673.19$	$T_{u_\omega}=7\ 650$	
$u_\omega=939.8$		$A_V=$ 100.23	$T_V=0.819$	$I_V=.04832$
		$\Delta A_1=1572.96$	$\Delta T_1=6.831$	

$\Delta A_1=1573$ ....log 3.19673 } Subtractive.
$\Delta S_1=9791.2$ ....log 3.99084 }

$\frac{\Delta A_1}{\Delta S_1}=.16065$ ....log 9.20589−10
$I_V=.04832$

$\frac{\Delta A_1}{\Delta S_1}-I_V=.11233$ ....log 9.05050−10
$\Delta T_1=6.831$ ....log 0.83448
$C_1=$ ....log 0.76503......log 0.76503

$2\phi_1=40°\ 50'\ 16''$ ....sin 9.81553−10
$\phi_1=20°\ 25'\ 08''$ (first approximation)................sec 0.02819

$T_1=$ ....log 1.62770

$T_1^2=$ ....log 3.25540
$g=32.2$ ....log 1.50786
8 ....log 0.90309....colog 9.09691−10

$Y_1=7247.1$ .... log 3.86017
$\frac{2}{3}Y_1=4831.4$, hence $f_1=1.1359$, from Table V

$f_1 = 1.1359$ .... log 0.05534
$C_1 =$ .... log 0.76503

$C_2 =$ .... log 0.82037 ...... colog 9.17963 − 10
$X = 57000$ .... log 4.75587

$\Delta S_2 =$ 8619.7 .... log 3.93550
$S_V =$ 2565.2 $\qquad A_{uω} = 1269.96 \qquad T_{uω} = 6.443$
$\qquad\qquad\qquad\quad A_V = 100.23 \qquad T_V = 0.819$
$S_{uω} = 11184.9$
$u_ω = 1007.1 \qquad \Delta A_2 = 1169.73 \qquad \Delta T_2 = 5.624$

$\Delta A_2 = 1169.7$ .... log 3.06808 } Subtractive.
$\Delta S_2 = 8619.7$ .... log 3.93550 }

$\dfrac{\Delta A_2}{\Delta S_2} = .13570$ .... log 9.13258 − 10
$I_V = .04832$

$\dfrac{\Delta A_2}{\Delta S_2} - I_V = .08738$ .... log 8.94141 − 10
$\Delta T_2 = 5.624$ .... log 0.75005
$C_2 =$ .... log 0.82037 $\qquad$ log 0.82037

$2\phi_2 = 35°\ 17'\ 48''$ .... sin 9.76178 − 10
$\phi_2 = 17°\ 38'\ 54''$ (second approximation) .... sec 0.02094

$T_2 =$ .... log 1.59136

$T_2^2 =$ .... log 3.18272
$g = 32.2$ .... log 1.50786
8 .... colog 9.09691 − 10

$Y_2 = 6130.4$ .... log 3.78749
$\tfrac{2}{3} Y_2 = 4086.9$, hence $f_2 = 1.1136$
$f_2 = 1.1136$ .... log 0.04673
$C_1 =$ .... log 0.76503

$C_3 =$ .... log 0.81176 ...... colog 9.18824 − 10
$X = 57000$ .... log 4.75587

$\Delta S_3 =$ 8792.4 .... log 3.94411
$S_V =$ 2565.2 $\qquad A_{uω} = 1323.79 \qquad T_{uω} = 6.617$
$\qquad\qquad\qquad\quad A_V = 100.23 \qquad T_V = 0.819$
$S_{uω} = 11357.6$
$u_ω = 996.05 \qquad \Delta A_3 = 1223.56 \qquad \Delta T_3 = 5.798$

$\Delta A_3 = 1223.56$ .... log 3.08764 } Subtractive.
$\Delta S_3 = 8792.4$ .... log 3.94411 }

$\frac{\Delta A_3}{\Delta S_3} = .13916$ .... log 9.14353

$I_V = .04832$

$\frac{\Delta A_3}{\Delta S_3} - I_V = .09084$ .... log 8.95828 − 10

$\Delta T_3 = 5.798$ .... log 0.76328

$C_3 =$ .... log 0.81176 ...... log 0.81176

$2\phi_3 = 36°\ 04'\ 46''$ .... sin 8.77004 − 10

$\phi_3 = 18°\ 02'\ 23''$ (third approximation) .... sec 0.02190

$T_3 =$ .... log 1.59694

$T_3^2 =$ .... log 3.19388

$g = 32.2$ .... log 1.50786

8 .... colog 9.09691 − 10

$Y_3 = 6290.0$ .... log 3.79865

$\frac{2}{3}Y_3 = 4193.3$, hence $f_3 = 1.1168$

$f_3 = 1.1168$ .... log 0.04797

$C_1 =$ .... log 0.76503

$C_4 =$ .... log 0.81300 colog 9.18700 − 10

$X = 57000$ .... log 4.75587

$\Delta S_4 = 8767.4$ .... log 3.94287

$S_V = 2565.2$	$A_{u_\omega} = 1315.96$	$T_{u_\omega} = 6.592$
$S_{u_\omega} = 11332.6$	$A_V = 100.23$	$T_V = 0.819$
$u_\omega = 997.6$	$\Delta A_4 = 1215.73$	$\Delta T_4 = 5.773$

$\Delta A_4 = 1215.73$ .... log 3.08483 } Subtractive.
$\Delta S_4 = 8767.4$ .... log 3.94287 }

$\frac{\Delta A_4}{\Delta S_4} = .13866$ .... log 9.14196 − 10

$I_V = .04832$

$\frac{\Delta A_4}{\Delta S_4} - I_V = .09034$ .... log 8.95588 − 10

$\Delta T_4 = 5.773$ .... log 0.76140

$C_4 =$ .... log 0.81300 ...... log 0.81300

$2\phi_4 = 35°\ 58'\ 04''$ .... sin 9.76888 − 10

$\phi_4 = 17°\ 59'\ 32''$ (fourth approximation) .... sec 0.02175

$T_4 =$ .... log 1.59615

$T_4^2 =$ .... log 3.19230

$g = 32.2$ .... log 1.50786

8 .... colog 9.09691 − 10

$Y_4 = 6267.2$ .... log 3.79707

$\frac{2}{3}Y_4 = 4178.1$, hence $f_4 = 1.1163$

$f_4=1.1163$ ....log 0.04778
$C_1=$ ....log 0.76503

$C_5=$ ....log 0.81281......colog 9.18719−10
$X=57000$ .... log 4.75587

$\Delta S_5=$ 8771.2 .... log 3.94306
$S_V=$ 2565.2 $A_{u_\omega}=1316.97$ $T_{u_\omega}=6.596$
$S_{u_\omega}=11336.4$ $A_V=$ 100.23 $T_V=0.819$
$u_\omega=$ 997.4 $\Delta A_5=1216.74$ $\Delta T_5=5.777$
$\Delta A_5=1216.7$ ....log 3.08518 } Subtractive.
$\Delta S_5=8771.2$ ....log 3.94306 }

$\frac{\Delta A_5}{\Delta S_5}=.13871$ ....log 9.14212−10
$I_V=.04832$

$\frac{\Delta A_5}{\Delta S_5}-I_V=.09039$ ....log 8.95612−10
$\Delta T_5=5.777$ ....log 0.76170
$C_5=$ ....log 0.81281......log 0.81281

$2\phi_5=35°\ 58'\ 20''$ ....sin 9.76893−10
$\phi_5=17°\ 59'\ 10''$ (fifth approximation)................sec 0.02176

$T_5=$ ....log 1.59627

$T_5^2=$ ....log 3.19254
$g=32.2$ ....log 1.50786
8 ....colog 9.09691−10

$Y_5=6270.6$ .... log 3.79731
$\frac{2}{3}Y_5=4180.4$, hence $f_5=1.1164$
$f_5=1.1164$ ....log 0.04782
$C_1=$ ....log 0.76503

$C_6=$ ....log 0.81285......colog 9.18715−10
$X=57000$ .... log 4.75587

$\Delta S_6=$ 8770.4 .... log 3.94302
$S_V=$ 2565.2 $A_{u_\omega}=1316.97$ $T_{u_\omega}=6.596$
$S_{u_\omega}=11335.6$ $A_V=$ 100.23 $T_V=0.819$
$u_\omega=$ 997.4 $\Delta A_6=1216.74$ $\Delta T_6=5.777$

$\Delta A_6 = 1216.7$ .... log 3.08518 } Subtractive.
$\Delta S_6 = 8769.5$ .... log 3.94302 }

$\frac{\Delta A_6}{\Delta S_6} = .13873$ .... log 9.14216 − 10

$I_V = .04832$

$\frac{\Delta A_6}{\Delta S_6} - I_V = .09041$ .... log 8.95622 − 10

$\Delta T_6 = 5.777$ .... log 0.76170

$C_6 =$ .... log 0.81285 ...... log 0.81285

$2\phi_6 = 35° \; 59' \; 10''$ .... sin 9.76907 − 10

$\phi_6 = 17° \; 59' \; 35''$ (sixth approximation) .... sec 0.02177

$T_6 =$ .... log 1.59632

$T_6^2 =$ .... log 3.19264

$g = 32.2$ .... log 1.50786

8 .... colog 9.09691 − 10

$Y_6 = 6272.0$ .... log 3.79741

$\frac{2}{3} Y_6 = 4181.3$, hence $f_6 = 1.1164$

$f_6 = 1.1164$ .... log 0.04782

$C_1 =$ .... log 0.76503

$C_7 =$ .... log 0.81285

We see that $C_7 = C_6$. Therefore further work will be simply a repetition of the last two approximations, and the limit of accuracy has been reached.

From the preceding work, therefore, we have the following data for the remainder of the problem:

$u_\omega = 997.4$ $\quad \frac{\Delta A}{\Delta S} = .13873$ $\quad \Delta T = 5.777$ $\quad \log C = 0.81285$

$\frac{\Delta A}{\Delta S} = .13873$ $\quad I_{u_\omega} = .31477$ $\quad$ From Table I.

$I_V = .04832$ $\quad \frac{\Delta A}{\Delta S} = .13873$

$\frac{\Delta A}{\Delta S} - I_V = .09041$ $\quad I_{u_\omega} - \frac{\Delta A}{\Delta S} = .17604$

$\frac{\Delta A}{\Delta S} - I_V = .09041$ ......log 8.95622−10

$I_{u_\omega} - \frac{\Delta A}{\Delta S} = .17604$ .... log 9.24561−10

$\Delta T = 5.777$ ....log 0.76170

$C =$ ....log 0.81285...... log 0.81285......log 0.81285

2 ....colog 9.69897−10

$u_\omega = 997.45$ ....log 2.99887

$2\phi = 35° 59' 10''$ ..sin 9.76907−10

$\phi = 17° 59' 35''$ ....2 sec 0.04354......sec 0.02177..cos 9.97823−1

$\omega = 32° 18' 28''$ .... tan 9.80097−10..............sec 0.07303

$T = 39.4745$ ....log 1.59632

$v_\omega = 1122.4$ ....log 3.05015

RESULTS.

ϕ.........17° 59′ 35″.
ω.........32° 18′ 28″.
T.........39.4745 seconds.
v_ω.........1122.4 foot-seconds.

Note to Form No. 3.—The number of approximations necessary to secure correct results increases with the range, therefore problems for shorter ranges will not involve as much labor as the one worked out on this form.

Form No. 4.

CHAPTER 9—EXAMPLE 1.

FORM FOR THE COMPUTATION OF THE ELEMENTS OF THE VERTEX FOR A GIVEN ANGLE OF DEPARTURE (ϕ) AND GIVEN ATMOSPHERIC DENSITY, CORRECTING FOR ALTITUDE BY A SERIES OF SUCCESSIVE APPROXIMATIONS.

FORMULÆ.

$$C=\frac{fw}{\delta cd^2}=\frac{f}{\delta}K;\ a_0'=A=\frac{\sin 2\phi}{C};\ Y=A''C\tan\phi;$$

$$\log\log f=\log Y+5.01765-10;\ x_0=Cz_0;\ t_0=Ct_0'\sec\phi;\ v_0=u_0\cos\phi$$

PROBLEM.

Cal. = 8″; $V=2750$ f. s.; $w=260$ pounds; $c=0.61$; Range = 19,000 yards; $\phi=15°\ 07'\ 00''$; Barometer = 29.42″; Thermometer = 75° F.

$K=$ .... log 0.82346
$\delta=.96344$ ....log 9.98383−10..colog 0.01617

$C_1=$ .... log 0.83963......colog 9.16037−10
$2\phi=30°\ 14'\ 00''$ .... sin 9.70202−10

$a_{0_1}'=.0728435$.. log 8.86239−10

$$A_1''=2670-\frac{50}{100}\times\frac{(-.0053)\times 69}{.0028}+\frac{50\times 0}{100}+\frac{.0001435\times 69}{.0028}=2738.8$$

$A_1''=2738.8$ ....log 3.43756
$C_1=$ ....log 0.83963
$\phi=15°\ 07'\ 00''$ ....tan 9.43158−10

$Y_1=$ ....log 3.70877
Constant ....log 5.01765−10

$f_1=$ ....log 0.05326......loglog 8.72642−10
$C_1=$ ....log 0.83963

$C_2=$ ....log 0.89289...... colog 9.10711−10
$2\phi=30°\ 14'\ 00''$ .... sin 9.70202−10

$a_{0_2}'=.0644355$ .... log 8.80913−10

$$A_2''=2398-\frac{50}{100}\times\frac{(-.0046)\times 67}{.0025}+\frac{50\times 0}{100}+\frac{.0020355\times 67}{.0025}=2514.2$$

$A_2''=2514.2$ ....log 3.40040
$C_2=$ ....log 0.89289
$\phi=15°\ 07'\ 00''$ ....tan 9.43158−10

$Y_2=$ ....log 3.72487
Constant ....log 5.01765−10

$f_2=$ ....log 0.05527......loglog 8.74252−10
$C_1=$ ....log 0.83963

$C_3=$ ....log 0.89490...... colog 9.10510−10
$2\phi=30°\ 14'\ 00''$ .... sin 9.70202−10

$a_{0_3}'=.0641385$ .... log 8.80712−10

$$A_3''=2398-\frac{50}{100}\times\frac{(-.0046)\times 67}{.0025}+\frac{50\times 0}{100}+\frac{.0017385\times 67}{.0025}=2506.2$$

$A_3''=2506.2$ .... log 3.39901
$C_3=$ .... log 0.89490
$\phi=15°\ 07'\ 00''$ .... tan 9.43158−10

$Y_3=$ .... log 3.72549
Constant .... log 5.01765−10

$f_3=$ .... log 0.05535 ...... loglog 8.74314−10
$C_1=$ .... log 0.83963

$C_4=$ .... log 0.89498 ...... colog 9.10502−10
$2\phi=30°\ 14'\ 00''$ .... sin 9.70202−10

$a_{0_4}'=.06417$ .... log 8.80704−10

$$A_4''=2398-\frac{50}{100}\times\frac{(-.0046)\times67}{.0025}+\frac{50\times0}{100}+\frac{.001727\times67}{.0025}=2505.9$$

$A_4''=2505.9$ .... log 3.39896
$C_4=$ .... log 0.89498
$\phi=15°\ 07'\ 00''$ .... tan 9.43158−10

$Y_4=5315.25$ .... log 3.72552
Constant .... log 5.01765−10

$f_4=$ .... log 0.05536 ...... loglog 8.74317−10
$C_1=$ .... log 0.83963

$C_5=$ .... log 0.89499 ...... colog 9.10501−10
$2\phi=30°\ 14'\ 00''$ .... sin 9.70202−10

$a_{0_5}'=.0641256$ .... log 8.80703−10

$$A_5''=2398-\frac{50}{100}\times\frac{(-.0046)\times67}{.0025}+\frac{50\times0}{100}+\frac{.0017256\times67}{.0025}=2505.9$$

$A_5''=A_4''$, therefore the limit of accuracy has been reached, and we have for the data for the remainder of the problem:

$a_0'=.0641256$ $\qquad\log C=0.89499$

$$z_0=4100+\frac{100}{.0025}\left[.0017256-\frac{50\times(-.0046)}{100}\right]=4261.0$$

$$t_0'=2.036+\frac{.063\times61}{100}-\frac{.079\times50}{100}=2.0349$$

$$u_0=1595-\frac{21\times61}{100}+\frac{66\times50}{100}=1615.2$$

$C=$ .... log 0.89499 ...... log 0.89499
$\phi=15°\ 07'\ 00''$ .... sec 0.01529 ...... cos 9.98471−10
$z_0=4261$ .... log 3.62951
$t_0'=2.0349$ .... log 0.30854
$u_0=1615.2$ .... log 3.20822

$x_0=33458$ .... log 4.52450

$t_0=16.551$ .... log 1.21882

$v_0=1559.3$ .... log 3.19293

RESULTS.

x_0 .... 11152.7 yards.
$y_0=Y$ .... 5315.25 feet.
t_0 .... 16.551 seconds.
v_0 .... 1559.3 foot-seconds.

Note to Form No. 4.—The number of approximations necessary to secure correct results increases with the range, therefore problems for shorter ranges will not involve as much labor as the one worked out on this form.

Form No. 5.

CHAPTER 9—EXAMPLE 2.

FORM FOR THE COMPUTATION OF THE ELEMENTS OF THE VERTEX FOR A GIVEN ANGLE OF DEPARTURE AND GIVEN ATMOSPHERIC DENSITY, GIVEN ALSO THE MEAN HEIGHT OF FLIGHT FROM WHICH TO CORRECT FOR ALTITUDE.

FORMULÆ.

$$C=\frac{f}{\delta}K;\ a_0'=A=\frac{\sin 2\phi}{C};\ y_0=Y=A''C\tan\phi;\ x_0=Cz_0;\ t_0=Ct_0'\sec\phi;\ v_0=u_0\cos\phi$$

PROBLEM.

Cal. = 8″; V = 2750 f. s.; w = 260 pounds; c = 0.61; Range = 19,000 yards; ϕ = 15° 07′ 00′; Barometer = 29.42″; Thermometer = 75° F.
Mean height of flight = 3543 feet.

K = ... log 0.82346
f = 1.0973 .... log 0.04033
δ = .96344 ....log 9.98383−10..colog 0.01617
C = ... log 0.87996......colog 9.12004−10
2ϕ = 30° 14′ 00″ .... sin 9.70202−10
a_0' = .0663835 .... log 8.82206−10

$$A''=2465-\frac{50}{100}\times\frac{(-.0048)\times 68}{.0025}+\frac{50\times 0}{100}+\frac{.0014835\times 68}{.0025}=2570.6$$

$$z_0=4200+\frac{100}{.0025}\left[.0014835-\frac{50\times(-.0048)}{100}\right]=4355.3$$

$$t_0'=2.099+\frac{.064\times 55.3}{100}-\frac{.082\times 50}{100}=2.0934$$

$$u_0=1574-\frac{20\times 55.3}{100}+\frac{66\times 50}{100}=1595.9$$

C = ...log 0.87996......log 0.87996..log 0.87996
A'' = 2570.6 .....log 3.41003
ϕ = 15° 07′ 00″ .tan 9.43158−10..............sec 0.01529..cos 9.98471−10
z_0 = 4355.3 ....log 3.63902
t_0' = 2.0934 ....log 0.32085
u_0 = 1595.9 ....log 3.20300
Y = 5267.1 .....log 3.72157
x_0 = 33035 ....log 4.51898
t_0 = 16.447 ....log 1.21610
v_0 = 1540.7 ....log 3.18771

RESULTS.

x_0........11011.7 yards. t_0.........16.447 seconds.
$y_0=Y$.....5267.1 feet. v_0........1540.7 foot-seconds.

NOTE TO FORM No. 5.—To solve the above problem with strict accuracy, the mean height of flight should not be used, but the approximation method employed in Form No. 4 should be followed, starting with a value of $C_1=\frac{K}{\delta}$, and proceeding as given on Form No. 4. In order to get a series of shorter problems for section room work, an approximately correct value of the mean height of flight is given in the above data (and in Example 2), from which, by the use of the value of f obtained from Table V, an approximately correct value of C may be determined without employing the longer method of Form No. 4. The results are sufficiently accurate to enable the process given in this form to be used for purposes of instruction in the use of the formulæ subsequently employed.

Form No. 6.

CHAPTER 9—EXAMPLE 3.

FORM FOR THE DERIVATION OF THE SPECIAL EQUATIONS FOR COMPUTING THE VALUES OF THE ORDINATE AND OF THE ANGLE OF INCLINATION OF THE CURVE TO THE HORIZONTAL AT ANY POINT OF THE TRAJECTORY WHOSE ABSCISSA IS KNOWN, WITH ATMOSPHERIC CONDITIONS STANDARD; CORRECTING FOR ALTITUDE.

FORMULÆ.

$$A=\frac{\sin 2\phi}{C}\ ;\ y=\frac{\tan\phi}{A}(A-a)x;\ \tan\theta=\frac{\tan\phi}{A}(A-a')$$

PROBLEM.

Cal. = 8"; $V=2750$ f. s.; $w=260$ pounds; $c=0.61$; Range = 19,000 yards; $\phi=15°\ 07'\ 00''$; $\log C=0.87827$ (value corrected for f from work in example on Form No. 1).

$C=$ ....colog 9.12173 − 10
$2\phi=30°\ 14'\ 00''$ .... sin 9.70202 − 10
$A=.066643$ .... log 8.82375 − 10......colog 1.17625
$\phi=15°\ 07'\ 00''$ .... tan 9.43158 − 10
$\frac{\tan\phi}{A}=4.0535$ .... log 0.60783

RESULTS.

$$y=4.0535(.066643-a)x$$
$$\tan\theta=4.0535(.066643-a')$$

NOTE TO FORM No. 6.—To determine the above equations with accuracy for any given trajectory in air, the value of $\log C$ must be determined by the process of approximation given on Form No. 1, for the range for which the special equations are desired. This value of $\log C$ must then be used as was done in the above problem. An approximate result may be obtained by determining the value of f by means of the maximum ordinate given in the range table, from which the value of K may be approximately corrected for altitude.

Form No. 7.

CHAPTER 9—EXAMPLE 4.

FORM FOR THE COMPUTATION, FOR ANY GIVEN TRAJECTORY, OF THE ABSCISSA AND ORDINATE OF THE VERTEX AND OF THE ORDINATE AND OF THE ANGLE OF INCLINATION OF THE CURVE TO THE HORIZONTAL AT ANY POINT OF THE TRAJECTORY WHOSE ABSCISSA IS KNOWN, HAVING GIVEN THE SPECIAL EQUATIONS FOR y AND TAN θ FOR THE GIVEN TRAJECTORY.

FORMULÆ.

$$y_0=Y=A''C\tan\phi;\quad x_0=Cz_0;\quad y=\frac{\tan\phi}{A}(A-a)x;\quad \tan\theta=\frac{\tan\phi}{A}(A-a')$$

PROBLEM.

Cal.$=8''$; $V=2750$ f. s.; $w=260$ pounds; $c=0.61$; Range$=19{,}000$ yards$=57{,}000$ feet; $\log C=0.87827$; $\phi=15°\ 07'\ 00''$; $y=4.0535(.066643-a)x$; $\tan\theta=4.0535(.066643-a')$; $x_1=8000$ yards$=24{,}000$ feet; $x_2=16{,}000$ yards$=42{,}000$ feet.

For Vertex: From data, $A=.066643$, and for vertex $a_0'=A$, therefore, from Table II for $a_0'=.066643$.

$$A''=2465-\frac{50}{100}\times\frac{(-.0048)\times 68}{.0025}+\frac{50\times 0}{100}+\frac{.001743\times 68}{.0025}=2577.7$$

$$z_0=4200+\frac{100}{.0025}\left[.001743-\frac{(-.0048)\times 50}{100}\right]=4365.7$$

$A''=2577.7$ ....log 3.41123
$C=$ ....log 0.87827......log 0.87827
$\phi=15°\ 07'\ 00''$ ....tan 9.43158−10
$z_0=4365.7$ ....log 3.64005
$x_0=32{,}985$ feet$=10{,}995$ yards...........log 4.51832
$y_0=Y=5261.1$ feet ....log 3.72108

For $x_1=8000$ yards$=24{,}000$ feet:

$C=$ ....colog 9.12173−10
$x_1=24000$ .... log 4.38021
$z=3176.4$ .... log 3.50194

$$a=.01781+\frac{.00075\times 76.4}{100}-\frac{.00131\times 50}{100}=.017728$$

$$a'=.0408+\frac{.0019\times 76.4}{100}-\frac{.0031\times 50}{100}=.040702$$

$A=.066643$ $\qquad$ $A=.066643$
$a=.017728$ $\qquad$ $a'=.040702$

$A-a=.048915$ ....log 8.68945−10
$A-a'=.025941$ ....log 8.41399−10
$\frac{\tan\phi}{A}=4.0535$ ....log 0.60783..........log 0.60783
$x_1=24000$ ....log 4.38021
$y_1=4758.7$ ....log 3.67749
$\theta=6°\ 02'\ 10''$ ....tan 9.02182−10

For $x_2 = 16{,}000$ yards $= 48{,}000$ feet:

$C =$ .... colog $9.12173-10$
$x_2 = 48000$ .... log 4.68124

$z = 6352.8$ .... log 3.80297

$$a = .05030 + \frac{.00137 \times 52.8}{100} - \frac{.00386 \times 50}{100} = .049093$$

$$a' = .1358 + \frac{.0044 \times 52.8}{100} - \frac{.0105 \times 50}{100} = .132873$$

$A = .066643$ $\quad A = .066643$
$a = .049093$ $\quad a' = .132873$

$A - a = .017550$ .... log $8.24428-10$
$A - a' = (-).066230$ .... $(-)$log $8.82105-10$

$\frac{\tan\phi}{A} = 4.0535$ .... log 0.60783 .... log 0.60783

$x_2 = 48000$ .... log 4.68124

$y_2 = 3414.7$ .... log 3.53335

$\theta_2 = (-)15°\ 01'\ 39''$ .... $(-)$tan $9.42888-10$

For point of fall, $x = X = 19{,}000$ yards $= 57{,}000$ feet:

$C =$ .... colog $9.12173-10$
$x = 57000$ .... log 4.75587

$z = 7544.0$ .... log 3.87760

$$a = .06851 + \frac{.00170 \times 44}{100} - \frac{.00520 \times 50}{100} = .066658$$

$$a' = .1946 + \frac{.0055 \times 44}{100} - \frac{.0140 \times 50}{100} = .190020$$

$A = .066643$ $\quad A = .066643$
$a = .066658$ $\quad a' = .190020$

$A - a = (-).000015$ .... $(-)$log $5.17609-10$
$A - a' = (-).123377$ .... $(-)$log $9.09125-10$

$\frac{\tan\phi}{A} = 4.0535$ .... log 0.60783 .... log 0.60783

$x = 57000$ .... log 4.75587

$y_\omega = (-)3.4657$ feet .... $(-)$log 0.53979

$\theta_\omega = (-)26°\ 34'\ 15''$ .... $(-)$tan $9.69908-10$

RESULTS.

For vertex.	For $x_1 = 8000$ yards.	For $x_2 = 16{,}000$ yards.	For point of fall.
$x_0 = 10{,}995$ yards	$y_1 = 4758.7$ feet	$y_2 = 3414.7$ feet	$y_\omega = (-)3.4657$ feet
$y_0 = Y = 5261.1$ feet	$\theta_1 = 6°\ 02'\ 10''$	$\theta_2 = (-)15°\ 01'\ 39''$	$\theta_\omega = (-)26°\ 34'\ 15''$

Note to Form No. 7.—In the above problem of course the ordinate at the point of fall should be zero. The angle θ at the point of fall should equal $-\omega$; for which the work gives $\theta = (-)26°\ 34'\ 15''$, and the range table gives $\omega = 26°\ 35'\ 00''$. These comparisons give an idea of the degree of accuracy of the above method.

Form No. 8.

CHAPTER 10—EXAMPLE 1.

FORM FOR THE COMPUTATION OF THE VALUES OF THE RANGE (R), ANGLE OF FALL (ω), TIME OF FLIGHT (T) AND STRIKING VELOCITY (v_ω) FOR A GIVEN ANGLE OF DEPARTURE (ϕ) AND ATMOSPHERIC CONDITION, CORRECTING FOR ALTITUDE BY A SERIES OF SUCCESSIVE APPROXIMATIONS.

FORMULÆ.

$C=\frac{f}{\delta}K$; $a_0'=A=\frac{\sin 2\phi}{C}$; $X=CZ$; $Y=A''C\tan\phi$; $\log\log f=\log Y+5.01765-10$;

$\tan\omega=B'\tan\phi$; $T=CT'\sec\phi$; $v_\omega=u_\omega\cos\phi\sec\omega$

PROBLEM.

Cal.=8″; V=2750 f. s.; w=260 pounds; c=0.61; ϕ=15° 07′ 00″;
Barometer=29.00″; Thermometer=82° F.

$K=$ .... log 0.82346
$\delta=.937$ .... log 9.97174−10..colog 0.02826

$C_1=$ .... log 0.85172......colog 9.14828−10
$2\phi=30°\ 14'\ 00''$ .... sin 9.70202−10

$a_{0_1}'=.0708435$ .... log 8.85030−10

$$A_1''=2601-\frac{50}{100}\times\frac{(-.0051)\times 69}{.0027}+\frac{50\times 0}{100}+\frac{.0008435\times 69}{.0027}=2687.7$$

$A_1''=2687.7$ .... log 3.42938
$C_1=$ .... log 0.85172
$\phi=15°\ 07'\ 00''$ .... tan 9.43158−10

$Y_1=$ .... log 3.71268
Constant .... log 5.01765−10

$f_1=$ .... log 0.05374......loglog 8.73033−10
$C_1=$ .... log 0.85172

$C_2=$ .... log 0.90546......colog 9.09454−10
$2\phi=30°\ 14'\ 00''$ .... sin 0.70202−10

$a_{0_2}'=.0625985$ .... log 8.79656−10.

$$A_2''=2398-\frac{50}{100}\times\frac{(-.0046)\times 67}{.0025}+\frac{50\times 0}{100}+\frac{.0001985\times 67}{.0025}=2465.0$$

$A_2''=2465$ .... log 3.39182
$C_2=$ .... log 0.90546
$\phi=15°\ 07'\ 00''$ .... tan 9.43158−10

$Y_2=$ .... log 3.72886
Constant .... log 5.01765−10

$f_2=$ .... log 0.05578......loglog 8.74651−10
$C_1=$ .... log 0.85172

$C_3=$ .... log 0.90750...... colog 9.09250−10
$2\phi=30°\ 14'\ 00''$ .... sin 9.70202−10

$a_{0_3}'=.062304$ .... log 8.79452−10

$$A_3''=2331-\frac{50}{100}\times\frac{(-.0045)\times 67}{.0024}+\frac{50\times 0}{100}+\frac{.002304\times 67}{.0024}=2458.1$$

$A_3''=2458.1$ ....log 3.39060
$C_3=$ ....log 0.90750
$\phi=15^\circ\ 07'\ 00''$ ....tan 9.43158−10

$Y_3=$ ....log 3.72968
Constant ....log 5.01765−10

$f_3=$ ....log 0.05589......loglog 8.74733−10
$C_1=$ ....log 0.85172

$C_4=$ ....log 0.90761...... colog 9.09239−10
$2\phi=30^\circ\ 14'\ 00''$ .... sin 9.70202−10

$a_{0_4}'=.0622885$ .... log 8.79441−10

$$A_4''=2331-\frac{50}{100}\times\frac{(-.0045)\times 67}{.0024}+\frac{50\times 0}{100}+\frac{.0022885\times 67}{.0024}=2457.7$$

$A_4''=2457.7$ ....log 3.39053
$C_4=$ ....log 0.90761
$\phi=15^\circ\ 07'\ 00''$ ....tan 9.43158−10

$Y_4=$ ....log 3.72972
Constant ....log 5.01765−10

$f_4=$ ....log 0.05589......loglog 8.74737−10
$C_1=$ ....log 0.85172

$C_5=$ ....log 0.90761

which equals log C_4; therefore the limit of approximation has been reached, and we have the following data:

$A=.0622885$ $\quad\log C=0.90761$ $\quad\phi=15^\circ\ 07'\ 00''$

$$Z=7100+\frac{100}{.00158}\left[.002785-\frac{50\times(-.00475)}{100}\right]=7267.9$$

$$\log B'=.2578+\frac{.0025\times 67.9}{100}+\frac{.0017\times 50}{100}=.26035$$

$$T'=4.327+\frac{.090\times 67.9}{100}-\frac{.165\times 50}{100}=4.3056$$

$$u_\omega=1114-\frac{10\times 67.9}{100}+\frac{33\times 50}{100}=1123.7$$

$C=$ ....log 0.90761.................log 0.90761
$Z=7267.9$ ......log 3.86141
$\phi=15^\circ\ 07'\ 00''$ ....tan 9.43158−10..sec 0.01529..cos 9.98471−10
$B'=$ ....log 0.26035
$T'=4.3056$ ....log 0.63403
$u_\omega=1123.7$ ....log 3.05065

$X=58752$ ......log 4.76902

$\omega=26^\circ\ 11'\ 44''$ ....tan 9.69193−10..............sec 0.04707

$T=36.052$ ....log 1.55693

$v_\omega=1208.9$ ....log 3.08243

RESULTS.

R........19,584 yards. $\quad$ T........36.052 seconds.

ω........26° 11′ 44″. $\quad$ v_ω........1208.9 foot-seconds.

Note to Form No. 8.—The number of approximations necessary to secure correct results increases with the angle of departure, therefore problems for a smaller angle of departure will not involve so much labor as the one worked out on the form.

Form No. 9.

CHAPTER 10—EXAMPLE 2.

FORM FOR THE COMPUTATION OF THE VALUES OF THE HORIZONTAL RANGE (R), ANGLE OF FALL (ω), TIME OF FLIGHT (T) AND STRIKING VELOCITY (v_ω) FOR A GIVEN ANGLE OF DEPARTURE (ϕ), ATMOSPHERIC CONDITION AND MAXIMUM ORDINATE.

FORMULÆ.

$$C=\frac{f}{\delta}K;\ A=\frac{\sin 2\phi}{C};\ X=CZ;\ \tan\omega=B'\tan\phi;\ T=CT'\sec\phi;$$

$$v_\omega=u_\omega\cos\phi\sec\omega$$

PROBLEM.

Cal. = 8″; V=2750 f. s.; w=260 pounds; c=0.61; ϕ=15° 07′ 00″; Barometer =29.00″; Thermometer=82° F.; Maximum ordinate=5400 feet; $\frac{2}{3}Y$=3600 feet.

K= .... log 0.82346
f=1.099 .... log 0.04100
δ=.937 ....log 9.97174−10..colog 0.02826
C= .... log 0.89272......colog 9.10728−10
2ϕ=30° 14′ 00″ .... sin 9.70202−10
A=.064461 .... log 8.80930−10

$$Z=7200+\frac{100}{.00161}\left[.000871-\frac{50\times(-.00486)}{100}\right]=7405.0$$

$$\log B'=.2620+\frac{.0024\times 5}{100}+\frac{.0023\times 50}{100}=.26407$$

$$T'=4.508+\frac{.092\times 5}{100}-\frac{.170\times 50}{100}=4.4276$$

$$u_\omega=1095-\frac{9\times 5}{100}+\frac{31\times 50}{100}=1110.1$$

C= ....log 0.89272..................log 0.89272
Z=7405 ....log 3.86953
ϕ=15° 07′ 00″ ....tan 9.43158−10..sec 0.01529..cos 9.98471−10
B'= ....log 0.26407
T'=4.4276 ....log 0.64617
u_ω=1110.1 ....log 3.04536
X=57843 ......log 4.76225
ω=26° 23′ 24″ ....tan 9.69565−10..............sec 0.04780
T=35.824 ....log 1.55418
v_ω=1196.4 ....log 3.07787

RESULTS.

	From above work.	From work with same data on Form No. 8.
R	19,281 yards	19,584 yards
ω	26° 23′ 24″	26° 11′ 44″
T	35.824 seconds	36.052 seconds
v_ω	1196.4 foot-seconds	1208.9 foot-seconds

NOTE TO FORM No. 9.—To solve the above problem with strict accuracy it must be done as shown on Form No. 8. In order to get a series of shorter problems for section room work, an approximately correct value of the maximum ordinate is given and employed as above. The comparison of results by the two methods given at the bottom of the above work gives an idea of the degree of inaccuracy resulting from the employment of the method given on this form.

Form No. 10A.

CHAPTER 11—EXAMPLE 1 (WHEN y IS POSITIVE).

FORM FOR THE COMPUTATION OF THE VALUES OF THE ANGLE OF ELEVATION (ψ) (THE JUMP BEING CONSIDERED AS ZERO), ANGLE OF INCLINATION TO THE HORIZONTAL AT THE POINT OF IMPACT (θ), AND TIME OF FLIGHT TO (t) AND REMAINING VELOCITY AT (v) THE POINT OF IMPACT WHEN FIRING AT A TARGET AT A KNOWN HORIZONTAL DISTANCE FROM THE GUN AND AT A KNOWN VERTICAL DISTANCE ABOVE THE HORIZONTAL PLANE OF THE GUN, FOR GIVEN ATMOSPHERIC CONDITIONS.

FORMULÆ.

$$C=\frac{f}{\delta}K;\ \tan p=\frac{y}{x};\ z=\frac{X}{C};\ \sin 2\phi_z=aC;\ \sin(2\phi-p)=\sin p(1+\cot p\sin 2\phi_z);$$

$$A=\frac{\sin 2\phi}{C};\ \tan\theta=\frac{\tan\phi}{A}(A-a');\ t=Ct'\sec\phi;\ v=u\cos\phi\sec\theta;\ \psi=\phi-p$$

PROBLEM.

Cal.$=8''$; $V=2750$ f. s.; $w=260$ pounds; $c=0.61$; Gun below target 900 feet; Horizontal distance$=18{,}000$ yards$=54{,}000$ feet; Maximum ordinate$=4470$ feet; Barometer$=29.00''$; Thermometer$=40°$ F.; $\frac{2}{3}Y=2980$ feet.

$K=$ .... log 0.82346
$f=1.0804$ .... log 0.03358
$\delta=1.021$ ....log 0.00903......colog 9.99097−10

$C=$ .... log 0.84801......colog 9.15199−10
$y=900$.............log 2.95424......Subtractive.
$x=54000$...........log 4.73239 .... log 4.73239

$p=0°\ 57'\ 18''$ ......tan 8.22185−10

$z=7662.6$ .... log 3.88438

$$a=.07021+\frac{.00172\times 62.6}{100}-\frac{.00532\times 50}{100}=.068627$$

$$a'=.2001+\frac{.0056\times 62.6}{100}-\frac{.0143\times 50}{100}=.19646$$

$$u=1077-\frac{8\times 62.6}{100}+\frac{29\times 50}{100}=1086.5$$

$$t'=4.692+\frac{.093\times 62.6}{100}-\frac{.175\times 50}{100}=4.6627$$

$C=$ ....log 0.84801
$a=.068627$ ....log 8.83649−10

$2\phi_s=$ ....sin 9.68450−10
$p=0°\ 57'\ 18''$ ....cot 1.77815

$\cot p \sin 2\phi_s=29.016$ ....log 1.46265
$1+\cot p \sin 2\phi_s=30.016$ ....log 1.47735
$p=\ 0°\ 57'\ 18''$ ....sin 8.22185−10

$2\phi-p=30°\ 01'\ 02''$ ....sin 9.69920−10
$p=\ 0°\ 57'\ 18''$

$2\phi=30°\ 58'\ 20''$ ....sin 9.71149−10
$\phi=15°\ 29'\ 10''$
$p=\ 0°\ 57'\ 18''$

$\psi=14°\ 31'\ 52''$
$C=$ ....colog 9.15199−10

$A=.07303$ .... log 8.86348−10
$A=$ .07303
$a'=$ .19646

$A-a'=(-).12343$ ....(−)log 9.09143−10
$\phi=15°\ 29'\ 10''$ .... tan 9.44258−10..sec 0.01606..cos 9.98394−10
$A=.07303$ ....log 8.86348−10..colog 1.13652
$t'=4.6627$ ....log 0.66864
$u=1086.5$ ....log 3.03603
$C=$ ....log 0.84801

$\theta=(-)25°\ 05'\ 38''$ ....(−)tan 9.67053−10.............sec 0.04306

$t=34.097$ ....log 1.53271

$v=1156.2$ ....log 3.06303

The range table gives for $R=18{,}500$ yards......$\phi=14°\ 26.9'$
for $R=18{,}600$ yards......$\phi=14°\ 34.9'$
Therefore, for an angle of elevation of $\psi=14°\ 31.9'$, the sight setting in range would be $R=18500+\dfrac{5\times 100}{8}=18562.5$ yards.

RESULTS.

ψ..........................14° 31′ 52″.
θ..........................(−)25° 05′ 38″.
t..........................34.097 seconds.
v..........................1156.2 foot-seconds.
Setting of sight in range....18,550 yards.

NOTE TO FORM No. 10A.—Note that the work on this form, for a target higher than the gun, is the same as that on Form No. 10B for the same problem with the gun higher than the target, down to and including the determination of the value of cot p sin $2\phi_s$, except that the sign of that quantity and of the position angle (p) is positive in Form No. 10A, and negative in Form No. 10B. Compare the results obtained on these two forms, having in mind the remarks made in paragraphs 191, 192 and 193 of Chapter 11 of the text.

Form No. 10B.

CHAPTER 11—EXAMPLE 1 (WHEN y IS NEGATIVE).

FORM FOR THE COMPUTATION OF THE VALUES OF THE ANGLE OF ELEVATION (ψ) (THE JUMP BEING CONSIDERED AS ZERO), ANGLE OF INCLINATION TO THE HORIZONTAL AT THE POINT OF IMPACT (θ), AND THE TIME OF FLIGHT TO (t) AND REMAINING VELOCITY AT (v) THE POINT OF IMPACT WHEN FIRING AT A TARGET AT A KNOWN HORIZONTAL DISTANCE FROM THE GUN AND AT A KNOWN VERTICAL DISTANCE BELOW THE HORIZONTAL PLANE OF THE GUN, FOR GIVEN ATMOSPHERIC CONDITIONS.

FORMULÆ.

$$C=\frac{f}{\delta}K;\ \tan p=\frac{y}{x};\ z=\frac{X}{C};\ \sin 2\phi_z=aC;\ \sin(2\phi-p)=\sin p(1+\cot p\sin 2\phi_z);$$

$$A=\frac{\sin 2\phi}{C};\ \tan\theta=\frac{\tan\phi}{A}(A-a');\ t=Ct'\sec\phi;\ v=u\cos\phi\sec\theta;\ \psi=\phi-p$$

PROBLEM.

Cal.=8″; V=2750 f. s.; w=260 pounds; c=0.61; Gun above target 900 feet; Horizontal distance=18,000 yards=54,000 feet; Maximum ordinate=4470 feet; Barometer=29.00″; Thermometer=40° F.; $\frac{2}{3}Y$=2980 feet.

$K=$ .... log 0.82346
f=1.0804 .... log 0.03358
δ=1.021 ....log 0.00903..colog 9.99097−10

$C=$ .... log 0.84801......colog 9.15199−10
y=(−)900.........(−)log 2.95424 } Subtractive.
x=54000 ....log 4.73239 } .... log 4.73239

p=(−)0° 57′ 18″...(−)tan 8.22185−10

z=7662.6 .... log 3.38438

$$a=.07021+\frac{.00172\times 62.6}{100}-\frac{.00532\times 50}{100}=.068627$$

$$a'=.2001+\frac{.0056\times 62.6}{100}-\frac{.0143\times 50}{100}=.19646$$

$$u=1077-\frac{8\times 62.6}{100}+\frac{29\times 50}{100}=1086.5$$

$$t'=4.692+\frac{.093\times 62.6}{100}-\frac{.175\times 50}{100}=4.6627$$

$C=$	................log	0.84801
$a=.068627$	................log	8.83649−10
$2\phi_x=$	................sin	9.68450−10
$p=(-)0°\ 57'\ 18''$	................(−)cot	1.77815
$\cot p \sin 2\phi_x=(-)29.016$	................(−)log	1.46265
$1+\cot p \sin 2\phi_x=(-)28.016$	........(−)log	1.44741
$p=(-)0°\ 57'\ 18''$	........(−)sin	8.22185−10
$2\phi-p=\ 27°\ 50'\ 10''$	.......(+)sin	9.66926−10
$p=(-)\ 0°\ 57'\ 18''$		
$2\phi=\ 26°\ 52'\ 52''$	................sin	9.65528−10
$\phi=\ 13°\ 26'\ 26''$		
$p=(-)\ 0°\ 57'\ 18''$		
$\psi=\ 14°\ 23'\ 44''$		
$C=$	................colog	9.15199−10
$A=.06416$	................log	8.80727−10

$A=\ \ .06416$
$a'=\ \ .19646$

$A-a'=(-).13230$ ....(−)log 9.12156−10

$\phi=13°\ 26'\ 26''$ .... tan 9.37836−10..sec 0.01206..cos 9.98794−10

$A=.06416$ ....log 8.80726−10..colog 1.19273

$t'=4.6627$ ....log 0.66864

$u=1086.5$ ....log 3.03603

$C=$ ....log 0.84801

$\theta=(-)26°\ 13'\ 58''$ ....(−)tan 9.69265−10..............sec 0.04720

$t=33.784$ ....log 1.52871

$v=1178.0$ ....log 3.07117

The range table gives for $R=18{,}400$ yards......$\phi=14°\ 19.0'$
for $R=18{,}500$ yards......$\phi=14°\ 26.9'$

Therefore, for an angle of elevation of $\psi=14°\ 23.7'$, the sight setting in range would be $R=18400+\dfrac{4.7\times100}{7.9}=18459.5$ yards.

RESULTS.

ψ..........................14° 23′ 44″.
θ..........................(−)26° 13′ 58″.
t..........................33.784 seconds.
v..........................1178.0 foot-seconds.
Setting of sight in range....18,450 yards.

Note to Form No. 10B.—Note that the work on this form, for a target lower than the gun, is the same as that on Form No. 10A for the same problem with the target higher than the gun, down to and including the determination of the value of $\cot p \sin 2\phi_x$, except that the sign of that quantity and of the angle of position (p) is minus in Form No. 10B and plus in Form No. 10A. Compare the results obtained in the two cases, having in mind the remarks made in paragraphs 191, 192 and 193 of Chapter 11 of the text.

Form No. 11.

CHAPTER 12—EXAMPLE 2.

FORM FOR THE COMPUTATION OF THE CHANGE IN RANGE RESULTING FROM A VARIATION FROM STANDARD IN THE INITIAL VELOCITY, OTHER CONDITIONS BEING STANDARD.

FORMULÆ.

$$C=\frac{fw}{cd^2}=fK;\ Z=\frac{X}{C};\ \Delta R_V=\frac{\Delta_{VA}}{B}\times\frac{\delta V}{\Delta V}\times R$$

PROBLEM.

Case 1.—Correcting for Altitude by Table V.

Cal.=8″; $V=2750$; $w=260$ pounds; $c=0.61$; Range=19,000 yards=57,000 feet; Maximum ordinate=5261 feet; Variation from standard of $V=+75$ f. s.; $\frac{2}{3}Y=3507$ feet.

$K=$	log 0.82346		
$f=1.0962$	log 0.03989		
$C=$	log 0.86335	colog	9.13665−10
$X=57000$		log	4.75587
$Z=7807.6$		log	3.89252

$$\Delta_{VA}=.00556+\frac{.00012\times 7.6}{100}-\frac{.00049\times 50}{100}=.0053241$$

$$B=.1377+\frac{.0040\times 7.6}{100}-\frac{.0093\times 50}{100}=.13335$$

$\Delta_{VA}=.0053241$		log	7.72625−10
$R=19000$		log	4.27875
$B=.13335$	log 9.12500−10	colog	0.87500
$\delta V=(+)75$		log	1.87506
$\Delta V=100$	log 2.00000	colog	8.00000−10
$\Delta R_V=(+)568.93$ yards		log	2.75506

PROBLEM.

Case 2.—Using Corrected Value of C Obtained by Successive Approximations on Form No. 1.

Cal.=8″; $V=2750$ f. s.; $w=260$ pounds; $c=0.61$; Range=19,000 yards=57,000 feet; log $C=0.87827$; Variation from standard of $V=+75$ f. s.

$C=$	colog	9.12173−10
$X=57000$	log	4.75587
$Z=7544.0$	log	3.87760

$$\Delta_{VA}=.00520+\frac{.00012\times 44}{100}-\frac{.00046\times 50}{100}=.0050228$$

$$B=.1261+\frac{.0038\times 44}{100}-\frac{.0038\times 50}{100}=.12337$$

$\Delta_{VA}=.0050228$		log 7.70094−10
$R=19000$		log 4.27875
$B=.12337$	log 9.09121−10	colog 0.90879
$\delta V=(+)75$		log 1.87506
$\Delta V=100$	log 2.00000	colog 8.00000−10
$\Delta R_V=(+)580.15$		log 2.76354

Note to Form No. 11.—The method of Case 2 is of course the more accurate, and gives the range table result. The method shown in Case 1 is introduced to give practice in the use of this formula without the necessity of taking up the successive approximation method in order to determine the value of *C* accurately.

Form No. 12.

CHAPTER 12—EXAMPLE 3.

FORM FOR THE COMPUTATION OF THE CHANGE IN RANGE RESULTING FROM A VARIATION FROM STANDARD IN THE DENSITY OF THE ATMOSPHERE, OTHER CONDITIONS BEING STANDARD.

FORMULÆ.

$$C=\frac{fw}{cd^2}\ ;\ Z=\frac{X}{C}\ ;\ \Delta R_\delta=-\frac{(B-A)R}{B}\times\frac{\Delta C}{C}$$

PROBLEM.

Case 1.—Correcting for Altitude by Table V.

Cal. = 8″; $V=2750$ f. s.; $w=260$ pounds; $c=0.61$; Range = 19,000 yards = 57,000 feet; Maximum ordinate = 5261 feet; Variation in density = +15 per cent; $\frac{2}{3}Y=3507$ feet.

$K=$ .... log 0.82346
$f=1.0962$ .... log 0.03989

$C=$ .... log 0.86335 ...... colog 9.13665−10
$X=57000$ .... log 4.75587

$Z=7807.6$ .... log 3.89252

$$A=.07368+\frac{.00178\times 7.6}{100}-\frac{.00556\times 50}{100}=.071035$$

$$B=.1377+\frac{.0040\times 7.6}{100}-\frac{.0093\times 50}{100}=.133354$$

$B=.133354$
$A=.071035$

$B-A=.062319$ .... log 8.79462−10
$R=19000$ .... log 4.27875
$B=.13335$ .... log 9.12500−10 ...... colog 0.87500
$\frac{\Delta C}{C}=.15$ .... log 9.17609−10
$\Delta R_\delta=(-)1331.9$ .... log 3.12446

PROBLEM.

Case 2.—Using Corrected Value of C Obtained by Successive Approximations on Form No. 1.

Cal. = 8″; $V=2750$ f. s.; $w=260$ pounds; $c=0.61$; Range = 19,000 yards = 57,000 feet; $\log C=0.87827$; Variation in density = +15 per cent.

$C=$ .... colog 9.12173−10
$X=57000$ .... log 4.75587

$Z=7544.0$ .... log 3.87760

$$A=.06851+\frac{.00170\times 44}{100}-\frac{.00520\times 50}{100}=.066658$$

$$B=.1261+\frac{.0038\times 44}{100}-\frac{.0088\times 50}{100}=.123372$$

$$
\begin{array}{llr}
B = .123372 & & \\
A = \underline{.066658} & & \\
B - A = .056714 & \ldots\ldots\ldots\ldots\ldots\ldots\ldots\ldots & \log 8.75369 - 10 \\
R = 19000 & \ldots\ldots\ldots\ldots\ldots\ldots\ldots\ldots & \log 4.27875 \\
B = .12337 & \ldots\ldots \log 9.09121 - 10 \ldots\ldots & \text{colog } 0.90879 \\
\frac{\Delta C}{C} = .15 & \ldots\ldots\ldots\ldots\ldots\ldots\ldots\ldots & \log \underline{9.17609 - 10} \\
\Delta R_\delta = (-)1310.1 & \ldots\ldots\ldots\ldots\ldots\ldots\ldots\ldots & \log 3.11732
\end{array}
$$

Note to Form No. 12.—The method of Case 2 is of course the more accurate, and gives the range table result. The method shown in Case 1 is introduced to give practice in the use of this formula without the necessity for taking up the successive approximation method in order to determine the value of *C* accurately.

Form No. 13.

CHAPTER 12—EXAMPLE 4.

FORM FOR THE COMPUTATION OF THE CHANGE IN RANGE RESULTING FROM A VARIATION FROM STANDARD IN THE WEIGHT OF THE PROJECTILE, OTHER CONDITIONS BEING STANDARD. DIRECT METHOD WITHOUT USING COLUMNS 10 AND 12 OF THE RANGE TABLES.

FORMULÆ.

$$C=\frac{fw}{cd^2};\ \delta V=-0.36\frac{\Delta w}{w}V;$$

$$\Delta R_W=\Delta R_W'+\Delta R_W''=\frac{\Delta_{VA}}{B}\times\frac{\delta V}{\Delta V}\times R+\frac{(B-A)R}{B}\times\frac{\Delta w}{w}$$

PROBLEM.

Case 1.—Correcting for Altitude by Table V.

Cal.=8″; V=2750 f. s.; w=260 pounds; c=0.61; Range=19,000 yards=57,000 feet; Maximum ordinate=5261 feet; Variation in weight=+10 pounds; $\frac{2}{3}Y$=3507 feet.

K= .... log 0.82346
f=1.0962 .... log 0.03989

C= .... log 0.86335 ..... colog 9.13665−10
X=57000 .... log 4.75587

Z=7807.6 .... log 3.89252

$$\Delta_{VA}=.00556+\frac{.00012\times7.6}{100}-\frac{.00049\times50}{100}=.0053\underset{\wedge}{2}412$$

$$A=.07368+\frac{.00178\times7.6}{100}-\frac{.00556\times50}{100}=.071035$$

$$B=.1377+\frac{.0040\times7.6}{100}-\frac{.0093\times50}{100}=.133354$$

Δw=+10 .... log 1.00000
w=260 .... colog 7.58503−10
V=2750 .... log 3.43933
.36 .... log 9.55630−10

δV=(−) .... log 1.58066

Δ_{VA}=.0053241 .... log 7.72625−10
R=19000 .... log 4.27875
B=.13335 .... log 9.12500−10 .... colog 0.87500
δV=(−) .... (−)log 1.58066
$\Delta V'$=100 .... log 2.00000 .... colog 8.00000−10

$\Delta R_w'$=(−)288.84 .... log 2.46066

B=.133354
A=.071035

$B-A$=.062319 .... log 8.79462−10
R=19000 .... log 4.27875
B=.13335 .... colog 0.87500
Δw=+10 .... log 1.00000
w=260 .... colog 7.58503−10

$\Delta R_w''$=(+)341.51 .... log 2.53340

ΔR_w= + 52.67 yards,

hence an increase in weight gives an increase in range for this gun at this range, therefore this quantity would carry a negative sign in Column 11 of the range table for this range.

PROBLEM.

Case 2.—Using Corrected Value of C Obtained by Successive Approximations on Form No. 1.

Cal. $=8''$; $V=2750$ f. s.; $w=260$ pounds; $c=0.61$; Range $=19{,}000$ yards $=57{,}000$ feet; $\log C=0.87827$; Variation in weight $=+10$ pounds.

$C=$ .... colog $9.12173-10$
$X=57000$ .... log 4.75587

$Z=7544.0$ .... log 3.87760

$$\Delta_{VA}=.00520+\frac{.00012\times 44}{100}-\frac{.00046\times 50}{100}=.0050228$$

$$A=.06851+\frac{.00170\times 44}{100}-\frac{.00520\times 50}{100}=.066658$$

$$B=.1261+\frac{.0038\times 44}{100}-\frac{.0088\times 50}{100}=.123372$$

$\Delta w=+10$ .... log 1.00000
$w=260$ .... colog $7.58503-10$

$V=2750$ .... log 3.43933
$.36$ .... log $9.55630-10$

$\delta V=(-)$ .... log 1.58066

$\Delta_{VA}=.0050228$ .... log $7.70094-10$
$R=19000$ .... log 4.27875
$B=.12337$ .... log $9.09121-10$ .... colog 0.90879
$\delta V=(-)$ .... log 1.58066
$\Delta V=100$ .... log 2.00000 .... colog $8.00000-10$

$\Delta R_w'=(-)294.53$ .... log 2.46914

$B=.123372$
$A=.066658$

$B-A=.056714$ .... log $8.75369-10$
$R=19000$ .... log 4.27875
$B=.12337$ .... colog 0.90879
$\Delta_w=+10$ .... log 1.00000
$w=260$ .... colog $7.58503-10$

$\Delta R_w''=(+)335.94$ .... log 2.52626

$\Delta R_w=(+)\ 41.44$

hence an increase in weight gives an increase in range for this gun at this range, and this quantity would carry a negative sign in Column 11 of the range table for this range.

Note to Form No. 13.—The method of Case 2 is of course the more accurate, and gives practically the range table results. The method shown in Case 1 is introduced to give practice in the use of these formulæ without the necessity for taking up the successive approximation method in order to determine the value of C accurately.

Form No. 14.

CHAPTER 12—EXAMPLE 5.

FORM FOR THE COMPUTATION OF THE CHANGE IN RANGE RESULTING FROM A VARIATION FROM STANDARD IN THE WEIGHT OF THE PROJECTILE, OTHER CONDITIONS BEING STANDARD. SHORT METHOD, USING DATA CONTAINED IN COLUMNS 10 AND 12 OF THE RANGE TABLES.

FORMULÆ.

$$\delta V = 0.36\,\frac{\Delta w}{w}\,V;\ \Delta R_w = \Delta R_w' + \Delta R_w'' = \Delta R_V \times \frac{\delta V}{\delta V'} + \frac{\Delta w}{w} \times \Delta R_C \times \Delta\delta$$

PROBLEM.

Cal. = 8″; $V = 2750$ f. s.; $w = 260$ pounds; $c = 0.61$; Range = 19,000 yards; From Column 10 of range table, $\Delta R_{50V} = 387$ yards; From Column 12 of range table, $\Delta R_{10C} = 874$ yards; Variation in weight = +10 pounds.

$\Delta w = +10$	log	1.00000
$w = 260$	colog	7.58503 − 10
$V = 2750$	log	3.43933
.36	log	9.55630 − 10
$\delta V = (-)$	log	1.58066
$\Delta R_{50V} = 387$	log	2.58771
$\delta V = (-)$	(−)log	1.58066
$\delta V' = 50$	colog	8.30103 − 10
$\Delta R_w' = (-)294.71$	(−)log	2.46940
$\Delta R_{10C} = 874$	log	2.94151
$\Delta w = +10$	log	1.00000
$w = 260$	colog	7.58503 − 10
$\Delta\delta = 10$	log	1.00000
$\Delta R_w'' = (+)336.15$	log	2.52654

$\Delta R_w = (+)$ 41.44 yards,

hence an increase in weight gives an increase in range for this gun at this range, therefore this quantity would carry a negative sign in Column 11 of the range table at this range.

NOTE TO FORM No. 14.—The method gives practically the range table result.

Form No. 15.

CHAPTER 12—EXAMPLE 6.

FORM FOR THE COMPUTATION OF THE CHANGE IN THE VERTICAL POSITION OF THE POINT OF IMPACT IN THE VERTICAL PLANE THROUGH THE TARGET RESULTING FROM A VARIATION IN THE SETTING OF THE SIGHT IN RANGE, ALL OTHER CONDITIONS BEING STANDARD.

FORMULA.

$$H = \Delta X \tan \omega$$

PROBLEM.

Cal. = 8″; $V = 2750$ f. s.; $w = 260$ pounds; $c = 0.61$; Range = 19,000 yards; $\omega = 26° 35' 00''$ (from range table); Variation in setting of sight = +150 yards.

$\Delta X = 450$	..........log	2.65321
$\omega = 26° 35' 00''$	..........tan	9.69932−10
$H = +225.18$ feet	..........log	2.35253

Form No. 16.

CHAPTER 13—EXAMPLE 1.

FORM FOR COMPUTATION OF THE DRIFT.

FORMULA.

$$D=\frac{\mu}{n}\times\frac{\lambda}{h}\times\frac{C^2D'}{\cos^3\phi}\times\text{Multiplier}$$

PROBLEM.

Case 1.—Correcting for Altitude by Table V.

Cal.=8″; V=2750 f. s.; w=260 pounds; c=0.61; Range=19,000 yards=57,000 feet; ϕ=15° 07′ 00″ (from range table); Maximum ordinate=5261 feet (from range table); $\frac{2}{3}Y$=3507 feet.

K=	log 0.82346	
f=1.0962	log 0.03989	
C=	log 0.86335	colog 9.13665−10
X=57000		log 4.75587
Z=7807.6		log 3.89252

$$D'=484+\frac{22\times 7.6}{100}-\frac{38\times 50}{100}=466.67$$

D'=466.67		log 2.66901
Multiplier=1.5		log 0.17609
μ=.53		log 9.72428−10
n=25	log 1.39794	colog 8.60206−10
$\frac{\lambda}{h}$=.32		log 9.50515−10
C=	log 0.86335	2 log 1.72670
ϕ=15° 07′ 00″	sec 0.01529	3 sec 0.04587
D=281.29 yards		log 2.44916

PROBLEM.

Case 2.—Using Corrected Value of C and ϕ Obtained by Successive Approximations on Form No. 1.

Cal.=8″; V=2750 f. s.; w=260 pounds; c=0.61; Range=19,000 yards=57,000 feet; log C=0.87827; ϕ=15° 07′ 15″ (from Form No. 1).

C=	colog 9.12173−10
X=57000	log 4.75587
Z=7544.0	log 3.87760

$$D'=422+\frac{20\times 44}{100}-\frac{33\times 50}{100}=414.3$$

$D'=414.3$			log 2.61731
Multiplier $=1.5$			log 0.17609
$\mu=.53$			log 9.72428−10
$n=25$	log 1.39794		colog 8.60206−10
$\frac{\lambda}{h}=.32$			log 9.50515−10
$C=$	log 0.87827		2 log 1.75654
$\phi=15°\ 07'\ 15''$	sec 0.01530		3 sec 0.04590
$D=267.50$ yards			log 2.42733

Note to Form No. 16.—The method of Case 2 is of course the more accurate, and gives practically the range table result. The method shown in Case 1 is introduced to give practice in the use of this formula without the necessity for taking up the successive approximation method in order to determine the exact values of C and ϕ.

Form No. 17.

CHAPTER 13—EXAMPLE 2.

FORM FOR COMPUTATION OF SIGHT BAR HEIGHTS AND SETTING OF SLIDING LEAF.

(Permanent Angle $=0°$.)

FORMULÆ.

$$h=l\tan\phi \qquad d=\frac{l\sec\phi}{R}D$$

PROBLEM.

Cal. $=8''$; $V=2750$ f. s.; $w=260$ pounds; $c=0.61$; Range $=19{,}000$ yards; $\phi=15°\ 07'\ 00''$; Sight radius $=41.125''$; Deflection $=266$ yards right.

$\phi=15°\ 07'\ 00''$		tan 9.43158−10	sec 0.01529
$l=41.125$		log 1.61411	log 1.61411
$R=19000$	log 4.27875		colog 5.72125−10
$D=266$			log 2.42488
$h=11.110''$		log 1.04569	
$d=0.59639''$ left			log 9.77553−10

Form No. 18.

CHAPTER 14—EXAMPLE 1.

FORM FOR THE COMPUTATION OF THE EFFECT OF WIND.

FORMULÆ.

$$W_x = \frac{W \times 6080}{60 \times 60 \times 3}\,;\; n = \frac{V^2 \sin 2\phi}{gX}\,;$$

$$\Delta R_W = W_x\left(T - \frac{n}{2n-1} \times \frac{X \cos\phi}{V}\right);\; D_W = W_z\left(T - \frac{X}{V\cos\phi}\right)$$

PROBLEM.

Cal. = 8″; V = 2750 f. s.; w = 260 pounds; c = 0.61; Range = 19,000 yards = 57,000 feet; ϕ = 15° 07′ 00″; T = 35.6 seconds (ϕ and T from range table); Wind component along line of fire = 15 knots an hour with the flight; Wind component perpendicular to the line of fire = 10 knots an hour to the right.

15	log 1.17609	
10		log 1.00000
6080	log 3.78390	log 3.78390
60 × 60 × 3 = 10800	colog 5.96658 − 10	colog 5.96658 − 10
W_x =	log 0.92657	
W_z =		log 0.75048
V = 2750		2 log 6.87866
2ϕ = 30° 14′ 00″		sin 9.70202 − 10
X = 57000	log 4.75587	colog 5.24413 − 10
g = 32.2		colog 8.49214 − 10
n = 2.0746		log 0.31695
$2n$ = 4.1492		
$2n - 1$ = 3.1492	log 0.49820	colog 9.50180 − 10
n = 2.0746		log 0.31695
ϕ = 15° 07′ 00		cos 9.98471 − 10
X = 57000		log 4.75587
V = 2750		colog 6.56067 − 10
13.182		log 1.12000
T = 35.640		
22.458		log 1.35137
W_x =		log 0.92657
ΔR_W = 189.64 yards over		log 2.27794
X = 57000		log 4.75587
V = 2750		colog 6.56067 − 10
ϕ = 15° 07′ 00″		sec 0.01529
21.47		log 1.33183
T = 35.64		
14.17		log 1.15137
W_z =		log 0.75048
D_W = 79.771 yards right		log 1.90185

Form No. 19.

CHAPTER 14—EXAMPLE 2.

FORM FOR THE COMPUTATION OF THE EFFECT OF THE MOTION OF THE GUN.

FORMULÆ.

$$G_x = \frac{G \times 6080}{60 \times 60 \times 3}\,;\quad n = \frac{V^2 \sin 2\phi}{gX}\,;$$

$$\Delta R_G = \frac{n}{2n-1} \times \frac{X \cos \phi}{V} G_x\,;\quad D_G = \frac{X}{V \cos \phi} G_s$$

PROBLEM.

Cal.=8″; V=2750 f. s.; w=260 pounds; c=0.61; Range=19,000 yards=57,000 feet; ϕ=15° 07′ 00″ (from range table); Speed component in line of fire=9 knots an hour against the flight; Speed component perpendicular to the line of fire=18 knots an hour to the left.

9	log 0.95424	
18		log 1.25527
6080	log 3.78390	log 3.78390
60×60×3=10800	colog 5.96658−10	colog 5.96658−10
G_x=	log 0.70472	
G_s=		log 1.00575
V=2750		2 log 6.87866
2ϕ=30° 14′ 00″		sin 9.70202−10
g=32.2		colog 8.49214−10
X=57000	log 4.75587	colog 5.24413−10
n=2.0746		log 0.31695
$2n$=4.1492		
$2n-1$=3.1492	log 0.49820	colog 9.50180−10
n=2.0746		log 0.31695
X=57000		log 4.75587
ϕ=15° 07′ 00″		cos 9.98471−10
V=2750		colog 6.56067−10
G_x=		log 0.70472
ΔR_G=66.791 yards short		log 1.82472
X=57000		log 4.75587
V=2750		colog 6.56067−10
ϕ=15° 07′ 00″		sec 0.01529
G_s=		log 1.00575
D_G=217.56 yards left		log 2.33758

Form No. 20.

CHAPTER 14—EXAMPLE 3.

FORM FOR THE COMPUTATION OF THE EFFECT OF MOTION OF THE TARGET.

FORMULÆ.

$$T_s = \frac{T \times 6080}{60 \times 60 \times 3}\ ;\ \Delta R_T = T_s T\ ;\ D_T = T_s T$$

PROBLEM.

Cal. = 8″; $V = 2750$ f. s.; $w = 260$ pounds; $c = 0.61$; Range = 19,000 yards; Time of flight = 35.64 seconds (from range table); S_x = Speed component in line of fire in knots per hour = 17 knots with flight; S_z = Speed component perpendicular to line of fire in knots per hour = 19 knots to left.

$T = 35.64$	log 1.55194......	log 1.55194
$S_x = 17$	log 1.23045	
$S_z = 19$		log 1.27875
6080	log 3.78390......	log 3.78390
$60 \times 60 \times 3 = 10800$	colog 5.96658−10..	colog 5.96658−10
$\Delta R_T = 341.09$ yards over.................	log 2.53287	
$D_T = 381.22$ yards right..........................		log 2.58117

NOTE TO FORM No. 20.—Note that this example is simply the arithmetical problem of determining how far the target will move in the given direction at the given speed during the time of flight; the speeds being given in knots per hour, and the results required in yards for the time of flight.

Form No. 21.

CHAPTER 16—EXAMPLE 1.

FORM FOR THE COMPUTATION OF THE PENETRATION OF HARVEYIZED (E_1) AND OF FACE-HARDENED (E_2) ARMOR BY CAPPED PROJECTILES.

FORMULÆ.

Harveyized Armor (Davis).

$$E_1^{0.8}=\frac{vw^{0.5}}{K'd^{0.5}}$$

$\log K'=3.25312$

Face-Hardened Armor (De Marre).

$$E_2^{0.7}=\frac{vw^{0.5}}{Kd^{0.75}}\times\frac{1}{\text{De Marre's Coefficient}}$$

$\log K=3.00945$

PROBLEM.

Cal. = 8″; V=2750 f. s.; w=260 pounds; c=0.61; Range=19,000 yards; v_ω=1184 f. s. (from range table); De Marre's coefficient=1.5.

w=260		log 2.41497 ....0.5	log 1.20748
v_ω=1184			log 3.07335
$v_\omega w^{0.5}$=		log 4.28083	log 4.28083
K'=		colog 6.74688−10	
K=			colog 8.99055−10
d=8	log 0.90309..0.5	colog 9.54846−10..0.75	colog 9.32268−10
$E_1^{0.8}$=		log 0.57617	
		10	
	8	log 5.76170	
E_1=5.2506″		log 0.72021	
			log 0.59406
			10
		7	log 5.94060
			log 0.84866
De Marre's coefficient=1.5			colog 9.82391−10
E_2=4.7051″			log 0.67257

FORM FOR THE COMPUTATION OF ϕ, ω, T, v_ω, D, Y, AND THE PENETRATION, GIVEN R AND f; ATMOSPHERIC CONDITIONS STANDARD.*

FORMULÆ.

$$C=\frac{fw}{cd^2}=fK;\ Z=\frac{X}{C};\ \sin 2\phi=AC;\ \tan\omega=B'\tan\phi;\ v_\omega=u_\omega\cos\phi\sec\omega$$

$$D=\frac{\mu\lambda}{nh}\times\frac{C^2D'}{\cos^3\phi};\ E_1{}^{0.5}=\frac{v_\omega w^{0.5}}{K'd^{0.5}}\ \text{(Harveyized—Davis)}$$

$$Y=A''C\tan\phi;\ (E_2\times 1.5)^{0.7}=\frac{v_\omega w^{0.5}}{Kd^{0.75}}\ \text{(Face hardened—De Marre)}$$

PROBLEM.

Cal.$=8''$; $V=2750$ f. s.; $w=260$ pounds; $c=0.61$; Range$=19,000$ yards$=57,000$ feet; $f=1.1345$.

$\log K$ 0.82346	
$\log f$ 0.05481	
$\log C$ 0.87827	
$\operatorname{colog} C$ ....9.12173 — 10	
$\log X$ 4.75587	
$\log Z$ 3.87760	
$Z=7544.0$	

(2) $\phi=15°\ 07'\ 15''$

$\log C$ 0 87827
$\log A$ ....8.82386 — 10
$\log \sin 2\phi$ ....9.70213 — 10
$2\phi=30°\ 14'\ 30''$

(3) $\omega=26°\ 34'\ 40''$

$\log B'$ 0.26751
$\log \tan\phi$ ....9.43170 — 10
$\log \tan\omega$ ....9.69921 — 10

(4) $T=35.642$ seconds

$\log C$ 0.87827
$\log T'$ 0.65839
$\log \sec\phi$ 0.01530
$\log T$ 1.55196

(5) $v_\omega=1184.2$

$\log u_\omega$ 3.04021
$\log \cos\phi$ ....9.98470 — 10
$\log \sec\omega$ 0.04850
$\log v_\omega$ 3.07341

(6) $D=267.50$

$\log \mu(.53)$ ....9.72428 — 10
$\operatorname{colog} n(25)$ ....8.60206 — 10
$\log \dfrac{\lambda}{h}(.32)$ ....9.50515 — 10
$\log \text{constant}$ ....7.83149 — 10
$\log C^2$ 1.75654
$\log \sec^3\phi$ 0.04590
$\log D'$ 2.61731
                        2.25124
$\log 1.5$ (if used)...........0.17609
$\log D$ 2.42733

$A=.06851+\dfrac{.00170\times 44}{100}$

$\quad -\dfrac{.00520\times 50}{100}=.066658$

$A''=2465-\dfrac{50}{100}\times\dfrac{(-.0048)\times 68}{.0025}$

$\quad +\dfrac{50\times 0}{100}+\dfrac{.001758\times 68}{.0025}$

$\quad =2578.1$

$\log B'=.2652+\dfrac{.0023\times 44}{100}$

$\quad -\dfrac{.0026\times 50}{100}=.267512$

$T'=4.600+\dfrac{.092\times 44}{100}-\dfrac{.173\times 50}{100}$

$\quad =4.55398$

$u_\omega=1086-\dfrac{9\times 44}{100}+\dfrac{30\times 50}{100}$

$\quad =1097.04$

$D'=422+\dfrac{20\times 44}{100}-\dfrac{33\times 50}{100}$

$\quad =414.30$

(8) $Y=5263.4$ feet

$\log A''$ 3.41130
$\log C$ 0.87827
$\log \tan\phi$ ....9.43170 — 10
$\log Y$ 3.72127

(9)   Harveyized armor. $E_1=5.2515$ in.

$\log w^{0.5}$ 1.20748
$\operatorname{colog} K'$ ....6.74688 — 10
$\operatorname{colog} d^{0.5}$ ....9.54846 — 10
$\log v_\omega$ 3.07341
$\log E_1{}^{0.5}$ 0.57623
$\log E_1$ 0.72028

(9)   Face hardened. $E_2=4.706$ in.

$\log w^{0.5}$ 1.20748
$\operatorname{colog} K$ ....6.99055 — 10
$\operatorname{colog} d^{0.75}$ ....9.32268 — 10
$\log v_\omega$ 3.07341
$\log (E_2\times 1.5)^{0.7}$ 0.59412
$\log(E_2\times 1.5)$ 0.84874
$\operatorname{colog} 1.5$ ....9.82391 — 10
$\log E_2$ 0.67265

RESULTS.

$\phi=15°\ 07'\ 15''$	$D=267.50$ yards.
$\omega=26°\ 34'\ 40''$	$Y=5263.4$ feet.
$T=35.642$ seconds.	$E_1=5.252$ inches.
$v_\omega=1184.2$ f. s.	$E_2=4.706$ inches.

* If we have a problem in which f is not known, then we must first determine the value of ϕ for the given range by the use of Form No. 1 in paragraph 273, Chapter 16.

Form No. 23.

CHAPTER 16—EXAMPLE 3.

FORM FOR THE COMPUTATION OF S, ΔR_V, ΔR_C, ΔR_w, FOR A GIVEN R AND f.

FORMULÆ.

$$C=\frac{fw}{cd^2}=fK;\ Z=\frac{X}{C};\ S=\frac{h}{3}\cot\omega\left(\frac{1+\frac{h}{3}\cot\omega}{R}\right);\ \Delta R_V=\frac{\Delta_{VA}}{B}\times\frac{\delta V}{\Delta V}\times R;$$

$$\Delta R_\delta=\frac{(B-A)R}{B}\times\frac{\Delta\delta}{\delta};\ \delta V=0.36\ \frac{\Delta w}{w}V;$$

$$\Delta R_w=\Delta R_w{}'+\Delta R_w{}''=\Delta R_V\times\frac{\delta V}{\delta V'}+\frac{\Delta w}{w}\times\Delta R_\delta\times\Delta\delta$$

PROBLEM.

Cal. $=8''$; $V=2750$ f. s.; $w=260$ pounds; $c=0.61$; Range $=19{,}000$ yards $=57{,}000$ feet; $\phi=15°\ 07'\ 15''$; $\omega=26°\ 34'\ 40''$; $f=1.1345$; $h=20$ feet; $\Delta w=\pm5$ pounds.

log K 0.82346
log f 0.05481
log C 0.87827
colog C .... 9.12173 — 10
log X 4.75587
log Z 3.87760
$Z = 7544.0$

(7) $S = 13.335$ yards

log $\frac{h}{3}$ (6.6667) 0.82391
log cot ω 0.30079
log(6.6667 cot ω) 1.12470
colog R .... 5.72125 — 10
log $\frac{6.6667}{R}$ cot ω .... 6.84595 — 10
$\frac{6.6667}{R}$ cot $\omega = .00070$
$1+\frac{6.6667}{R}$ cot ω
$= 1.0007$ .... log 0.00030
6.6667 cot ω .... log 1.12470
log S 1.12500

(10) $\Delta R_V = 386.77$ yards

log Δ_{VA} .... 7.70094 — 10
colog B 0.90879
log δV (50) 1.69897
colog ΔV (100) .... 8.00000 — 10
log R 4.27875
log ΔR_{wV} 2.58745

RESULTS.

$S = 13.335$ yards.
$\Delta R_{wV} = 386.77$ yards.
$\Delta R_{w\delta} = 873.43$ yards.
$\Delta R_w = \pm\ 20.70$ yards.

$\Delta_{VA} = .00520 + \frac{.00012\times44}{100} - \frac{.00046\times50}{100} = .0050228$

$A = .06851 + \frac{.00170\times44}{100} - \frac{.00520\times50}{100} = .066658$

$B = .1261 + \frac{.0038\times44}{100} - \frac{.0088\times50}{100}$
$= .123372$

(12) $\Delta R_\delta = 873.43$ yards

log $(B-A)$ .... 8.75369 — 10
log R 4.27875
colog B 0.90879
log (0.1) .... 9.00000 — 10
log ΔR_δ 2.94123

(11) $\Delta R_w = \pm\ 20.70$ yards

log Δw 0.69897
colog w .... 7.58503 — 10
log V 3.43933
log 0.36 .... 9.55630 — 10
log δV 1.27963
log ΔR_{wV} 2.58745
log δV 1.27963
colog $\delta V'$ (50) .... 8.30103 — 10
log $\Delta R_w{}'$ 2.16811
log $\Delta R_{w\delta}$ 2.94123
log Δw 0.69897
colog w .... 7.58503 — 10
log $\Delta\delta$ (10) 1.00000
log $\Delta R_w{}''$ 2.22523
$\Delta R_w{}' = \mp\ 147.27$
$\Delta R_w{}'' = \pm\ 167.97$
$\Delta R_w = \pm\ 20.70$

An increase in weight gives an increase in range for this gun at this range, therefore this quantity would carry a negative sign in Column 11 of the range table for this range.

Form No. 24.

CHAPTER 16—EXAMPLE 4.

FORM FOR THE COMPUTATION OF EFFECTS OF WIND AND OF MOTION OF GUN AND TARGET; ALSO CHANGE IN HEIGHT OF POINT OF IMPACT FOR VARIATION IN SETTING OF SIGHT IN RANGE FOR A GIVEN *R* AND *f*.

FORMULÆ.

$$n=\frac{V^2\sin 2\phi}{gX};\ \Delta R_W=W_s\left(T-\frac{n}{2n-1}\times\frac{X\cos\phi}{V}\right);\ D_W=W_z\left(T-\frac{X}{V\cos\phi}\right);$$

$$\Delta R_G=\left(\frac{n}{2n-1}\times\frac{X\cos\phi}{V}\right)G_s;\ D_G=\frac{X}{V\cos\phi}G_z;\ \Delta R_T=T_sT;$$

$$D_T=T_zT;\ W_s=\text{Etc.}=\frac{W\times 6080}{3\times 60\times 60}$$

PROBLEM.

Cal.=8″; V=2750 f. s.; w=260 pounds; c=0.61; Range=19,000 yards=57,000 feet; ϕ=15° 07′ 15″; T=35.642 seconds; ω=26° 34′ 40″.

Value of n

log V^2 .... 6.87866
log sin 2ϕ .... 9.70213 — 10
colog g (32.2) .... 8.49214 — 10
colog X .... 5.24413 — 10
log n 0.31706

n = 2.0752
$2n$ = 4.1504
$2n-1$ = 3.1504

(13) ΔR_W = 151.74 yards

log n 0.31706
log X 4.75587
log cos ϕ .... 9.98470 — 10
colog $(2n-1)$ .... 9.50163 — 10
colog V .... 6.56067 — 10
log $\frac{nX\cos\phi}{(2n-1)V}$ 1.11993

$\frac{nX\cos\phi}{(2n-1)V}$ = 13.180
T = 35.642

log .... 22.462 ..... 1.35145
log W_s 0.82966
log ΔR_W 2.18111

(16) D_W = 95.740 yards

log X 4.75587
colog V .... 6.56067 — 10
log sec ϕ 0.01530
log $\frac{X}{V\cos\phi}$ 1.33184

$\frac{X}{V\cos\phi}$ = 21.470
T = 35.642

log .... 14.172 ..... 1.1[illegible]143
log W_z 0.82966
log D_W 1.98109

Value of W_s, W_z, G_s, G_z, T_s, T_z for a component of 12 knots.

log 12 .... 1.07918
log 6080 .... 3.78390
colog 3 .... 9.52288 — 10
colog $(60)^2$ .... 6.44370 — 10
log W_s, etc. 0.82966

(14) ΔR_G = 89.040 yards

log $\frac{nX\cos\phi}{(2n-1)V}$ 1.11993
log G_s 0.82966
log ΔR_G 1.94959

(17) D_G = 145.04 yards

log $\frac{X}{V\cos\phi}$ 1.33184
log G_z 0.82966
log D_G 2.16150

(15) $\Delta R_T = D_T$ = 240.78 yards

log $T_s = T_z$ 0.82966
log T 1.55196
log $\Delta R_T = D_T$ 2.38162

(19) H = 150.08 feet

log X = 300 .... 2.47712
log tan ω .... 9.69921 — 10
log H_{100} 2.17633

RESULTS.

n = 2.0752.
ΔR_W = 151.74 yards.
D_W = 95.740 yards.
ΔR_G = 89.040 yards.
D_G = 145.04 yards.
$\Delta R_T = D_T$ = 240.78 yards.
H = 150.08 feet.

Form No. 25A.

CHAPTER 17—EXAMPLE 8.

FORM FOR THE SOLUTION OF REAL WIND AND SPEED PROBLEMS.

PROBLEM.

Cal.=8″; V=2750 f. s.; w=260 pounds; c=0.61; Range=7500 yards; Real wind, direction from, 225° true; velocity, 15 knots an hour; Motion of gun, course, 355° true; speed, 20 knots an hour; Motion of target, course, 320° true; speed, 25 knots an hour; Target at moment of firing, 75° true; distant, 7500 yards; Barometer=30.00″; Thermometer=10° F.; Temperature of powder=75° F.; Weight of projectile=263 pounds.

Temperature of powder, $\frac{-35}{10} \times 15 = -52.5$ foot-seconds.

Use Table IV to correct for density. Use traverse tables for resolution of wind and speeds.

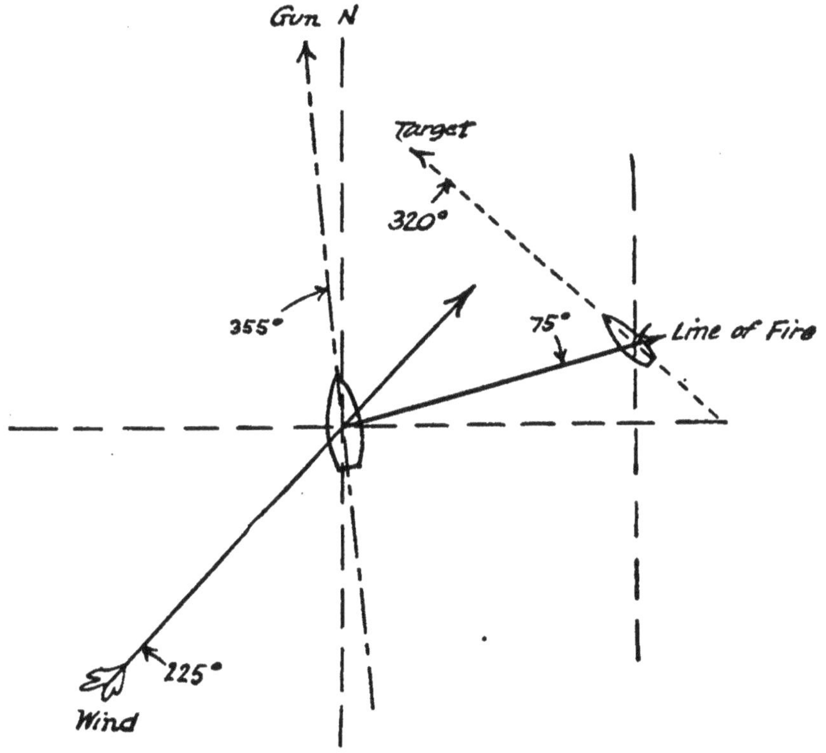

Cause of error. Speed of or variation in.	Affects.	Formulæ.	Errors in—			
			Range.		Deflection.	
			Short. Yds.	Over. Yds.	Right. Yds.	Left. Yds.
Gun	Range.....	$20 \cos 80 \times \frac{44}{12} = \frac{3.5 \times 44}{12}$	....	12.8	....	....
	Deflection..	$20 \sin 80 \times \frac{55}{12} = \frac{19.7 \times 55}{12}$	....	....	....	90.3
Target..........	Range.....	$25 \cos 65 \times \frac{68}{12} = \frac{10.6 \times 68}{12}$	....	60.1	....	....
	Deflection..	$25 \sin 65 \times \frac{68}{12} = \frac{22.7 \times 68}{12}$	....	....	128.6	....
Wind	Range.....	$15 \cos 30 \times \frac{24}{12} = \frac{13 \times 24}{12}$	....	26.0	....	....
	Deflection..	$15 \sin 30 \times \frac{13}{12} = \frac{7.5 \times 13}{12}$	....	....	....	8.1
Initial velocity ...	Range.....	$52.5 \times \frac{207}{50}$	217.4	....	....	....
w...............	Range.....	$3 \times \frac{43}{5}$	25.8	....	....	....
Density...........	Range.....	1.25×180	225.0	....	....	....
			468.2	98.9	128.6	98.4
			98.9		98.4	
			369.3		30.2	

$30.2 \text{ yards} \times \frac{12}{68} = 5.3$ knots on deflection scale.

Set sights at:

Exactly..........in range, 7869.3 yards; in deflection, 44.7 knots.

Actually.........in range, 7850.0 yards; in deflection, 45.0 knots.

Remember to shoot short rather than over.

Form No. 25B.

CHAPTER 17—EXAMPLE 8.

FORM FOR THE SOLUTION OF REAL WIND AND SPEED PROBLEMS.

PROBLEM.

Cal. = 8″; $V = 2750$ f. s.; $w = 260$ pounds; $c = 0.61$; Range = 7000 yards; Real wind, direction from, 160° true; velocity, 20 knots an hour; Motion of gun, course, 260° true; speed, 18 knots an hour; Motion of target, course, 170° true; speed, 23 knots an hour; Target at moment of firing bearing, 115° true; distant, 7000 yards; Barometer = 29.00″; Thermometer = 85° F.; Temperature of powder = 95° F.; Weight of projectile = 258 pounds.

Temperature of powder, $\frac{+35}{10} \times 5 = +17.5$ foot-seconds.

Use Table IV for correction for density. Use traverse tables for resolving speeds.

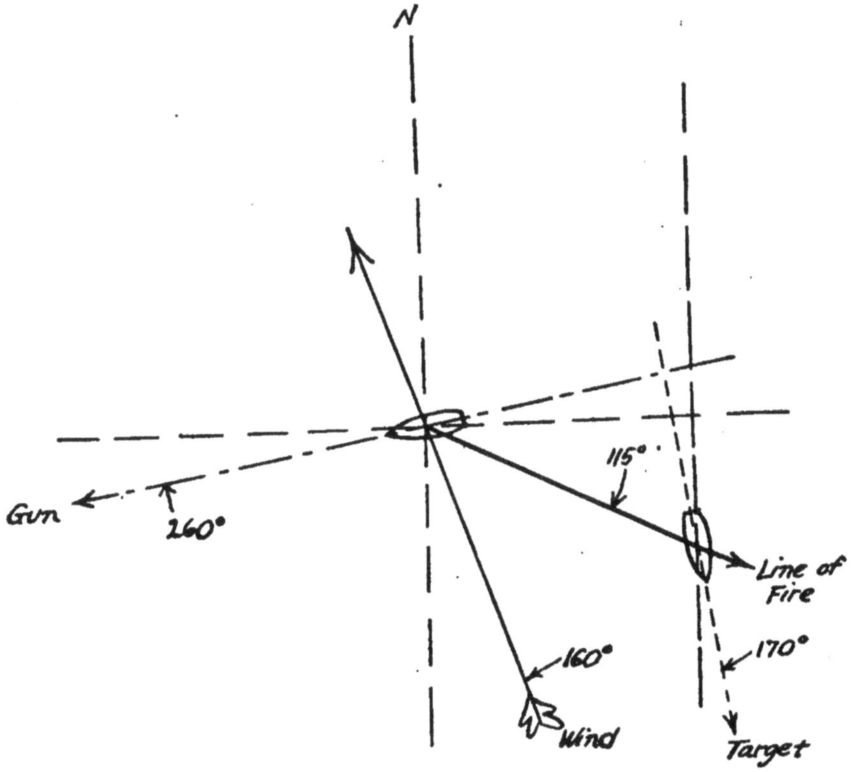

Cause of error. Speed of or variation in.	Affects.	Formulæ.	Errors in — Range. Short. Yds.	Range. Over. Yds.	Deflection. Right. Yds.	Deflection. Left. Yds.
Gun	Range.....	$18 \cos 35 \times \frac{42}{12} = \frac{14.7 \times 42}{12}$	51.5	....	....	....
	Deflection..	$18 \sin 35 \times \frac{52}{12} = \frac{10.3 \times 52}{12}$	....	....	44.6	....
Target	Range.....	$23 \cos 55 \times \frac{63}{12} = \frac{13.2 \times 63}{12}$	69.3	....	....	....
	Deflection..	$23 \sin 55 \times \frac{63}{12} = \frac{18.8 \times 63}{12}$	....	....	....	98.7
Wind	Range.....	$20 \cos 45 \times \frac{21}{12} = \frac{14.1 \times 21}{12}$	24.7	....	....	....
	Deflection..	$20 \sin 45 \times \frac{11}{12} = \frac{14.1 \times 11}{12}$	....	....	....	12.9
Initial velocity ...	Range.....	$17.5 \times \frac{197}{50}$	....	69.0	....	....
w................	Range.....	$2 \times \frac{43}{5}$	....	17.2	....	....
Density..........	Range.....	$.69 \times 157$	....	108.3	....	....
			145.5	194.5	44.6	111.6
$67 \text{ yards} \times \frac{12}{63} = 12.8$ knots on deflection scale.				145.5		44.6
				49.0		67.0

Set sights at:

Exactly..........in range, 6951 yards; in deflection, 62.8 knots.

Actually.........in range, 6950 yards; in deflection, 62.0 knots.

Remember to shoot short rather than over.

Form No. 26.

CHAPTER 17—EXAMPLE 9.

FORM FOR THE SOLUTION OF APPARENT WIND AND SPEED PROBLEMS.

PROBLEM.

Cal. = 8″; V = 2750 f. s.; w = 260 pounds; c = 0.61; Range = 7300 yards; Apparent wind, direction from, 45° true; velocity, 30 knots an hour; Motion of gun, course, 80° true; speed, 21 knots an hour; Motion of target, course, 100° true; speed, 28 knots an hour; Target at moment of firing bearing, 300° true; distant, 7300 yards; Barometer = 28.50″; Thermometer = 10° F.; Temperature of powder = 60° F.; Weight of projectile = 255 pounds.

Temperature of powder, $\frac{-35}{10} \times 30 = -105$ foot-seconds.

Use Table IV for correction for density. Use traverse tables for resolution of speeds.

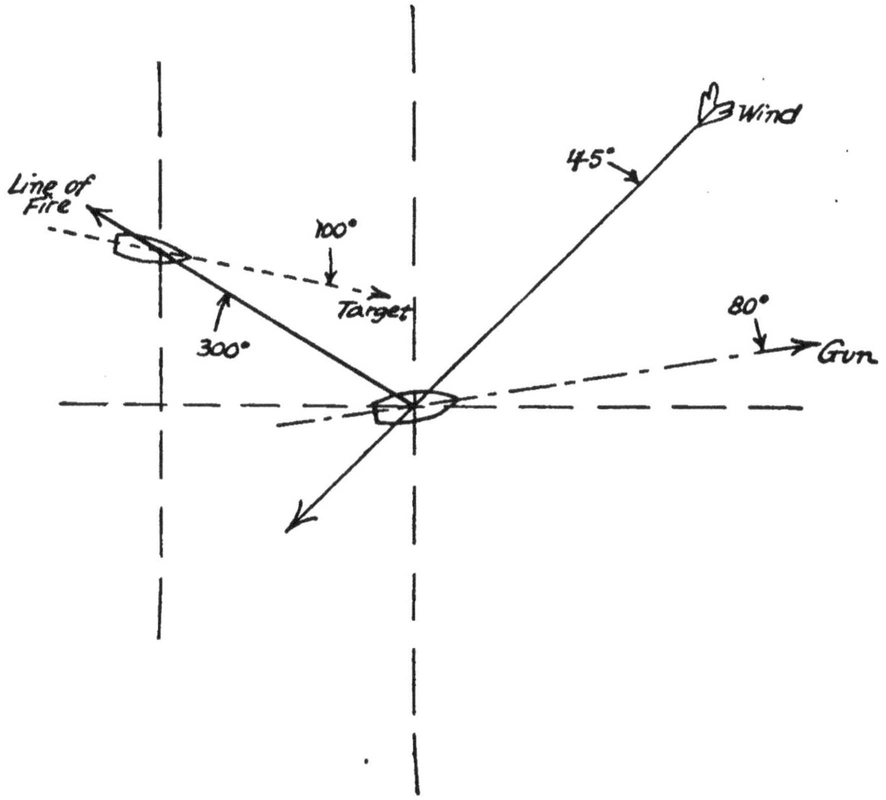

Cause of error. Speed of or variation in.	Affects.	Formulæ.	Errors in— Range. Short. Yds.	Errors in— Range. Over. Yds.	Errors in— Deflection. Right. Yds.	Errors in— Deflection. Left. Yds.
Gun	Range	$21 \cos 40 \times \frac{66}{12} = \frac{16.1 \times 66}{12}$	88.6	....	....	....
	Deflection	$21 \sin 40 \times \frac{66}{12} = \frac{13.5 \times 66}{12}$	....	....	74.3	....
Target	Range	$28 \cos 20 \times \frac{66}{12} = \frac{26.3 \times 66}{12}$	....	144.7	....	....
	Deflection	$28 \sin 20 \times \frac{66}{12} = \frac{9.6 \times 66}{12}$	....	....	....	52.8
Wind	Range	$30 \cos 75 \times \frac{23}{12} = \frac{7.8 \times 23}{12}$	....	14.9	....	....
	Deflection	$30 \sin 75 \times \frac{12}{12} = \frac{29 \times 12}{12}$	....	....	....	29.0
Initial velocity	Range	$105 \times \frac{203}{50}$	426.3	....	....	....
w	Range	$43 \times \frac{5}{5}$	....	43.0	....	....
Density	Range	$.69 \times 171$	118.0	....	....	....
			632.9	202.6	74.3	81.8
			202.6			74.3
		7.5 yards deflection $\times \frac{12}{66} = 1.4$ knots on deflection scale.	430.3			7.5

Set sights at:

Exactly..........in range, 7730.3 yards; in deflection, 51.4 knots.

Actually.........in range, 7700.0 yards; in deflection, 51.0 knots.

Remember to shoot short rather than over.

Form No. 27A.

CHAPTER 18—EXAMPLE 13.

FORM FOR THE COMPUTATION OF THE CORRECT SIGHT-SETTING IN RANGE USING REDUCED VELOCITY, WITHOUT THE USE OF REDUCED VELOCITY RANGE TABLE.

FORMULÆ.

$$C=fK;\ Z=\frac{X}{C};\ \sin 2\phi=AC$$

PROBLEM.

Cal. $=6''$, $V_1=2800$ f. s.; $V_2=2600$ f. s.; $w=105$ pounds; $c=.61$; Range$=3000$ yards $=9000$ feet; maximum ordinate$=53$ feet; $\frac{2}{3}Y=35$ feet, hence $f=1.0011$ from Table V.

$K=$ (from Table VI) .... log 0.67956
$f=1.0011$ .... log 0.00047

$C=$ .... log 0.68003...... colog 9.31997−10
$X=9000$ .... log 3.95424

$Z=1880.2$ .... log 3.27421

From Table II

$$A=.00994+\frac{.00065\times 80.2}{100}=.010461$$

$A=.010461$ .... log 8.01957−10
$C=$ .... log 0.68003

$2\phi=2°\ 52'\ 13''$ .... sin 8.69960−10
$\phi=1°\ 26.1'$

From Range Table "H" this ϕ corresponds to

$$R=3400+13=3413 \text{ yards}$$

Form No. 27B.

CHAPTER 18—EXAMPLE 14.

FORM FOR THE COMPUTATION OF THE CORRECT SIGHT-SETTING IN RANGE USING REDUCED VELOCITY, WITH THE USE OF REDUCED VELOCITY RANGE TABLE.

PROBLEM.

Cal. = 6″; $V_1 = 2800$ f. s.; $V_2 = 2600$ f. s.; $w = 105$ pounds; $c = .61$; Range = 3000 yards. From Range Table " F " for Range = 3000 yards, we have

$$\phi = 1^\circ\ 26.1'$$

This angle of departure in Range Table " H " gives

$$R = 3400 + 13 = 3413 \text{ yards}$$

Form No. 28.

CHAPTER 18—EXAMPLES 1 AND 2.

FORM FOR THE COMPUTATIONS FOR THE CALIBRATION OF A SINGLE GUN AND FOR DETERMINING THE MEAN DISPERSION.

PROBLEM.

Cal.=8″; V=2750 f. s.; w=260 pounds; c=0.61; Actual range=8500 yards; Sights set at, in range, 8500 yards; in deflection, 40 knots; Center of bull's eye above water, 12 feet; Bearing of target from gun, 37° true; Wind blowing from 350° true, with velocity of 8 knots an hour; Barometer=29.85″; Thermometer =80° F.; Temperature of powder=100° F.; Weight of shell=268 pounds; Number of shot=4, falling as follows:

Shot.	Range.		Deflection.	
	Short. Yds.	Over. Yds.	Right. Yds.	Left. Yds.
1....................	100	....	....	85
2....................	125	....	....	80
3....................	85	....	....	60
4....................	90	....	....	55
Mean errors on foot of perpendicular through bull's eye...	4|400.0 100.0 short			4|280 70.0 left

Correction in range due to height of bull's eye:

$$\frac{100}{31}\times 12 = 38.7 \text{ yards over}$$

Correction in deflection due to intentional displacement:

$$\frac{80}{12}\times 10 = 66.7 \text{ yards left}$$

Temperature of powder:

$$\frac{+35}{10}\times 10 = +35 \text{ foot-seconds}$$

Use Table IV for density correction and traverse tables for resolution of wind forces.

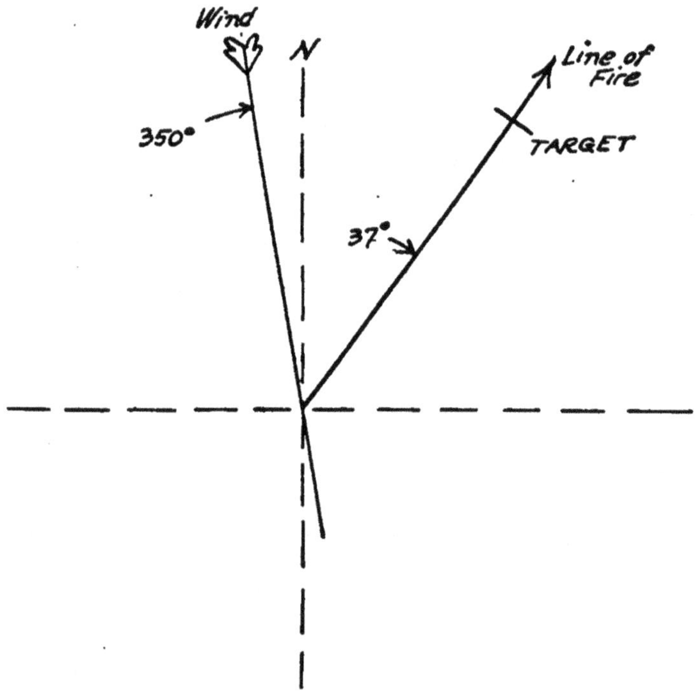

			Short. Yds.	Over. Yds.	Right. Yds.	Left. Yds.
Wind	Range	$8 \cos 47 \times \frac{31}{12} = \frac{5.5 \times 31}{12}$	14.2	....	....	....
	Deflection	$8 \sin 47 \times \frac{17}{12} = \frac{5.9 \times 17}{12}$	....	....	8.4	....
w	Range	$8 \times \frac{41}{5}$	65.6	....	....	....
Density	Range	$.318 \times 229$	....	72.8	....	....
Initial velocity	Range	$35 \times \frac{227}{50}$	....	158.0	....	....
Height of bull's eye	Range	$12 \times \frac{100}{31}$	....	38.7	....	....
Intentional deflection	Deflection	$10 \times \frac{80}{12}$	....	....	....	66.7
			79.8	270.4 79.8	8.4	66.7 8.4
Errors on point *P* as an origin for standard conditions				190.6		58.3

Observed distance from target in range	100.0 yards short.
Error (where shot should have fallen)	190.6 yards over.
True mean error in range under standard conditions	290.6 yards short.
Observed distance from target in deflection	70.7 yards left.
Error (where shot should have fallen)	58.3 yards left.
True mean error in deflection under standard conditions	11.7 yards left.

That is, under standard conditions the mean point of impact of the gun is 290.6 yards short of and 11.7 yards to the left of the point *P*. We wish to adjust the sight scales so that the actual mean point of impact of the gun shall be at *P*. To do this we:

1. Run up the sight until the pointer indicates 8790.6 yards in range, then slide the scale under the pointer until the latter is over the 8500-yard mark on the former, and then clamp the scale.

2. 11.7 yards in deflection equals $\frac{12}{80} \times 11.7 = 1.8$ knots on the deflection scale at the given range. Set the sight for a deflection of 51.8 knots, then slide the scale until the 50-knot mark is under the pointer, and then clamp the scale.

MEAN DISPERSION FROM MEAN POINT OF IMPACT.

Number of shot.	In range.			In deflection.		
	Fall relative to target. Short or over. Yds.	Position of mean point of impact relative to target. Short or over. Yds.	Variation of each shot from mean point of impact. Short or over. Yds.	Fall relative to target. Right or left. Yds.	Position of mean point of impact relative to target. Right or left. Yds.	Variation of each shot from mean point of impact. Right or left. Yds.
1	100 short	100 short	0	85 left	70 left	15
2	125 short	100 short	25	80 left	70 left	10
3	85 short	100 short	15	60 left	70 left	10
4	90 short	100 short	10	65 left	70 left	15
			4|50			4|50
			12.5			12.5

Mean dispersion from mean point of impact:
In range.................................. 12.5 yards.
In deflection.............................. 12.5 yards.

Form No. 29.

CHAPTER 19—EXAMPLE 1.

FORM FOR THE COMPUTATIONS FOR THE CALIBRATION OF A SHIP'S BATTERY.

PROBLEM.

Cal.=8"; $V=2750$; $w=260$ pounds; $c=0.61$; Range=8500 yards.

For a battery of eight of the above guns, having determined the true mean errors to be as given below (by previous calibration practice), how should the sights of the guns be adjusted to make all the guns shoot together?

Note that no one of the guns shoots closely enough to be taken as a standard gun. At 8500 yards, one yard in deflection equals $\frac{12}{80}=.15$ knot on deflection scale.

Number of gun.	Errors.		With reference to point P, each gun shot.			To bring [illegible]ights together [illegible] them for each gun as follows:	
	Range. Yds.	Deflection. Yds.	In range. Yds.	In deflection. Yards.	In deflection. Knots.	In range. Yds.	In deflection. Kts.
1..........	25 short	25 left	25 short	25 left	3.75 left	8525	53.75
2..........	100 over	50 left	100 over	50 left	7.5 left	8400	57.50
3..........	100 short	75 right	100 short	75 right	11.25 right	8600	38.75
4........	75 short	50 right	75 short	50 right	7.5 right	8575	42.50
5..........	150 over	100 left	150 over	100 left	15.0 left	8350	65.00
6..........	75 short	75 left	75 short	75 left	11.25 left	8575	61.25
7..........	80 short	80 right	80 short	80 right	12.0 right	8580	38.00
8..........	90 over	25 right	90 over	25 right	3.75 right	8410	46.25

After the sights have been set as indicated above, move the sight scales under the pointers until the latter are over the 8500-yard marks in range and over the 50-knot marks in deflection, and then clamp the scales.

APPENDIX B.

THE FARNSWORTH GUN ERROR COMPUTER.

PURPOSE AND USE.

1. This instrument was devised by Midshipman J. S. Farnsworth, U. S. N., class of 1915, during his first class year at the Naval Academy.

2. It is intended for the purpose of determining quickly and accurately, by mechanical means and without computations, the errors in range and in deflection introduced into gun fire by: *

(a) Wind.

(b) Motion of firing ship.

(c) Motion of target ship.

(d) Variation from standard in the temperature of the powder.

(e) Variation from standard in the density of the atmosphere.

Plate I shows the device on an enlarged scale, so that the graduations can be clearly seen. The radial arm shown at the right of the drawing is secured to the same axis as the discs.

3. The uses and advantages of the instrument are readily apparent. It can be used by both spotting and plotting groups if desired, but presumably it would be used in the plotting room. Its use will enable the initial errors to be allowed for in firing ranging shots to be accurately and quickly determined, so that with it a spotter has a vastly greater chance of having the ranging shot strike within good spotting distance of the target than by any "judgment" or "rule of thumb" methods. This should enable a ship to begin to place her salvos properly in a shorter time and with less waste of ammunition than could be done without the device.

4. Errors due to changes in courses, speeds, wind, or other conditions during firing can be similarly quickly obtained by the use of the computer.

5. The accompanying drawing (Plate I) shows the device arranged for working with apparent wind, and for determining deflection errors directly in knots of the deflection scale of the sight, and not in yards. The device could be equally well arranged for real wind, for deflections in yards, or for any other desired system, by simply drawing the proper spiral curves on the smaller disc; but the arrangement shown here is believed to be the most useful one for service conditions. The drawing

---

* Throughout this description the "errors" have been considered and not the "corrections." In the practical use of the computer it must be remembered that, having determined an "error" the "correction" to compensate for it is numerically equal but of opposite sign. Thus, an "error" of 100 short calls for a correction of "up 100," etc.

A very clear and concise statement of the purpose and principle of the gun error computer is contained in the following extract from a report thereon submitted to the commander-in-chief of the United States Atlantic fleet by Ensign H. L. Abbott, U. S. N.:

"The gun error computer is a combination of a set of curves showing the correction to be applied at various ranges to range and deflection for unit variation from normal of the conditions considered, such as wind; and of a specially graduated numerical or circular slide rule for modifying the correction for unit variation to give the correction for the actual variation. This instrument can be made to take the place of the range tables, and with its aid the corrections for any particular set of conditions can be picked out with much greater ease and facility than with the present cumbrous range tables and accompanying necessary calculations."

does not show the three curves in colors, as they should be drawn on a working device, each curve being of a radically different color from the others; and the powder temperature error and density error curves are not shown on the drawing. In the following descriptions it is assumed that the several curves would be drawn as follows:

Wind range curve in red.
Wind deflection curve in green.
Target and gun range curve in black.
Powder temperature error curve in blue.
Density error curve in yellow.

METHOD OF CONSTRUCTION.

6. In external appearance and in some principles of construction, the device is similar to an omnimeter. It consists, as shown on the plate, of two circular discs, an outer or larger, and an inner or smaller one, concentrically secured on the same axis and capable of independent rotary motion around that axis; and, in addition, of a radial arm secured on the same axis and capable of free rotary motion around that axis. These parts should be so arranged that the radial arm can be clamped to the inner disc without clamping the two discs together, and so that the two discs can be clamped together without clamping the radial arm to the inner disc. The radial arm should be made of some transparent material, with the range scale line scribed radially from the center of the axis down the middle of the arm.

7. The salient features of the device are:

(a) **The Range Circle.**—The graduations on the outside of the larger circle on the larger disc.

(b) **The Deflection Circle.**—The graduations on the inside of the larger circle on the larger disc.

(c) **The Speed Circle.**—The graduations on the outside of the smaller circle on the larger disc. This circle is in coincidence with the periphery of the smaller or inner disc.

(d) **The Correction Circle.**—The graduations on the periphery of the smaller disc.

(e) **The Range and Deflection Curves.**—Drawn on the face of the smaller disc, spirally, from the center of the disc outward. They are the:

(1) *Wind range curve.*
(2) *Wind deflection curve.*
(3) *Target and gun range curve.*
(4) *Powder temperature curve.*
(5) *Density curve.*

(f) **The Radial Arm.**—Bearing the range scale.

Of the above, *a*, *b* and *c* are all on the larger disc, and their positions relative to one another are therefore fixed. Also *d* and *e* are both on the smaller disc, and their positions relative to each other are therefore fixed. However, *a*, *b* and *c* can be rotated relative to *d* and *e*. The range scale, being on *f*, can be rotated relative to either or to both of the discs.

8. Of the above, only the curves vary for different guns. It would therefore be necessary to construct the apparatus and then have the curves scribed on it for the particular type of gun with which the individual instrument is to be used. Thus, there would be one computer for each caliber of gun on board. Plate I shows the device as arranged for the 12″ gun for which $V=2900$ f. s., $w=870$ pounds and $c=0.61$; the necessary data for its construction having been obtained from the range table for that gun.

9. The mathematical principles involved in the construction of the several elements of the device are described herein (the description being based on the assumption that the reader is not familiar with the omnimeter).

(a) **Range Circle.**—The entire circumference is divided into parts representing logarithmic increments in the secant of the angle, from zero degrees to the angle whose logarithmic secant is unity (84° +). These increments are laid down on the circle in a counter-clockwise direction according to the logarithmic secants, and the scale is marked with the angles corresponding to the given logarithmic secants. For example, the point marked 23° lies in a counter-clockwise direction from the zero of the scale, and at a distance from it equal to .03597 of the circumference (log sec 23° = 0.03597).

(b) **Deflection Circle.**—The entire circumference is divided into parts representing logarithmic increments in the sine of the angle, from the angle whose logarithmic sine is 9.00000 − 10 (5° +) to 90°. These increments are laid down on the circle in a clockwise direction according to the logarithmic sines, and the scale is marked with the angles corresponding to the given logarithmic sines. For example, the point marked 23° lies in a clockwise direction from the zero of the scale, and at a distance from it equal to .59188 of the circumference (log sine 23° = 9.59188 − 10). The zero of the scale coincides with the zero of the scale of the range circle.

(c) **Speed Circle.**—The entire circumference is divided into parts representing logarithmic increments in the natural numbers from 1.0 to 10 (the decimal point may be placed wherever necessary, and the point marked "10" may be considered as the "zero" of this scale, and will hereafter be referred to as such in this description). The increments are laid down on the circle in a counter-clockwise direction from zero, and the divisions of the scale are marked with the numbers corresponding to the given logarithms. For example, the number 2.3 lies in a counter-clockwise direction from the zero, and at a distance from it equal to .36173 of the circumference (log 2.3 = 0.36173). The zero of this scale coincides with the zeros of the range and deflection circles.

(d) **Correction Circle.**—The construction of the correction circle is exactly the same as that of the speed circle, except that the scale is laid down in a clockwise direction from the zero.*

(e) **Range and Deflection Curves.**—Each of these is based on the data in the appropriate column of the range table for the given gun, and these curves are therefore different for different guns. The method of plotting them is described below.

(f) **Range Scale.**—A radius of appropriate length to fit the discs is subdivided as a range scale. These divisions are purely arbitrary, and Plate I shows the increments in range as decreasing in relative magnitude on the scale as the range increases; so that the divisions are larger and more easily and accurately read at the ranges that will most likely be used; becoming smaller as the range becomes very great. The size of these divisions, either actual or relative to one another, does not affect the work of the instrument, provided this range scale be prepared first and then used in plotting the error curves in the manner described below.†

* Those familiar with the omnimeter will perceive that up to this point the principles of that instrument have been followed; but that the scales of the range circle (logarithmic secants) and speed circle (logarithms of numbers) have been laid down in the opposite direction from those on the omnimeter.

† If the device be made of a good working size, these divisions may all be made of the same size and still be clearly read, and this is the best way to construct it.

10. To plot the range and deflection curves for wind and for motion of firing or target ship, the data is obtained from the proper column in the range table for the error and gun under consideration (Columns 13, 14, 15, 16, 17 and 18). Thus, for instance, to locate the point of the **wind range curve** for a range of 10,000 yards for the given 12″ gun, Column 13 of the range table (Bureau Ordnance Pamphlet No. 298) shows that the error in range caused by a 12-knot wind blowing along the line of fire is 27 yards, and it would therefore be 2.25 yards for a 1-knot wind. Therefore the desired point of the curve is plotted on the inner disc on a radius passing through the 2.25 mark on the correction circle, and at a distance from the center corresponding to 10,000 yards on the range scale. Enough points are plotted in this manner to enable an accurate curve to be scribed through them. The other curves are plotted in a similar manner, but instead of plotting deflection curves in "yards error," they are plotted in "knots error of the deflection scale of the sight," thus enabling the deflection error to be determined directly in knots for application to the sight drums. For example, for the wind deflection curve, the data for plotting would be found by dividing the data in Column 16 of the range table for the given range by the corresponding data in Column 18. Approximate values of the correction scale reading are marked at intervals along the curves to aid the operator in placing the decimal point correctly and in getting the result in correct units.

11. To plot the **powder temperature curve,** it will be seen from Column 10 of the range table that, for a range of 15,000 yards, 50 f. s. variation from standard in the initial velocity causes 379.65 yards error in range, therefore 1 foot-second variation in initial velocity would cause 7.593 yards error in range. From the notes to the range table, it will be seen that, for this gun, 10° variation from standard in the temperature of the powder (90° being the standard) causes a change of 35 f. s. in initial velocity, but recent experiments show that this value is too high, and that for each 10° variation in temperature, the change in initial velocity is only 20 f. s. Consequently, a variation of one degree from standard in the temperature of the powder would cause an error of $2.0 \times 7.593 = 15.186$ yards in range. Therefore, to locate the point on the curve corresponding to 15,000 yards range, place the desired point on the face of the smaller disc on a radius passing through the 15.186 mark on the correction circle, and at a distance from the center corresponding to 15,000 yards on the range scale.

12. Before proceeding to a description of the method of plotting the **density curve,** a brief preliminary discussion of another point is necessary. As the density of the air depends upon two different variables, one being the barometric reading and the other the temperature of the air (assuming, as is done in present methods, that the air is always half saturated), it is not practicable from a point of view of easy operation to lay down a single curve for use in determining the density corresponding to given readings of barometer and thermometer. Therefore a sheet of auxiliary curves is necessary for this purpose, for use in connection with the computer. Such a set of curves is shown on Plate II, and is good for any gun. It is really a graphic representation of Table IV of the Ballistic Tables (the table of multipliers for Column 12), and values of the multiplier can be taken from these curves much more quickly than they can be obtained from the table by interpolation. These curves have been designated **atmospheric condition curves,** and on Plate II show as straight lines, giving values for the multipliers ten times as great as those given in the table. This has been done in order to have the computer retain the principle on which it is constructed for all other errors; namely, that the first reading taken from the correction circle by bringing the range mark on the range scale into coincidence with the proper curve shall show the error due to unit variation in the quantity under consideration. (The same thing could be done in this case by plotting the curve for

the full errors due to 10 per cent variation in the density, and then using the values of the multipliers as given in the table; but this would make the principle of construction different in this case from what it is in all the others, and it was deemed best to adhere to the same principle throughout.) It will also be seen that the curves in question are plotted as straight lines, whereas they would not be quite that if accurately plotted from the table. The straight lines have been plotted as representing as nearly as possible the mean value of the curve that would be obtained by plotting accurately from the table. At the end of this description will be found a mathematical demonstration of the fact that these curves must be straight lines, whence it follows that the table is theoretically slightly in error in so far as it departs from this requirement.

13. To plot the **density curve**, it will be seen from Column 12 of the range table that, for a range of 15,000 yards, a variation from standard in the density of the atmosphere of 10 per cent will cause an error in range of 451 yards; therefore, a variation of 1 per cent in density will cause an error of 45.1 yards. Therefore to plot the point on the curve corresponding to 15,000 yards range, place the desired point on the face of the disc on a radius passing through the 45.1 mark on the correction circle, and at a distance from the center corresponding to the 15,000-yard mark on the range scale. Proceed in a similar manner to plot points corresponding to enough other ranges to enable the curve to be accurately scribed.

METHOD OF USE.

14. Before proceeding to describe the use of the computer, the following rule must be laid down:

(a) Always use the angle that is less than 90° that any of the directions makes with the line of fire, in order that we may always:

(b) Determine all range errors involving angles by multiplying results in the line of fire by the cosine of the angle; that is, by dividing by the secant.

(c) Determine all deflection errors involving angles by multiplying results perpendicular to the line of fire by the sine of the angle.

15. As an illustration of the method of using the computer, its manipulation will now be described in finding the error in range that would be caused by an apparent wind of 45 knots an hour blowing at an angle of 50° to the line of fire, for a range of 15,000 yards. The gun is the same 12″ gun.

16. Move the radial arm until the 15,000-yard mark on the range scale cuts the wind range curve (red curve). The value on the correction circle where it is now cut by the range scale line is the error for 1-knot wind in the line of fire, and will show as 5 yards. Now swing the inner disc and radial arm together until the range scale line and 5 on the correction circle are in coincidence with the 45 mark of the speed circle and clamp the two discs together. The reading now showing on the correction circle in coincidence with the zero of the speed circle is 225 yards, or the product of 5×45, and this would be the error caused by a 45-knot wind blowing along the line of fire. This is not what is wanted in this case, however, so with the two discs still clamped together, swing the radial arm until the range scale line is in coincidence with the 50° mark on the range circle, and then read across by the range scale line to the correction circle, where the coincident mark will be 144 yards, which is the desired result, and will be found to check with the results of work with the range table by ordinary methods.

17. The above process may be more fully explained as follows, for the benefit of those who are not familiar with the omnimeter. As a result of the manner in which the wind range curve (red) was plotted, when the 15,000-yard mark on the range

scale was brought to cut the wind range curve, and the reading was noted where the range scale line cut the correction circle, that reading was 5 yards, or the error due to a 1-knot wind blowing along the line of fire. Now had the zeros of the correction and speed circles been in coincidence when this was done, when the inner disc was moved around in a counter-clockwise direction until the five of the correction circle coincided with the zero of the speed circle, the zero of the correction circle moved a distance equal to log 5. Now when the motion of the inner disc was continued in the same direction until the 5 of the correction circle coincided with the 45 of the speed circle, the zero of the correction circle moved a further distance in the same direction equal to log 45. The total travel of the zero of the correction circle must therefore have been $\log 5 + \log 45 = \log 225$; and the reading on the speed circle now coincident with the zero of the correction circle (the measure of the total travel of that zero) must be 225 yards, which is the error in range due to a 45-knot wind in the line of fire. The decimal point has moved one digit to the right because of the fact that the zero of the correction circle traveled between one and two complete circumferences during the operation. Now clamp the two discs together as they stand. If the range scale on the radial arm be first placed at the zero of the speed circle (where we read 225 on the correction circle), which is also the zero of the range or log secant circle; and then be moved in a counter-clockwise direction until the range scale line is coincident with the 50° mark on the range circle, the range scale line will have traveled a distance from the 225 mark on the correction circle equal to log sec 50°, and if the range scale line be then followed across from the 50° mark on the range circle to the correction circle, the reading on the latter will be $\log 225 - \log \sec 50°$, or $\log 225 + \log \cos 50°$; that is, the logarithm of $225 \times \cos 50°$, which is the desired result; and reading off the anti-logarithm on the correction circle corresponding to the above result, the reading will be 144 yards, which is the desired error; that is, the error in range caused by an apparent wind of 45 knots blowing at an angle of 50° with the line of fire. The sign of the error, that is, whether it is a "short" or an "over," will at once be apparent from a glance at the plotting board, on which the direction of the apparent wind should be indicated relative to the line of fire.

18. To determine the deflection due to the wind, proceed in a similar manner, using the wind deflection curve (green), and taking the angle from the deflection circle. Setting the radial arm with the 15,000-yard mark of the range scale in coincidence with the wind deflection curve gives, from the correction circle, that a 1-knot wind perpendicular to the line of fire causes an error of 0.245 knots (on the deflection scale of the sight) in deflection. Moving the .245 mark of the correction circle around to coincide with the 45-knot mark on the speed circle and reading the zero of the correction (or speed) circle will give 11.0 knots as the error due to a 45-knot wind perpendicular to the line of fire (this would not be noted in actual practice unless the wind were actually blowing perpendicularly to the line of fire, in which case it would be the desired result); and reading across from the 50° mark on the deflection circle to the correction circle would give 8.5 knots as the amount of error in deflection. As before, the sign of the error must be determined from the plotting board. What was really done here, after determining the value 0.245, was to perform the addition $\log 0.245 + \log 45 = \log 11$, and then the addition $\log 11 + \log \sin 50° = \log 8.5$. That is, the value 0.245 was first found mechanically, and then the compound operation $0.245 \times 45 \times \sin 50° = 8.5$ was mechanically performed.

19. As the apparent wind was used in the preceding operations, the errors for the motion of the gun would be taken from the same curve as those for the motion of the target. For the error in range the method is exactly the same for both gun motion and target motion as for the wind error in range, using the target and gun

range curve (black). For the error in deflection the work might be done in either one of two ways, as follows:

(a) Use the target and gun range curve (black) for deflection errors as well as for range errors (Columns 15 and 18 of the range table are numerically the same) proceeding as before, which would give the deflection error in yards, which would then have to be transformed into knots of the sight deflection scale.

(b) Solve by the principles laid down in paragraph 24, subparagraph (b), below, for the solution of right triangles. This can be done because what we desire is the resolution of the speed into a line at right angles to the line of fire, which is the speed in knots multiplied by the sine of the angle, the result being in knots of the deflection scale. This is the shortest method, requires no curve on the computer, and is the one actually used in practice. Suppose the firing ship were steaming at 15 knots on a course making an angle of 36° with the line of fire. Bring the 15 on the correction circle into coincidence with the zero of the speed circle. Then read across from the 36° mark on the deflection circle to the correction circle, where the 8.8 mark shows that the required error is 8.8 knots of the deflection scale of the sight. The operation here performed was $15 \times \sin 36°$.

20. For the error in range due to the motion of the target, proceed exactly as was done in the case of motion of the gun, using the same curve; the target and gun range curve (black). The process for the deflection error is also the same as before. Suppose the target were moving at 18 knots at an angle of 40° with the line of fire. Put 18 on the correction circle in coincidence with the zero of the speed circle. Then read across from 40° on the deflection circle to the correction circle, and 11.6 knots will there be shown as the required error.

21. To use the powder temperature curve, bring the range scale into coincidence with the powder temperature curve at the given range mark, and clamp the radial arm and smaller disc together. Determine the variation from standard (90° F.) in the temperature of the powder ($90° \sim t° = T°$; where $t°$ is the temperature of the charge, and $T°$ is the variation from standard). Turn the smaller disc and radial arm together until the range scale line cuts the speed circle at the $T°$ mark. Then read the mark on the correction circle that is coincident with the zero mark on the speed circle (or the mark on the speed circle that is coincident with the zero mark on the correction circle), and this reading will be the desired error in yards resulting from a variation of $T°$ from standard (90° F.) in the temperature of the powder. A powder temperature higher than standard always gives an increase in range, and the reverse.

22. To use the density curve, bring the range scale into coincidence with the density error curve for the given range, and clamp the radial arm and smaller disc together. Determine the value of the multiplier for the given barometer and thermometer readings from the atmospheric condition curves. Turn the smaller disc and radial arm together until the range scale line cuts the speed circle at the mark indicating the value of the multiplier thus determined. Then read the mark on the correction circle that is coincident with the zero mark on the speed circle (or the mark on the speed circle that is coincident with the zero of the correction circle), and this reading will be the desired error in yards resulting from the variation from standard in the density of the atmosphere due to the given barometric and thermometric readings. A multiplier carrying a negative sign (that is, one taken from a red point on the atmospheric condition curves) always gives a "short" (density greater than unity); and one carrying a positive sign (that is, one taken from a black point on the atmospheric condition curves) always means an "over" (density less than unity).

23. Having shown how to manipulate the computer in detail, it will be seen that the process of use in the plotting room would be about as follows:

FORM FOR USE IN CONNECTION WITH FARNSWORTH ERROR COMPUTER.

Range, yards.	Errors in.			
	Range. Yds.		Deflection. Knots.	
	Short.	Over.	Right.	Left.
Temperature of powder: Standard, 90°; actual, —°.				
Atmospheric conditions: Barometer, —"; ther., —°.				
Motion of gun: Speed, — knots; angle, —°.				
Apparent wind: Velocity, — knots; angle, —°.				
Sums.				
Preliminary errors.				
Motion of target: Speed, — knots; angle, —°.				
Final errors (signs to be changed to give "corrections").				

(a) By "angle" is meant that angle *less than* 90° which the course of the firing ship, direction of the apparent wind, or course of the target ship makes with the line of fire.

(b) The **preliminary errors** include all those that will presumably be known long enough in advance to afford reasonable time for their determination.

(c) The temperature of the powder and the readings of the barometer and thermometer will be known before starting the approach. The first two lines of the above form may therefore be filled out when work begins, and will presumably remain constant throughout the action.

(d) As soon as plotting begins and the proposed line of fire and range are determined with sufficient accuracy, the plotter determines the angles made by the course of the firing ship and by the apparent wind (the information relative to the latter being sent down by the spotter) with the proposed line of fire, and the errors for gun motion and wind are determined and entered in their proper columns. The algebraic additions necessary to give the preliminary errors are then made and entered. This leaves only target motion to be accounted for, and as soon as the plotter has the necessary information he gives the "angle" and speed of the target ship, the errors caused thereby are taken from the computer and entered in their columns, and then two simple algebraic additions give the total errors required. The necessary corrections for application to the sights for the ranging shot can then be sent to the guns.

24. The computer is readily available for the solution of any right triangle, in addition to the purpose for which it was devised. In the case of angle from 84° to 90°, the sines are practically equal to unity and the cosines are negligible, and

oppositely for angles from 0° to 6°. For this reason the graduations for these angles have been omitted from the circles. For examples in the solution of right triangles we have:

(a) Given One Angle and the Hypothenuse to Find the Side Adjacent.—Given that the angle is 30° and the hypothenuse is 27. Put 27 on the correction circle in coincidence with zero on the speed circle. Then find 30° on the range circle and read across to the correction circle, where 23.5 will be found for the side adjacent. ($27 \times \cos 30° = 27$ divided by $\sec 30° = 23.4$ by the traverse tables.)

(b) Given One Angle and the Hypothenuse to Find the Side Opposite.—Given that the angle is 30° and the hypothenuse is 27. Put 27 on the correction circle in coincidence with zero on the speed circle. Then find 30° on the deflection circle and read across to the correction circle, where 13.5 will be found for the side opposite. ($27 \times \sin 30° = 13.5$ by the traverse tables.)

(c) Given One Angle and the Side Opposite to Find the Hypothenuse.—Given that the angle is 30° and the side opposite is 15. Put 15 on the correction circle in coincidence with 30° on the deflection circle, and coinciding with the zero of the correction circle will be 30+ on the speed circle for the hypothenuse. ($15 \times \operatorname{cosec} 30° = 15$ divided by $\sin 30° = 30+$ by the traverse tables.)

(d) Given One Angle and the Side Adjacent to Find the Hypothenuse.—Given that the angle is 30° and the side adjacent is 15. Put 15 on the correction circle in coincidence with 30° on the range circle, and coinciding with the zero of the correction circle will be 17.25 on the speed circle for the hypothenuse. ($15 \times \sec 30° = 17.3$ by the traverse tables.)

(e) Given One Angle and the Side Adjacent to Find the Side Opposite.—Given the side adjacent as 15 and the angle as 30°, first find the hypothenuse as in (d), which is 17.25. Put 17.25 on the correction circle in coincidence with zero on the speed circle, and in coincidence with 30° on the deflection circle will be found 8.65 on the correction circle for the side opposite. ($17.25 \times \sin 30° = 8.62$ by the traverse tables.)

(f) Given One Angle and the Side Opposite to Find the Side Adjacent.—Given the side opposite as 15 and the angle as 30°, first find the hypothenuse as in (c), which is 30+. Bring 30+ on the correction circle into coincidence with zero on the speed circle, and in coincidence with 30° on the range circle will be 26+ on the correction circle for the side adjacent. ($30+ \times \cos 30° = 30+$ divided by $\sec 30° = 26+$ by traverse tables.)

(g) Given the Two Sides to Find the Angles and Hypothenuse.—The computer does not handle this case as easily as the traverse tables; but it is not one usually encountered in the class of work where the instrument would habitually be used.

INSTRUCTIONS FOR USE.

25. To summarize, the following brief instructions should be used in connection with the instrument:

(a) To Determine the Error in Range Resulting from a Variation from Standard in the Temperature of the Powder.

Error in Range.—(Use blue curve, Column 10 of range table.)

(1) Bring the given range on the range scale into coincidence with the powder temperature curve, and clamp the radial arm and smaller disc together.

(2) Determine the variation from standard (90° F.) in the temperature of the powder ($90° \sim t° = T°$).

(3) Turn the smaller disc and radial arm together until the range scale line cuts the speed circle at the $T°$ mark. Read the desired error on the correction circle coincident with the zero of the speed circle.

(4) A powder temperature higher than the standard always gives an increase in range, and the reverse.

(b) To Determine the Error in Range Resulting from a Variation from Standard in the Density of the Atmosphere.

Error in Range.—(Use yellow curve, Column 12.)

(1) Bring the given range on the range scale into coincidence with the density curve, and clamp the radial arm and smaller disc together.

(2) Determine the value of the multiplier from the atmospheric condition curves for the given readings of barometer and thermometer.

(3) Turn the smaller disc and radial arm together until the range scale line cuts the speed circle at the mark indicating the value of the multiplier determined from the atmospheric condition curves. Read the desired error on the correction circle coincident with the zero of the speed circle.

(4) A negative sign on the multiplier always means a "short," and a positive sign an "over."

(c) To Determine Errors Due to an Apparent Wind of Known Velocity and at a Known Angle to the Line of Fire.

Error in Range.—(Use red curve, Column 13.)

(1) Rotate radial arm until wind range curve intersects range scale on runner at given range, and clamp radial arm to upper disc.

(2) Rotate lower disc until range scale line on radial arm intersects speed circle at apparent wind velocity in knots. Clamp discs together; unclamp radial arm.

(3) Rotate radial arm until range scale line intersects range circle at angle to line of fire at which wind is blowing.

(4) Read across by range scale line to correction circle, and note result; the desired range error in yards.

(5) Determine sign of error by glance at plotting board.

Error in Deflection. (Use green curve, Column 16.)

(1) Rotate radial arm until wind deflection curve intersects range scale on radial arm at given range, and clamp radial arm to inner disc.

(2) Rotate lower disc until range scale line on radial arm intersects speed circle at apparent wind velocity in knots. Clamp discs together; unclamp radial arm.

(3) Rotate radial arm until range scale line intersects deflection circle at angle to line of fire at which wind is blowing.

(4) Read across by range scale line to correction circle, and note result; the desired error in knots.

(5) Determine sign of error by glance at plotting board.

(d) To Determine Errors Due to Motion of Gun (or Target) at Given Speed and Angle with Line of Fire.

Error in Range.—(Use black curve, Column 15.)

(1) Rotate radial arm until target and gun range curve intersects range scale on radial arm at given range, and clamp radial arm to upper disc.

(2) Rotate lower disc until range scale line on radial arm intersects speed circle at speed of gun (or target) in knots. Clamp discs together and unclamp radial arm.

(3) Rotate radial arm until range scale line intersects range circle at angle to line of fire made by course of gun (or target).

(4) Read across by range scale line to correction circle, and note result; the desired range error in yards due to motion of gun (or target).

APPENDIX C.

ARBITRARY DEFLECTION SCALES FOR GUN SIGHTS.

INTRODUCTORY.

1. In many cases, notably in turret sights, the system of marking the deflection scales of sights in "knots," as described in this text book, is no longer carried out; these scales being marked in arbitrary divisions instead, the manner of constructing and using which scales will now be explained.

2. The method of controlling deflection by means of "deflection boards" and "arbitrary scales" was devised for the purpose of relieving the sight setters of the responsibility of keeping the deflection pointer on a designated deflection curve. The principle upon which the method is based is in no way different from the standard method of controlling deflection by means of knot curves. It differs in the method of application, in that one curve sheet upon which the knot curves are drawn performs the functions of the curve drums formerly fitted upon each individual sight. Many of the sights still in service are adapted for the use of either method of deflection control, and it will be seen by trying both methods that they give the same results, regardless of which one is used.

3. The method of bringing the point of impact on the target in deflection in no way differs from that of bringing the point of impact on the target in range, except that deflection correction controls the angle of the sight with respect to the axis of the gun in the horizontal plane, while range correction controls it in the vertical plane. If the point of impact be short of the target, or, in other words, too low, the sight is raised; if the point of impact is to the left in deflection, the rear end of the telescopic sight is moved to the right, and *vice versa*. In either case it is the angle between the axis of the telescope and the axis of the gun that is changed, for range in the vertical plane, and for deflection in the horizontal plane.

4. To arrive at a clear understanding of the principle of deflection, it should be comprehended that all deflection measurements can be reduced to angular measurements. If the horizontal angle between the axis of the gun and the line of sight be the same for all the guns of the same caliber firing, then the corresponding deflection, whether measured in knots or in yards, will also be the same for all those guns. It is thus seen that the sights for all types can be so constructed that the unit of measurement for deflection is an angle.

PRINCIPLE OF ARBITRARY SCALES.

5. In the method of controlling deflection by the use of "deflection boards" and "arbitrary scales," the unit of measurement, that is, the angle corresponding to one division of the scale, is the angle that is subtended by one-half of a chord of 0.2 of an inch at 100″ radius; that is, it is the angle whose tangent is .001. By using this unit of measurement, the divisions on the arbitrary scale (*G*, Plate III), are all equal to 0.1 of an inch on all deflection boards for all sights for all guns, and all deflection boards are therefore uniform in construction. The arbitrary scale fitted to each sight is graduated so that one division of the sight scale corresponds to this

standard angle, whatever the value of the sight radius, and the actual magnitude of each such division in fractions of an inch therefore depends upon the value of the sight radius, and is determined from it by proportion, as follows:

$$\frac{x}{l} = \frac{0.1}{100}, \text{ whence } x = \frac{l}{1000}$$

where x (in fractions of an inch) is the magnitude of the arbitrary division, and l is the sight radius in inches. These arbitrary scales, when once graduated, become permanent, regardless of any change in initial velocity or other modifications affecting the trajectory. The necessary corrections to provide for a change in initial velocity, for instance, would be made on the curve sheet (*J*, Plate III), and expensive and troublesome modifications in the manufactured scales on the sights would therefore be unnecessary. As the above-mentioned curve sheets are made on drawing paper, quickly and at small cost, it will be seen that changes in the ballistics of the guns could be made without great expense or delay in the supply of the necessary means for deflection control.

6. In the triangle under consideration, the "side opposite" to the angle adopted as the standard angular unit of deflection, that is, the angle whose tangent is .001, is sometimes known as a "mill," because the side opposite is always one one-thousandth part of the side adjacent. In this case it is therefore the angle that corresponds to a deflection of 1 yard at 1000 yards range, and to a deflection of 10 yards at 10,000 yards range, etc.

GENERAL DESCRIPTION OF THE SIGHT DEFLECTION BOARD.

7. The "sight deflection board," as shown on Plate III, as furnished to ships, is simply a means of mechanically turning a determined deflection in knots into the units of the arbitrary scale, and at the same time applying the drift correction for the given range. It consists of a wood or aluminum board, *A*, about 20" square. On each side is a rack, *B*, which is secured by wing nuts, *C*. Across the top, and also held by the wing nuts *C*, is a metal strip, *D*, which carries the sliding pointer, *E*. The scale of arbitrary divisions, *G*, slides up and down the board parallel to itself upon the racks, *B*, as guides. A pinion on each end of the shaft, *F*, runs upon the racks, *B*, and prevents canting of the scale, *G*. The sliding pointer, *H*, is carried upon the scale, *G*, for use in keeping track of the divisions of the scale used. The curve sheet, *J*, is cut to fit under the racks, *B*, where it is held from slipping, after being properly adjusted, by the wing nuts, *C*. In placing the sheet on the board, it must be so adjusted that the reference line, *XX*, will always be under the "50" mark of the scale *G* as the latter is run up and down from top to bottom of the board. (It will be noted on the plate that the line *XX*, which should intersect the 50 curve at zero yards range, is slightly to the right of that curve at the 1000-yard range mark at the top of the curve sheet, which is of course as it should be. The slight divergence of the 50 mark of the scale *G* from the line *XX* that is noticeable on the plate is undoubtedly due to parallax in taking the photograph, the camera apparently not having been set up directly in front of that point.)

8. The legend on the curve sheet shows for what sights, for what caliber of gun, and for what initial velocity it is to be used; and also indicates, for the information of the spotters and sight setters, the value in knots at some given range to which the divisions on the arbitrary scale correspond.

METHOD OF USE.

9. The deflection board is designed primarily for use in the plotting room, but it can be used at any other point that may be desired, such as the spotter's top or in the turrets.

10. When about to open fire, the knot curve to be used should be determined by computation (or by the use of the gun error computer) in the same manner as has been explained for the deflection sight scale marked in knots; but this would no longer be sent out to the guns as the setting of the sights in deflection. Instead, the pointer *E* is placed at the top to indicate the curve to be used (the 45-knot curve on Plate III). The scale *G* is then run down the board to correspond to the range to be used (14,000 yards on the plate). The pointer *H* is then run along the scale *G* until it is over the proper curve on the sheet (45 knots), and the reading under the same pointer on the scale *G* will then be the number of divisions of the arbitrary sight scale at which the sights should be set to give the desired deflection (40 divisions on the plate). As the curves on the sheet are the drift curves for the gun, the sight setting in arbitrary divisions of the scale thus found will of course include the drift correction.

11. As the range varies during the firing, the scale *G* is moved up and down to follow it, and the pointer *H* is moved to the right or left to keep it over the proper curve on the sheet (45 on the plate). The pointer *H* will then always indicate on the scale *G* the proper sight setting in deflection in the markings of the arbitrary scale.

12. In case the spotter's corrections indicate the use of a new curve at any time, the pointer *E* is shifted to that curve, and the new readings for the arbitrary scale are read off from the scale *G* by the pointer *H* (which is now following the new curve) and sent to the sight setters.

13. By this process the sight setters are relieved of all responsibility in regard to the deflection setting other than that of setting the sight for the scale readings which they receive from time to time from the deflection operator, and it is no longer necessary for them to be continually following a drift curve on the sight drum as the range increases or decreases.

CONTROL OF DEFLECTION WITHOUT THE USE OF KNOT CURVES.

14. If preferred, or if no deflection board be at hand, a table may be made up showing the value in knots of one or more divisions of the arbitrary deflection scale at different ranges, from which the spotter can estimate first his initial sight setting in deflection, and afterwards any changes that he may desire to make. So far as the deflection in yards is concerned, all that is necessary is a knowledge of the fact that for all guns, at all ranges, with all arbitrary deflection scale sights, one division of the arbitrary scale causes or corrects a deflection in yards equal to one one-thousandth of the range; while for the transformation from "knots" to "arbitrary divisions" and the reverse, a table can be used similar to:

Range in Yards.	Deflection in—	
	Knots.	Divisions of Arbitrary Scale.
5000	5	3.5
10000	5	4.0
15000	5	4+
20000	5	4.5

It will be seen from the above table that, for the gun in question, the variation between knots and divisions is so slight for all probable battle ranges that no great error would result from assuming that 5 knots always equal 4 divisions at all such ranges.

15. The method of control described above involving the use of the board gives greater accuracy than the one using curve drums on the sights, as the deflection board permits the curve sheets to be made on a larger scale. It is not necessary, however, to continue the use of the deflection board after the initial data has been obtained for opening fire. The board may be used to determine the setting of the sights in deflection by the arbitrary scale for firing the first shot; and after that the spotter can indicate the deflection changes in terms of the arbitrary scale, providing he knows approximately the value of the arbitrary divisions in knots or yards at the target, for the approximate range at which the firing is being conducted (in yards, this is one one-thousandth of the range in yards, as already seen); and, after shots are seen to be hitting at the proper point, they can then be held at that point by giving the spotter's corrections in terms of the arbitrary scale, as soon as the point of impact appears to creep to the right or to the left, and before it can creep off the target.

PROPOSED USE OF ARBITRARY DIVISIONS FOR RANGE SCALES.

16. The advisability of using the "arbitrary scale" method for ranges as well as for deflection (replacing "yards" in range) is under consideration, and should it be done, the sume division (one mill) would be used. This, with a sight radius of 100 inches, would give clearly readable divisions on the sight scale corresponding to angular differences of two minutes in arc in elevation.

17. The use of the arbitrary scale in range would avoid any changes in sight graduations due to possible changes in initial velocity, as the divisions of the arbitrary scale could be taken from a range chart drawn on paper. This chart could be so drawn as to permit of compensation for slight changes in initial velocity due to variations in the powder, in powder temperature, etc. Also, as all divisions of the sight scale would be of equal magnitude, this system would lend itself readily to the employment of some step by step mechanical means of setting the sights directly from the plotting room or elsewhere, without the interposition of any person as a sight setter.

Lightning Source UK Ltd.
Milton Keynes UK
UKOW07f2011250817
307996UK00004B/149/P

9 781165 687824